Publisher
Jim Scheikofer
The Family Handyman®

Director, Publication Services
Sue Baalman-Pohlman
HDA, Inc. *(Home Design Alternatives)*

Publication Manager
Kimberly King
HDA, Inc. *(Home Design Alternatives)*

Newsstand Sales
David Algire
Reader's Digest Association, Inc.

Marketing Manager
Andrea Vecchio
The Family Handyman

Production Manager
Judy Rodriguez
The Family Handyman

Home Plans Manager
Curtis Cadenhead
HDA, Inc. *(Home Design Alternatives)*

Copyright 2005 by
Home Service Publications, Inc.,
publishers of
The Family Handyman Magazine,
2915 Commers Drive, Suite 700,
Eagan, MN 55121.
Plan copyrights held by home
designer/architect.

The Family Handyman is a
registered trademark of
RD Publications, Inc.

RD Publications, Inc.
is a subsidiary of The Reader's
Digest Association, Inc.

Reader's Digest and The Family
Handyman logo are registered
trademarks of The Reader's
Digest Association, Inc.
All rights reserved.
Unauthorized reproduction,
in any manner is prohibited.

Artist drawings and photos shown
in this publication may vary
slightly from the actual working
drawings. Some photos are
shown in mirror reverse. Please
refer to the floor plan for accurate
layout. All plans appearing in this
publication are protected under
copyright law.

Reproduction of the illustrations
or working drawings by any
means is strictly prohibited. The
right of building only one structure
from the plans purchased is
licensed exclusively to the buyer
and the plans may not be
resold unless by express
written authorization.

Reader's Digest

The Family Handyman Contents

Vol. 19, No. 11

Featured Homes

Plan #718-007D-0010 is featured on page 35.
Photo courtesy of Bill Wood Remodeling; St. Louis, MO

Plan #718-016D-0048 is featured on page 37.
Photo courtesy of Axelrod Designs; Commack, NY

Sections

Home Plans	2-320
Our Blueprint Packages Offer...	12
What Kind of Plan Package Do You Need?	
Other Helpful Building Aids...	13
Home Plans Index	14
To Order Home Plans	15
Quick & Easy Customizing	16

The Family Handyman magazine and HDA, Inc. (Home Design Alternatives) are pleased to join together and bring you this collection of charming and comfortable home plans including Country and Victorian plans featuring many different styles for many different budgets from some of the nation's leading designers and architects.

Technical Specifications - At the time the construction drawings were prepared, every effort was made to ensure that these plans and specifications meet nationally recognized building codes (BOCA, Southern Building Code Congress and others). Because national building codes change or vary from area to area some drawing modifications and/or the assistance of a professional designer or architect may be necessary to comply with your local codes or to accommodate specific building conditions. We advise you to consult with your local building official for information regarding codes governing your area.

On The Cover...

Plan #718-065D-0013 is featured on page 310.
Photo courtesy of Studer Residential Designs, Inc., Cold Springs, KY; photographer: Exposures Unlimited, Ron and Donna Kolb.

Plan #718-024D-0006

1,618 total square feet of living area

Loaded With Charm

Special features

- Secondary bedrooms with walk-in closets are located on the second floor and share a bath
- Utility room is tucked away in the kitchen for convenience but is out of sight
- Dining area is brightened by a large bay window
- 3 bedrooms, 2 1/2 baths
- Slab or crawl space foundation, please specify when ordering

Price Code C

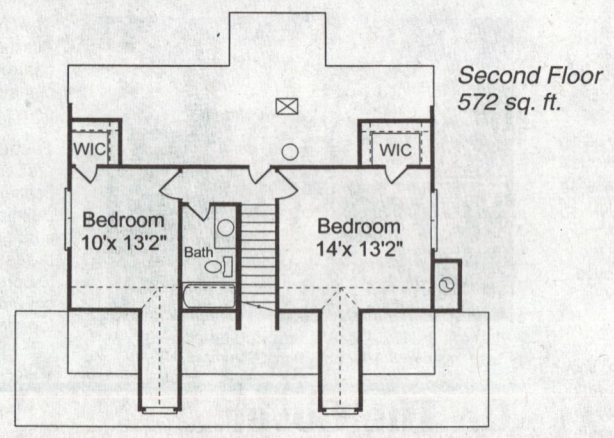

Second Floor 572 sq. ft.

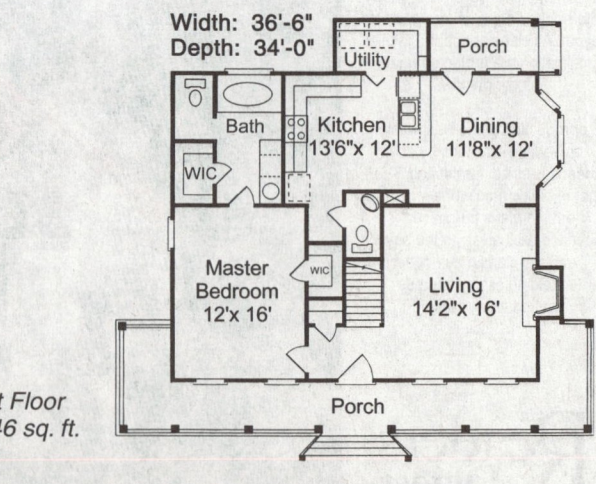

Width: 36'-6"
Depth: 34'-0"

First Floor 1,046 sq. ft.

Plan #718-008D-0045

1,540 total square feet of living area

Cheerful And Sunny Kitchen

Special features

- Porch entrance into foyer leads to an impressive dining area with full window and a half-circle window above
- Kitchen/breakfast room features a center island and cathedral ceiling
- Great room with cathedral ceiling and exposed beams is accessible from the foyer
- Master bedroom includes a full bath and walk-in closet
- Two additional bedrooms share a full bath
- 3 bedrooms, 2 baths, 2-car garage
- Basement foundation, drawings also include crawl space and slab foundations

Price Code B

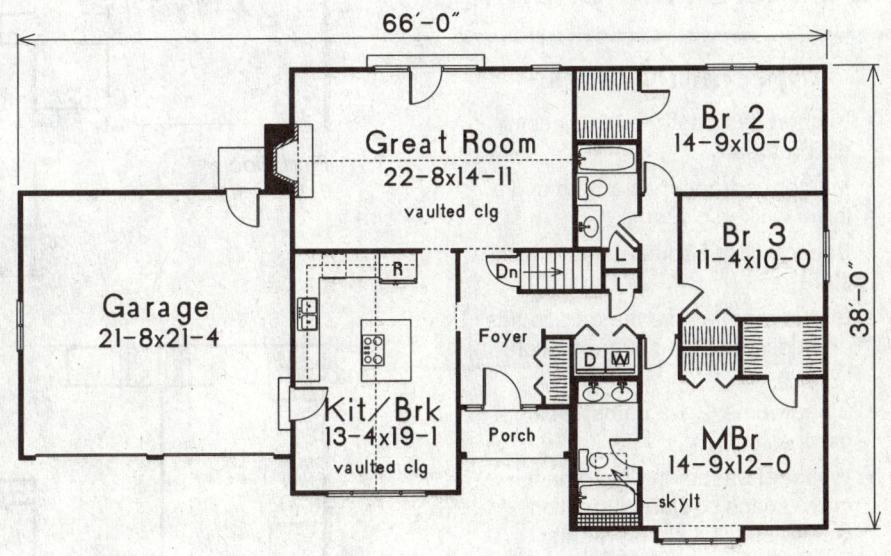

Plan #718-055D-0022

2,107 total square feet of living area

Dormers Add Charm

Special features

- Kitchen has pantry and adjacent dining area
- Master bedroom has a bath and a large walk-in closet
- Second floor bedrooms have attic storage
- Bonus room above the garage has an additional 324 square feet of living area
- 3 bedrooms, 2 1/2 baths, 2-car garage
- Walk-out basement, basement, crawl space or slab foundation, please specify when ordering

Price Code C

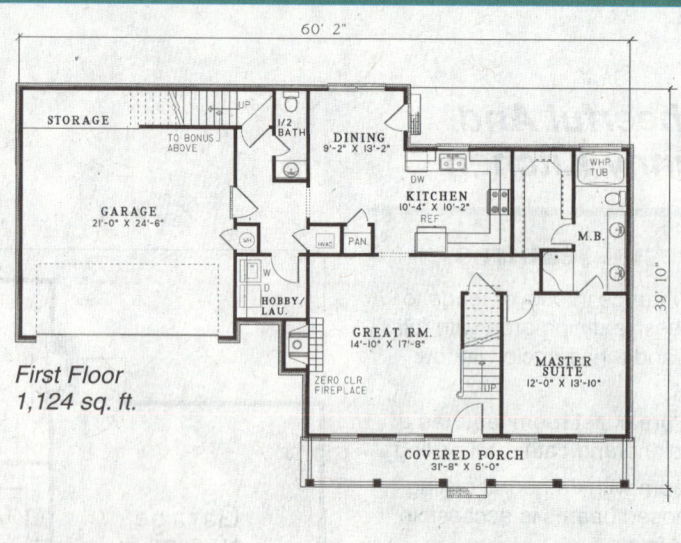

First Floor
1,124 sq. ft.

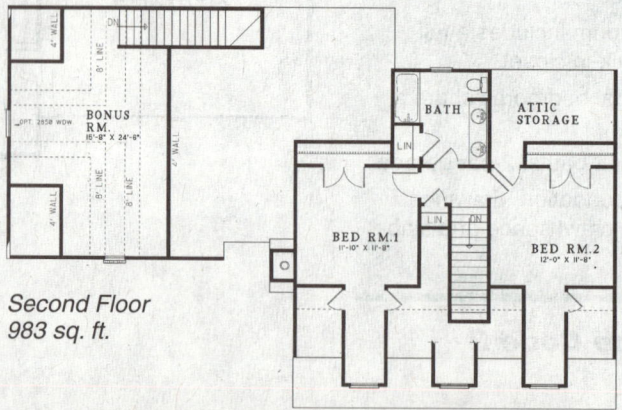

Second Floor
983 sq. ft.

TO ORDER BLUEPRINTS USE THE FORM ON PAGE 15 OR CALL TOLL-FREE 1-877-671-6036
View thousands more home plans online at www.familyhandyman.com/HOMEPLANS

Plan #718-008D-0072

1,200 total square feet of living area

Perfect Home For Escaping To The Outdoors

Special features

- Enjoy lazy summer evenings on this magnificent porch
- Activity area has a fireplace and ascending stair from the cozy loft
- Kitchen features a built-in pantry
- Master bedroom enjoys a large bath, walk-in closet and cozy loft overlooking the room below
- 2 bedrooms, 2 baths
- Crawl space foundation

Price Code A

Second Floor 416 sq. ft.

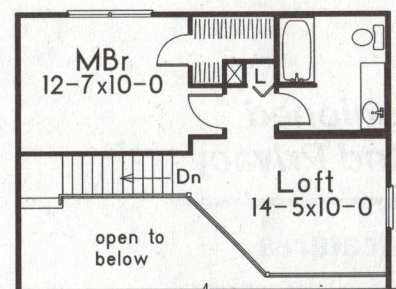

First Floor 784 sq. ft.

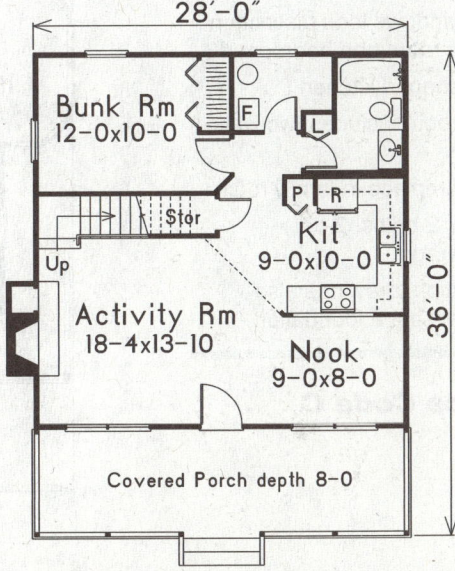

TO ORDER BLUEPRINTS USE THE FORM ON PAGE 15 OR CALL TOLL-FREE 1-877-671-6036
View thousands more home plans online at www.familyhandyman.com/homeplans

Plan #718-037D-0006

1,772 total square feet of living area

Old-Fashioned Comfort And Privacy

Special features

- Extended porches in front and rear provide a charming touch
- Large bay windows lend distinction to the dining room and bedroom #3
- Efficient U-shaped kitchen
- Master bedroom includes two walk-in closets
- Full corner fireplace in family room
- 3 bedrooms, 2 baths, 2-car detached garage
- Slab foundation, drawings also include crawl space foundation

Price Code C

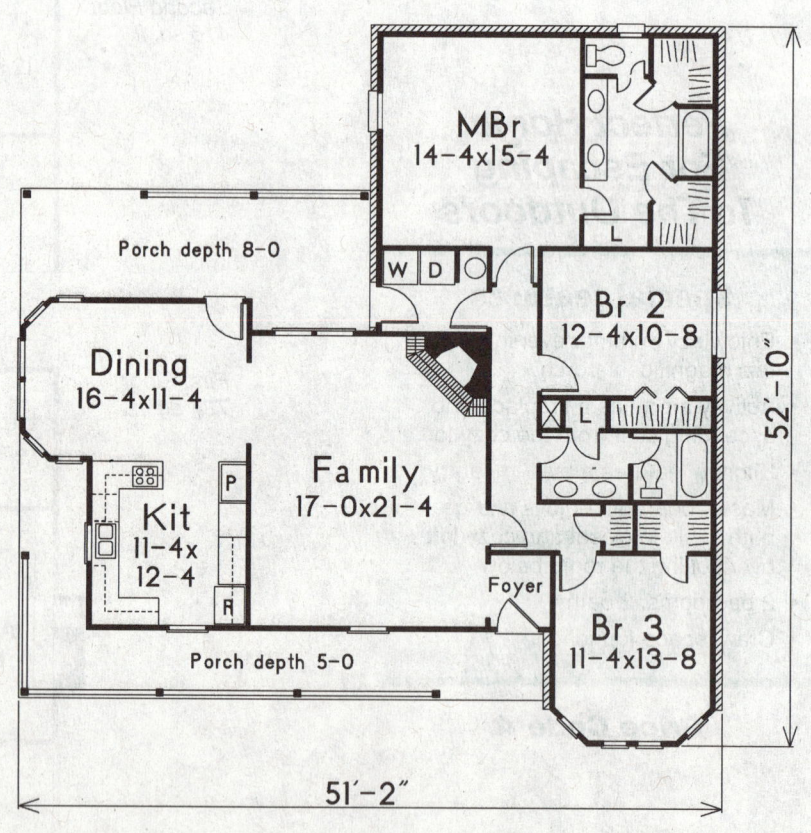

TO ORDER BLUEPRINTS USE THE FORM ON PAGE 15 OR CALL TOLL-FREE 1-877-671-6036
View thousands more home plans online at www.familyhandyman.com/homeplans

Plan #718-008D-0079

2,253 total square feet of living area

Distinct Country Look And Feel

Special features

- Great room is joined by the rear covered porch
- Secluded parlor provides area for peace and quiet or a private office
- Sloped ceiling adds drama to the master bedroom
- Great room, kitchen and breakfast area combine for a large open living area
- 3 bedrooms, 2 1/2 baths, 2-car garage
- Basement foundation

Price Code D

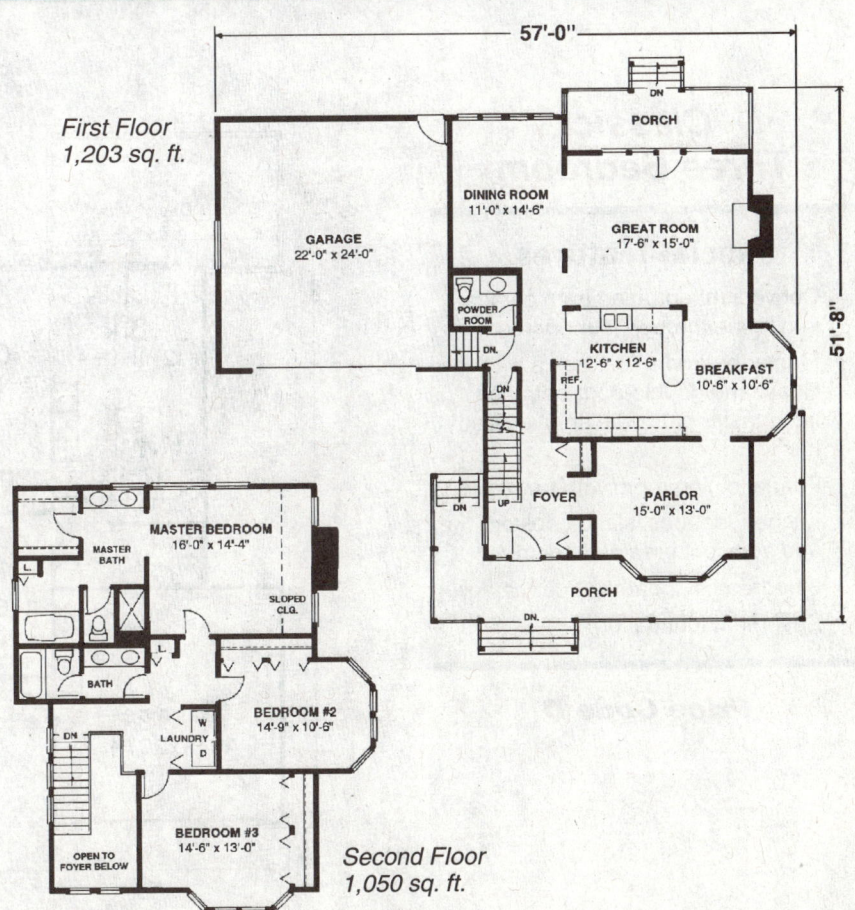

TO ORDER BLUEPRINTS USE THE FORM ON PAGE 15 OR CALL TOLL-FREE 1-877-671-6036
View thousands more home plans online at www.familyhandyman.com/HOMEPLANS

Plan #718-027D-0003

2,061 total square feet of living area

Classic Three Bedroom

Special features

- Convenient entrance from garage into home through laundry room
- Master bedroom features a walk-in closet and double-door entrance into master bath with an oversized tub
- Formal dining room with tray ceiling
- Kitchen features island cooktop and adjacent breakfast room
- 3 bedrooms, 2 baths, 2-car garage
- Basement foundation

Price Code D

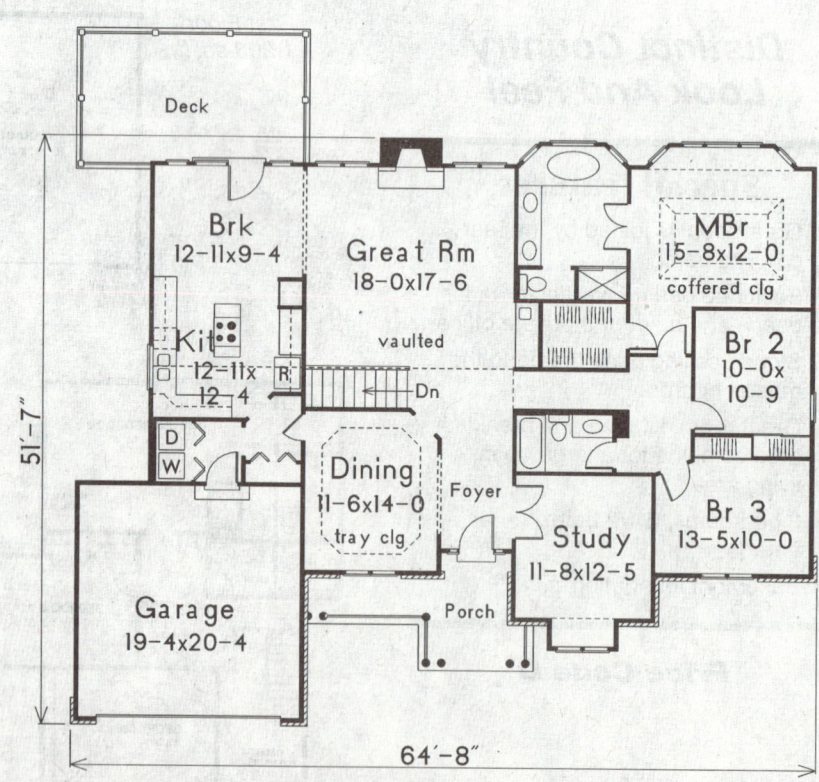

TO ORDER BLUEPRINTS USE THE FORM ON PAGE 15 OR CALL TOLL-FREE 1-877-671-6036
View thousands more home plans online at www.familyhandyman.com/HOMEPLANS

Plan #718-008D-0080

2,009 total square feet of living area

Extra Amenities Enhance Living

Special features

- Spacious master bedroom has a dramatic sloped ceiling and private bath with double sinks and walk-in closet
- Bedroom #3 has extra storage inside closet
- Versatile screened porch is ideal for entertaining year-round
- Sunny breakfast area is located near the kitchen and screened porch for convenience
- 3 bedrooms, 2 1/2 baths
- Basement foundation

Price Code C

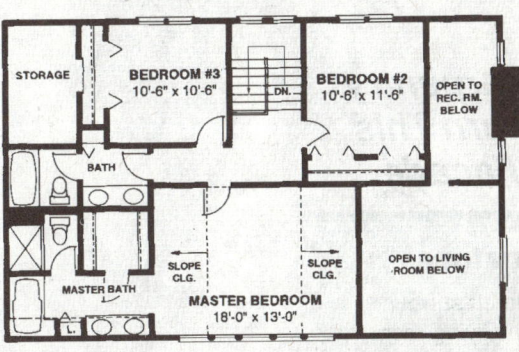

Second Floor 847 sq. ft.

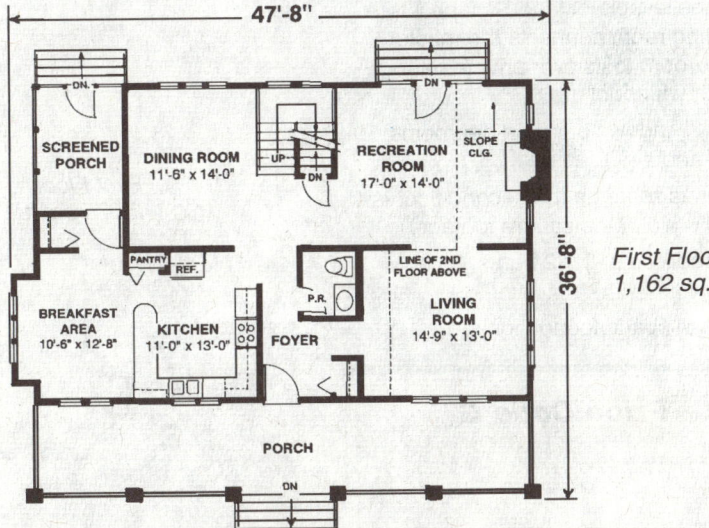

First Floor 1,162 sq. ft.

TO ORDER BLUEPRINTS USE THE FORM ON PAGE 15 OR CALL TOLL-FREE 1-877-671-6036
View thousands more home plans online at www.familyhandyman.com/HOMEPLANS

Plan #718-071D-0007

4,220 total square feet of living area

Amazing Carpentry Details Adorn This Home's Facade

Special features

- A large covered porch surrounds and connects to the living room with fireplace
- Unbelievable octagon-shaped sitting room connects the master bedroom to its own private bath with whirlpool tub
- Bay windows brighten bedrooms #3 and #4
- Bonus room on the second floor is included in the square footage
- 4 bedrooms, 3 1/2 baths, 3-car garage
- Crawl space foundation

Price Code G

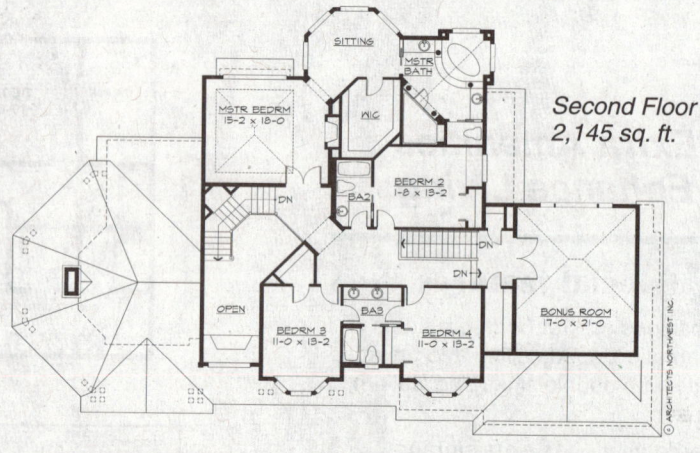

Second Floor 2,145 sq. ft.

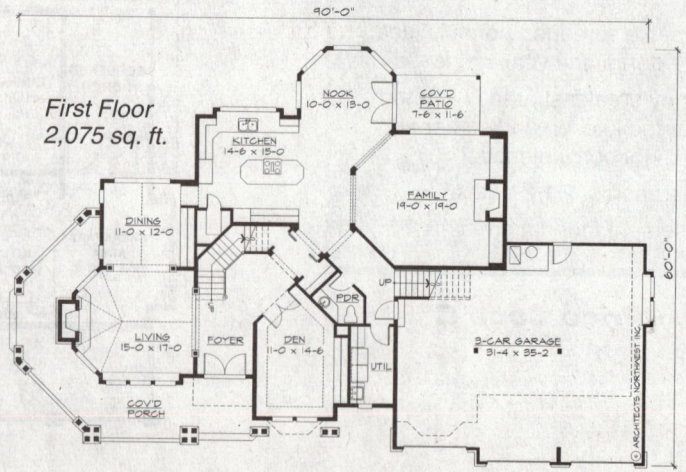

First Floor 2,075 sq. ft.

Plan #718-008D-0081

2,420 total square feet of living area

Superb Home Accented With Victorian Details

Special features

- Master bedroom is filled with extras such as a unique master bath and lots of storage
- Extending off great room is a bright sunroom with access to a deck
- Compact kitchen with nook creates a useful breakfast area
- 4 bedrooms, 2 1/2 baths, 2-car garage
- Basement foundation

Price Code D

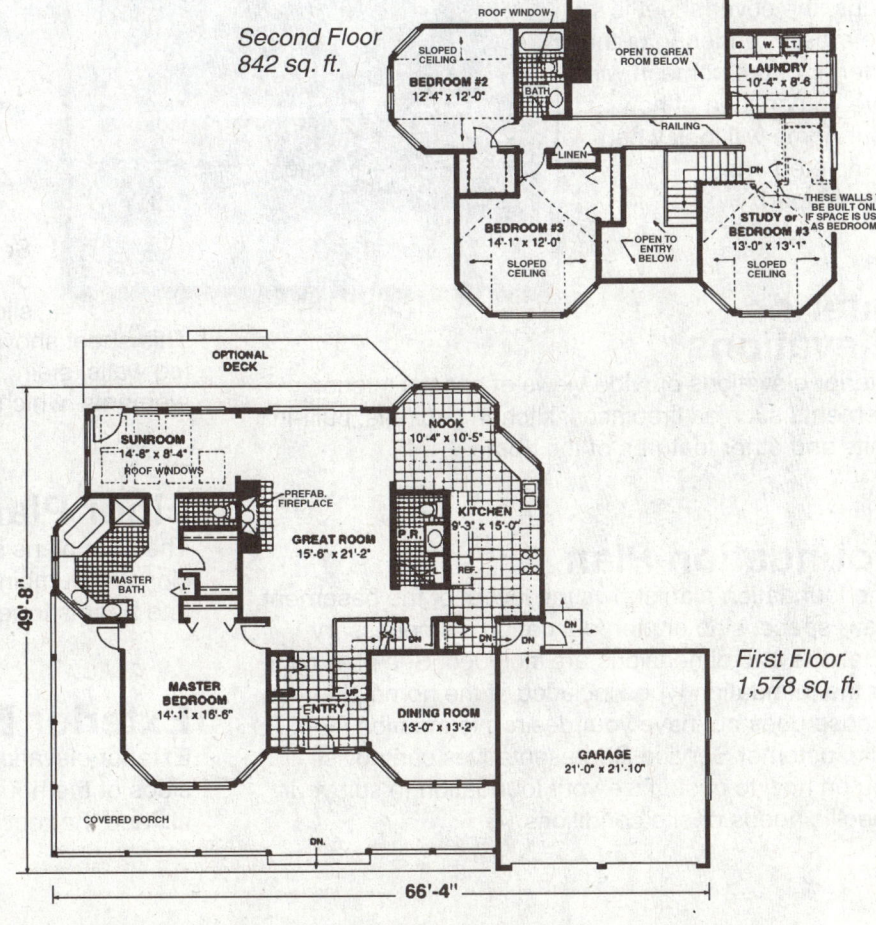

Second Floor 842 sq. ft.

First Floor 1,578 sq. ft.

TO ORDER BLUEPRINTS USE THE FORM ON PAGE 15 OR CALL TOLL-FREE 1-877-671-6036
View thousands more home plans online at www.familyhandyman.com/HOMEPLANS

Our Blueprint Packages Offer...

Quality plans for building your future, with extras that provide unsurpassed value, ensure good construction and long-term enjoyment.

A quality home - one that looks good, functions well, and provides years of enjoyment - is a product of many things - design, materials, craftsmanship.

But it's also the result of outstanding blueprints - the actual plans and specifications that tell the builder exactly how to build your home.

And with our BLUEPRINT PACKAGES you get the absolute best. A complete set of blueprints is available for every design in this book. These "working drawings" are highly detailed, resulting in two key benefits:

☐ Better understanding by the contractor of how to build your home and...

☐ More accurate construction estimates.

Other helpful building aids are also available to help make your dream home a reality.

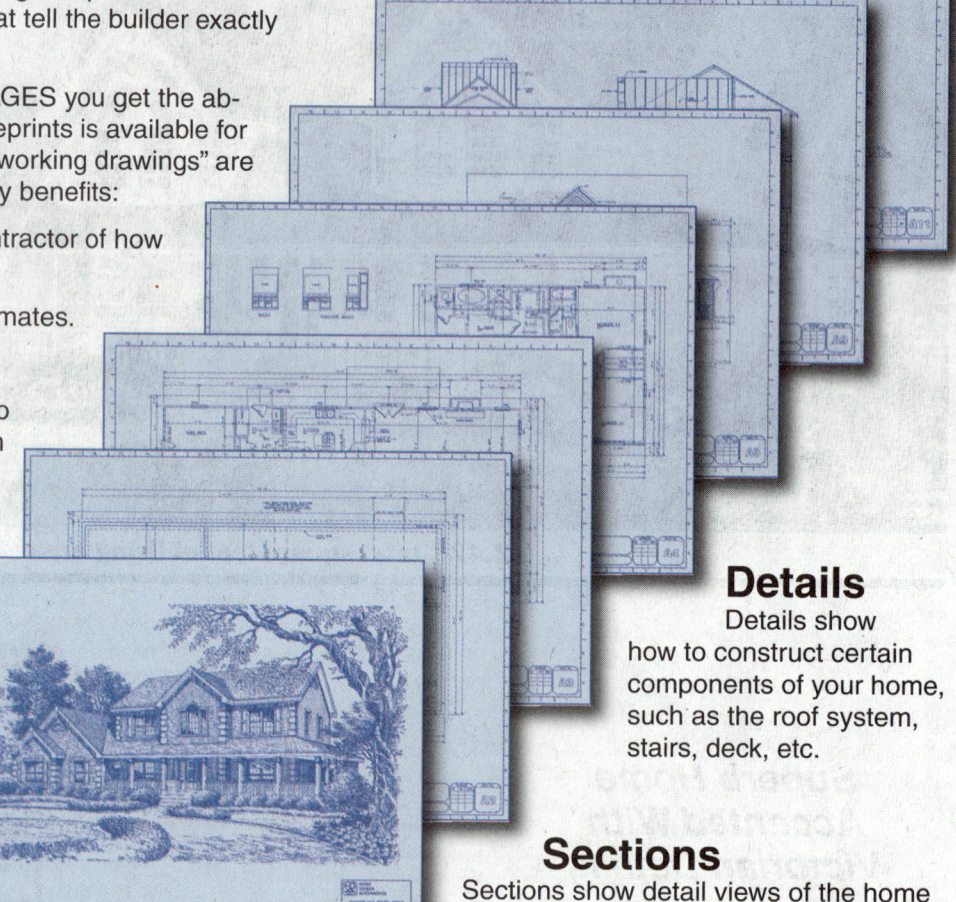

Cover Sheet
Included with many of the plans, the cover sheet is the artist's rendering of the exterior of the home. It will give you an idea of how your home will look when completed and landscaped.

Interior Elevations
Interior elevations provide views of special interior elements such as fireplaces, kitchen cabinets, built-in units and other features of the home.

Foundation Plan
The foundation plan shows the layout of the basement, crawl space, slab or pier foundation. All necessary notations and dimensions are included. See plan page for the foundation types included. If the home plan you choose does not have your desired foundation type, our Customer Service Representatives can advise you on how to customize your foundation to suit your specific needs or site conditions.

Details
Details show how to construct certain components of your home, such as the roof system, stairs, deck, etc.

Sections
Sections show detail views of the home or portions of the home as if it were sliced from the roof to the foundation. This sheet shows important areas such as load-bearing walls, stairs, joists, trusses and other structural elements, which are critical for proper construction.

Floor Plans
The floor plans show the placement of walls, doors, closets, plumbing fixtures, electrical outlets, columns, and beams for each level of the home.

Exterior Elevations
Exterior elevations illustrate the front, rear and both sides of the house, with all details of exterior materials and the required dimensions.

What Kind Of Plan Package Do You Need?

Now that you've found the home you've been looking for, here are some suggestions on how to make your Dream Home a reality. To get started, order the type of plans that fit your particular situation.

YOUR CHOICES

- **The 1-Set Study Package -** We offer a 1-set plan package so you can study your home in detail. This one set is considered a study set and is marked "not for construction." It is a copyright violation to reproduce blueprints.

- **The Minimum 5-Set Package -** If you're ready to start the construction process, this 5-set package is the minimum number of blueprint sets you will need. It will require keeping close track of each set so they can be used by multiple subcontractors and tradespeople.

- **The Standard 8-Set Package -** For best results in terms of cost, schedule and quality of construction, we recommend you order eight (or more) sets of blueprints. Besides one set for yourself, additional sets of blueprints will be required by your mortgage lender, local building department, general contractor and all subcontractors working on foundation, electrical, plumbing, heating/air conditioning, carpentry work, etc.

- **Reproducible Masters -** If you wish to make some minor design changes, you'll want to order reproducible masters. These drawings contain the same information as the blueprints but are printed on erasable and reproducible paper which clearly indicates your right to copy or reproduce. This will allow your builder or a local design professional to make the necessary drawing changes without the major expense of redrawing the plans. This package also allows you to print copies of the modified plans as needed. The right of building only one structure from these plans is licensed exclusively to the buyer. You may not use this design to build a second or multiple dwelling(s) without purchasing another blueprint. Each violation of the Copyright Law is punishable in a fine.

- **Mirror Reverse Sets -** Plans can be printed in mirror reverse. These plans are useful when the house would fit your site better if all the rooms were on the opposite side than shown. They are simply a mirror image of the original drawings causing the lettering and dimensions to read backwards. Therefore, when ordering mirror reverse drawings, you must purchase at least one set of right-reading plans. Some of our plans are offered mirror reverse right-reading. This means the plan, lettering and dimensions are flipped but read correctly. See the Home Plans Index on page 14 for availability.

Other Helpful Building Aids...

Your Blueprint Package will contain the necessary construction information to build your home. We also offer the following products and services to save you time and money in the building process.

Material Lists

Material lists are available for many of the plans in this book. Each list gives you the quantity, dimensions and description of the building materials necessary to construct your home. You'll get faster and more accurate bids from your contractor while saving money by paying for only the materials you need. See the Home Plans Index on page 14 for availability.
Cost: $125.00
Note: Material lists are not refundable.

Detail Plan Packages

Framing, Plumbing & Electrical Plan Packages: Three separate packages offer homebuilders details for constructing various foundations; numerous floor, wall and roof framing techniques; simple to complex residential wiring; sump and water softener hookups; plumbing connection methods; installation of septic systems and more. Each package includes three-dimensional illustrations and a glossary of terms. Purchase one or all three.
Cost: $20.00 each or all three for $40.00.
Note: These drawings do not pertain to a specific home plan.

The Legal Kit™

Our Legal Kit provides contracts and legal forms to help protect you from the potential pitfalls inherent in the building process. The Kit supplies commonly used forms and contracts suitable for homeowners and builders. It can save you a considerable amount of time and help protect you and your assets during and after construction.
Cost: $35.00

Express Delivery

Most orders are processed within 24 hours of receipt. Please allow 7-10 business days for delivery. If you need to place a rush order, please call us by 11:00 a.m. Monday-Friday CST and ask for express service (allow 1-2 business days).

Technical Assistance

If you have questions, call our technical support line at 1-314-770-2228 between 8:00 a.m. and 5:00 p.m. Monday-Friday CST. Whether it involves design modifications or field assistance, our designers are extremely familiar with all of our designs and will be happy to help you. We want your home to be everything you expect it to be.

HD HOME DESIGN ALTERNATIVES, INC.

COPYRIGHT

These plans are protected under Copyright Law. Reproduction by any means is strictly prohibited. The right of building only one structure from these plans is licensed exclusively to the buyer and these plans may not be resold unless by express written authorization from home designer/architect. You may not use this design to build a second or multiple dwelling(s) without purchasing another blueprint or blueprints or paying additional design fees. Each violation of the Copyright Law is punishable in a fine.

Home Plans Index

Plan Number	Square Feet	Price Code	Page	Mat. List	Right Read. Reverse	Can. Shipping
718-001D-0003	2,286	E	289	•		
718-001D-0007	2,874	E	17	•		
718-001D-0008	2,935	E	114	•		
718-001D-0013	1,882	D	210	•		
718-001D-0016	2,847	E	105	•		
718-001D-0024	1,360	A	306	•		
718-001D-0028	2,461	D	293	•		
718-001D-0031	1,501	B	95	•		
718-001D-0037	3,216	F	192	•		
718-001D-0059	2,050	C	288	•		
718-001D-0060	1,818	C	32	•		
718-001D-0061	1,875	C	29	•		
718-001D-0064	2,262	D	200	•		
718-001D-0066	2,511	D	129	•		
718-001D-0067	1,285	B	111	•		
718-001D-0080	1,832	C	224	•		
718-003D-0001	2,058	C	96	•		
718-003D-0002	1,676	B	191	•		
718-003D-0005	1,708	B	287	•		
718-004D-0001	2,505	D	19	•		
718-004D-0002	1,823	C	100	•		
718-005D-0001	1,400	B	116	•		
718-006D-0003	1,674	B	209	•		
718-006D-0004	1,996	C	93	•		
718-007D-0003	2,806	E	284	•		
718-007D-0004	2,531	D	199	•		
718-007D-0005	2,336	D	188	•		
718-007D-0008	2,452	D	121	•		
718-007D-0010	1,721	C	35	•		
718-007D-0011	2,182	D	134	•		
718-007D-0015	2,828	F	201	•		
718-007D-0017	1,882	C	228	•		
718-007D-0030	1,140	AA	78	•		
718-007D-0032	1,294	A	174	•		
718-007D-0038	1,524	B	270	•		
718-007D-0039	1,563	B	28	•		
718-007D-0041	1,700	B	202	•		
718-007D-0048	2,758	E	125	•		
718-007D-0049	1,791	C	219	•		
718-007D-0050	2,723	E	80	•		
718-007D-0052	2,521	D	217	•		
718-007D-0053	2,334	D	206	•		
718-007D-0054	1,575	B	257	•		
718-007D-0055	2,029	D	163	•		
718-007D-0056	3,199	E	55	•		
718-007D-0062	2,483	D	102	•		
718-007D-0064	2,967	E	147	•		
718-007D-0065	2,218	D	248	•		
718-007D-0067	1,761	B	66	•		
718-007D-0068	1,384	B	176	•		
718-007D-0072	2,900	E	275	•		
718-007D-0075	1,684	B	303	•		
718-007D-0077	1,977	C	23	•		
718-007D-0078	2,514	D	138	•		
718-007D-0079	2,727	E	232	•		
718-007D-0085	1,787	B	86	•		
718-007D-0088	1,299	A	252	•		
718-007D-0089	2,125	C	168	•		
718-007D-0100	2,409	D	110	•		
718-007D-0101	2,384	D	38	•		
718-007D-0103	1,231	A	119	•		
718-007D-0105	1,084	AA	214	•		
718-007D-0106	1,200	A	75	•		
718-007D-0112	1,062	AA	183			
718-007D-0113	2,547	D	298	•		
718-007D-0116	2,100	C	262			
718-007D-0117	2,695	E	42	•		
718-007D-0118	1,991	C	131	•		
718-007D-0119	1,621	B	236	•		
718-007D-0121	1,559	B	70	•		
718-007D-0122	2,054	C	160			
718-007D-0123	1,308	A	279	•		
718-007D-0124	1,944	C	51			
718-007D-0126	1,365	A	144	•		
718-007D-0134	1,310	A	242			
718-007D-0136	1,533	B	60			
718-007D-0137	1,568	B	153			
718-007D-0140	1,591	B	266	•		
718-007D-0146	1,929	C	49			
718-007D-0157	1,599	B	150			
718-007D-0162	1,519	B	196			
718-007D-0163	1,580	B	245			
718-007D-0164	1,741	B	314			
718-008D-0045	1,540	B	3	•		
718-008D-0072	1,200	A	5	•		
718-008D-0079	2,253	D	7			
718-008D-0080	2,009	C	9	•		
718-008D-0081	2,420	D	11	•		
718-011D-0003	1,693	C	20		•	
718-011D-0004	1,997	D	112		•	
718-011D-0006	1,873	D	108		•	
718-011D-0007	1,580	C	212	•	•	
718-011D-0010	2,197	C	120	•	•	
718-011D-0025	2,287	E	205	•	•	
718-011D-0035	6,088	H	90		•	
718-011D-0041	3,231	G	203	•	•	
718-011D-0042	2,561	F	187		•	
718-011D-0045	2,850	F	283		•	
718-013D-0009	1,598	C	292			
718-013D-0011	1,643	B	221			
718-013D-0015	1,787	B	25			
718-013D-0020	1,985	C	207			
718-013D-0022	1,992	C	123	•	•	
718-013D-0025	2,097	C	216	•		
718-013D-0028	2,239	D	313			
718-013D-0033	2,340	D	273	•		
718-016D-0021	1,892	D	308	•		
718-016D-0048	2,567	F	37	•		
718-016D-0049	1,793	B	227	•		
718-016D-0051	1,945	D	132	•		
718-016D-0055	1,040	B	77	•		
718-016D-0058	2,874	G	296	•		
718-017D-0001	2,043	D	41	•		
718-017D-0006	3,006	E	99	•		
718-017D-0007	1,567	C	141	•		
718-020D-0005	1,770	B	230			
718-020D-0010	2,194	C	305			
718-020D-0013	3,012	E	193			
718-020D-0039	3,059	E	52			
718-021D-0003	3,035	E	31	•		
718-021D-0006	1,600	C	148	•		
718-021D-0008	1,266	A	127	•		
718-021D-0011	1,800	D	241	•		
718-021D-0012	1,672	C	104	•		
718-021D-0020	2,360	D	57	•		
718-023D-0001	3,149	E	154	•		
718-023D-0006	2,357	D	247	•		
718-023D-0009	2,333	D	65	•		
718-024D-0006	1,618	C	2			
718-024D-0011	1,819	C	309			
718-024D-0017	2,697	E	291			
718-024D-0019	2,331	D	164			
718-024D-0040	2,503	D	259			
718-027D-0001	2,147	C	82	•		
718-027D-0003	2,061	D	8	•		
718-027D-0005	2,135	D	167	•		
718-027D-0006	2,076	C	299	•		
718-028D-0003	1,716	B	260			
718-028D-0004	1,785	B	18		•	
718-028D-0006	1,700	B	178			
718-028D-0008	2,156	C	220		•	
718-028D-0010	2,214	D	98		•	
718-028D-0011	2,123	C	45		•	
718-028D-0030	1,856	C	126		•	
718-028D-0043	2,052	C	295			
718-028D-0049	2,214	D	107		•	
718-029D-0002	1,619	B	137	•		
718-030D-0001	1,374	A	39			
718-030D-0003	1,753	B	136			
718-030D-0005	1,815	C	235			
718-030D-0009	1,772	B	198			
718-030D-0010	1,919	C	301			
718-030D-0011	2,089	C	282			
718-030D-0012	2,143	C	195			
718-035D-0001	1,715	B	231	•		
718-035D-0006	1,671	B	54			
718-035D-0013	1,497	A	152	•		
718-035D-0017	1,373	A	244	•		
718-035D-0019	1,676	B	73			
718-035D-0021	1,978	C	162	•		
718-035D-0025	1,614	B	263			
718-035D-0028	1,779	B	89	•		
718-035D-0032	1,856	C	184	•		
718-035D-0036	2,193	C	286	•		
718-035D-0045	1,749	B	59	•		
718-035D-0051	1,491	A	315	•		
718-035D-0052	2,072	C	43	•	•	
718-036D-0001	2,267	D	140			
718-036D-0012	2,470	D	233			
718-036D-0013	2,200	D	56			
718-036D-0048	1,830	C	156			
718-036D-0058	2,529	D	250			
718-036D-0059	2,674	E	69			
718-037D-0002	1,816	C	171	•		
718-037D-0004	2,449	E	265	•		
718-037D-0005	3,050	E	85	•		
718-037D-0006	1,772	C	6	•		
718-037D-0007	2,282	D	177	•		
718-037D-0009	2,059	C	277	•		
718-037D-0013	2,213	E	91	•		
718-037D-0014	2,932	F	155	•		
718-037D-0015	2,772	E	186	•		
718-037D-0016	2,066	C	312	•		
718-038D-0036	1,470	A	26	•		
718-038D-0039	1,771	B	246	•		
718-038D-0040	1,642	B	118	•		
718-038D-0044	1,982	C	223	•		
718-038D-0045	2,044	C	46	•		
718-038D-0054	1,560	B	142	•		
718-038D-0055	1,763	C	239	•	•	
718-038D-0056	1,712	B	62	•		
718-039D-0012	1,815	C	159	•		
718-039D-0020	2,010	C	255	•		
718-040D-0001	1,814	D	72	•		
718-040D-0003	1,475	B	172	•		
718-040D-0007	2,073	D	74	•		
718-040D-0016	3,013	E	297	•		
718-040D-0019	1,854	D	109	•		
718-040D-0022	2,327	D	166	•		
718-040D-0026	1,393	B	268	•		
718-040D-0027	1,597	C	88	•		
718-043D-0003	1,890	C	185			
718-043D-0005	1,734	B	280			
718-043D-0006	2,355	D	316			
718-043D-0007	2,788	E	271			
718-043D-0008	1,496	A	30			
718-043D-0011	2,422	D	122			
718-043D-0018	3,502	F	218			
718-043D-0019	3,230	F	44			
718-047D-0005	1,885	C	34			
718-047D-0020	1,783	B	157			
718-047D-0024	1,786	B	133			
718-047D-0025	1,806	C	226			
718-047D-0032	1,963	C	237			
718-047D-0035	2,077	C	253			
718-047D-0050	2,293	D	53			
718-047D-0062	3,359	G	146			
718-047D-0075	2,052	C	58			
718-047D-0077	2,326	D	106			
718-047D-0079	2,508	D	240			
718-047D-0086	3,570	F	290			
718-047D-0090	3,882	F	64			
718-048D-0001	1,865	D	161	•		
718-048D-0011	1,550	B	261	•		
718-051D-0006	2,171	C	81			
718-051D-0011	2,155	C	180			
718-051D-0020	2,491	D	281			
718-051D-0030	2,034	F	21			
718-051D-0055	1,907	C	124			
718-051D-0057	2,229	D	211			
718-051D-0117	2,128	C	33			
718-051D-0124	2,236	E	135			
718-052D-0043	1,854	C	234			
718-052D-0044	1,856	C	319	•		
718-052D-0052	1,936	C	48			
718-052D-0089	2,911	E	145			
718-053D-0001	1,582	B	175	•		
718-053D-0002	1,668	C	267	•		
718-053D-0003	1,992	C	197	•		
718-053D-0007	1,922	C	243	•		
718-053D-0015	2,214	D	67	•		
718-053D-0016	2,216	D	165	•		
718-053D-0021	2,826	E	304	•		
718-053D-0030	1,657	B	256	•		
718-053D-0053	1,609	B	76	•		
718-053D-0058	1,818	C	83	•		
718-053D-0060	2,636	E	311	•		
718-055D-0016	2,698	E	179	•	•	
718-055D-0017	1,525	B	272	•	•	
718-055D-0022	2,107	C	4	•	•	
718-055D-0023	4,237	G	208	•	•	
718-055D-0032	2,439	D	22	•	•	
718-055D-0035	3,059	E	113	•	•	
718-055D-0038	2,247	D	213	•	•	
718-055D-0088	2,261	D	36	•	•	
718-055D-0089	2,635	E	139	•	•	
718-055D-0091	2,499	D	225	•	•	
718-055D-0098	3,060	E	61	•	•	
718-055D-0099	1,897	C	300	•	•	
718-055D-0103	2,716	E	149	•	•	
718-055D-0109	2,217	C	249	•	•	
718-055D-0118	2,789	E	97	•	•	
718-056D-0001	1,624	E	204			
718-056D-0003	2,272	G	189			
718-056D-0005	2,111	H	276			
718-056D-0007	1,985	G	47			
718-056D-0008	1,821	E	101			
718-056D-0027	1,580	E	143			
718-058D-0002	2,059	C	68	•		
718-058D-0016	1,558	B	169	•		
718-058D-0020	1,428	A	258	•		
718-058D-0032	1,879	C	87	•		
718-058D-0038	1,680	B	181	•		
718-058D-0048	3,556	F	285	•		
718-058D-0052	2,140	C	24	•		
718-060D-0005	1,742	B	115			
718-060D-0006	1,945	C	215			
718-060D-0007	2,079	C	40			
718-060D-0008	2,281	D	128			
718-060D-0027	1,628	B	238			
718-060D-0028	2,287	D	229			
718-060D-0032	2,969	E	307			
718-062D-0034	2,020	C	63			•
718-062D-0039	2,493	D	158	•		•
718-062D-0041	1,541	B	50	•	•	•
718-062D-0042	2,582	D	194	•	•	•
718-062D-0043	2,750	E	151	•		•
718-062D-0045	2,516	D	251	•		•
718-062D-0046	2,632	E	254	•		•
718-062D-0055	1,583	B	71	•		•
718-062D-0059	1,588	B	173	•	•	•
718-065D-0013	2,041	C	310			
718-065D-0037	2,241	D	294	•		
718-065D-0038	1,663	B	317			
718-065D-0042	2,362	D	79	•		
718-065D-0043	3,816	F	170			
718-065D-0046	2,049	C	269	•	•	
718-067D-0004	1,698	B	94		•	
718-067D-0006	1,840	C	264		•	
718-067D-0007	2,651	E	84			
718-067D-0008	2,327	D	182		•	
718-067D-0010	2,431	D	103		•	
718-067D-0014	2,599	D	274		•	
718-071D-0002	2,770	E	27		•	
718-071D-0003	2,890	E	190		•	
718-071D-0005	3,688	G	318		•	
718-071D-0006	3,746	G	278		•	
718-071D-0007	4,220	G	10		•	
718-071D-0008	4,100	G	130		•	
718-071D-0010	5,250	H	320		•	
718-077D-0002	1,855	D	222	•		
718-077D-0003	1,896	D	92			
718-077D-0004	2,024	D	302	•		
718-077D-0006	2,307	D	117			

Important Information To Know Before You Order

- **Exchange Policies** - Since blueprints are printed in response to your order, we cannot honor requests for refunds. However, if for some reason you find that the plan you have purchased does not meet your requirements, you may exchange that plan for another plan in our collection within 90 days of purchase. At the time of the exchange, you will be charged a processing fee of 25% of your original plan package price, plus the difference in price between the plan packages (if applicable) and the cost to ship the new plans to you.
  Please note: Reproducible drawings can only be exchanged if the package is unopened.

- **Building Codes & Requirements** - At the time the construction drawings were prepared, every effort was made to ensure that these plans and specifications meet nationally recognized codes. Our plans conform to most national building codes. Because building codes vary from area to area, some drawing modifications and/or the assistance of a professional designer or architect may be necessary to comply with your local codes or to accommodate specific building site conditions. We advise you to consult with your local building official for information regarding codes governing your area.

Questions? Call Our Customer Service Number 1-877-671-6036

Blueprint Price Schedule — BEST VALUE

Price Code	1-Set*	SAVE $110 5-Sets	SAVE $200 8-Sets	Reproducible Masters
AAA	$225	$295	$340	$440
AA	$325	$395	$440	$540
A	$385	$455	$500	$600
B	$445	$515	$560	$660
C	$500	$570	$615	$715
D	$560	$630	$675	$775
E	$620	$690	$735	$835
F	$675	$745	$790	$890
G	$765	$835	$880	$980
H	$890	$960	$1005	$1105

Plan prices subject to change without notice.
Please note that plans and material lists are not refundable.

- **Additional Sets*** - Additional sets of the plan ordered are available for $45.00 each. Five-set, eight-set, and reproducible packages offer considerable savings.

- **Mirror Reverse Plans*** - Available for an additional $15.00 per set, these plans are simply a mirror image of the original drawings causing the dimensions and lettering to read backwards. Therefore, when ordering mirror reverse plans, you must purchase at least one set of right-reading plans. Some of our plans are offered mirror reverse right-reading. This means the plan, lettering and dimensions are flipped but read correctly. To purchase a mirror reverse right-reading set, the cost is an additional $150.00. See the Home Plans Index on page 14 for availability.

- **One-Set Study Package*** - We offer a one-set plan package so you can study your home in detail. This one set is considered a study set and is marked "not for construction." It is a copyright violation to reproduce blueprints.

*Available only within 90 days after purchase of plan package or reproducible masters of same plan.

Shipping & Handling Charges

U.S. SHIPPING - HI and AK express only

	1-4 Sets	5-7 Sets	8 Sets or Reproducibles
Regular (allow 7-10 business days)	$15.00	$17.50	$25.00
Priority (allow 3-5 business days)	$25.00	$30.00	$35.00
Express* (allow 1-2 business days)	$35.00	$40.00	$45.00

CANADA SHIPPING (to/from) - Plans with suffix 62D

	1-4 Sets	5-7 Sets	8 Sets or Reproducibles
Standard (allow 8-12 business days)	$25.00	$30.00	$35.00
Express* (allow 3-5 business days)	$40.00	$40.00	$45.00

Overseas Shipping/International - Call, fax, or e-mail (plans@hdainc.com) for shipping costs.

* For express delivery please call us by 11:00 a.m. Monday-Friday CST

How To Order

For fastest service, Call Toll-Free
1-877-671-6036
24 HOURS A DAY

Four Easy Ways To Order

1. CALL toll-free 1-877-671-6036 for credit card orders. MasterCard, Visa, Discover and American Express are accepted.
2. FAX your order to 1-314-770-2226.
3. MAIL the Order Form to: HDA, Inc.
   944 Anglum Road
   St. Louis, MO 63042
4. ONLINE visit
   www.familyhandyman.com/homeplans

Order Form

Please send me -

PLAN NUMBER 718BT - _____

PRICE CODE _____ (see page 14)

Specify Foundation Type (see plan page for availability)
☐ Slab ☐ Crawl space ☐ Pier
☐ Basement ☐ Walk-out basement

☐ Reproducible Masters $ _____
☐ Eight-Set Plan Package $ _____
☐ Five-Set Plan Package $ _____
☐ One-Set Study Package (no mirror reverse) $ _____
☐ Additional Plan Sets*
   _____ (Qty.) at $45.00 each $ _____

Mirror Reverse*
☐ Right-reading $150 one-time charge
   (see index on page 14 for availability) $ _____
☐ Print in Mirror Reverse (where right-reading is not available)
   _____ (Qty.) at $15.00 each $ _____
☐ Material List* $125 (see page 14 for avail.) $ _____
☐ Legal Kit (see page 13) $ _____

Detail Plan Packages: (see page 13)
☐ Framing ☐ Electrical ☐ Plumbing $ _____

SUBTOTAL $ _____
Sales Tax - MO residents add 6% $ _____
☐ Shipping / Handling (see chart at left) $ _____
TOTAL ENCLOSED (US funds only) $ _____

I hereby authorize HDA, Inc. to charge this purchase to my credit card account (check one):

☐ MasterCard ☐ Visa ☐ Discover ☐ American Express

Credit Card number _____

Expiration date _____

Signature _____

Name _____
      (Please print or type)

Street Address _____
      (Please **do not** use PO Box)

City _____

State _____ Zip _____

Daytime phone number (___) - _____

Email _____

I'm a ☐ Builder/Contractor   I ☐ have
      ☐ Homeowner   ☐ have not
      ☐ Renter   selected my
                               general contractor

Thank you for your order!

Quick & Easy Customizing
Make Changes To Your Home Plan In 4 Steps

Here's an affordable and efficient way to make changes to your plan.

1. **Select the house plan that most closely meets your needs.** Purchase of a reproducible master is necessary in order to make changes to a plan.

2. **Call 1-877-671-6036 to place your order.** Tell the sales representative you're interested in customizing a plan. A $50 nonrefundable consultation fee will be charged. You will then be instructed to complete a customization checklist indicating all the changes you wish to make to your plan. You may attach sketches if necessary. If you proceed with the custom changes the $50 will be credited to the total amount charged.

3. **FAX the completed customization checklist** to our design consultant at 1-866-477-5173 or e-mail customize@hdainc.com. Within 24-48* business hours you will be provided with a written cost estimate to modify your plan. Our design consultant will contact you by phone if you wish to discuss any of your changes in greater detail.

4. **Once you approve the estimate,** a 75% retainer fee is collected and customization work gets underway. Preliminary drawings can usually be completed within 5-10* business days. Following approval of the preliminary drawings your design changes are completed within 5-10* business days. Your remaining 25% balance due is collected prior to shipment of your completed drawings. You will be shipped five sets of revised blueprints or a reproducible master, plus a customized materials list if required.

Sample Modification Pricing Guide

The average prices specified below are provided as examples only. They refer to the most commonly requested changes, and are subject to change without notice. Prices for changes will vary or differ, from the prices below, depending on the number of modifications requested, the plan size, style, quality of original plan, format provided to us (originally drawn by hand or computer), and method of design used by the original designer. To obtain a detailed cost estimate or to get more information, please contact us.

Categories	Average Cost*
Adding or removing living space	Quote required
Adding or removing a garage	Starting at $400
Garage: Front entry to side load or vice versa	Starting at $300
Adding a screened porch	Starting at $280
Adding a bonus room in the attic	Starting at $450
Changing full basement to crawl space or vice versa	Starting at $495
Changing full basement to slab or vice versa	Starting at $495
Changing exterior building material	Starting at $200
Changing roof lines	Starting at $360
Adjusting ceiling height	Starting at $280
Adding, moving or removing an exterior opening	$65 per opening
Adding or removing a fireplace	Starting at $90
Modifying a non-bearing wall or room	$65 per room
Changing exterior walls from 2"x4" to 2"x6"	Starting at $200
Redesigning a bathroom or a kitchen	Starting at $120
Reverse plan right reading	Quote required
Adapting plans for local building code requirements	Quote required
Engineering and Architectural stamping and services	Quote required
Adjust plan for handicapped accessibility	Quote required
Interactive Illustrations (choices of exterior materials)	Quote required
Metric conversion of home plan	Starting at $400

*Prices and Terms are subject to change without notice.

Plan #718-001D-0007

2,874 total square feet of living area

Massive Ranch With Classy Features

Special features

- Large family room with sloped ceiling and wood beams adjoins the kitchen and breakfast area with windows on two walls
- Large foyer opens to family room with massive stone fireplace and open stairs to the basement
- Private master bedroom includes a raised tub under the bay window, dramatic dressing area and a huge walk-in closet
- 4 bedrooms, 2 1/2 baths, 2-car side entry garage
- Basement foundation

Price Code E

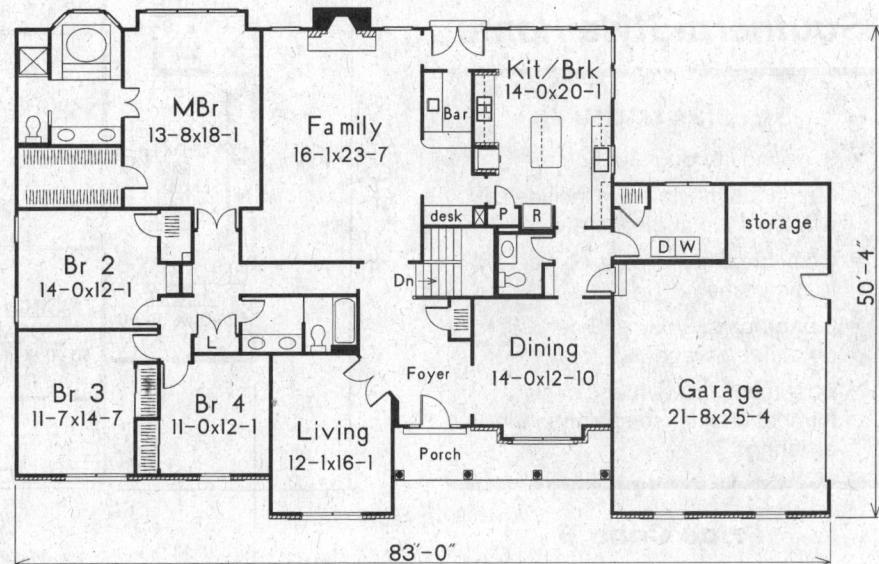

TO ORDER BLUEPRINTS USE THE FORM ON PAGE 15 OR CALL TOLL-FREE 1-877-671-6036
View thousands more home plans online at www.familyhandyman.com/HOMEPLANS

The Family Handyman

Plan #718-028D-0004

1,785 total square feet of living area

Traditional Southern-Style Home

Special features

- 9' ceilings throughout home
- Luxurious master bath includes a whirlpool tub and separate shower
- Cozy breakfast area is convenient to the kitchen
- 3 bedrooms, 3 baths, 2-car detached garage
- Basement, crawl space or slab foundation, please specify when ordering

Price Code B

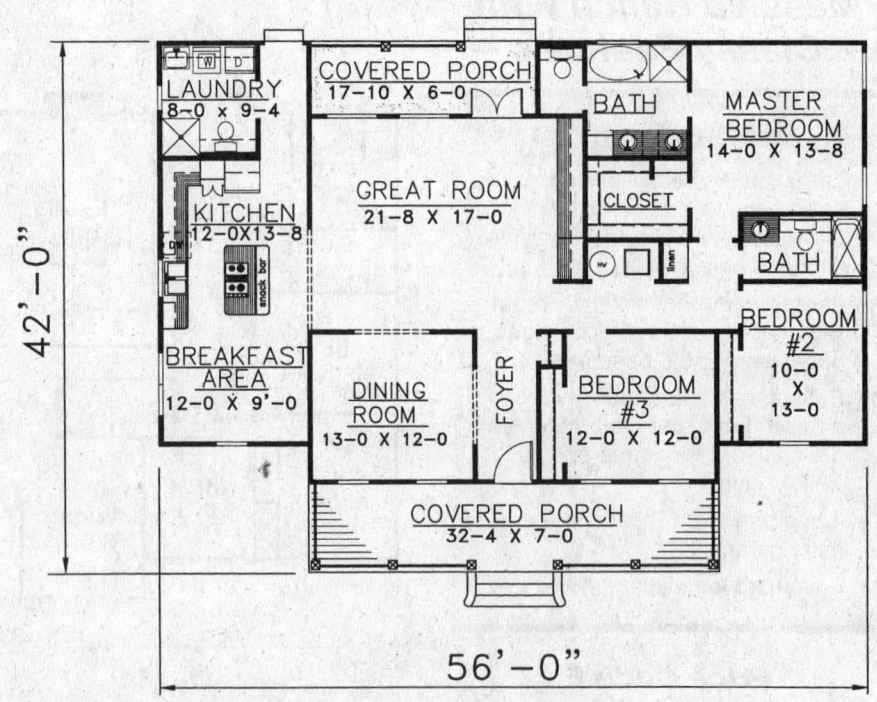

TO ORDER BLUEPRINTS USE THE FORM ON PAGE 15 OR CALL TOLL-FREE 1-877-671-6036
View thousands more home plans online at www.familyhandyman.com/HOMEPLANS

Plan #718-004D-0001

2,505 total square feet of living area

Charming House, Spacious And Functional

Special features

- The garage features extra storage area and ample workspace
- Laundry room is accessible from the garage and the outdoors
- Deluxe raised tub and immense walk-in closet grace master bath
- 3 bedrooms, 2 1/2 baths, 2-car side entry garage
- Basement foundation, drawings also include crawl space foundation

Price Code D

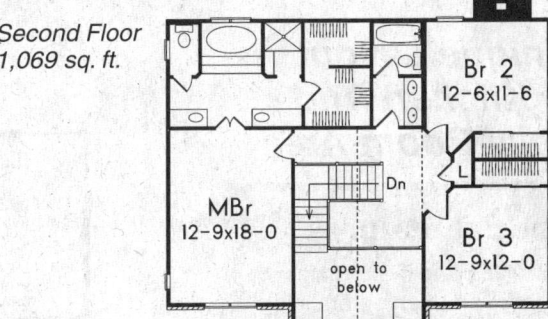

Second Floor 1,069 sq. ft.

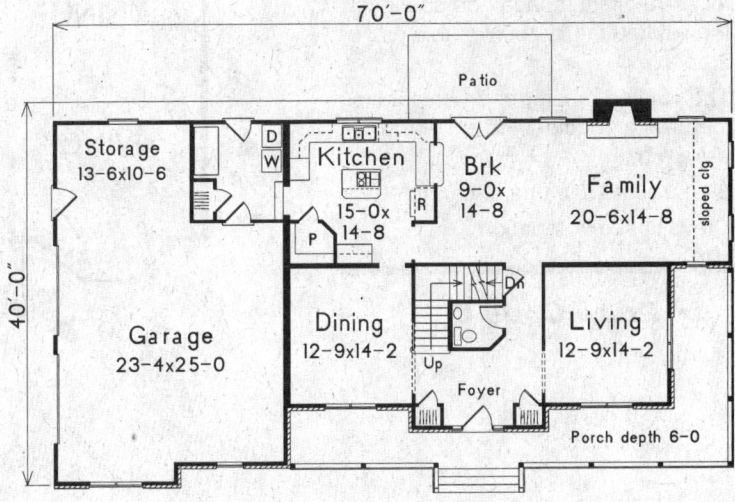

First Floor 1,436 sq. ft.

TO ORDER BLUEPRINTS USE THE FORM ON PAGE 15 OR CALL TOLL-FREE 1-877-671-6036
View thousands more home plans online at www.familyhandyman.com/homeplans

Plan #718-011D-0003

1,693 total square feet of living area

Unique Layout In Kitchen And Family Room Area

Special features

- Formal dining and living rooms combine for an open entertaining area
- The kitchen includes a bayed nook for extra dining space and opens to the vaulted family room with a cozy fireplace
- The vaulted master bedroom features a double-door entry and private bath
- 3 bedrooms, 2 baths, 2-car garage
- Crawl space foundation

Price Code C

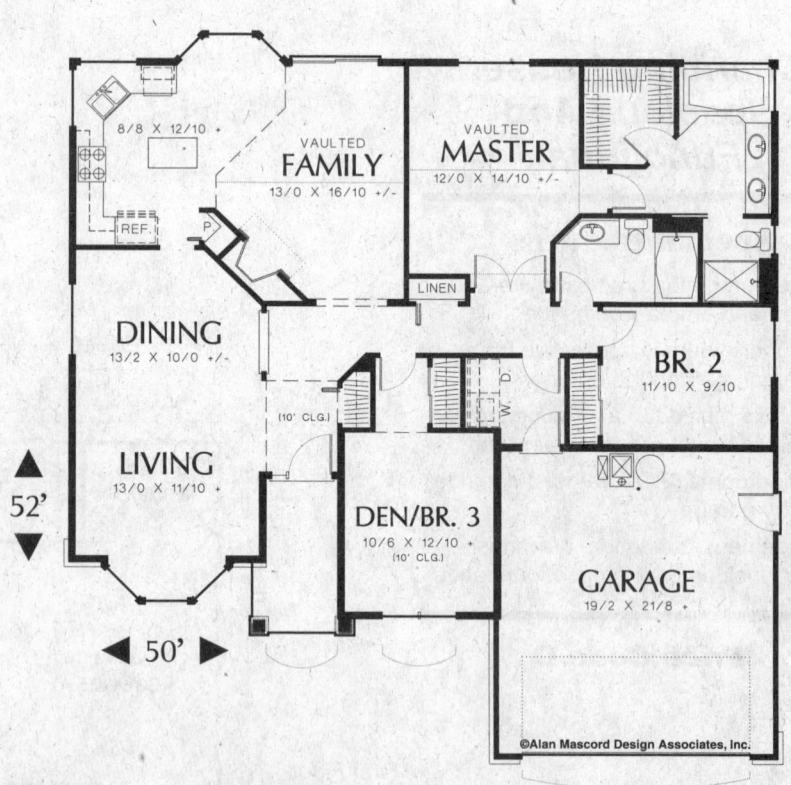

TO ORDER BLUEPRINTS USE THE FORM ON PAGE 15 OR CALL TOLL-FREE 1-877-671-6036
View thousands more home plans online at www.familyhandyman.com/homeplans

Plan #718-051D-0030

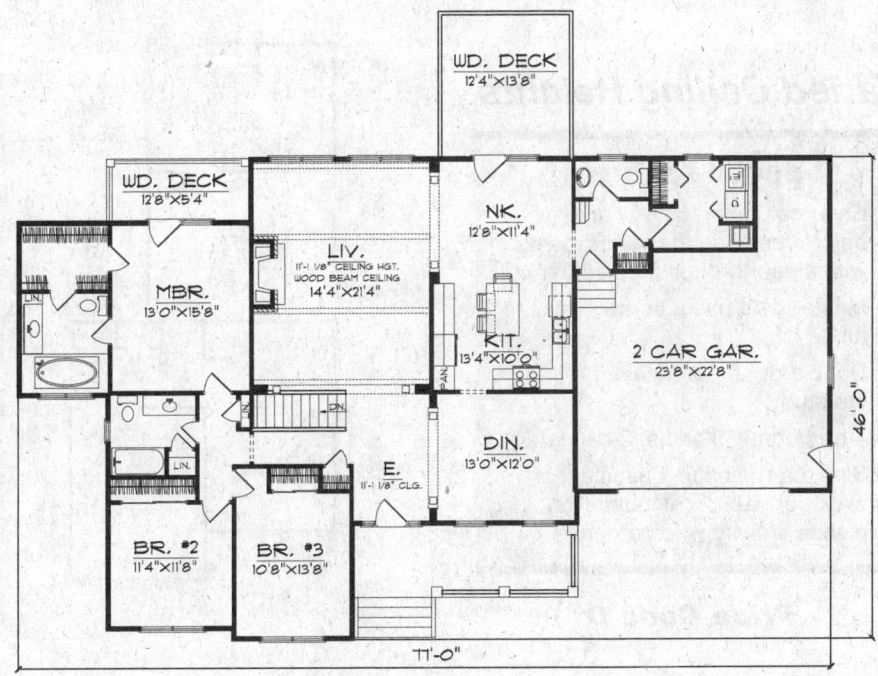

2,034 total square feet of living area

Inviting Covered Porch Entry

Special features

- Oversized tub in master bath adds luxury
- Rustic touches are present in the great room which features a beamed ceiling and a large brick fireplace
- Center island in kitchen features extra seating
- 3 bedrooms, 2 1/2 baths, 2-car garage
- Basement foundation

Price Code F

TO ORDER BLUEPRINTS USE THE FORM ON PAGE 15 OR CALL TOLL-FREE 1-877-671-6036
View thousands more home plans online at www.familyhandyman.com/HOMEPLANS

Plan #718-055D-0032

2,439 total square feet of living area

Varied Ceiling Heights

Special features

- Enter columned gallery area just before reaching the family room with a see-through fireplace
- Master bath has a corner whirlpool tub
- Double-door entrance leads into the study
- 4 bedrooms, 3 baths, 2-car garage
- Slab, crawl space, basement or walk-out basement foundation, please specify when ordering

Price Code D

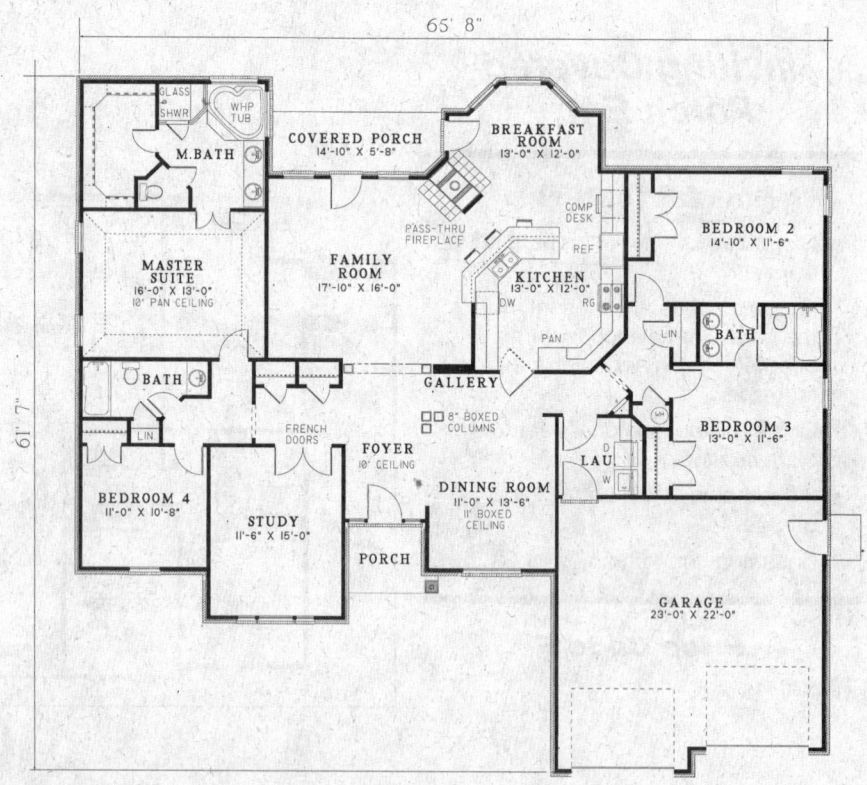

TO ORDER BLUEPRINTS USE THE FORM ON PAGE 15 OR CALL TOLL-FREE 1-877-671-6036
View thousands more home plans online at www.familyhandyman.com/HOMEPLANS

Plan #718-007D-0077

1,977 total square feet of living area

Classic Atrium Ranch With Rooms To Spare

Special features

- Classic traditional exterior is always in style
- Spacious great room boasts a vaulted ceiling, dining area, atrium with elegant staircase and feature windows
- Atrium opens to 1,416 square feet of optional living area below which consists of a family room, two bedrooms, two baths and a study
- 4 bedrooms, 2 1/2 baths, 3-car side entry garage
- Walk-out basement foundation

Price Code C

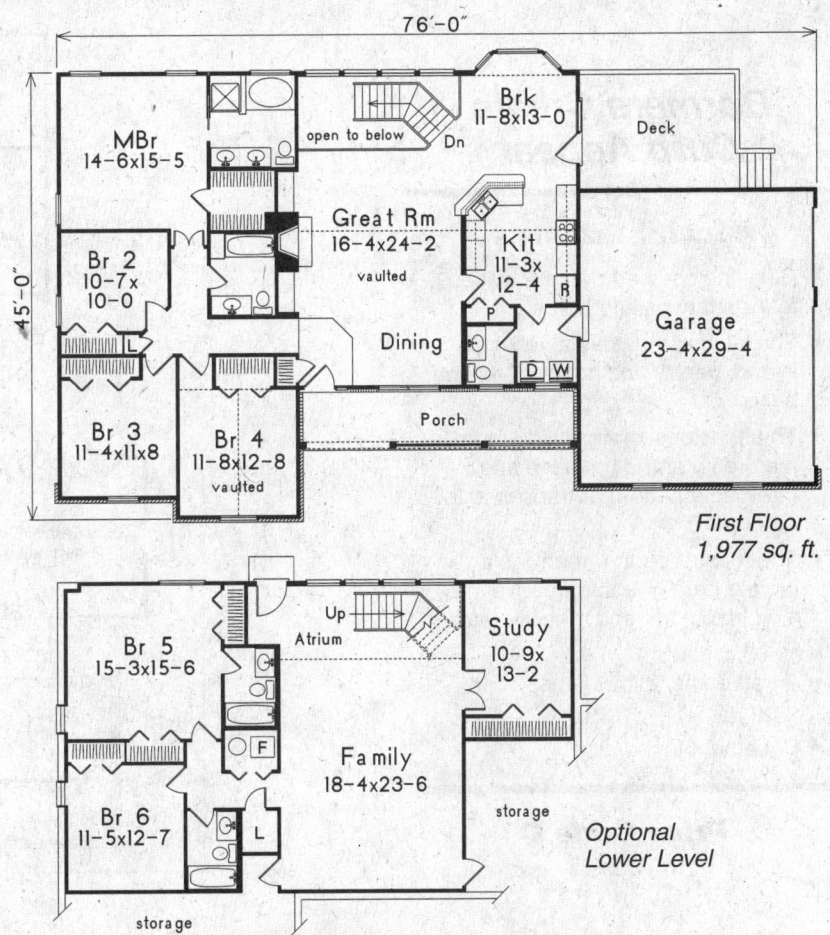

First Floor 1,977 sq. ft.

Optional Lower Level

TO ORDER BLUEPRINTS USE THE FORM ON PAGE 15 OR CALL TOLL-FREE 1-877-671-6036
View thousands more home plans online at www.familyhandyman.com/homeplans

Plan #718-058D-0052

2,140 total square feet of living area

Dormers Create Curb Appeal

Special features

- Relaxing covered porch provides four entrances into home
- The kitchen includes a cooktop island, pantry and connects eating bar
- The spacious family/dining room features a grand fireplace and three double-door entrances to the outdoors
- The master bedroom enjoys a private bath with separate vanities, a whirlpool tub and massive walk-in closet
- 3 bedrooms, 2 1/2 baths, 2-car garage
- Basement foundation

Price Code C

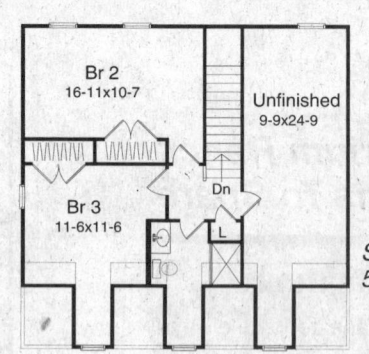

Second Floor 536 sq. ft.

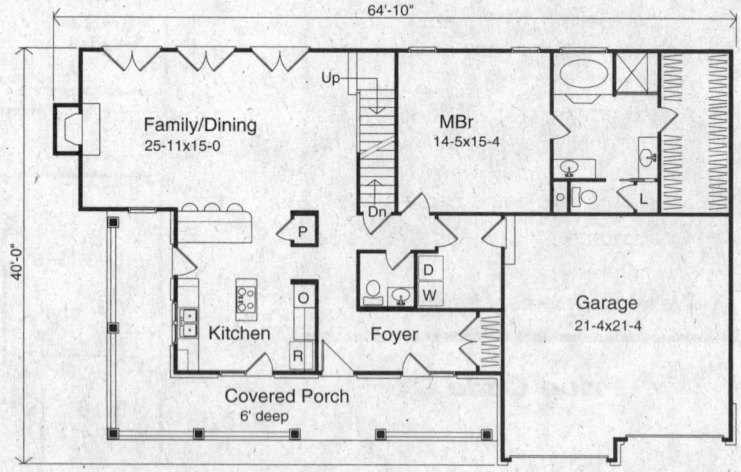

First Floor 1,604 sq. ft.

TO ORDER BLUEPRINTS USE THE FORM ON PAGE 15 OR CALL TOLL-FREE 1-877-671-6036
View thousands more home plans online at www.familyhandyman.com/HOMEPLANS

The Family Handyman

Plan #718-013D-0015

1,787 total square feet of living area

Uncommonly Styled Ranch

Special features

- Skylights brighten screen porch which connects to the family room and deck outdoors
- Master bedroom features a comfortable sitting area, large private bath and direct access to screen porch
- Kitchen has a serving bar which extends dining into the family room
- 3 bedrooms, 2 baths, 2-car side entry garage
- Basement, crawl space or slab foundation, please specify when ordering

Price Code B

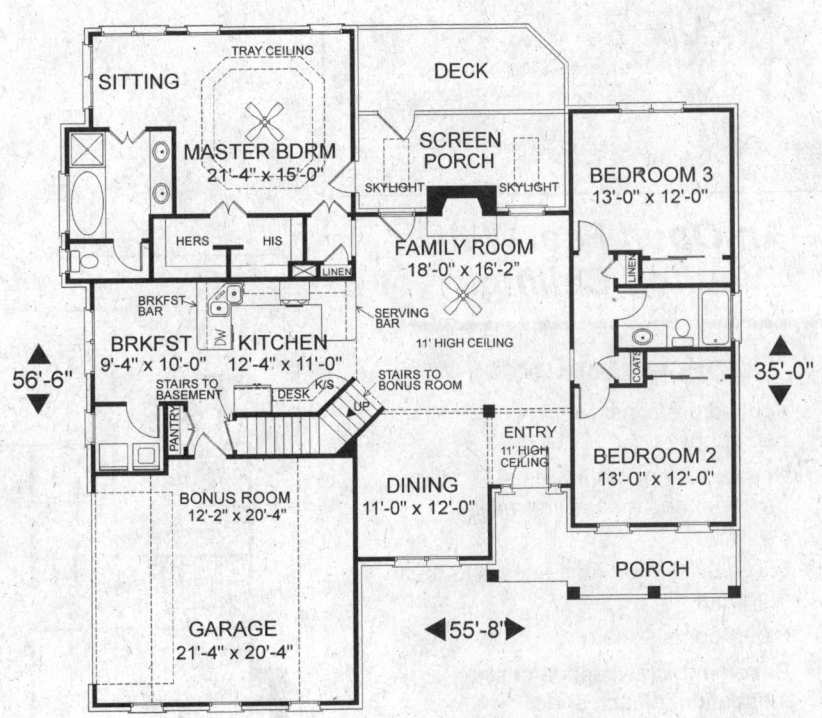

TO ORDER BLUEPRINTS USE THE FORM ON PAGE 15 OR CALL TOLL-FREE 1-877-671-6036
View thousands more home plans online at www.familyhandyman.com/homeplans

The Family Handyman

Plan #718-038D-0036

1,470 total square feet of living area

Rear View

An Open Feel With Vaulted Ceilings

Special features

- Vaulted breakfast room is cheerful and sunny
- Private second floor master bedroom has a bath and walk-in closet
- Large utility room has access to the outdoors
- 3 bedrooms, 2 baths
- Basement, crawl space or slab foundation, please specify when ordering

Price Code A

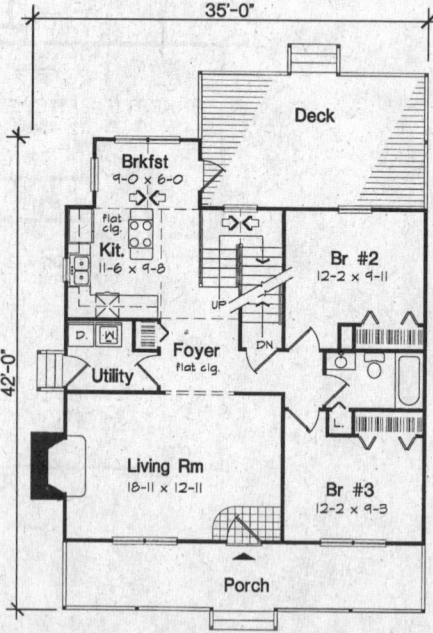

Second Floor
435 sq. ft.

First Floor
1,035 sq. ft.

TO ORDER BLUEPRINTS USE THE FORM ON PAGE 15 OR CALL TOLL-FREE 1-877-671-6036
View thousands more home plans online at www.familyhandyman.com/HOMEPLANS

Plan #718-071D-0002

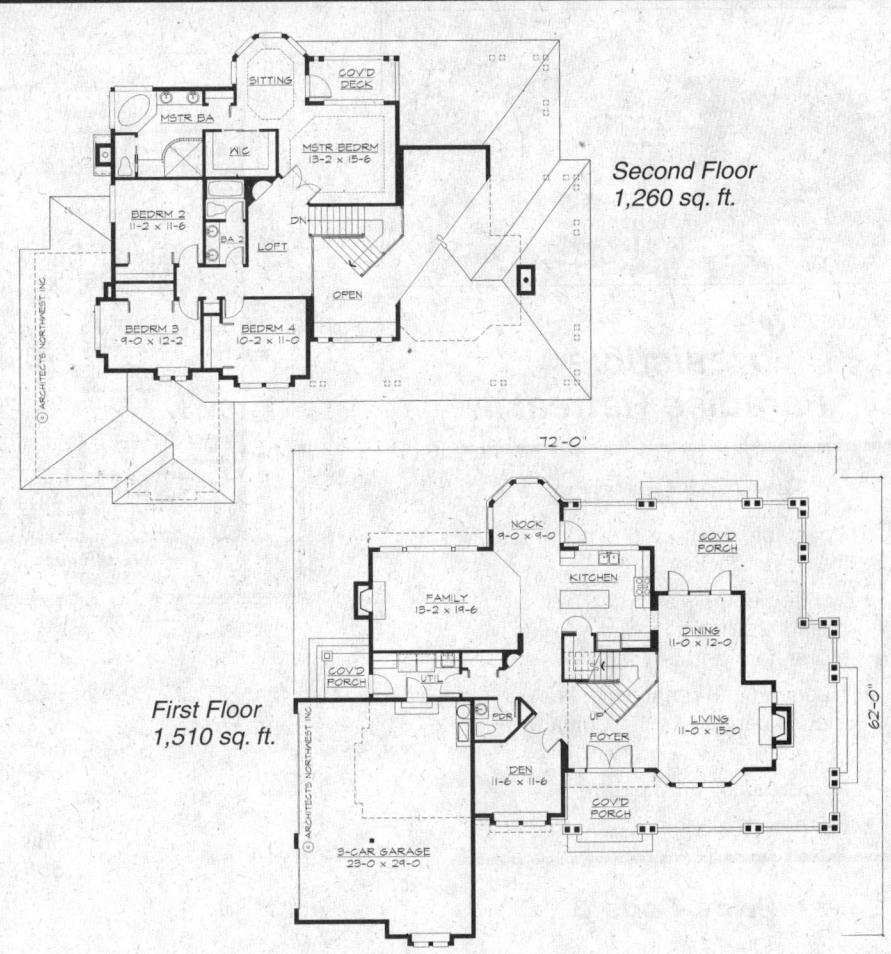

2,770 total square feet of living area

Outdoor Living Areas Surround Home

Special features

- Formal living and dining areas combine for optimal entertaining possibilities including access outdoors and a fireplace
- The cheerful family and breakfast rooms connect for added spaciousness
- A double-door entry into the master bedroom leads to a private covered deck, sitting area and luxurious bath
- 4 bedrooms, 2 1/2 baths, 3-car side entry garage
- Crawl space foundation

Price Code E

TO ORDER BLUEPRINTS USE THE FORM ON PAGE 15 OR CALL TOLL-FREE 1-877-671-6036
View thousands more home plans online at www.familyhandyman.com/HOMEPLANS

Plan #718-007D-0039

1,563 total square feet of living area

Rear View

Irresistible Paradise Retreat

Special features

- Enjoyable wrap-around porch and lower sundeck
- Vaulted entry is adorned with a palladian window, plant shelves, stone floor and fireplace
- Huge vaulted great room has magnificent views through a two-story atrium window wall
- 2 bedrooms, 1 1/2 baths
- Basement foundation

Price Code B

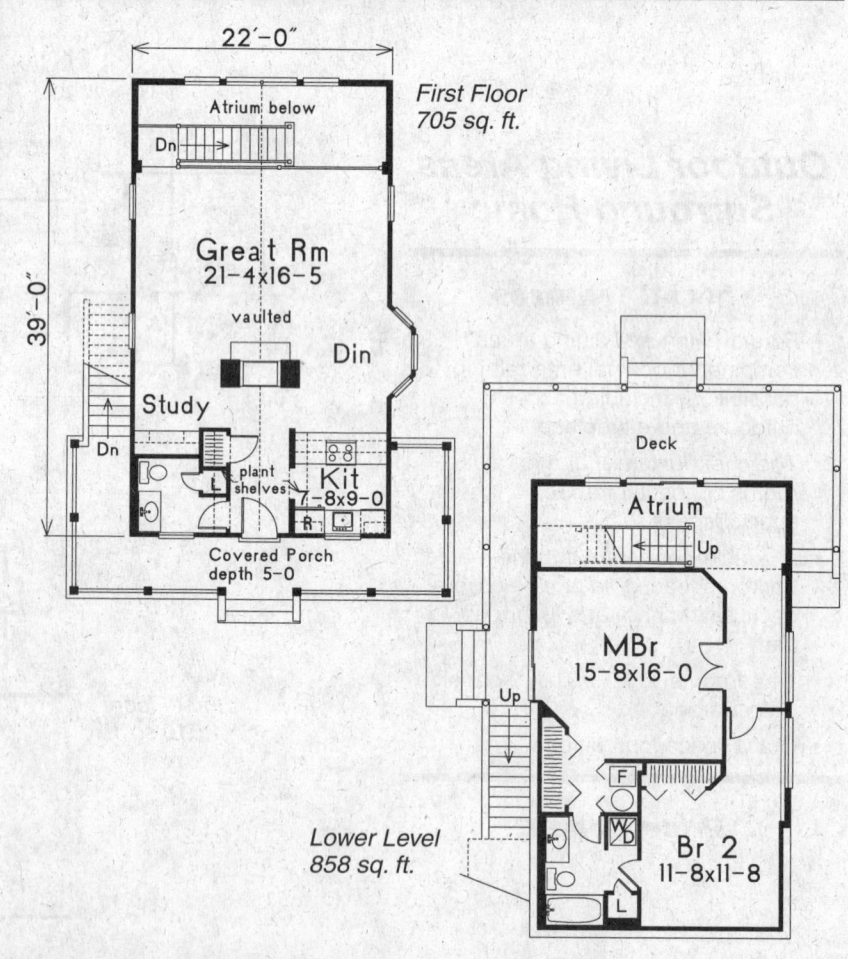

TO ORDER BLUEPRINTS USE THE FORM ON PAGE 15 OR CALL TOLL-FREE 1-877-671-6036
View thousands more home plans online at www.familyhandyman.com/homeplans

Plan #718-001D-0061

1,875 total square feet of living area

Wrap-Around Country Porch

Special features

- Country-style exterior with wrap-around porch and dormers
- Large second floor bedrooms share a dressing area and bath
- Master bedroom includes a bay window, walk-in closet, dressing area and bath
- 3 bedrooms, 2 baths, 2-car side entry garage
- Crawl space foundation, drawings also include basement and slab foundations

Price Code C

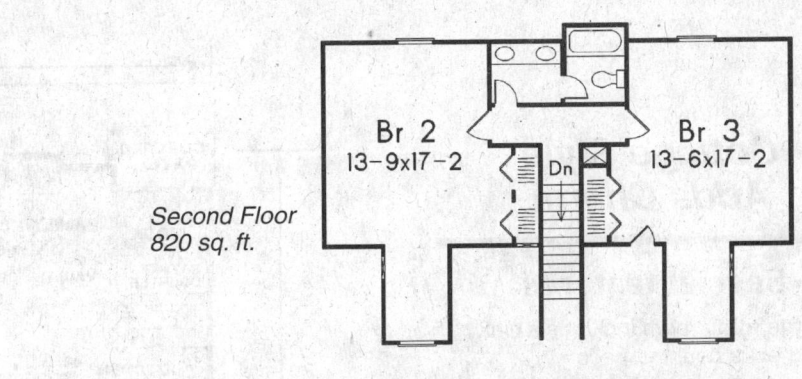

Second Floor 820 sq. ft.

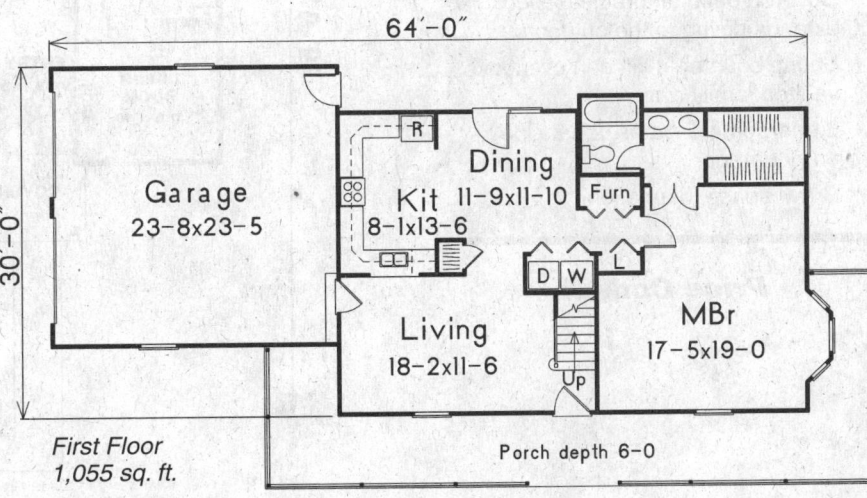

First Floor 1,055 sq. ft.

TO ORDER BLUEPRINTS USE THE FORM ON PAGE 15 OR CALL TOLL-FREE 1-877-671-6036
View thousands more home plans online at www.familyhandyman.com/HOMEPLANS

The Family Handyman

Plan #718-043D-0008

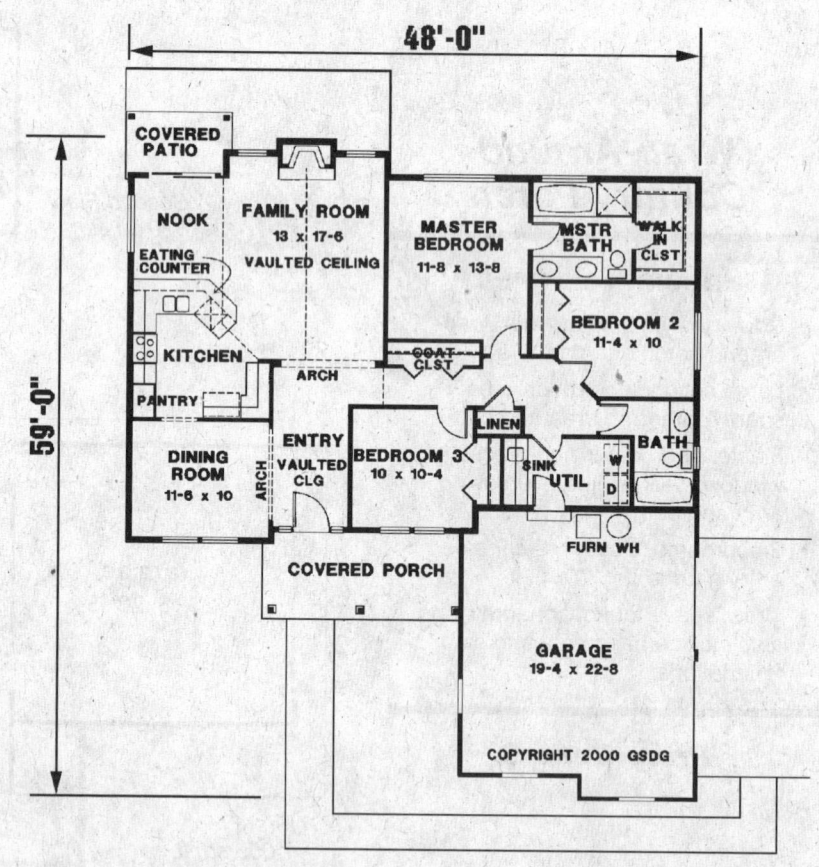

1,496 total square feet of living area

Cottage Style Adds Charm

Special features

- Large utility room includes a sink and extra counterspace
- Covered patio off breakfast nook extends dining to the outdoors
- Eating counter in kitchen overlooks vaulted family room
- 3 bedrooms, 2 baths, 2-car side entry garage
- Crawl space foundation

Price Code A

TO ORDER BLUEPRINTS USE THE FORM ON PAGE 15 OR CALL TOLL-FREE 1-877-671-6036
View thousands more home plans online at www.familyhandyman.com/HOMEPLANS

Plan #718-021D-0003

3,035 total square feet of living area

Traditional Classic, Modern Features Abound

Special features

- Front facade includes large porch
- Private master bedroom with windowed sitting area, walk-in closet, sloped ceiling and skylight
- Formal living and dining rooms adjoin the family room through attractive French doors
- Energy efficient home with 2" x 6" exterior walls
- 4 bedrooms, 3 1/2 baths, 2-car detached side entry garage
- Crawl space foundation, drawings also include slab and basement foundations

Price Code E

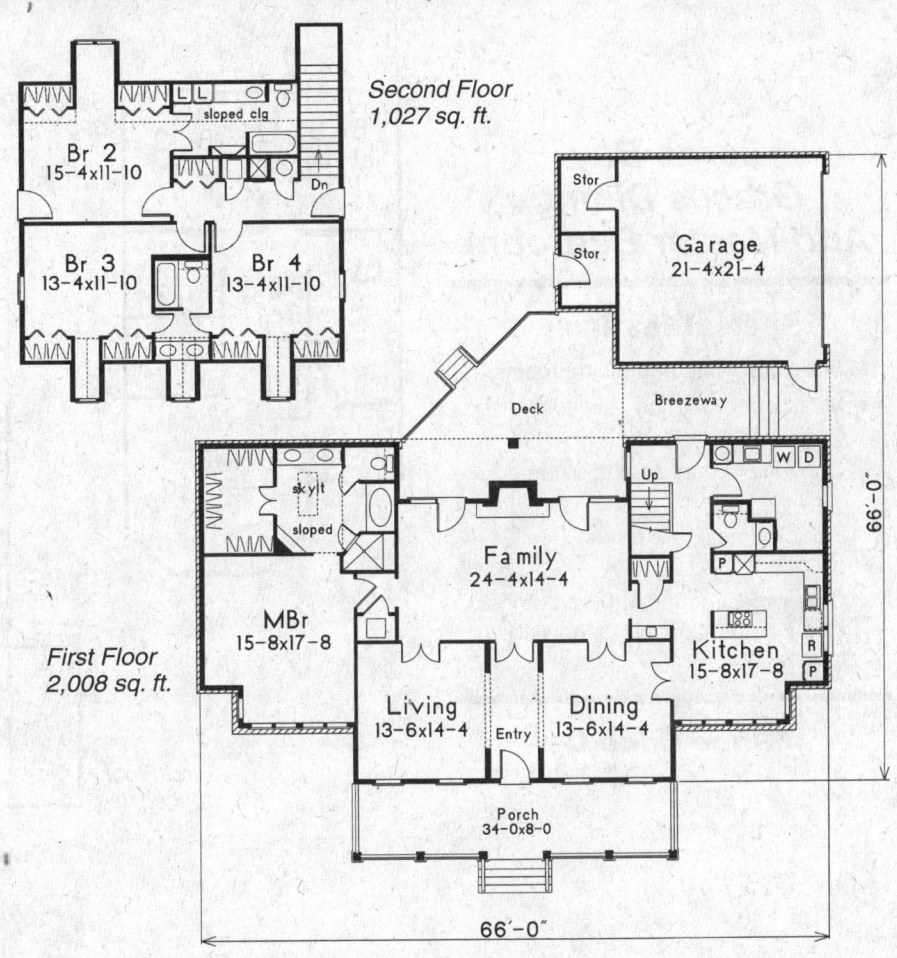

TO ORDER BLUEPRINTS USE THE FORM ON PAGE 15 OR CALL TOLL-FREE 1-877-671-6036
View thousands more home plans online at www.familyhandyman.com/HOMEPLANS

The Family Handyman

Plan #718-001D-0060

1,818 total square feet of living area

Large Bay Graces Dining And Master Bedroom

Special features
- Spacious living and dining rooms
- Master bedroom has a walk-in closet, dressing area and bath
- Convenient carport and storage area
- 3 bedrooms, 2 1/2 baths, 1-car carport
- Crawl space foundation, drawings also include basement and slab foundations

Price Code C

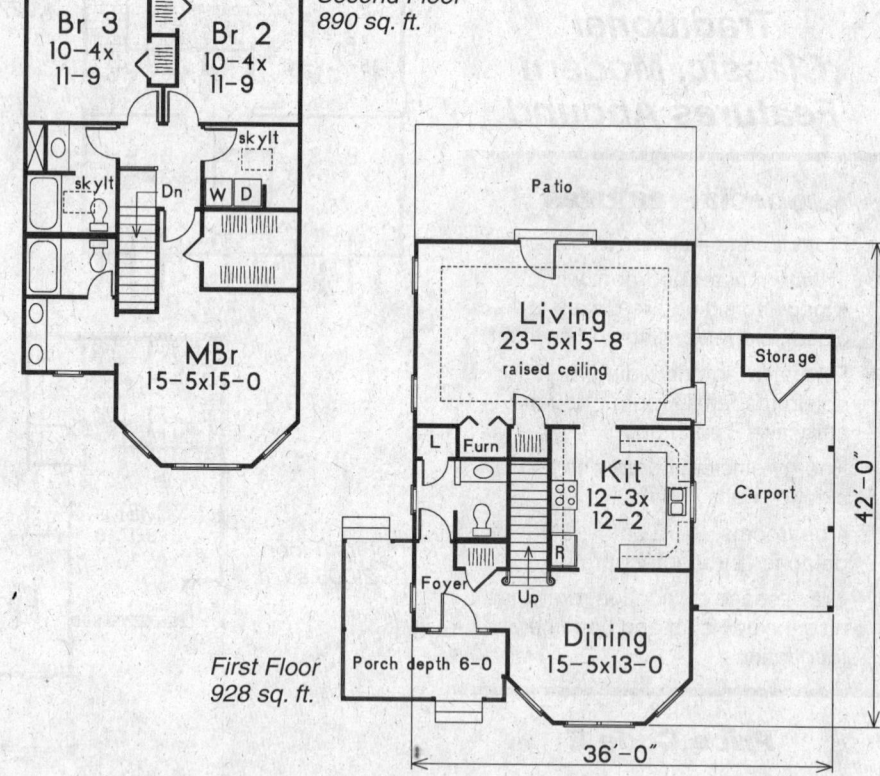

Second Floor 890 sq. ft.

Br 3 10-4x 11-9
Br 2 10-4x 11-9
MBr 15-5x15-0

First Floor 928 sq. ft.

Patio
Living 23-5x15-8 raised ceiling
Storage
Kit 12-3x 12-2
Carport
Foyer
Porch depth 6-0
Dining 15-5x13-0
42'-0"
36'-0"

TO ORDER BLUEPRINTS USE THE FORM ON PAGE 15 OR CALL TOLL-FREE 1-877-671-6036
View thousands more home plans online at www.familyhandyman.com/homeplans

Plan #718-051D-0117

2,128 total square feet of living area

Charming Two-Story Traditional

Special features

- The elegant great room boasts a 10' ceiling and grand fireplace flanked by built-in shelves
- An island with extra seating connects the kitchen and the cozy nook
- The master bedroom retreat enjoys a walk-in closet and private bath with a whirlpool tub
- Secondary bedrooms enjoy walk-in closets and share bath with a double-bowl vanity
- 3 bedrooms, 2 1/2 baths, 2-car garage
- Basement foundation

Price Code C

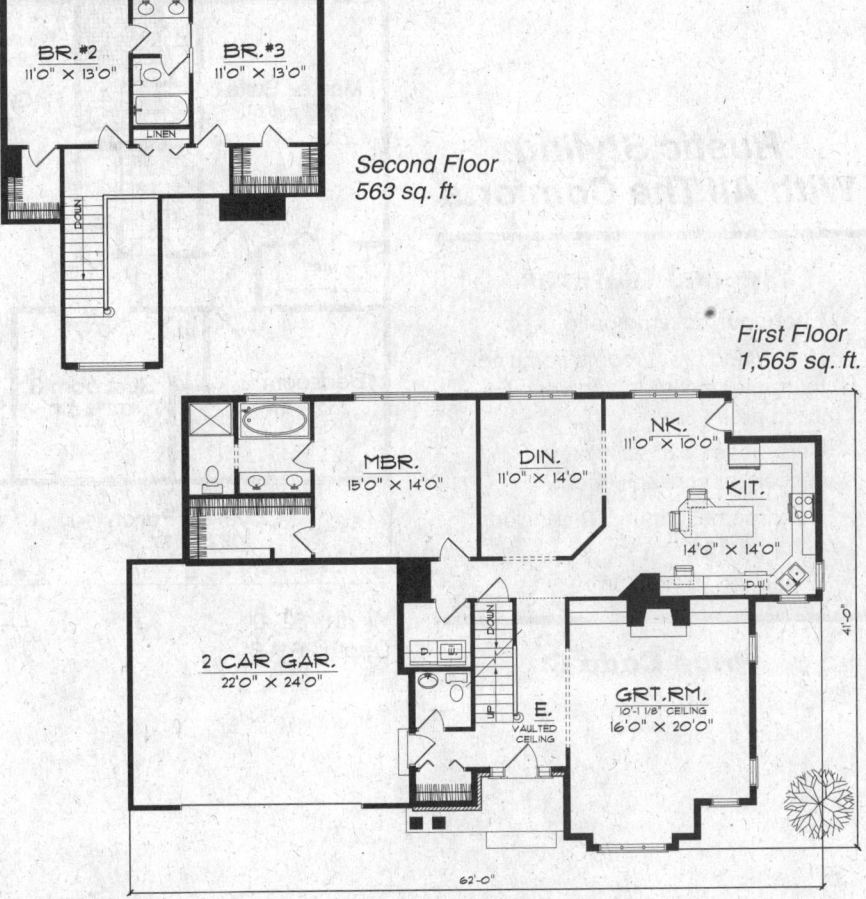

Second Floor 563 sq. ft.

First Floor 1,565 sq. ft.

TO ORDER BLUEPRINTS USE THE FORM ON PAGE 15 OR CALL TOLL-FREE 1-877-671-6036
View thousands more home plans online at www.familyhandyman.com/HOMEPLANS

Plan #718-047D-0005

1,885 total square feet of living area

Rustic Styling With All The Comforts

Special features

- Enormous covered patio
- Dining and great rooms combine to create one large and versatile living area
- Utility room is directly off the kitchen for convenience
- 3 bedrooms, 2 baths, 2-car side entry garage
- Basement foundation

Price Code C

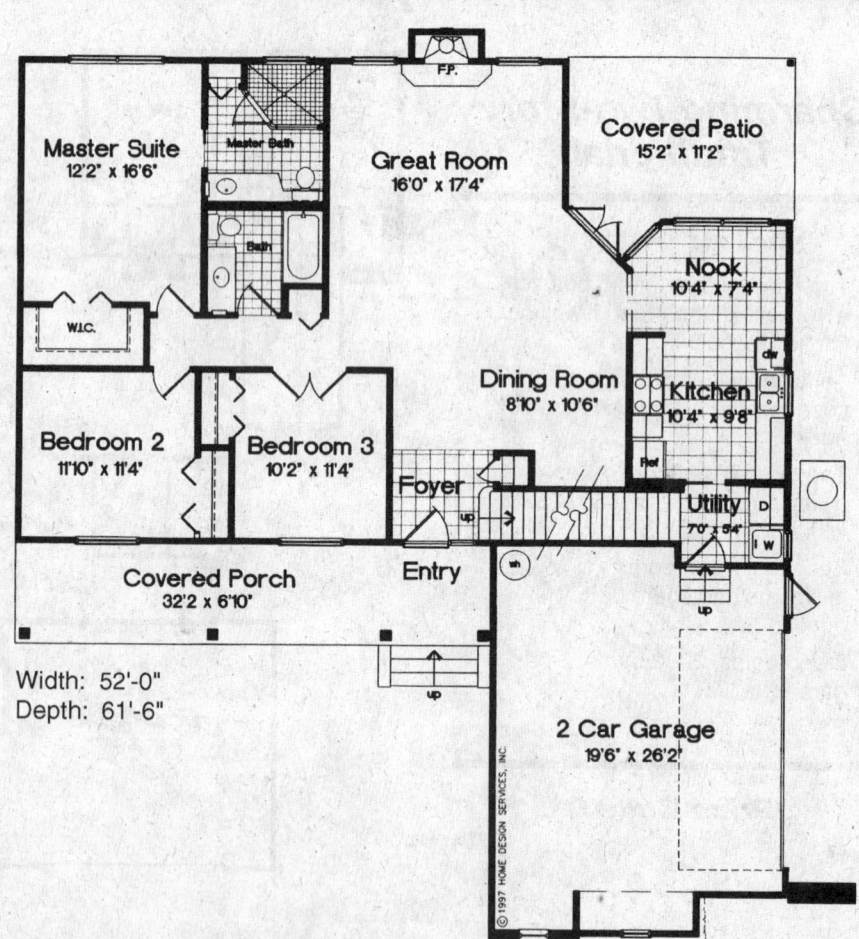

Width: 52'-0"
Depth: 61'-6"

Plan #718-007D-0010

1,721 total square feet of living area

Rear View

Atrium Creates A Dramatic Ambiance

Special features

- Roof dormers add great curb appeal
- Vaulted dining and great rooms are immersed in light from the atrium window wall
- Breakfast room opens onto the covered porch
- Functionally designed kitchen
- 3 bedrooms, 2 baths, 3-car garage
- Walk-out basement foundation, drawings also include crawl space and slab foundations
- 1,604 square feet on the first floor and 117 square feet on the lower level

Price Code C

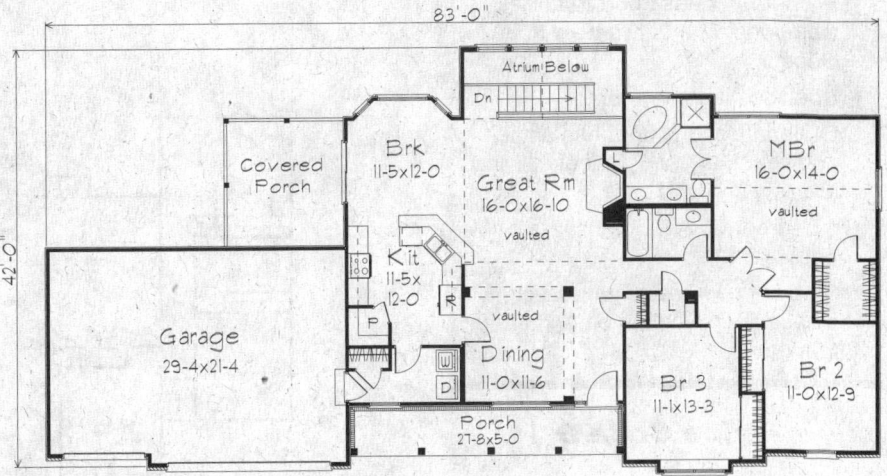

TO ORDER BLUEPRINTS USE THE FORM ON PAGE 15 OR CALL TOLL-FREE 1-877-671-6036
View thousands more home plans online at www.familyhandyman.com/HOMEPLANS

The Family Handyman

Plan #718-055D-0088

2,261 total square feet of living area

Sunny Breakfast Room

Special features

- Efficiently designed kitchen with work island and snack bar
- Master bath has double vanities, whirlpool tub and two walk-in closets
- Spacious laundry room
- Optional second floor has an additional 367 square feet of living area
- 4 bedrooms, 3 1/2 baths, 2-car side entry garage
- Slab or crawl space foundation, please specify when ordering foundation

Price Code D

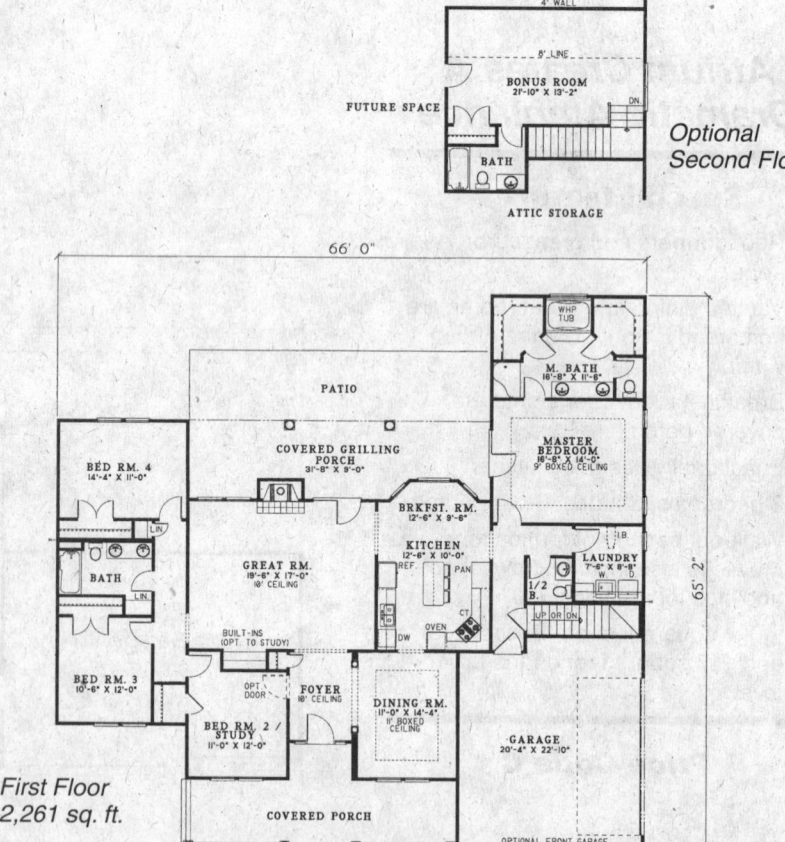

Optional Second Floor

First Floor
2,261 sq. ft.

TO ORDER BLUEPRINTS USE THE FORM ON PAGE 15 OR CALL TOLL-FREE 1-877-671-6036
View thousands more home plans online at www.familyhandyman.com/HOMEPLANS

Plan #718-016D-0048

2,567 total square feet of living area

Country-Style Home With Inviting Porch

Special features

- Breakfast room has a 12' cathedral ceiling and a bayed area full of windows
- Great room has a stepped ceiling, built-in media center and a corner fireplace
- Bonus room on the second floor has an additional 300 square feet of living area
- 4 bedrooms, 3 baths, 2-car side entry garage
- Basement, crawl space or slab foundation, please specify when ordering

Price Code F

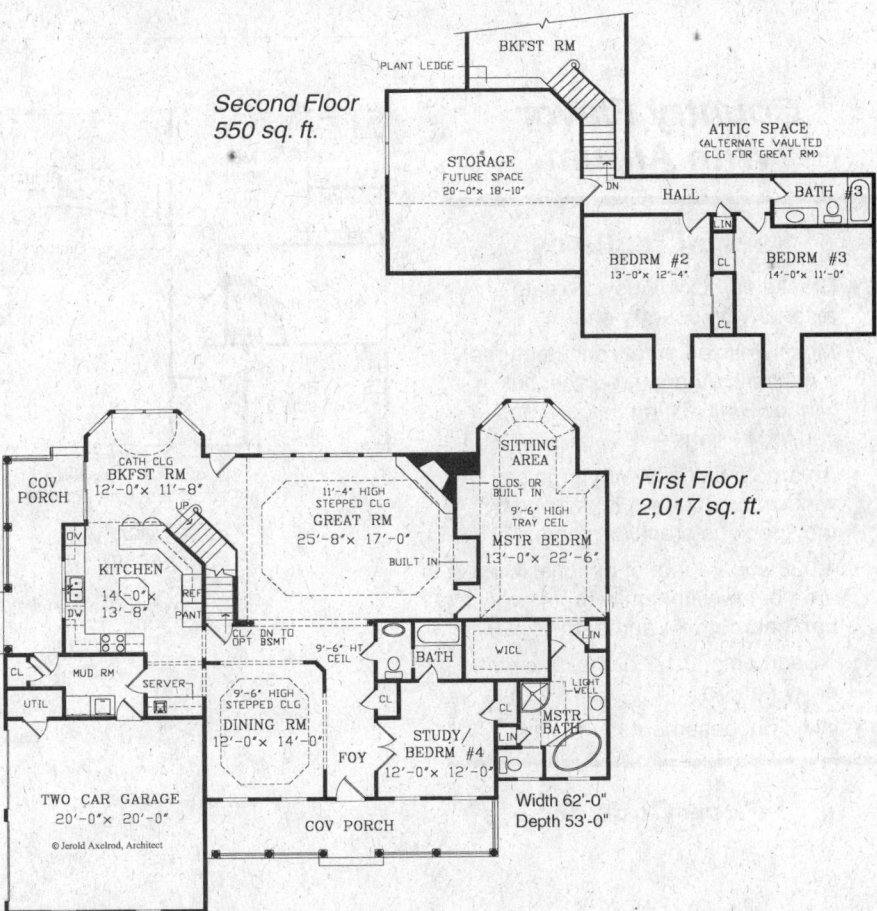

Second Floor 550 sq. ft.

First Floor 2,017 sq. ft.

Width 62'-0"
Depth 53'-0"

© Jerold Axelrod, Architect

TO ORDER BLUEPRINTS USE THE FORM ON PAGE 15 OR CALL TOLL-FREE 1-877-671-6036
View thousands more home plans online at www.familyhandyman.com/HOMEPLANS

Plan #718-007D-0101

2,384 total square feet of living area

Country Flavor With Atrium

Special features

- Bracketed box windows create an exterior with country charm
- Massive-sized great room features a majestic atrium, fireplace, box window wall, dining balcony and vaulted ceilings
- An atrium balcony with large bay window off sundeck is enjoyed by the spacious breakfast room
- 1,038 square feet of optional living area below with family room, wet bar, bedroom #4 and bath
- 3 bedrooms, 2 1/2 baths, 2-car side entry garage
- Walk-out basement foundation

Price Code D

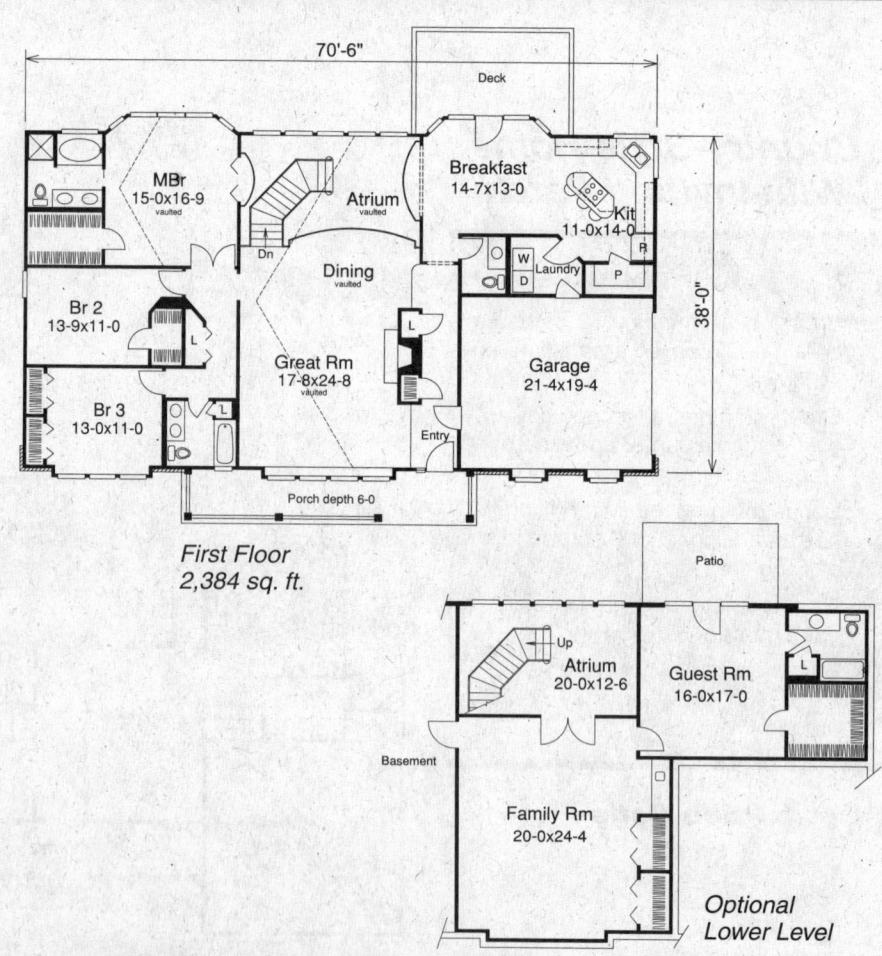

TO ORDER BLUEPRINTS USE THE FORM ON PAGE 15 OR CALL TOLL-FREE 1-877-671-6036
View thousands more home plans online at www.familyhandyman.com/HOMEPLANS

Plan #718-030D-0001

1,374 total square feet of living area

Scalloped Front Porch

Special features

- Garage has extra storage space
- Spacious living room has a fireplace
- Well-designed kitchen enjoys an adjacent breakfast nook
- Secluded master suite maintains privacy
- 3 bedrooms, 2 baths, 2-car garage
- Slab or crawl space foundation, please specify when ordering

Price Code A

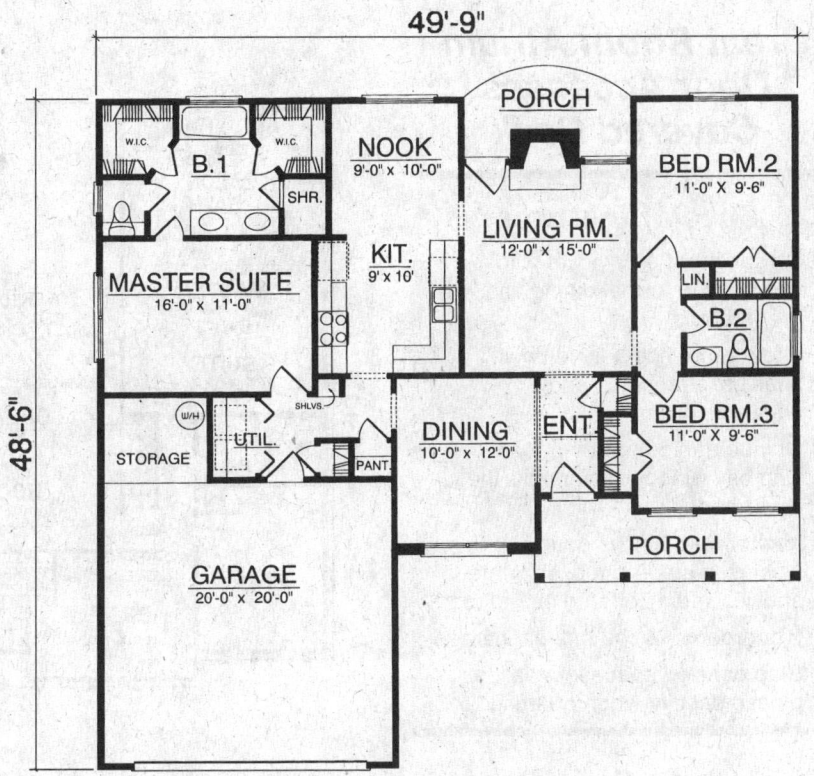

TO ORDER BLUEPRINTS USE THE FORM ON PAGE 15 OR CALL TOLL-FREE 1-877-671-6036
View thousands more home plans online at www.familyhandyman.com/homeplans

The Family Handyman

Plan #718-060D-0007

2,079 total square feet of living area

Great Room Atrium Door Accesses Covered Deck

Special features

- Large formal entry foyer with openings to formal dining and great rooms
- Great room has built-in bookshelves, a fireplace and a coffered ceiling
- Unique angled morning room with bay windows overlooks the covered deck
- Master bath enjoys double walk-in closets, a step-up tub, separate shower and a coffered ceiling
- 3 bedrooms, 2 baths, 2-car garage
- Slab or crawl space foundation, please specify when ordering

Price Code C

TO ORDER BLUEPRINTS USE THE FORM ON PAGE 15 OR CALL TOLL-FREE 1-877-671-6036
View thousands more home plans online at www.familyhandyman.com/homeplans

Family Handyman

Plan #718-017D-0001

2,043 total square feet of living area

Welcoming Front Porch, A Country Touch

Special features

- Energy efficient home with 2" x 6" exterior walls
- Two-story central foyer includes two coat closets
- Large combined space is provided by the kitchen, family and breakfast rooms
- Breakfast nook for informal dining looks out to the deck and screened porch
- 3 bedrooms, 2 1/2 baths, 2-car side entry garage
- Basement foundation, drawings also include slab foundation

Price Code D

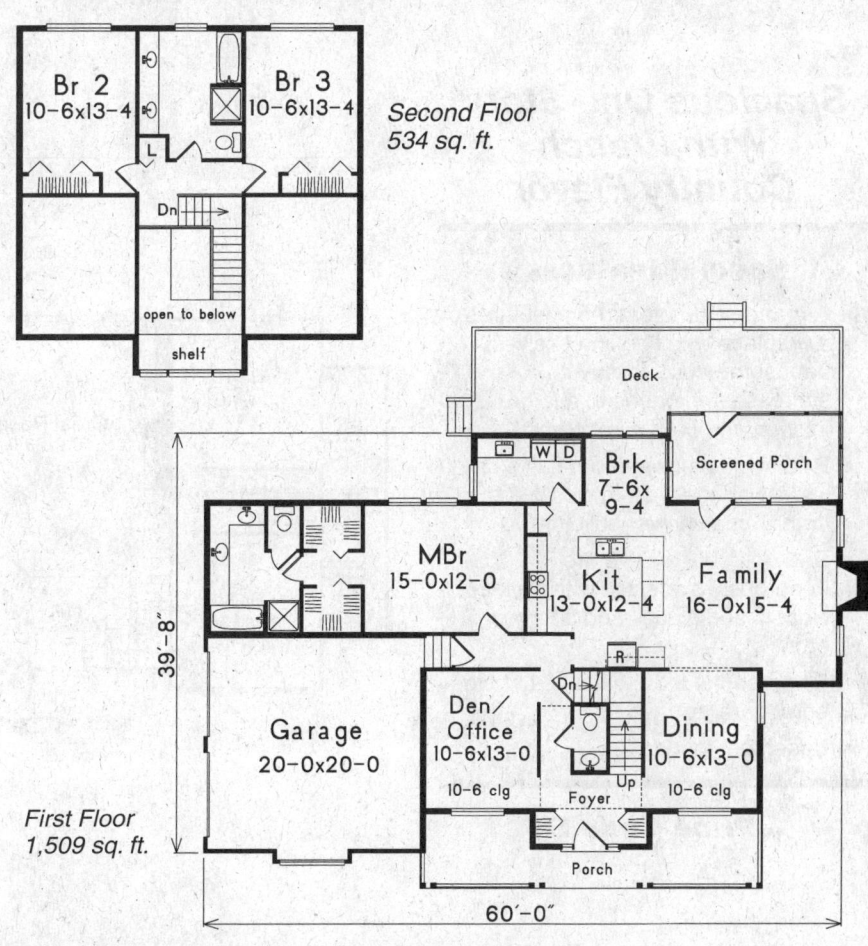

TO ORDER BLUEPRINTS USE THE FORM ON PAGE 15 OR CALL TOLL-FREE 1-877-671-6036

View thousands more home plans online at www.familyhandyman.com/homeplans

Plan #718-007D-0117

2,695 total square feet of living area

Spacious One-Story With French Country Flavor

Special features

- A grand-scale great room features a fireplace with flanking shelves, handsome entry foyer with staircase and opens to a large kitchen and breakfast room
- Roomy master bedroom has a bay window, huge walk-in closet and bath with a shower built for two
- Bedrooms #2 and #3 are generously oversized with walk-in closets and a Jack and Jill style bath
- 3 bedrooms, 2 1/2 baths, 2-car side entry garage
- Basement foundation

Price Code E

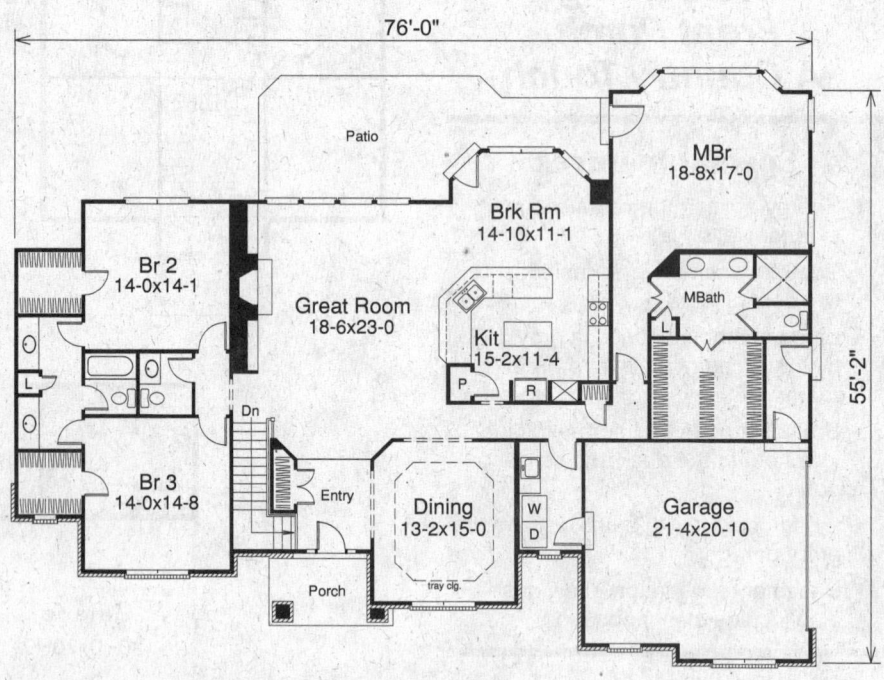

TO ORDER BLUEPRINTS USE THE FORM ON PAGE 15 OR CALL TOLL-FREE 1-877-671-6036
View thousands more home plans online at www.familyhandyman.com/HOMEPLANS

Plan #718-035D-0052

2,072 total square feet of living area

Serving Bar In Kitchen

Special features

- Master suite has a large bay sitting area, private vaulted bath and an enormous walk-in closet
- Tray ceilings in the breakfast and dining rooms are charming touches
- Great room has a centered fireplace and a French door leading outdoors
- 3 bedrooms, 2 1/2 baths, 2-car side entry garage
- Walk-out basement, slab or crawl space foundation, please specify when ordering

Price Code C

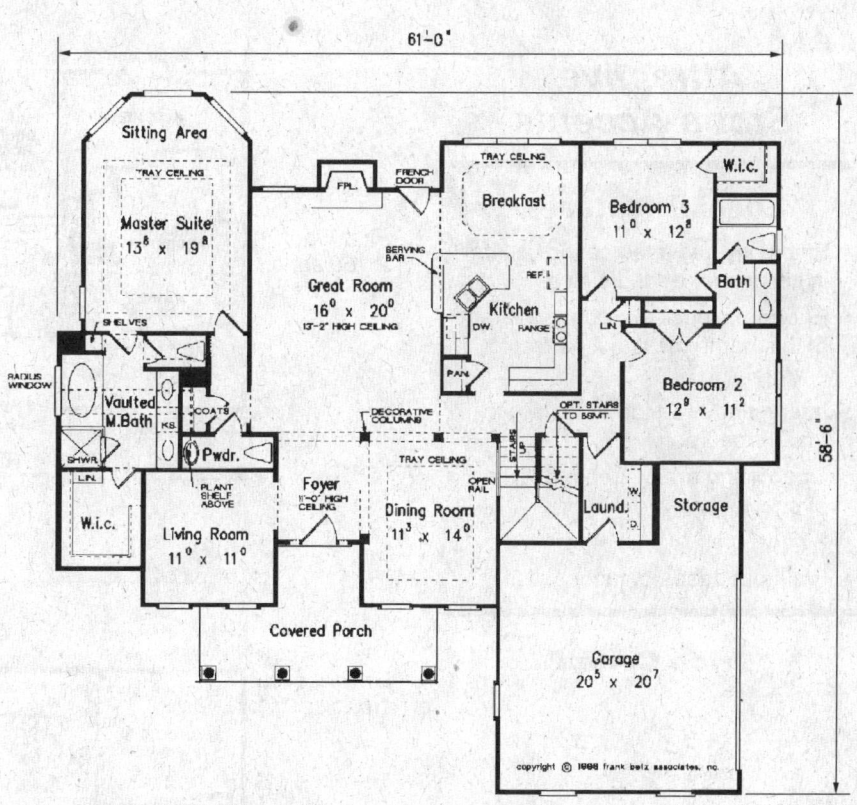

TO ORDER BLUEPRINTS USE THE FORM ON PAGE 15 OR CALL TOLL-FREE 1-877-671-6036
View thousands more home plans online at www.familyhandyman.com/HOMEPLANS

Plan #718-043D-0019

3,230 total square feet of living area

WIDTH: 66'-0"
DEPTH: 44'-0"

Attractive Stone Accents

Special features

- Efficiently designed eating counter in kitchen for added dining
- Enormous deck surrounds the rear of this home making it perfect for entertaining
- Interesting two-sided fireplace in master bedroom
- Open living areas create a feeling of spaciousness
- 3 bedrooms, 2 1/2 baths
- Walk-out basement foundation

Price Code F

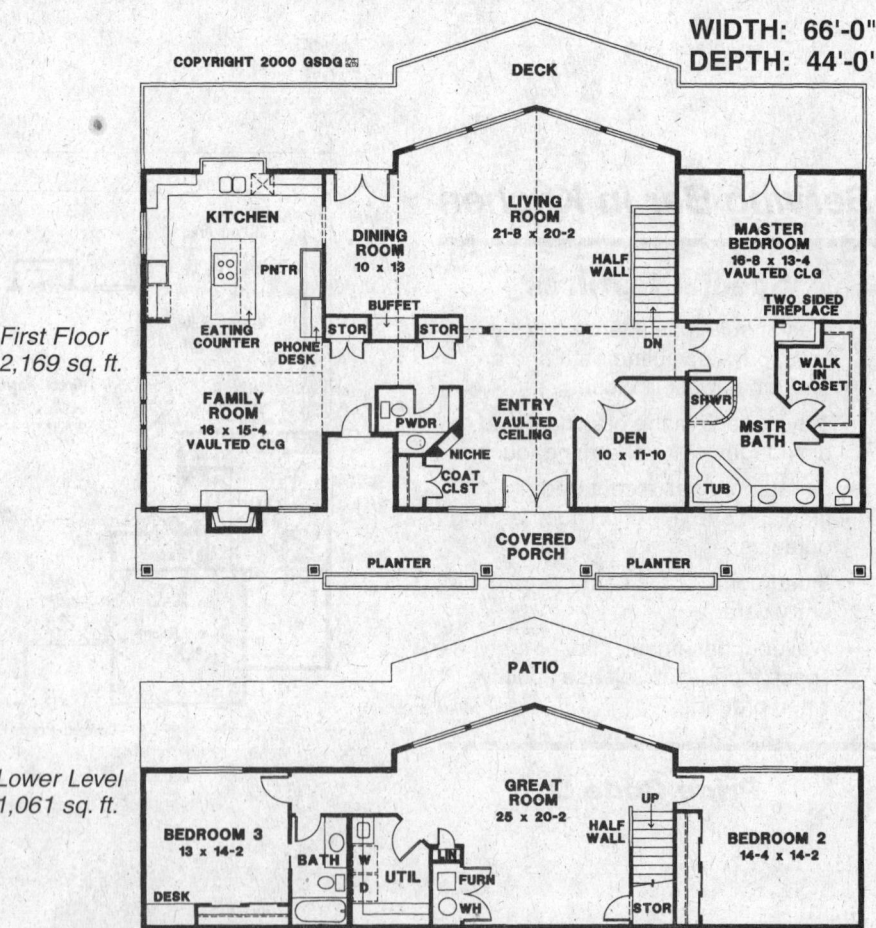

First Floor 2,169 sq. ft.

Lower Level 1,061 sq. ft.

TO ORDER BLUEPRINTS USE THE FORM ON PAGE 15 OR CALL TOLL-FREE 1-877-671-6036
View thousands more home plans online at www.familyhandyman.com/homeplans

Plan #718-028D-0011

2,123 total square feet of living area

Spacious Country Home

Special features

- L-shaped porch extends the entire length of this home creating lots of extra space for outdoor living
- Master bedroom is secluded for privacy and has two closets, double vanity in bath and a double-door entry onto covered porch
- Efficiently designed kitchen
- 3 bedrooms, 2 1/2 baths
- Crawl space or slab foundation, please specify when ordering

Price Code C

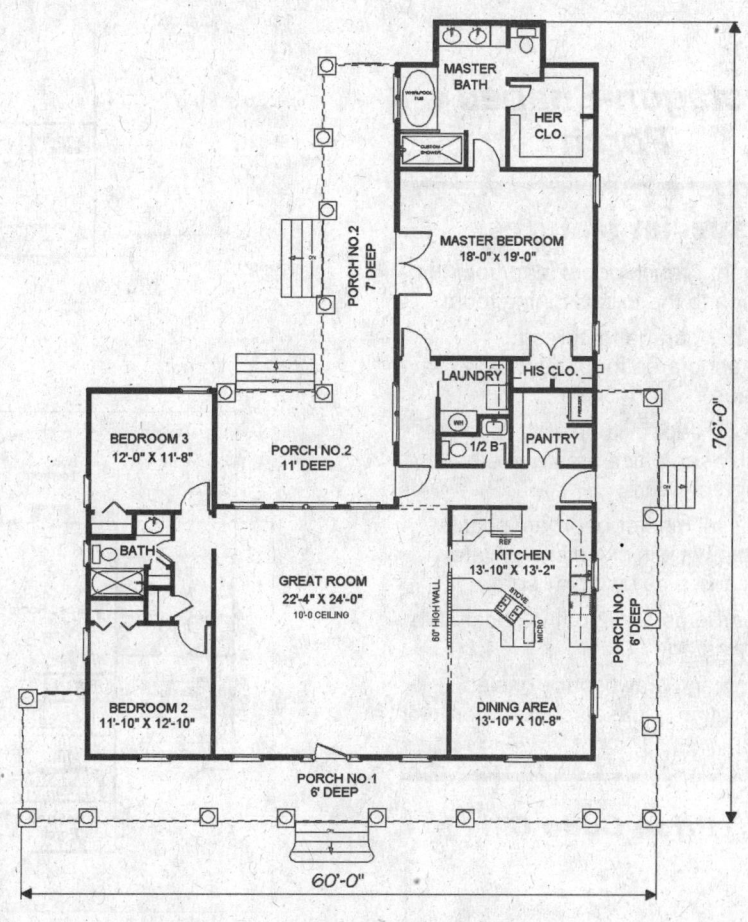

TO ORDER BLUEPRINTS USE THE FORM ON PAGE 15 OR CALL TOLL-FREE 1-877-671-6036
View thousands more home plans online at www.familyhandyman.com/HOMEPLANS

Plan #718-038D-0045

2,044 total square feet of living area

Octagon-Shaped Porch

Special features

- Elegant French doors lead from the kitchen to the formal dining room
- Two-car garage features a workshop area for projects or extra storage
- Second floor includes loft space ideal for an office area and a handy computer center
- Colossal master bedroom boasts double walk-in closets, a private bath and a bay window seat
- 3 bedrooms, 2 1/2 baths, 2-car side entry garage
- Basement, crawl space or slab foundation, please specify when ordering

Price Code C

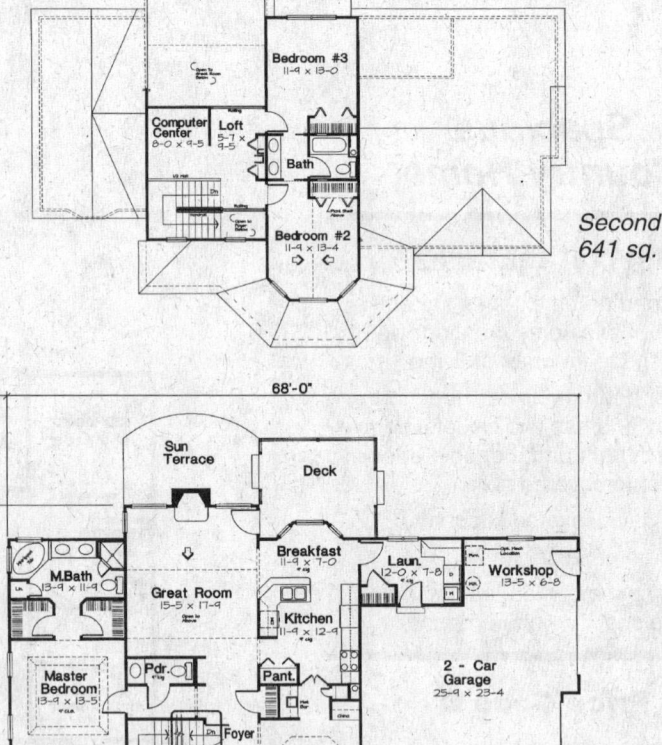

Second Floor 641 sq. ft.

First Floor 1,403 sq. ft.

TO ORDER BLUEPRINTS USE THE FORM ON PAGE 15 OR CALL TOLL-FREE 1-877-671-6036
View thousands more home plans online at www.familyhandyman.com/HOMEPLANS

Plan #718-056D-0007

1,985 total square feet of living area

Ranch With Traditional Feel

Special features

- 9' ceilings throughout home
- Master suite has direct access into the sunroom
- Sunny breakfast room features a bay window
- Bonus room on the second floor has an additional 191 square feet of living area
- 3 bedrooms, 3 baths, 2-car side entry garage
- Slab foundation

Price Code G

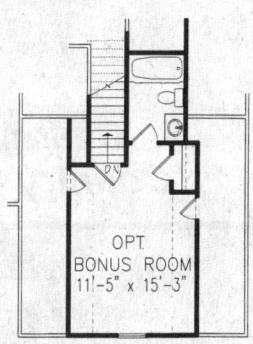

Optional Second Floor

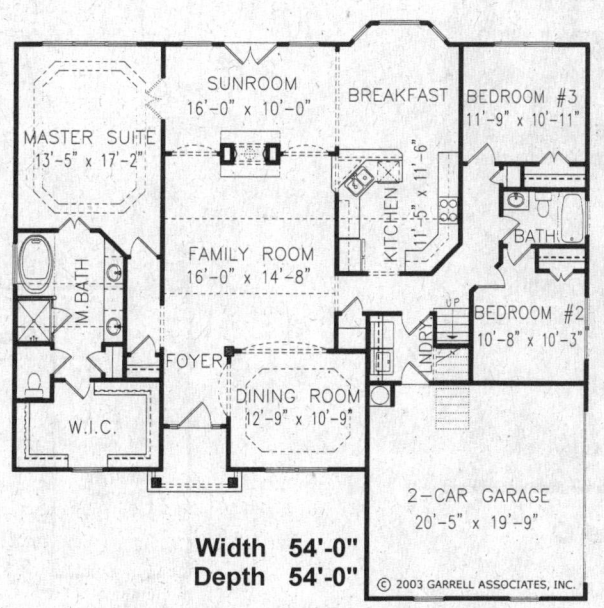

First Floor 1,985 sq. ft.

Width 54'-0"
Depth 54'-0"

© 2003 GARRELL ASSOCIATES, INC.

TO ORDER BLUEPRINTS USE THE FORM ON PAGE 15 OR CALL TOLL-FREE 1-877-671-6036
View thousands more home plans online at www.familyhandyman.com/HOMEPLANS

The Family Handyman

Plan #718-052D-0052

1,936 total square feet of living area

Charming Country Home

Special features

- Covered porch creates an inviting entrance
- Kitchen, breakfast and great rooms combine for an open area and include double-door access to the rear sundeck
- Second floor includes an abundance of storage area
- Bonus room on the second floor has an additional 528 square feet of living area
- 3 bedrooms, 2 1/2 baths, 2-car side entry garage
- Walk-out basement foundation

Price Code C

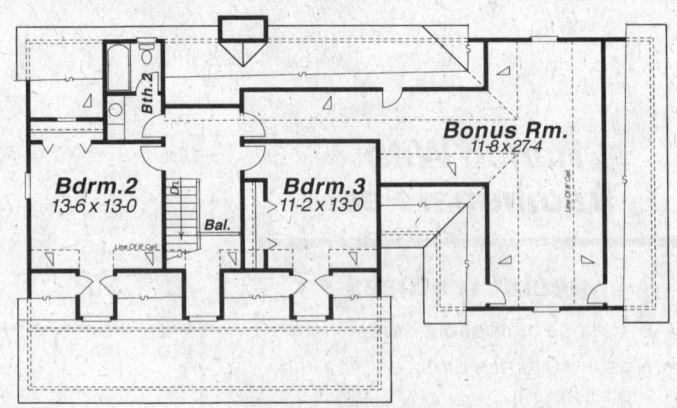

Second Floor 624 sq. ft.

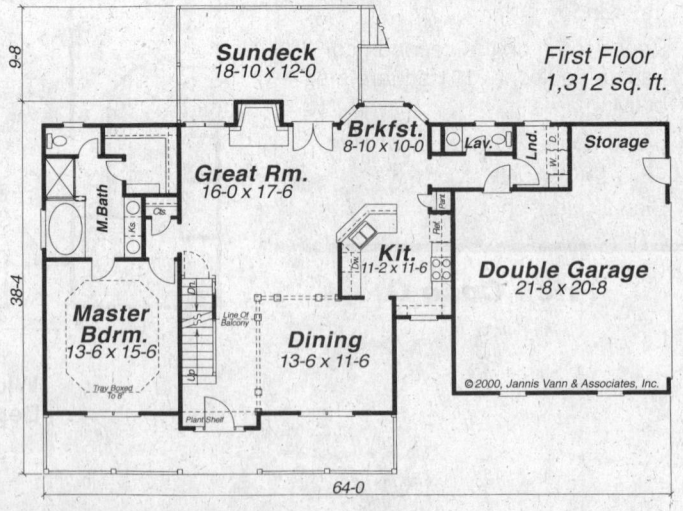

First Floor 1,312 sq. ft.

TO ORDER BLUEPRINTS USE THE FORM ON PAGE 15 OR CALL TOLL-FREE 1-877-671-6036
View thousands more home plans online at www.familyhandyman.com/HOMEPLANS

Plan #718-007D-0146

1,929 total square feet of living area

The Plan That Has It All

Special features

- A classic traditional exterior for timeless elegance
- More than a great room for this size home, the grand room features a vaulted ceiling and a brick and wood mantle fireplace flanked by doors to the rear patio
- State-of-the-art U-shaped kitchen has a built-in pantry, computer desk, snack bar and breakfast room with bay window
- The master bedroom includes a vaulted ceiling, large walk-in closet, luxury bath and access to the rear patio
- 4 bedrooms, 3 baths, 3-car side entry garage
- Crawl space foundation, drawings also include slab and basement foundations

Price Code C

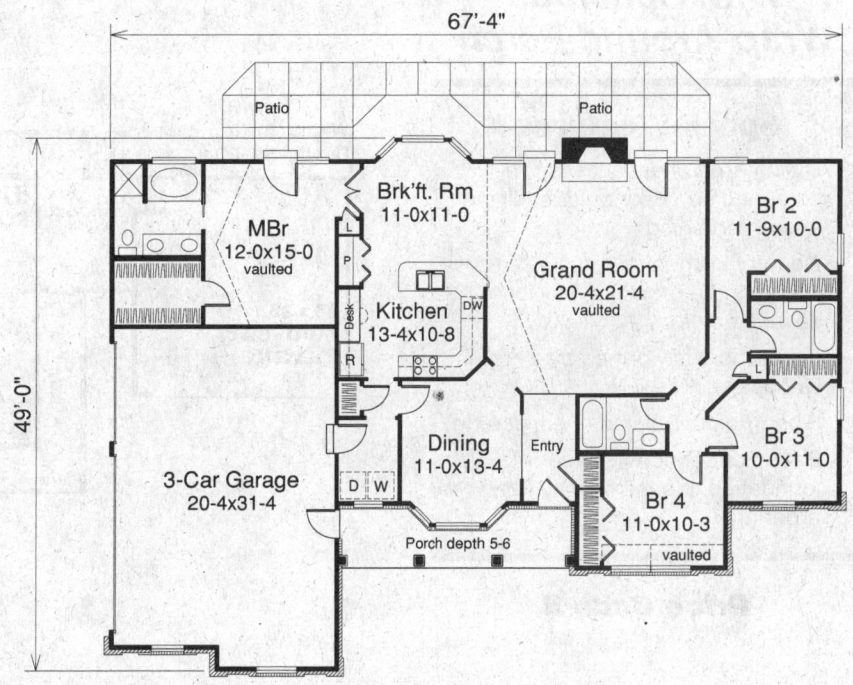

TO ORDER BLUEPRINTS USE THE FORM ON PAGE 15 OR CALL TOLL-FREE 1-877-671-6036
View thousands more home plans online at www.familyhandyman.com/HOMEPLANS

Plan #718-062D-0041

1,541 total square feet of living area

Country Ranch With Spacious Wrap-Around Porch

Special features

- Dining area offers access to a screened porch for outdoor dining and entertaining
- Country kitchen features a center island and a breakfast bay for casual meals
- Great room is warmed by a woodstove
- 3 bedrooms, 2 baths, 2-car garage
- Basement or crawl space foundation, please specify when ordering

Price Code B

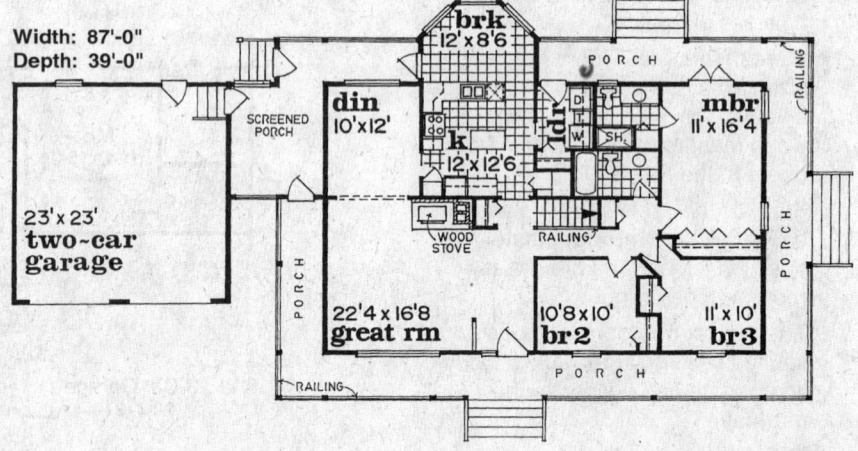

Plan #718-007D-0124

1,944 total square feet of living area

Country Ranch Enjoys Large Great Room

Special features

- Spacious surrounding porch, covered patio and stone fireplace create an expansive ponderosa appearance
- The large entry leads to a grand-sized great room featuring a vaulted ceiling, fireplace, wet bar and access to the porch through three patio doors
- The U-shaped kitchen is open to the hearth room and enjoys a snack bar, fireplace and patio access
- A luxury bath, walk-in closet and doors to the porch are a few of the amenities of the master bedroom
- 3 bedrooms, 2 baths, 3-car detached garage
- Basement foundation

Price Code C

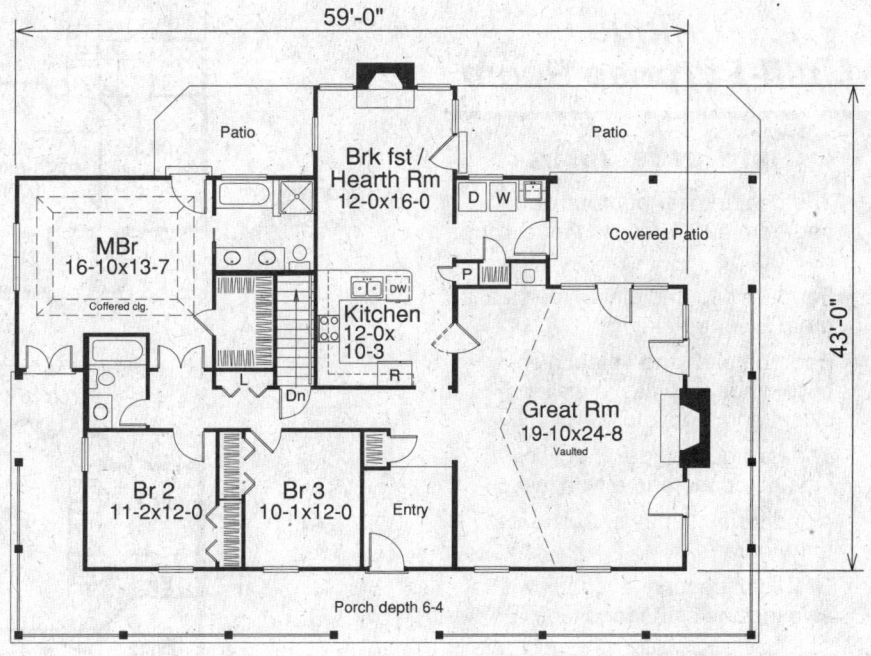

TO ORDER BLUEPRINTS USE THE FORM ON PAGE 15 OR CALL TOLL-FREE 1-877-671-6036
View thousands more home plans online at www.familyhandyman.com/homeplans

Plan #718-020D-0039

3,059 total square feet of living area

Unique Multi-Purpose Room

Special features

- The den, master bedroom and bedroom #2 all access the relaxing rear porch
- Formal living and dining rooms are great for entertaining
- Bedrooms #3 and #4 each enjoy built-in bookshelves, a walk-in closet and a private bath
- The garage includes plenty of storage space and a work bench
- 4 bedrooms, 4 baths, 2-car side entry garage
- Crawl space foundation, drawings also include slab foundation

Price Code E

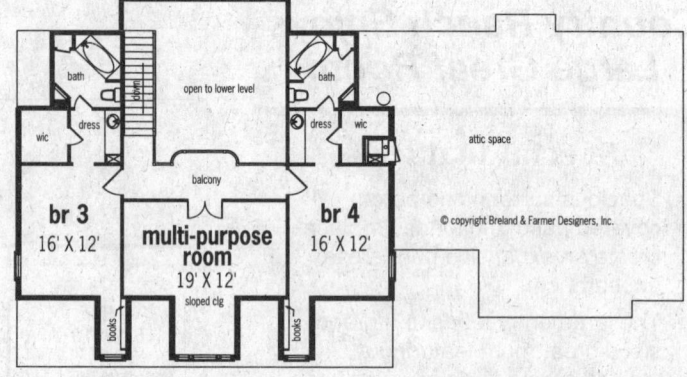

Second Floor 1,134 sq. ft.

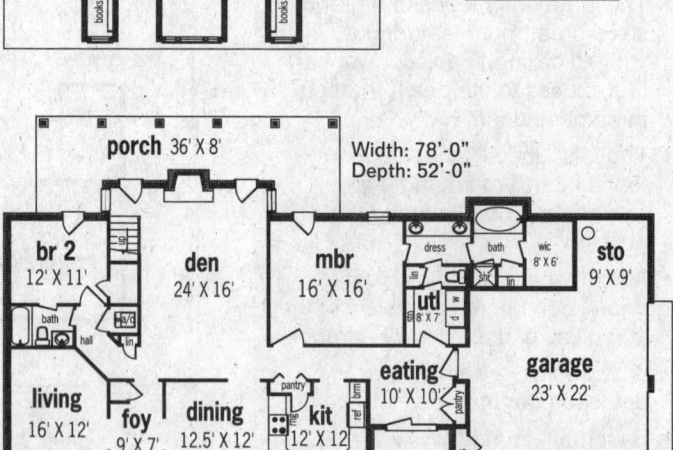

First Floor 1,925 sq. ft.

Width: 78'-0"
Depth: 52'-0"

TO ORDER BLUEPRINTS USE THE FORM ON PAGE 15 OR CALL TOLL-FREE 1-877-671-6036
View thousands more home plans online at www.familyhandyman.com/HOMEPLANS

Plan #718-047D-0050

2,293 total square feet of living area

Pillars And Dormers Add Charm

Special features

- Formal dining area flows into large family room making great use of space
- Cozy nook off kitchen makes an ideal breakfast area
- Covered patio attaches to master bedroom and family room
- Optional second floor has an additional 509 square feet of living area
- Framing - only concrete block available
- 4 bedrooms, 2 baths, 2-car side entry garage
- Slab foundation

Price Code D

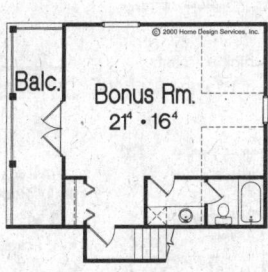

Optional Second Floor

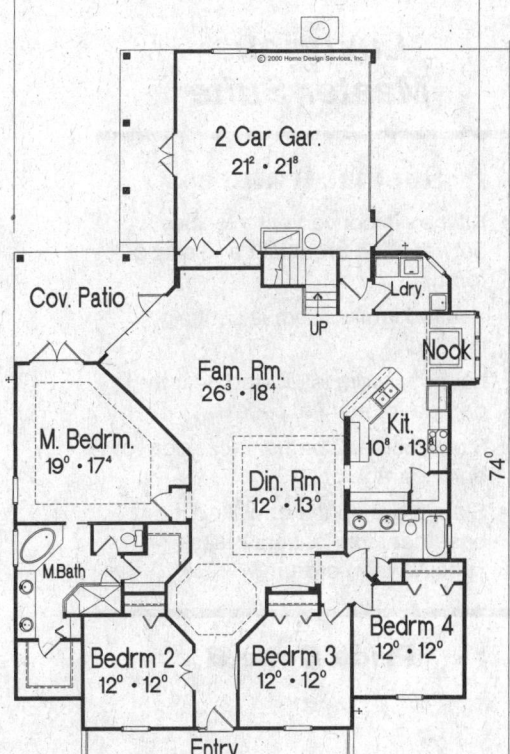

First Floor 2,293 sq. ft.

TO ORDER BLUEPRINTS USE THE FORM ON PAGE 15 OR CALL TOLL-FREE 1-877-671-6036
View thousands more home plans online at www.familyhandyman.com/HOMEPLANS

Plan #718-035D-0006

1,671 total square feet of living area

Luxurious Master Suite

Special features

- Kitchen is conveniently located between the breakfast and dining rooms
- Vaulted family room is centrally located
- Laundry room is located near the garage for easy access
- 3 bedrooms, 2 baths, 2-car side entry garage
- Slab, crawl space or walk-out basement foundation, please specify when ordering

Price Code B

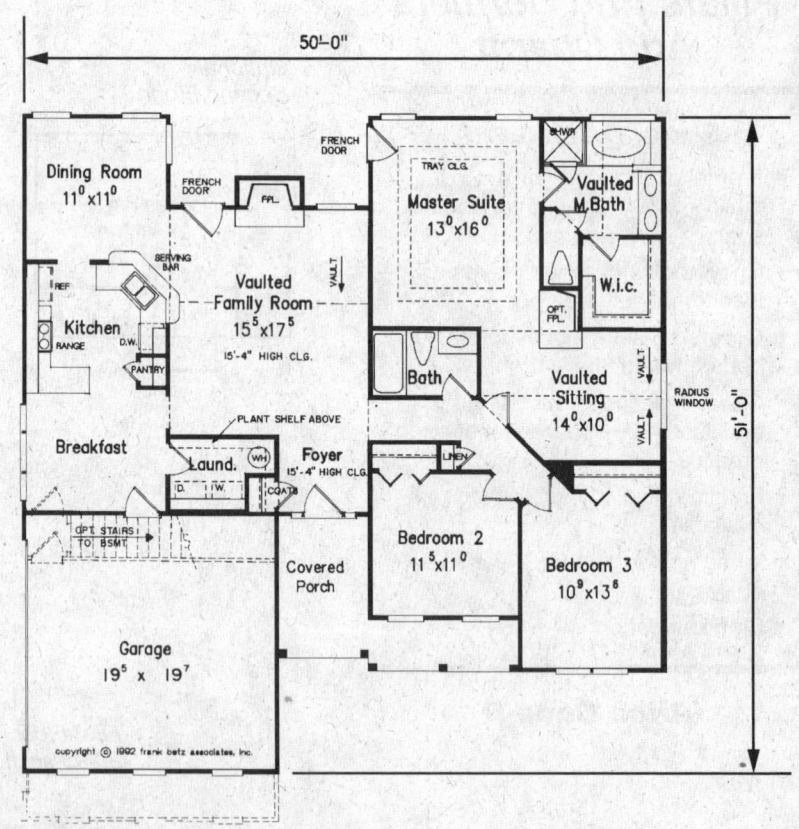

Plan #718-007D-0056

3,199 total square feet of living area

Double Atrium Embraces The Sun

Special features

- Kitchen features bay-shaped cabinetry built over an atrium overlooking a two-story window wall
- A second atrium dominates the master bedroom that boasts a sitting area and a luxurious bath that has a whirlpool tub open to a garden and lower level study
- 3 bedrooms, 2 1/2 baths, 3-car side entry garage
- Walk-out basement foundation

Price Code E

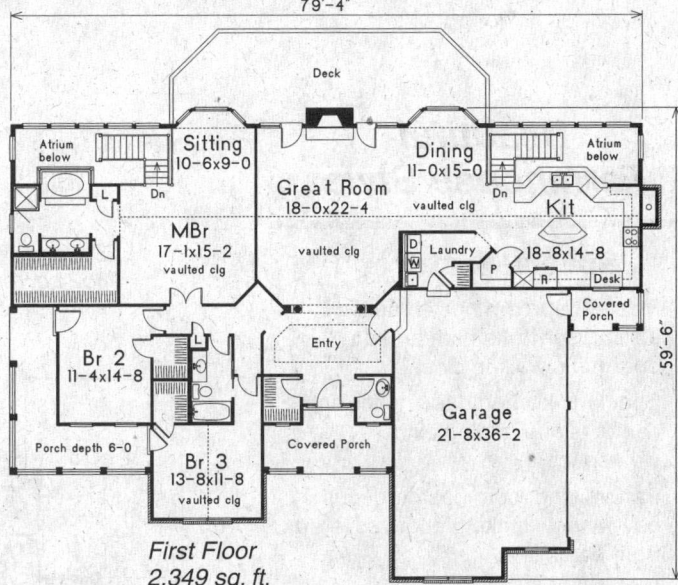

First Floor 2,349 sq. ft.

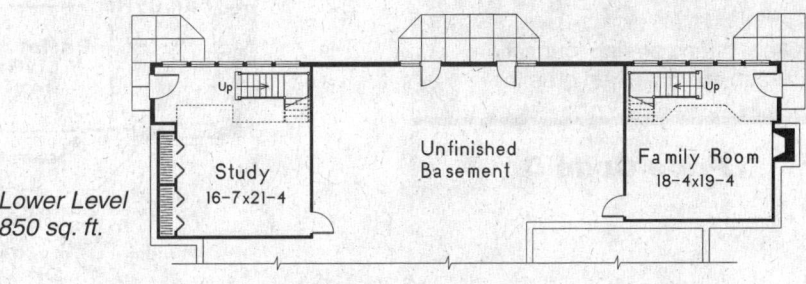

Lower Level 850 sq. ft.

Plan #718-036D-0013

2,200 total square feet of living area

Beautiful Farmhouse Style

Special features

- Master bedroom has a vaulted ceiling, spacious bath and an enormous walk-in closet
- Spacious kitchen has an efficient center island adding extra workspace
- Parlor/living room has gorgeous bay window looking out to covered front porch
- 9' ceilings throughout the first floor
- 3 bedrooms, 2 1/2 baths, 2-car garage
- Crawl space or slab foundation, please specify when ordering

Price Code D

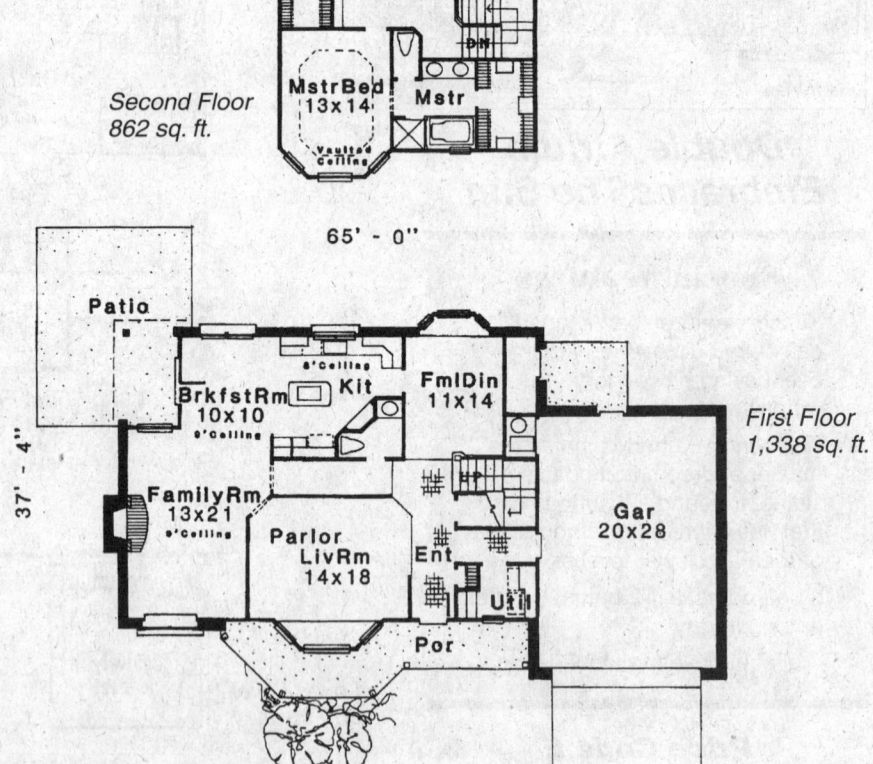

Second Floor 862 sq. ft.

First Floor 1,338 sq. ft.

TO ORDER BLUEPRINTS USE THE FORM ON PAGE 15 OR CALL TOLL-FREE 1-877-671-6036
View thousands more home plans online at www.familyhandyman.com/homeplans

Plan #718-021D-0020

2,360 total square feet of living area

Circular Stairway Adds To Front Entry

Special features

- Master bedroom includes a sitting area and large bath
- Sloped family room ceiling provides a view from the second floor balcony
- Kitchen features an island bar and walk-in butler's pantry
- 3 bedrooms, 2 1/2 baths, 2-car side entry garage
- Crawl space foundation, drawings also include slab and basement foundations

Price Code D

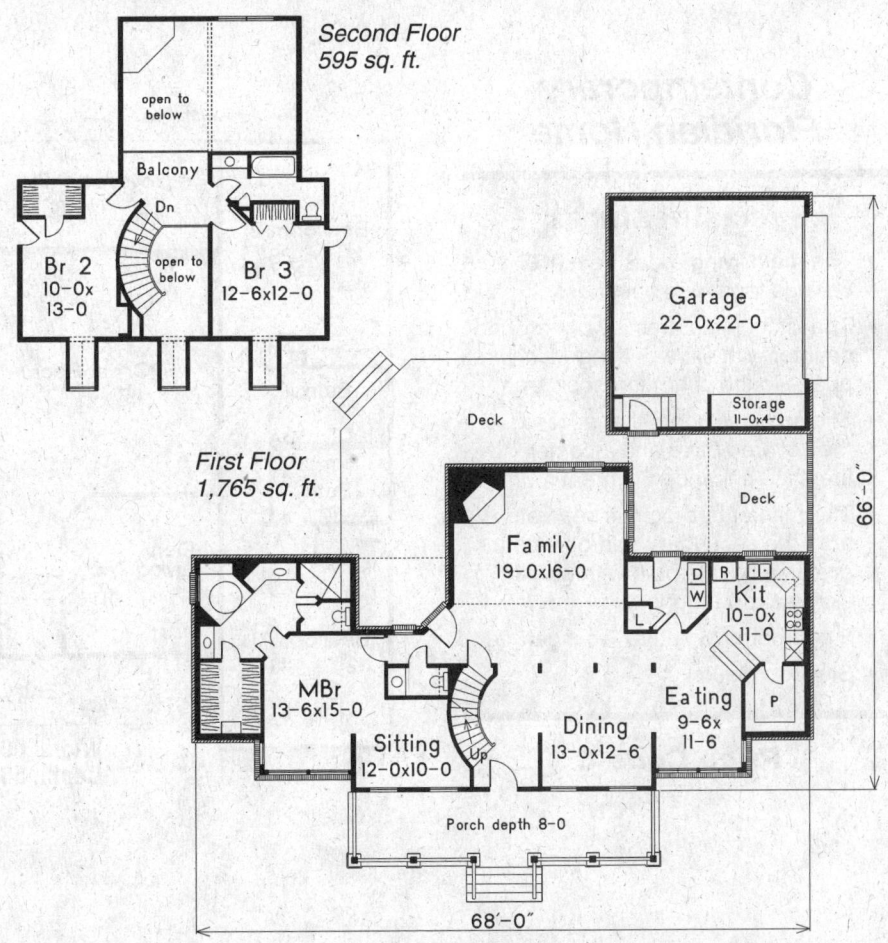

TO ORDER BLUEPRINTS USE THE FORM ON PAGE 15 OR CALL TOLL-FREE 1-877-671-6036
View thousands more home plans online at www.familyhandyman.com/HOMEPLANS

57

Plan #718-047D-0075

2,052 total square feet of living area

Contemporary Floridian Home

Special features

- The main living areas boast 10' ceilings for added openness
- The kitchen features a wrap-around counter with extra seating which opens to the charming nook area
- Sliding glass doors that access the covered patio and a corner fireplace enhance the great room
- The master bedroom is separate from the secondary bedrooms and enjoys a private bath with walk-in closet and whirlpool tub
- 3 bedrooms, 3 baths, 2-car garage
- Slab foundation

Price Code C

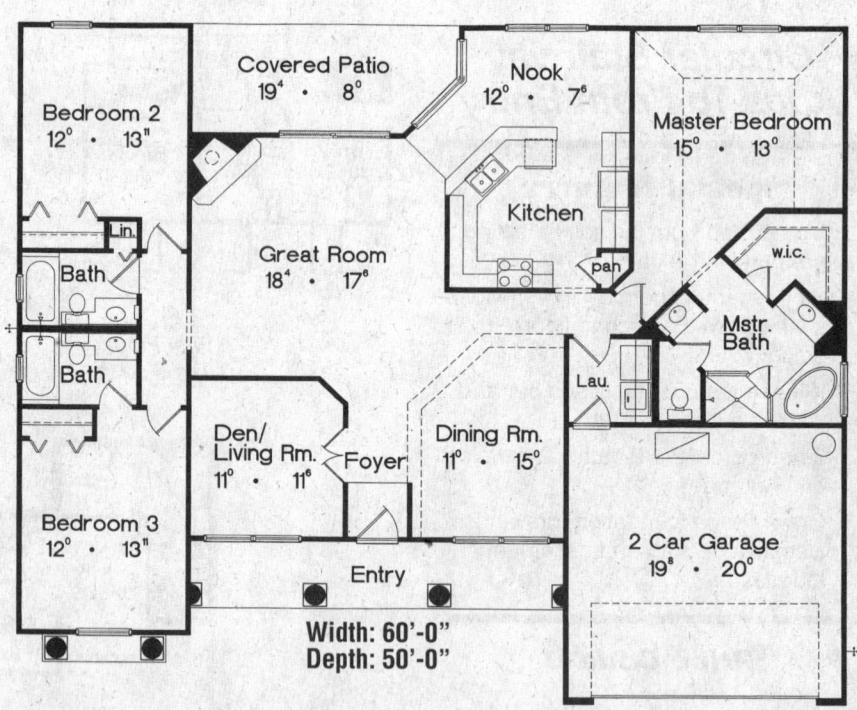

TO ORDER BLUEPRINTS USE THE FORM ON PAGE 15 OR CALL TOLL-FREE 1-877-671-6036
View thousands more home plans online at www.familyhandyman.com/homeplans

Plan #718-035D-0045

1,749 total square feet of living area

Cozy Covered Front Porch

Special features

- Tray ceiling in master suite
- A breakfast bar overlooks the vaulted great room
- Additional bedrooms are located away from the master suite for privacy
- Optional bonus room above the garage has an additional 308 square feet of living area
- 3 bedrooms, 2 baths, 2-car garage
- Walk-out basement, slab or crawl space foundation, please specify when ordering

Price Code B

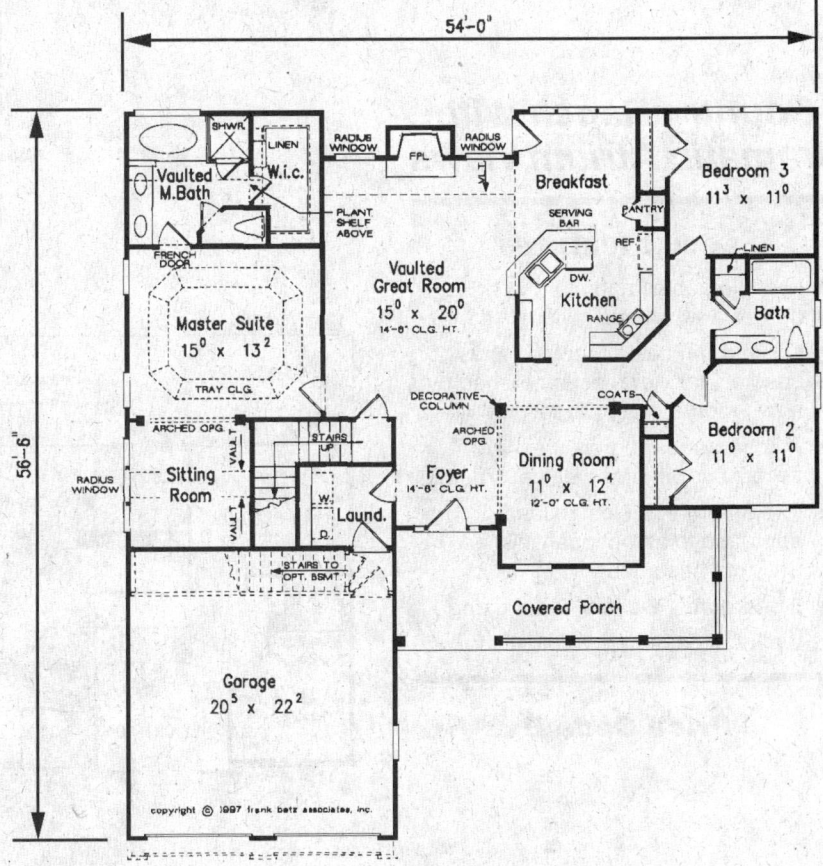

TO ORDER BLUEPRINTS USE THE FORM ON PAGE 15 OR CALL TOLL-FREE 1-877-671-6036
View thousands more home plans online at www.familyhandyman.com/homeplans

Plan #718-007D-0136

1,533 total square feet of living area

Rear View

Country Ranch With Dramatic Atrium Views

Special features

- Multiple gables and stonework deliver a warm and inviting exterior
- Great room has a fireplace and spectacular views accomplished by a two-story atrium window wall
- A covered rear porch is easily accessed from the breakfast room
- The atrium provides an ideal approach to an optional finished walk-out basement
- 3 bedrooms, 2 baths, 2-car garage
- Walk-out basement foundation

Price Code B

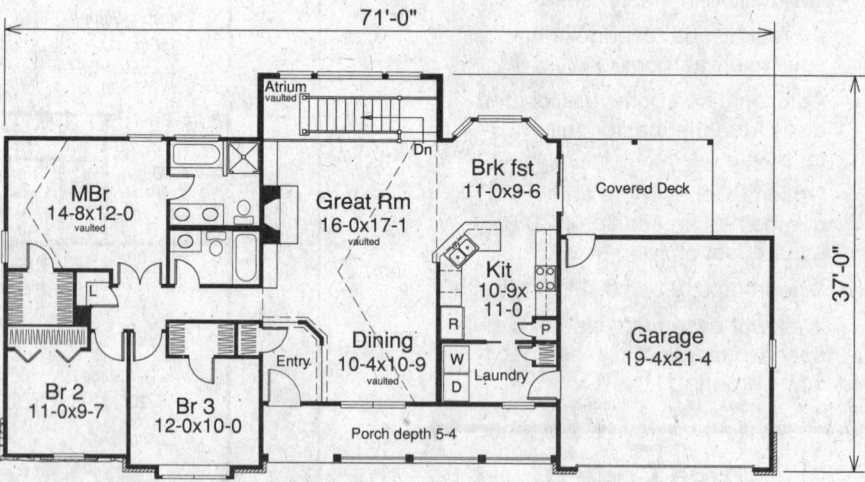

TO ORDER BLUEPRINTS USE THE FORM ON PAGE 15 OR CALL TOLL-FREE 1-877-671-6036
View thousands more home plans online at www.familyhandyman.com/homeplans

Plan #718-055D-0098

3,060 total square feet of living area

Triple Dormers Add Charm To This Country Home

Special features

- French doors in hearth room lead into a private study with built-in shelves
- Kitchen includes a large wrap-around style eating counter capable of serving five
- Breakfast area has access onto a large covered grilling porch
- 3 bedrooms, 2 1/2 baths, 2-car side entry garage
- Crawl space or slab foundation, please specify when ordering

Price Code E

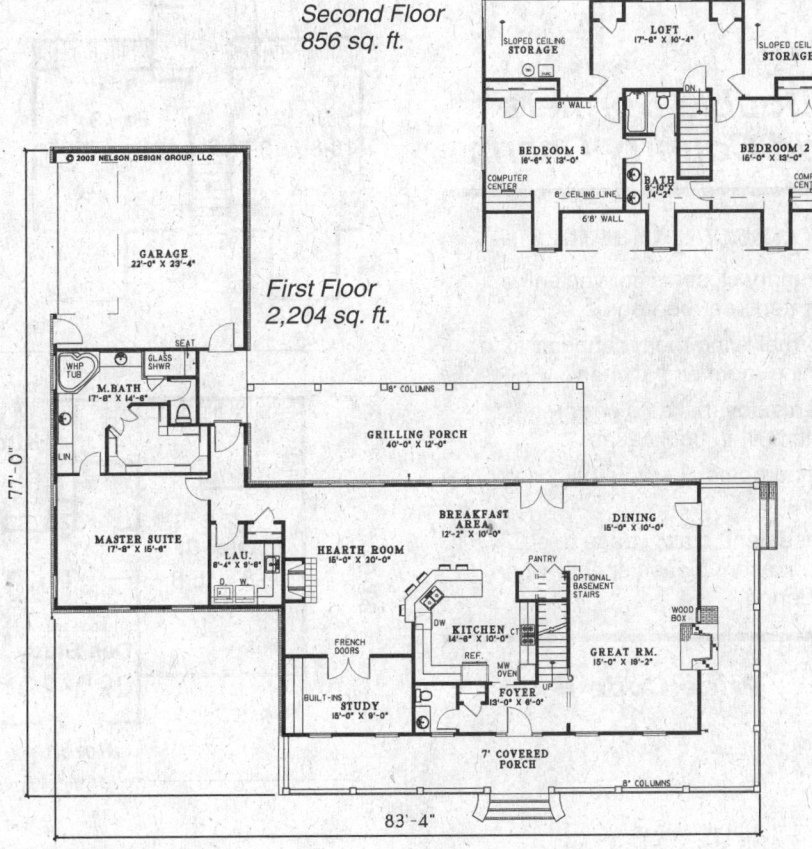

TO ORDER BLUEPRINTS USE THE FORM ON PAGE 15 OR CALL TOLL-FREE 1-877-671-6036
View thousands more home plans online at www.familyhandyman.com/homeplans

Plan #718-038D-0056

1,712 total square feet of living area

Double Dormers Add Country Charm

Special features

- Laundry closet is conveniently located near bedrooms
- Formal living room connects to the dining room and kitchen
- Den/study makes a cozy retreat with built-in bookcases
- 3 bedrooms, 2 1/2 baths, 2-car garage
- Basement, crawl space or slab foundation, please specify when ordering

Price Code B

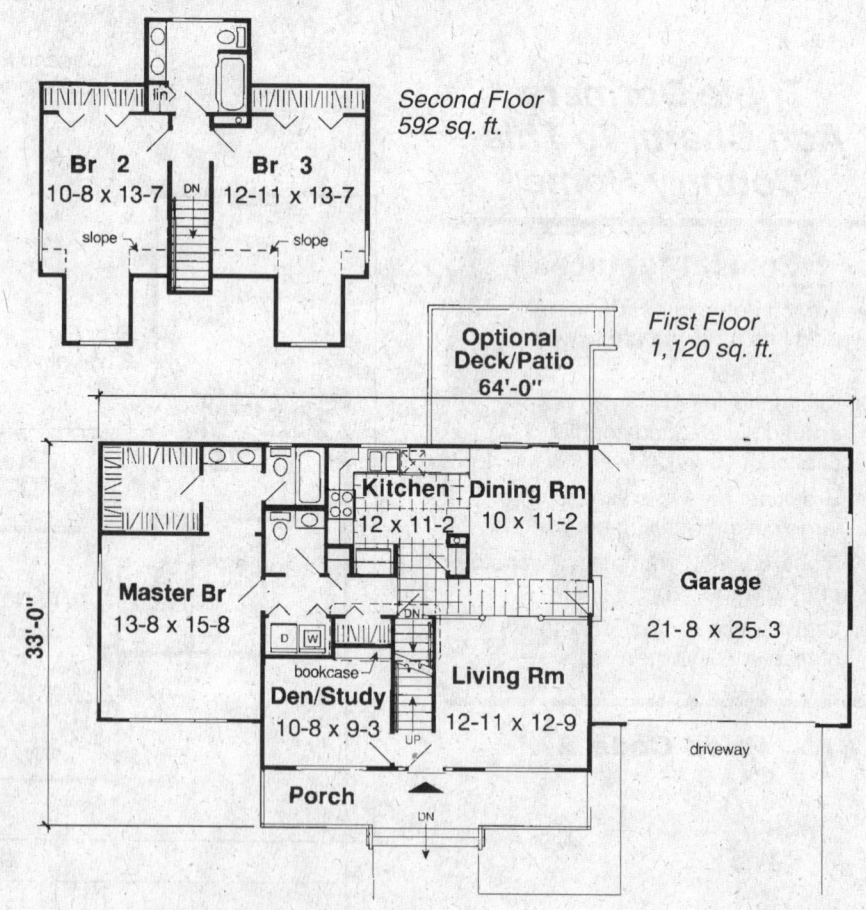

TO ORDER BLUEPRINTS USE THE FORM ON PAGE 15 OR CALL TOLL-FREE 1-877-671-6036
View thousands more home plans online at www.familyhandyman.com/homeplans

Plan #718-062D-0034

2,020 total square feet of living area

A Rustic Family Home

Special features

- All bedrooms on second floor for privacy
- Unique gallery hall on second floor is brightened by light from dormer window and is the perfect place to spotlight artwork
- Large living room has front and rear views along with a cozy fireplace
- Bonus room on the second floor has an additional 377 square feet of living area
- 3 bedrooms, 2 1/2 baths, 2-car garage
- Basement foundation

Price Code C

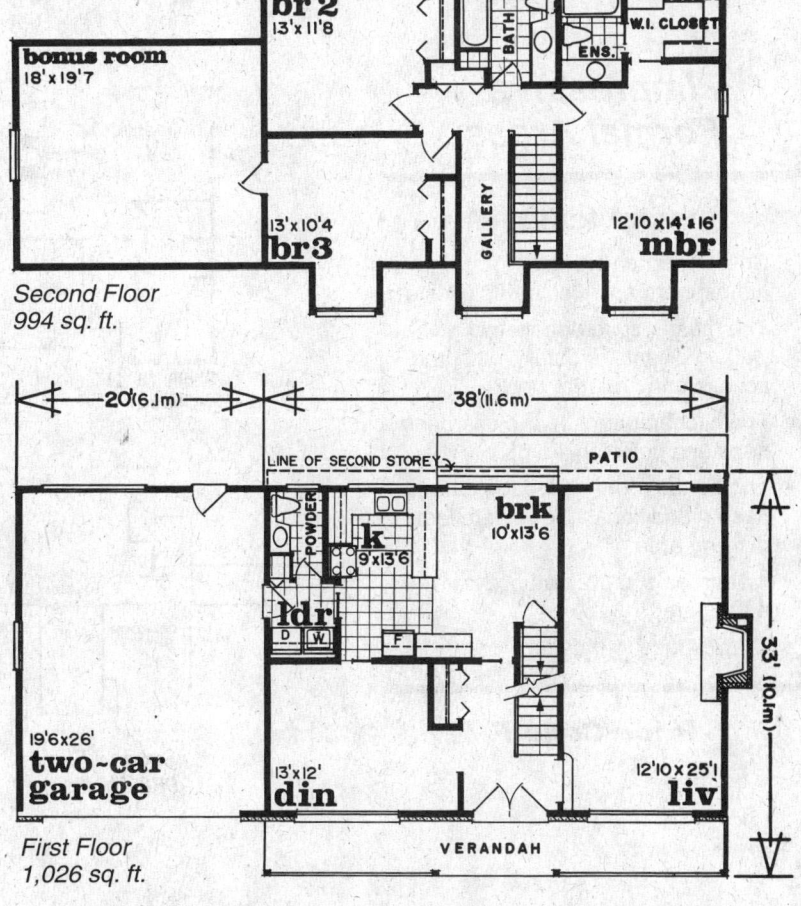

Second Floor
994 sq. ft.

First Floor
1,026 sq. ft.

TO ORDER BLUEPRINTS USE THE FORM ON PAGE 15 OR CALL TOLL-FREE 1-877-671-6036
View thousands more home plans online at www.familyhandyman.com/HOMEPLANS

Plan #718-047D-0090

3,882 total square feet of living area

Impressive Formal Areas

Special features

- Covered porch creates a relaxing atmosphere and welcomes guests
- The master suite boasts two walk-in closets, a deluxe bath and access onto the rear deck
- The kitchen opens to the charming nook and cozy family room
- The bonus room above the garage has an additional 480 square feet of living area
- 4 bedrooms, 3 1/2 baths, 2-car rear entry garage
- Crawl space foundation

Price Code F

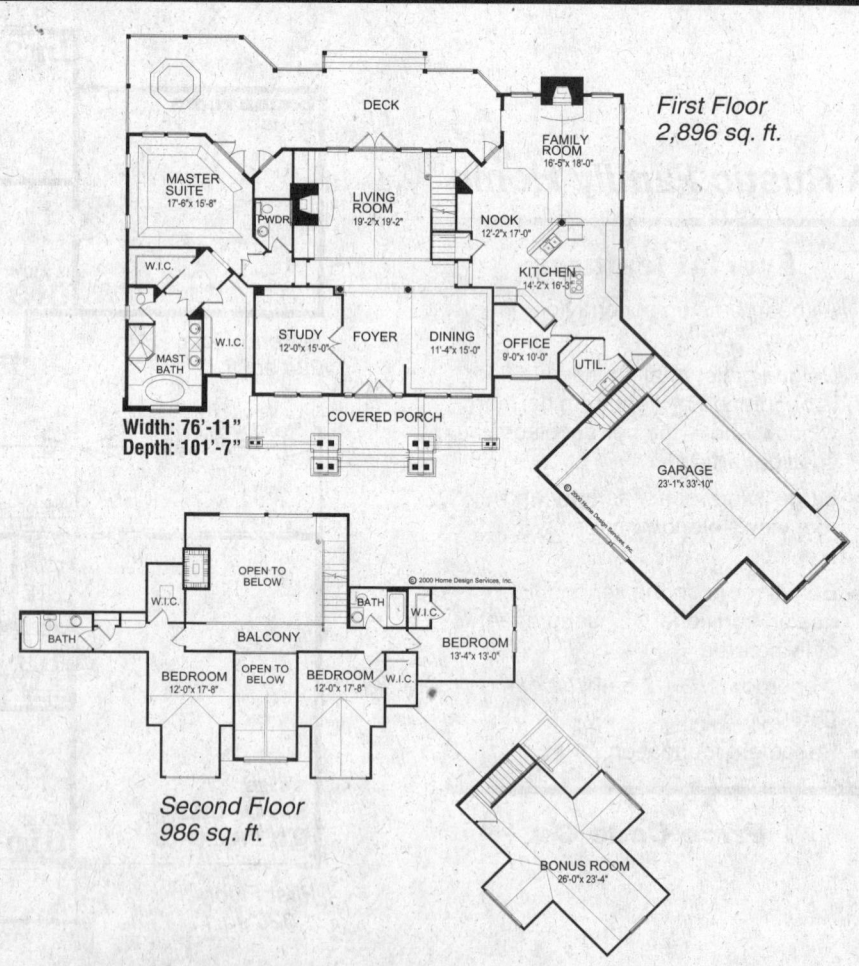

Plan #718-023D-0009

2,333 total square feet of living area

Double French Doors Grace Living Room

Special features

- 9' ceilings on the first floor
- Master bedroom features a large walk-in closet and an inviting double-door entry into a spacious bath
- Convenient laundry room is located near the kitchen
- 4 bedrooms, 3 baths, 2-car side entry garage
- Slab foundation, drawings also include crawl space and partial crawl space/basement foundations

Price Code D

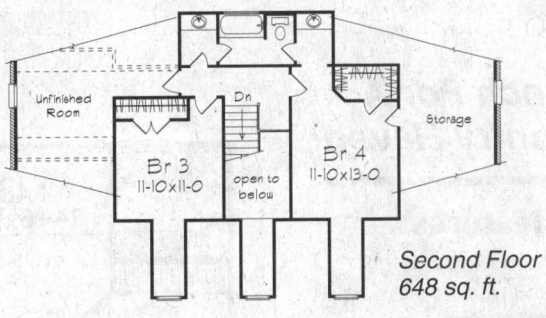

Second Floor 648 sq. ft.

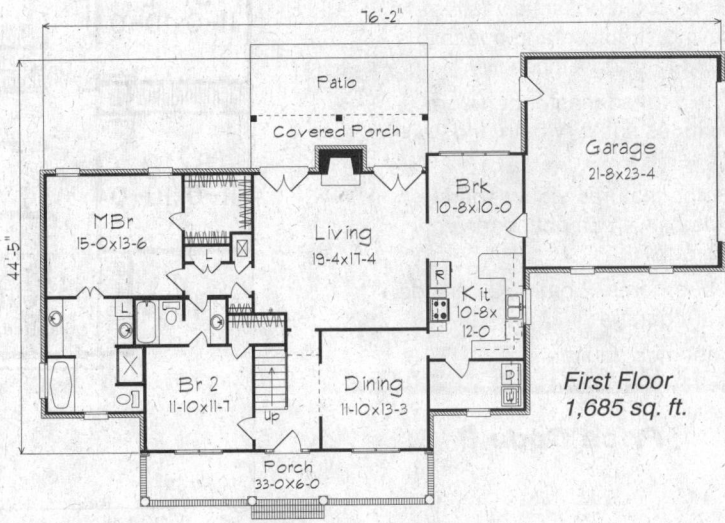

First Floor 1,685 sq. ft.

TO ORDER BLUEPRINTS USE THE FORM ON PAGE 15 OR CALL TOLL-FREE 1-877-671-6036
View thousands more home plans online at www.familyhandyman.com/HOMEPLANS

Plan #718-007D-0067

1,761 total square feet of living area

Small Ranch For A Perfect Country Haven

Special features

- Exterior window dressing, roof dormers and planter boxes provide visual warmth and charm
- Great room boasts a vaulted ceiling, fireplace and opens to a pass-through kitchen
- The vaulted master bedroom includes a luxury bath and walk-in closet
- Home features eight separate closets with an abundance of storage
- 4 bedrooms, 2 baths, 2-car side entry garage
- Basement foundation

Price Code B

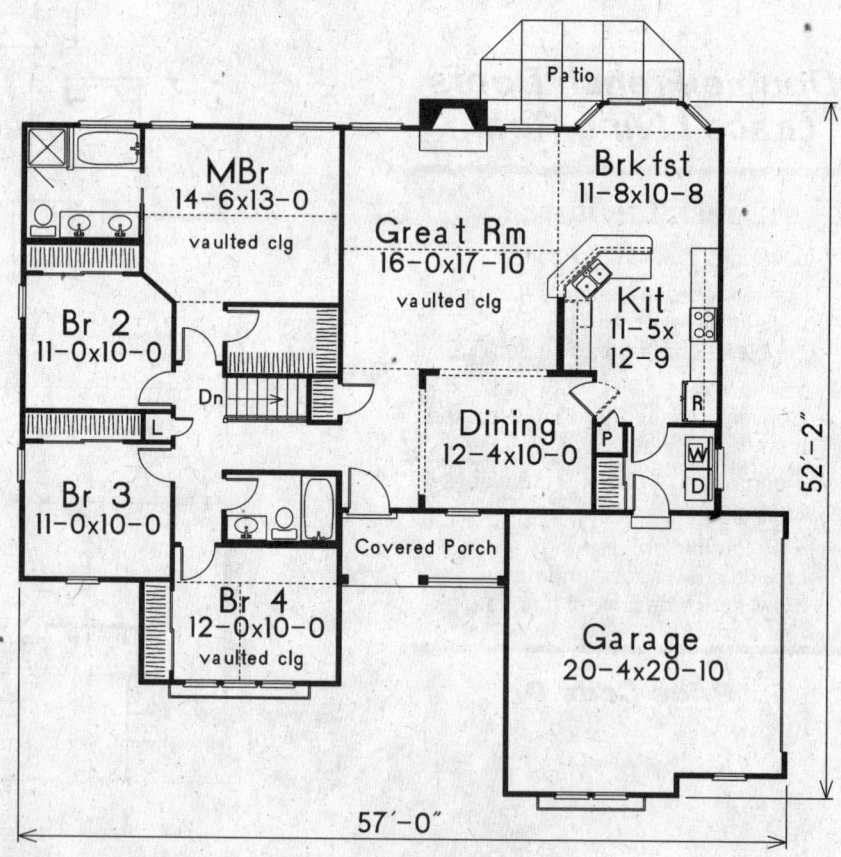

Plan #718-053D-0015

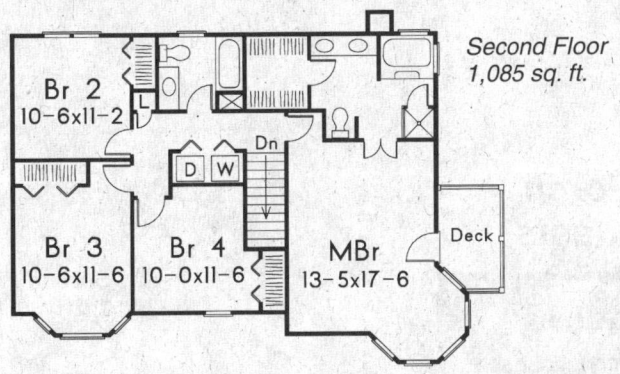

2,214 total square feet of living area

Second Floor 1,085 sq. ft.

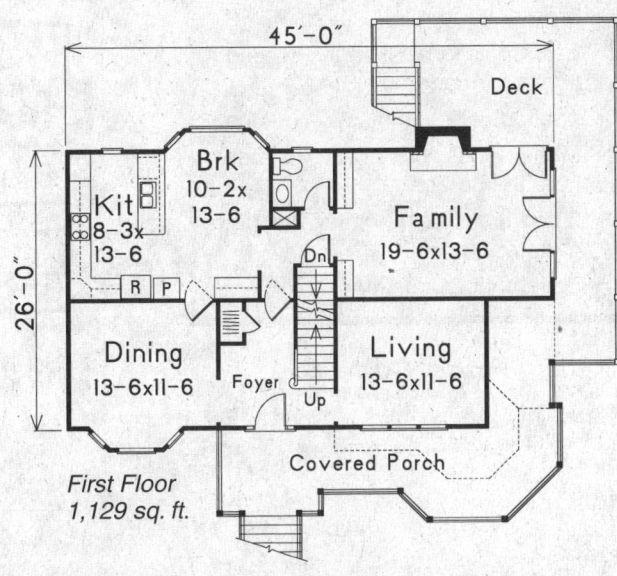

First Floor 1,129 sq. ft.

Victorian Turret Provides Dramatic Focus

Special features

- Victorian accents dominate facade
- Covered porches and decks fan out to connect front and rear entries and add to outdoor living space
- Elegant master bedroom suite features a five-sided windowed alcove and private deck
- Corner kitchen with a sink-top peninsula
- 4 bedrooms, 2 1/2 baths, 2-car drive under garage
- Basement foundation

Price Code D

TO ORDER BLUEPRINTS USE THE FORM ON PAGE 15 OR CALL TOLL-FREE 1-877-671-6036
View thousands more home plans online at www.familyhandyman.com/homeplans

The Family Handyman

Plan #718-058D-0002

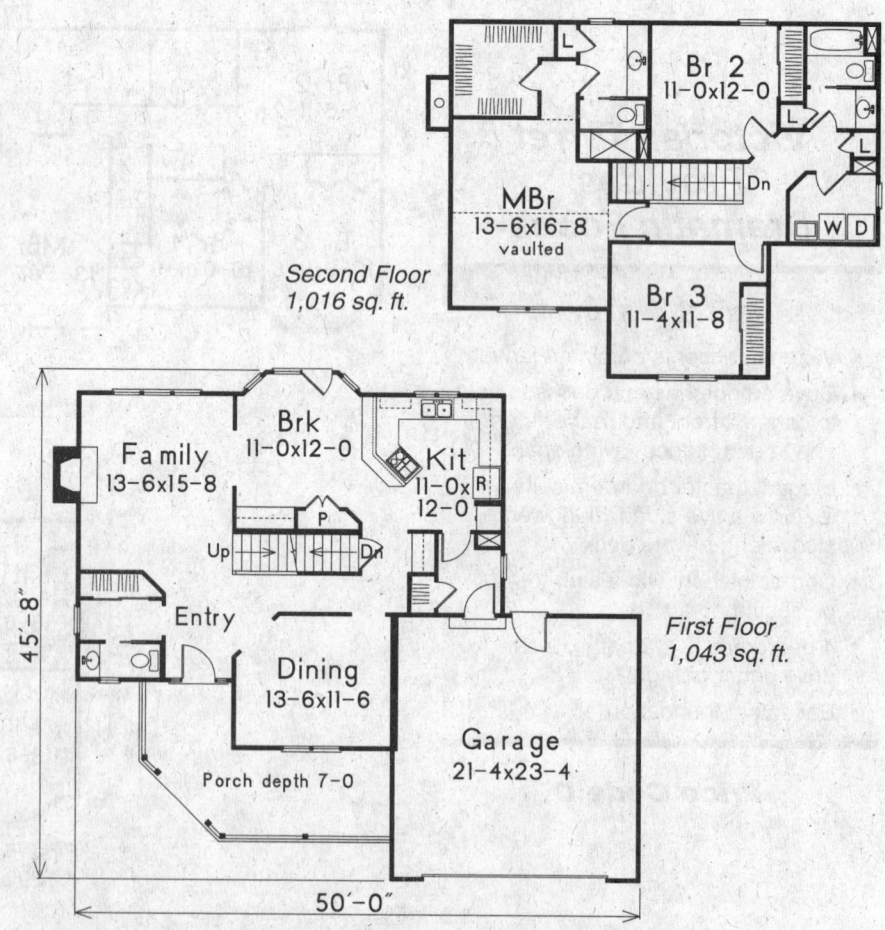

2,059 total square feet of living area

Angled Porch Greets Guests

Special features

- Large desk and pantry add to the breakfast room
- Laundry is located on the second floor near bedrooms
- Vaulted ceiling in master bedroom
- Mud room is conveniently located near the garage
- 3 bedrooms, 2 1/2 baths, 2-car garage
- Basement foundation

Price Code C

Second Floor 1,016 sq. ft.

First Floor 1,043 sq. ft.

TO ORDER BLUEPRINTS USE THE FORM ON PAGE 15 OR CALL TOLL-FREE 1-877-671-6036
View thousands more home plans online at www.familyhandyman.com/homeplans

Plan #718-036D-0059

2,674 total square feet of living area

Impressive Gallery

Special features

- First floor master bedroom has a convenient location
- Kitchen and breakfast area have an island and access to the covered front porch
- Second floor bedrooms have dormer window seats for added charm
- Optional future rooms on the second floor have an additional 520 square feet of living area
- 4 bedrooms, 3 baths, 3-car side entry garage
- Basement or slab foundation, please specify when ordering

Price Code E

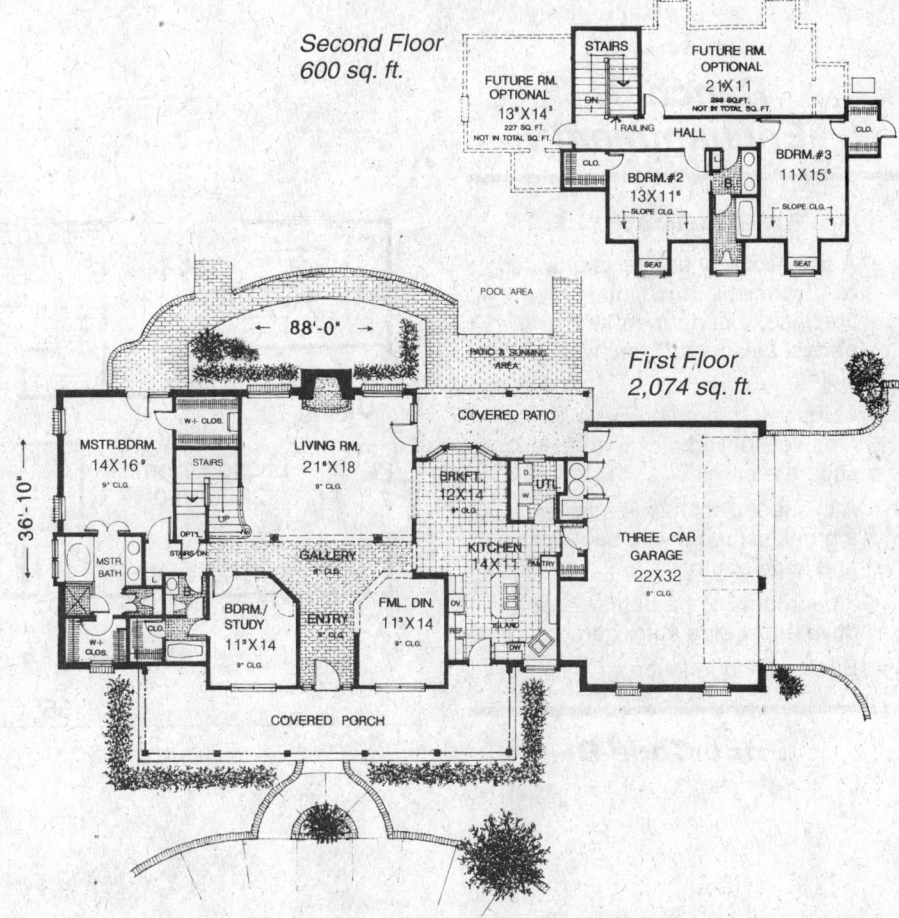

Second Floor 600 sq. ft.

First Floor 2,074 sq. ft.

TO ORDER BLUEPRINTS USE THE FORM ON PAGE 15 OR CALL TOLL-FREE 1-877-671-6036
View thousands more home plans online at www.familyhandyman.com/homeplans

Plan #718-007D-0121

1,559 total square feet of living area

Ranch Of Enchantment

Special features

- A cozy country appeal is provided by a spacious porch, masonry fireplace, roof dormers and a perfect balance of stonework and siding
- Large living room enjoys a fireplace, bayed dining area and separate entry
- A U-shaped kitchen is adjoined by a breakfast room with bay window and large pantry
- 3 bedrooms, 2 1/2 baths, 2-car drive under side entry garage
- Basement foundation

Price Code B

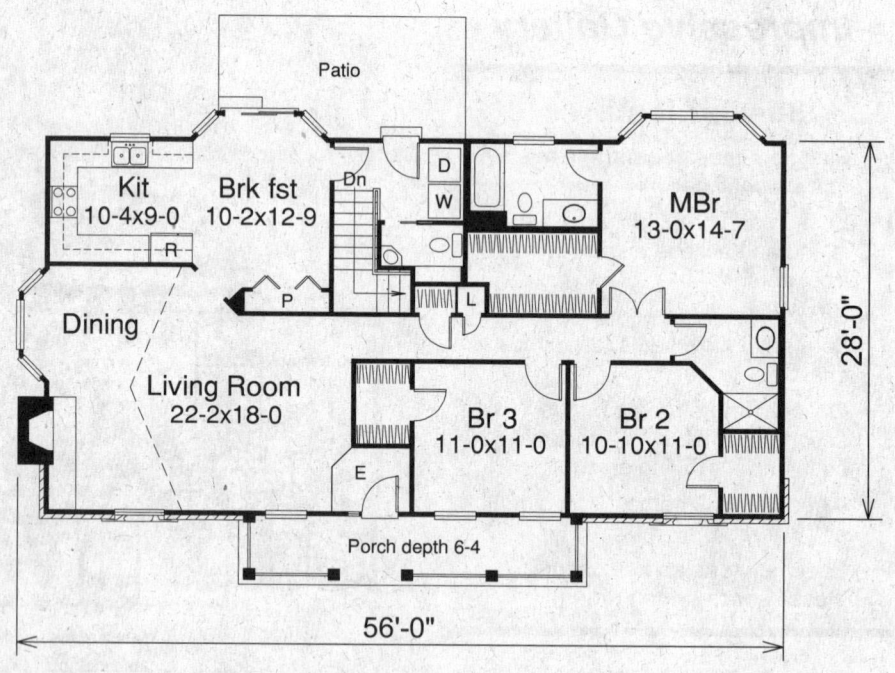

TO ORDER BLUEPRINTS USE THE FORM ON PAGE 15 OR CALL TOLL-FREE 1-877-671-6036
View thousands more home plans online at www.familyhandyman.com/homeplans

Plan #718-062D-0055

1,583 total square feet of living area

Charming Turn Of The Century Exterior

Special features

- Energy efficient home with 2" x 6" exterior walls
- Open kitchen includes a preparation island
- Wrap-around railed porch and rear deck expand the living space to outdoor entertaining
- 3 bedrooms, 2 baths
- Basement or crawl space foundation, please specify when ordering

Price Code B

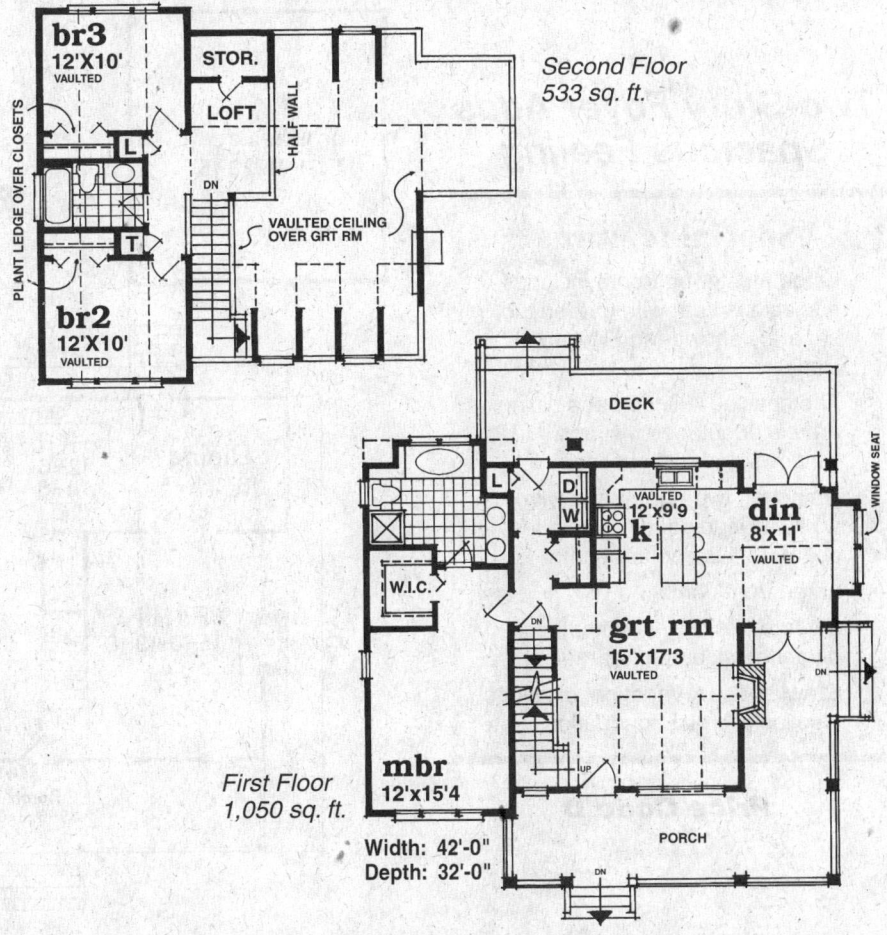

TO ORDER BLUEPRINTS USE THE FORM ON PAGE 15 OR CALL TOLL-FREE 1-877-671-6036
View thousands more home plans online at www.familyhandyman.com/homeplans

The Family Handyman

Plan #718-040D-0001

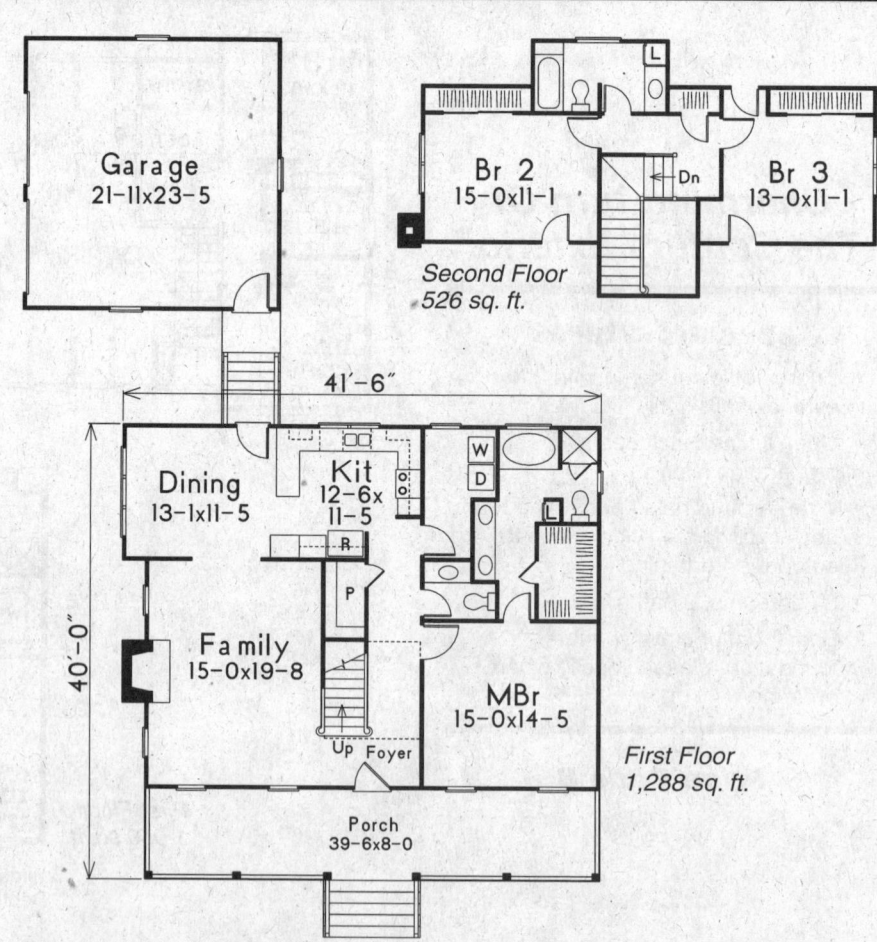

1,814 total square feet of living area

Two-Story Foyer Adds Spacious Feeling

Special features

- Large master bedroom includes a spacious bath with garden tub, separate shower and large walk-in closet
- The spacious kitchen and dining area is brightened by large windows and patio access
- Detached two-car garage with walkway leading to house adds charm to this country home
- Large front porch
- 3 bedrooms, 2 1/2 baths, 2-car detached side entry garage
- Crawl space foundation, drawings also include slab foundation

Price Code D

TO ORDER BLUEPRINTS USE THE FORM ON PAGE 15 OR CALL TOLL-FREE 1-877-671-6036
View thousands more home plans online at www.familyhandyman.com/HOMEPLANS

Plan #718-035D-0019

1,676 total square feet of living area

Charming Single Dormer Above Entry

Special features

- Vaulted master suite has private bath and a massive walk-in closet
- Vaulted family room includes pass-through serving bar from kitchen for convenience
- Architectural details include arched openings into dining room
- 3 bedrooms, 2 baths, 2-car drive under garage
- Walk-out basement foundation

Price Code B

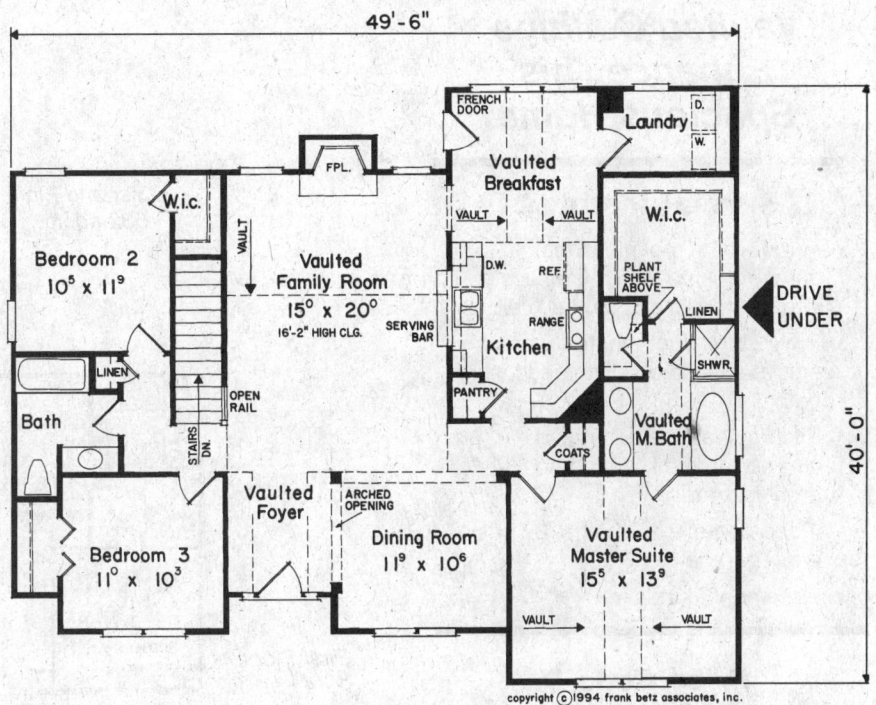

TO ORDER BLUEPRINTS USE THE FORM ON PAGE 15 OR CALL TOLL-FREE 1-877-671-6036
View thousands more home plans online at www.familyhandyman.com/HOMEPLANS

The Family Handyman

Plan #718-040D-0007

2,073 total square feet of living area

Vaulted Ceilings Enhance This Spacious Home

Special features

- Family room provides ideal gathering area with a fireplace, large windows and vaulted ceiling
- Private first floor master bedroom enjoys a vaulted ceiling and luxury bath
- Kitchen features an angled bar connecting the kitchen and breakfast area
- 4 bedrooms, 2 1/2 baths, 2-car side entry garage
- Basement foundation

Price Code D

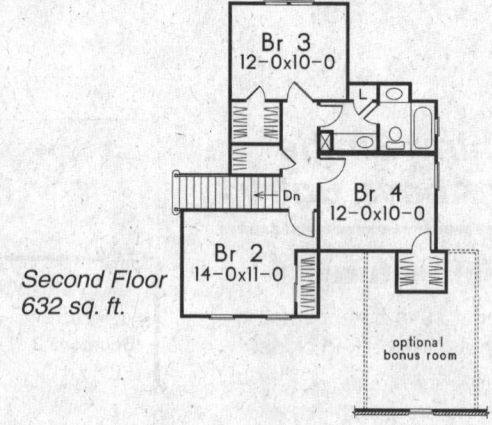

Second Floor 632 sq. ft.

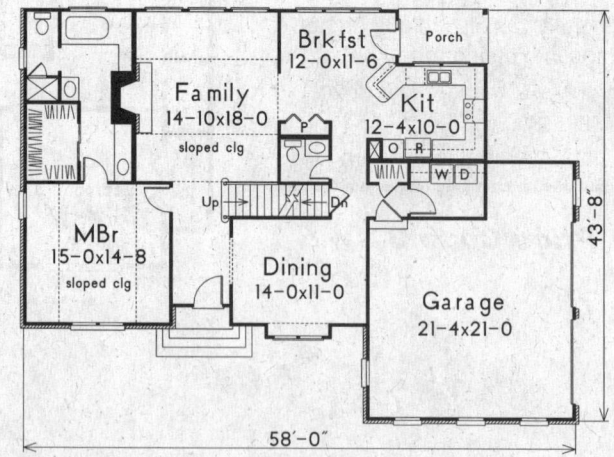

First Floor 1,441 sq. ft.

TO ORDER BLUEPRINTS USE THE FORM ON PAGE 15 OR CALL TOLL-FREE 1-877-671-6036
View thousands more home plans online at www.familyhandyman.com/homeplans

Plan #718-007D-0106

1,200 total square feet of living area

Exciting Living For A Narrow Sloping Lot

Special features

- Entry leads to a large dining area which opens to the kitchen and sun-drenched living room
- An expansive window wall in the two-story atrium lends space and light to living room with fireplace
- The large kitchen features a breakfast bar, built-in pantry and storage galore
- 697 square feet of optional living area on the lower level includes a family room, bedroom #3 and a bath
- 2 bedrooms, 1 bath
- Walk-out basement foundation

Price Code A

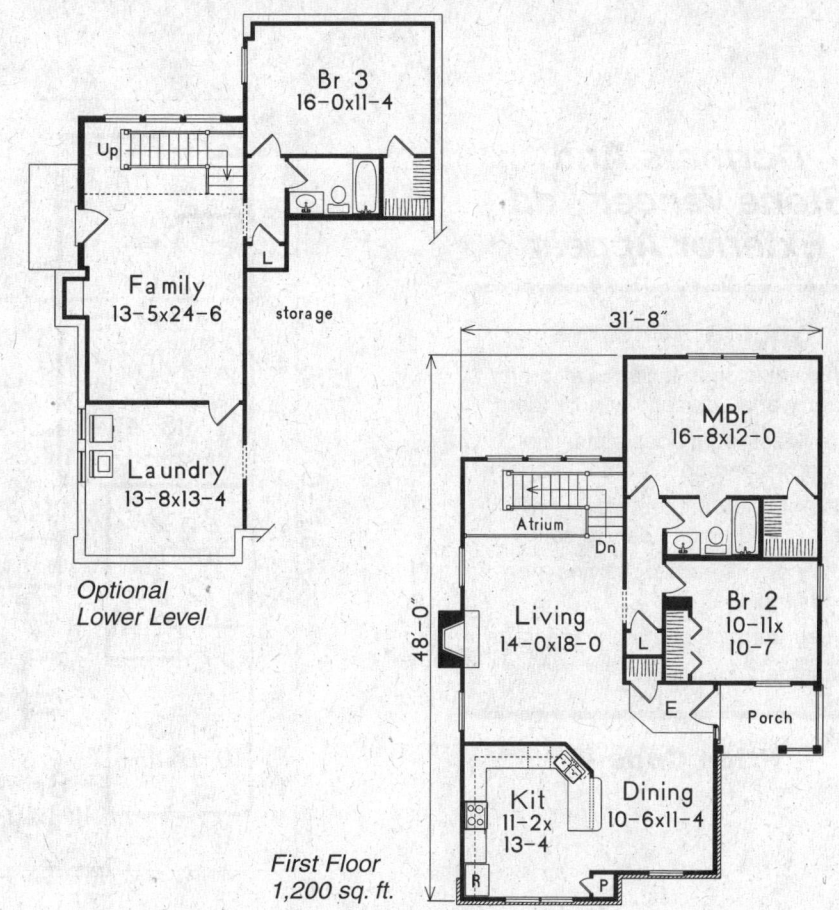

TO ORDER BLUEPRINTS USE THE FORM ON PAGE 15 OR CALL TOLL-FREE 1-877-671-6036
View thousands more home plans online at www.familyhandyman.com/HOMEPLANS

Plan #718-053D-0053

1,609 total square feet of living area

Dormers And Stone Veneer Add Exterior Appeal

Special features

- Efficient kitchen includes a corner pantry and adjacent laundry room
- Breakfast room boasts plenty of windows and opens onto rear deck
- Master bedroom features a tray ceiling and private deluxe bath
- Entry opens into large living area with fireplace
- 4 bedrooms, 2 baths, 2-car garage
- Basement foundation

Price Code B

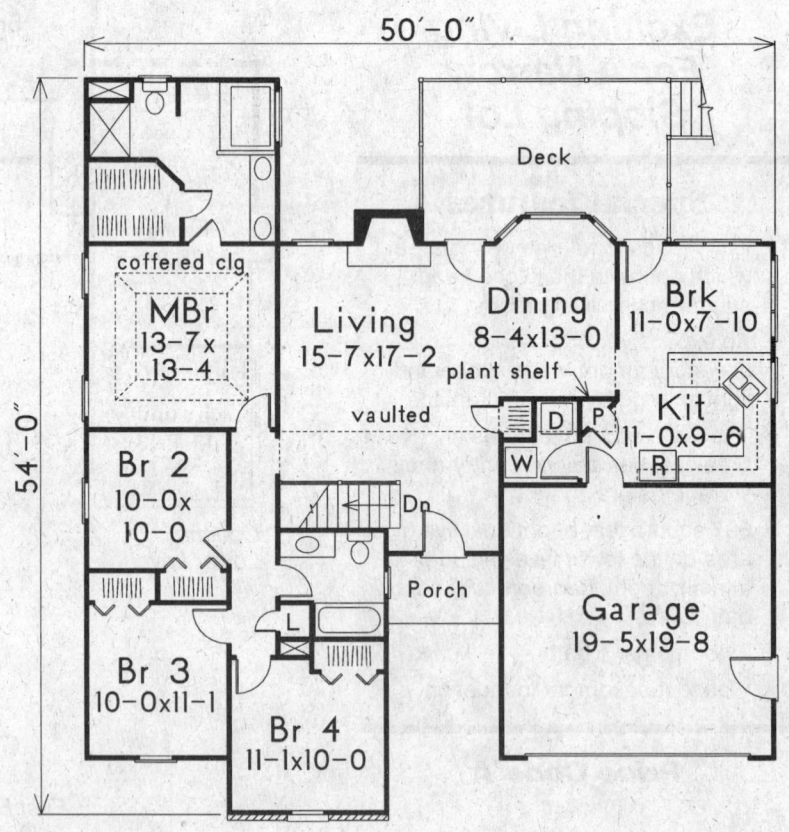

TO ORDER BLUEPRINTS USE THE FORM ON PAGE 15 OR CALL TOLL-FREE 1-877-671-6036
View thousands more home plans online at www.familyhandyman.com/homeplans

Plan #718-016D-0055

1,040 total square feet of living area

Nostalgic Porch And Charming Interior

Special features

- An island in the kitchen greatly simplifies your food preparation efforts
- A wide archway joins the formal living room to the dramatic angled kitchen and dining room
- Optional second floor has an additional 597 square feet of living area
- Optional first floor design has 2 bedrooms including a large master bedroom that enjoys a private luxury bath
- 3 bedrooms, 1 1/2 baths
- Basement, crawl space or slab foundation, please specify when ordering

Price Code B

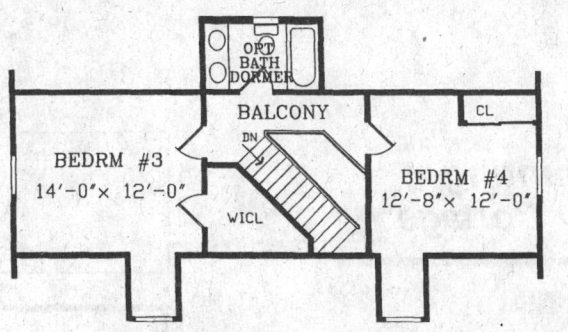

Optional Second Floor

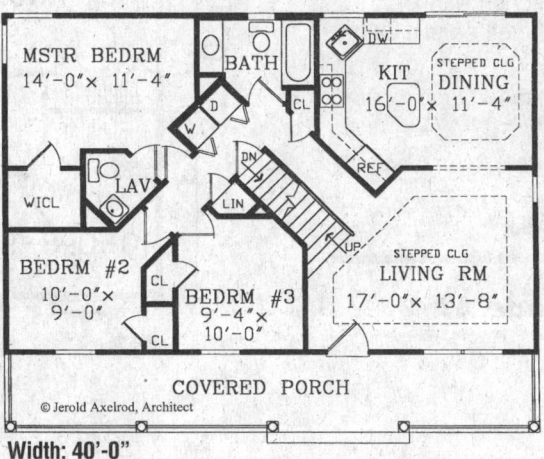

First Floor 1,040 sq. ft.

Width: 40'-0"
Depth: 26'-0"

TO ORDER BLUEPRINTS USE THE FORM ON PAGE 15 OR CALL TOLL-FREE 1-877-671-6036
View thousands more home plans online at www.familyhandyman.com/homeplans

Plan #718-007D-0030

1,140 total square feet of living area

Enchanting Country Cottage

Special features

- Open and spacious living and dining areas for family gatherings
- Well-organized kitchen with an abundance of cabinetry and a built-in pantry
- Roomy master bath features a double-bowl vanity
- 3 bedrooms, 2 baths, 2-car drive under garage
- Basement foundation

Price Code AA

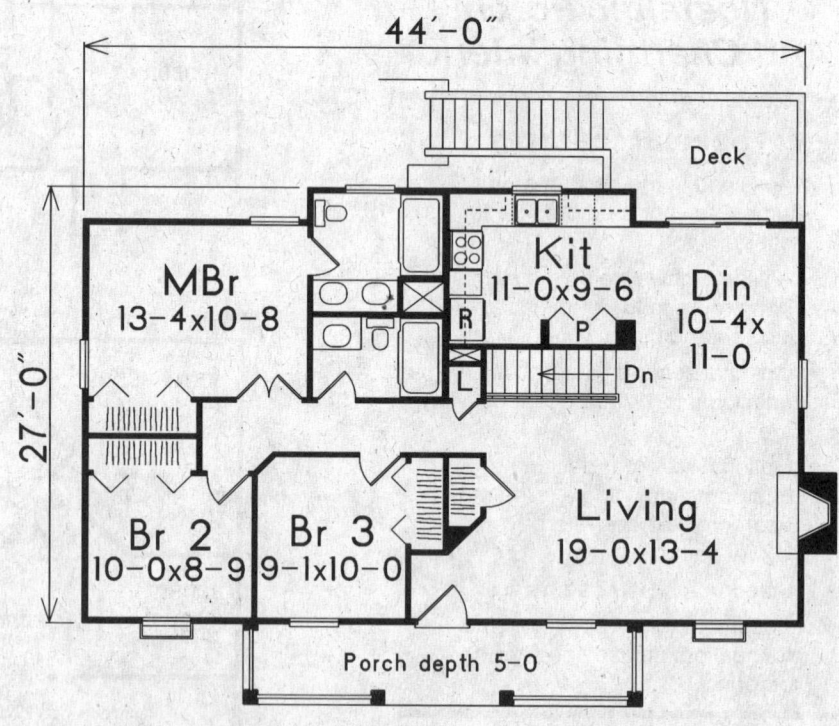

Plan #718-065D-0042

2,362 total square feet of living area

Front Porch Is An Inviting Entrance

Special features

- A spacious kitchen with an oversized island, breakfast area and delightful screened porch combine for family enjoyment
- The second floor offers a computer area in addition to the two bedrooms
- Bonus room on the second floor has an additional 271 square feet of living area
- 3 bedrooms, 2 1/2 baths, 2-car side entry garage
- Basement foundation

Price Code D

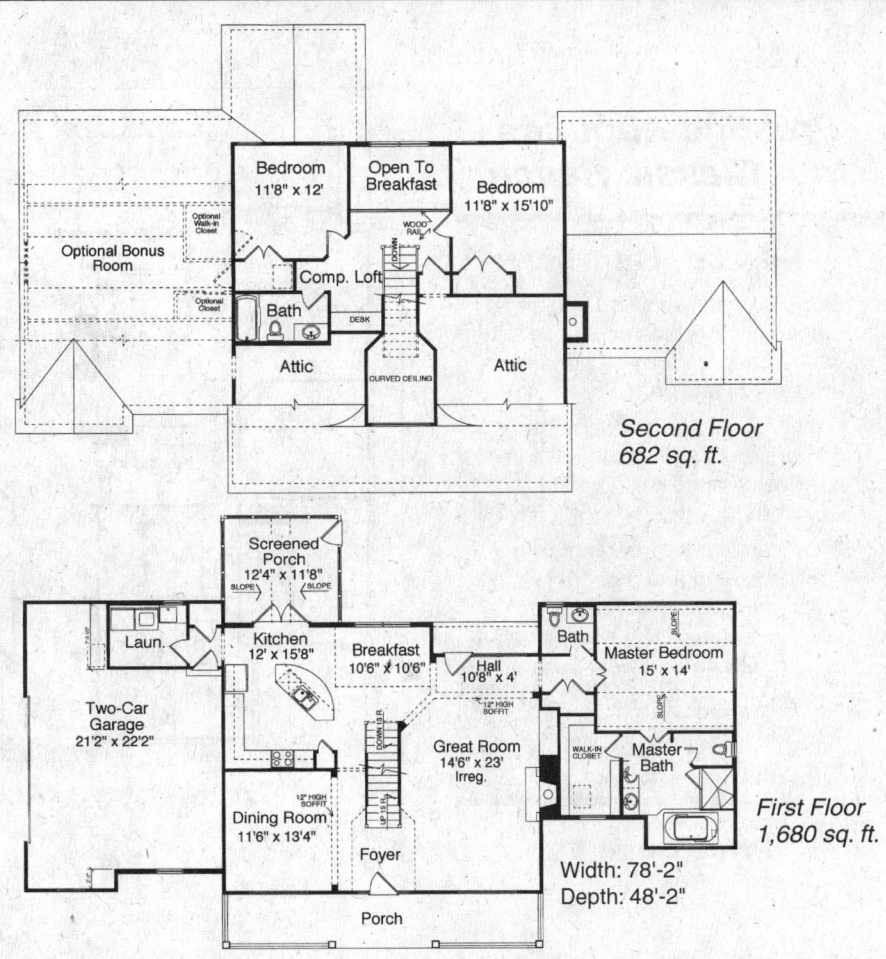

TO ORDER BLUEPRINTS USE THE FORM ON PAGE 15 OR CALL TOLL-FREE 1-877-671-6036
View thousands more home plans online at www.familyhandyman.com/HOMEPLANS

Plan #718-007D-0050

2,723 total square feet of living area

Prestige Abounds In A Classic Ranch

Special features

- Large porch invites you into an elegant foyer which accesses a vaulted bedroom #4/study with private hall and coat closet
- Great room is second to none, comprised of a fireplace, built-in shelves, vaulted ceiling and a 1 1/2 story window wall
- A spectacular hearth room with vaulted ceiling and masonry fireplace opens to an elaborate kitchen featuring two snack bars, a cooking island and walk-in pantry
- 4 bedrooms, 2 1/2 baths, 3-car side entry garage
- Basement foundation

Price Code E

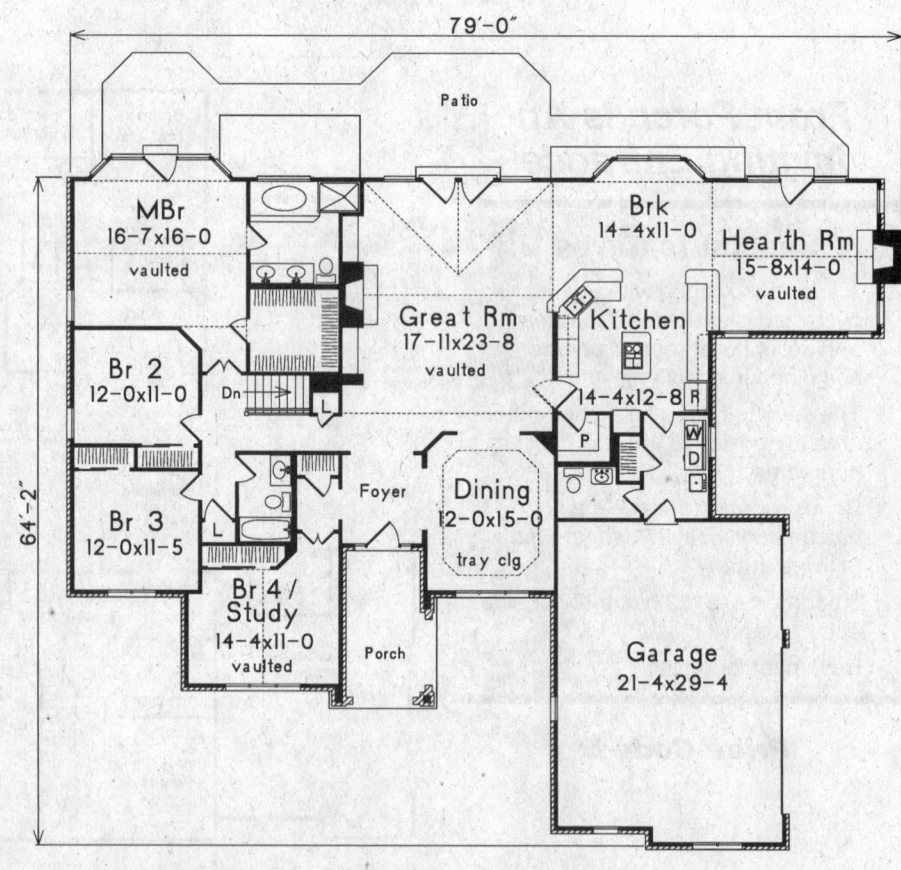

TO ORDER BLUEPRINTS USE THE FORM ON PAGE 15 OR CALL TOLL-FREE 1-877-671-6036
View thousands more home plans online at www.familyhandyman.com/HOMEPLANS

Plan #718-051D-0006

2,171 total square feet of living area

Dormers Create Curb Appeal

Special features

- The kitchen boasts an abundance of counterspace and opens into the nook for extra dining space
- The spacious great room features a 10' ceiling and grand fireplace
- A formal dining room provides an elegant entertaining space
- The relaxing master bedroom enjoys a walk-in closet, whirlpool tub and double vanity
- 3 bedrooms, 2 baths, 3-car garage
- Basement foundation

Price Code C

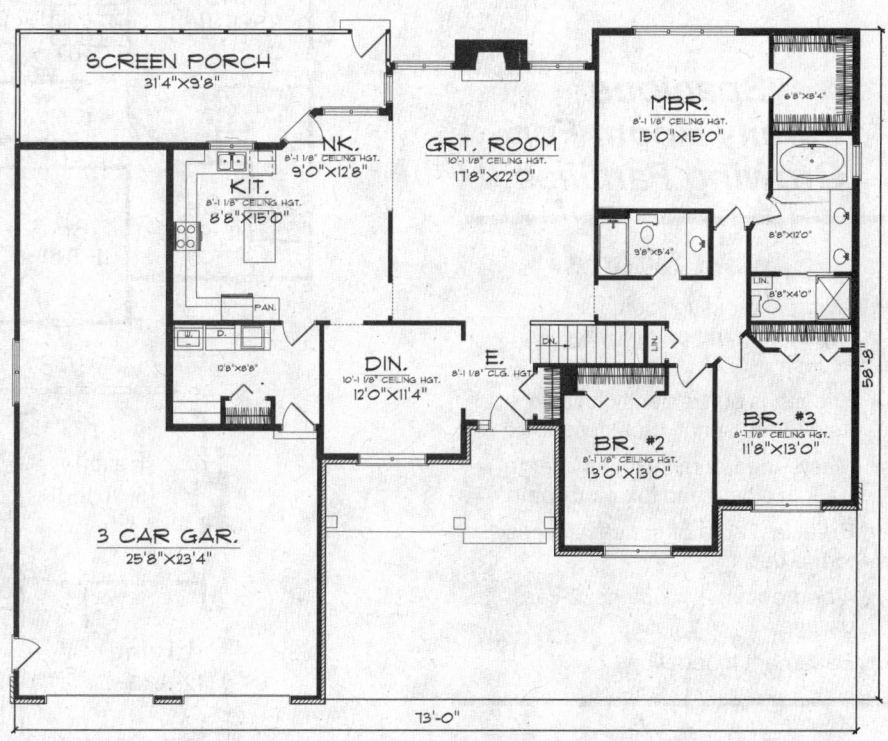

TO ORDER BLUEPRINTS USE THE FORM ON PAGE 15 OR CALL TOLL-FREE 1-877-671-6036
View thousands more home plans online at www.familyhandyman.com/homeplans

Plan #718-027D-0001

2,147 total square feet of living area

Spacious Family Room For Growing Families

Special features

- Living and dining rooms are adjacent to the entry foyer for easy access
- Kitchen is conveniently located next to the sunny breakfast nook
- Master bedroom includes a large walk-in closet and luxurious bath
- Breakfast area offers easy access to the deck
- 4 bedrooms, 2 1/2 baths, 2-car garage
- Basement foundation

Price Code C

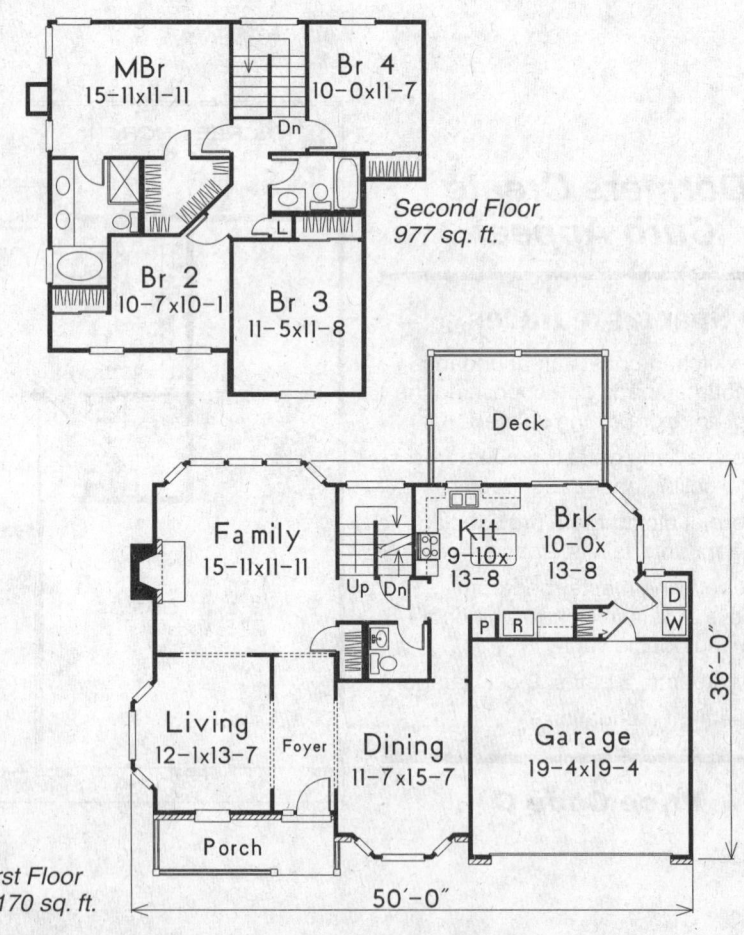

TO ORDER BLUEPRINTS USE THE FORM ON PAGE 15 OR CALL TOLL-FREE 1-877-671-6036
View thousands more home plans online at www.familyhandyman.com/homeplans

Plan #718-053D-0058

1,818 total square feet of living area

Dormers Accent Country Home

Special features

- Breakfast room is tucked behind the kitchen and has a laundry closet and deck access
- Living and dining areas share a vaulted ceiling and fireplace
- Master bedroom has two closets, a large double-bowl vanity and a separate tub and shower
- Large front porch wraps around the home
- 4 bedrooms, 2 1/2 baths, 2-car drive under garage
- Basement foundation

Price Code C

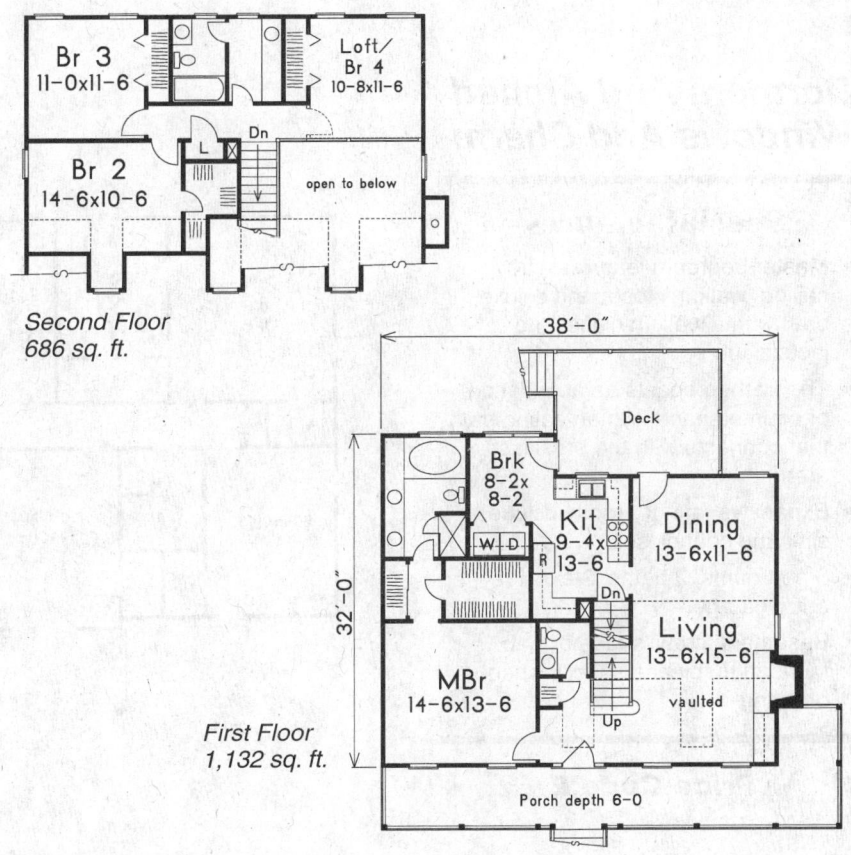

TO ORDER BLUEPRINTS USE THE FORM ON PAGE 15 OR CALL TOLL-FREE 1-877-671-6036
View thousands more home plans online at www.familyhandyman.com/HOMEPLANS

Plan #718-067D-0007

2,651 total square feet of living area

Dormers And Arched Windows Add Charm

Special features

- Master bedroom features a tray ceiling, walk-in closet and deluxe bath with a walk-in closet and jacuzzi tub
- The kitchen boasts an abundance of counterspace with an eating bar that connects with the breakfast area
- Expansive laundry room includes a sink and coat closet
- 3 bedrooms, 2 baths, 2-car side entry garage
- Basement, crawl space or slab foundation, please specify when ordering

Price Code E

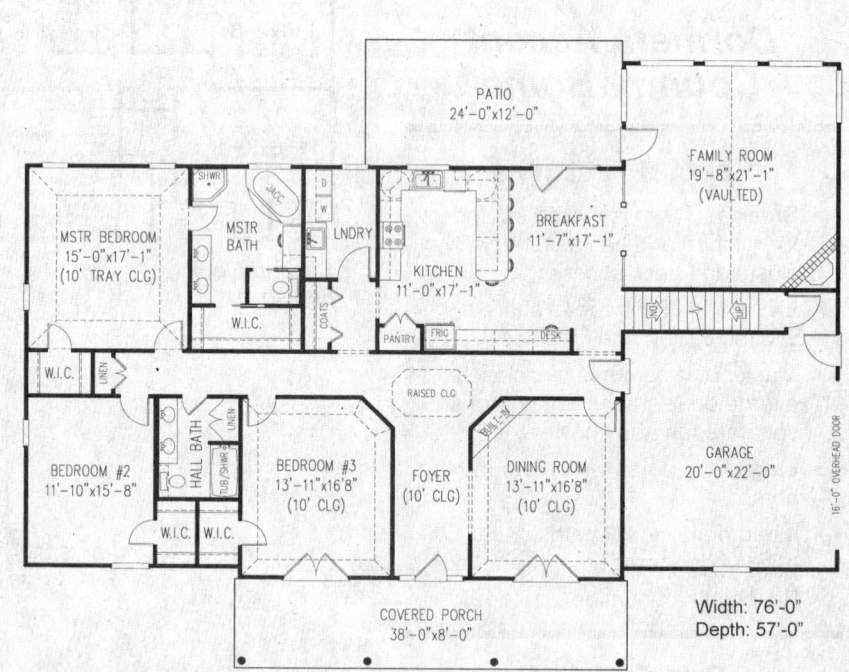

Width: 76'-0"
Depth: 57'-0"

TO ORDER BLUEPRINTS USE THE FORM ON PAGE 15 OR CALL TOLL-FREE 1-877-671-6036
View thousands more home plans online at www.familyhandyman.com/HOMEPLANS

Plan #718-037D-0005

3,050 total square feet of living area

Spacious Styling For Gracious Living

Special features

- Sunny garden room and two-way fireplace create a bright, airy living room
- Front porch is enhanced by arched transom windows and bold columns
- Sitting alcove, French door access to side patio, walk-in closets and abundant storage enhance the master bedroom
- 4 bedrooms, 3 1/2 baths, 2-car detached garage
- Slab foundation, drawings also include crawl space foundation

Price Code E

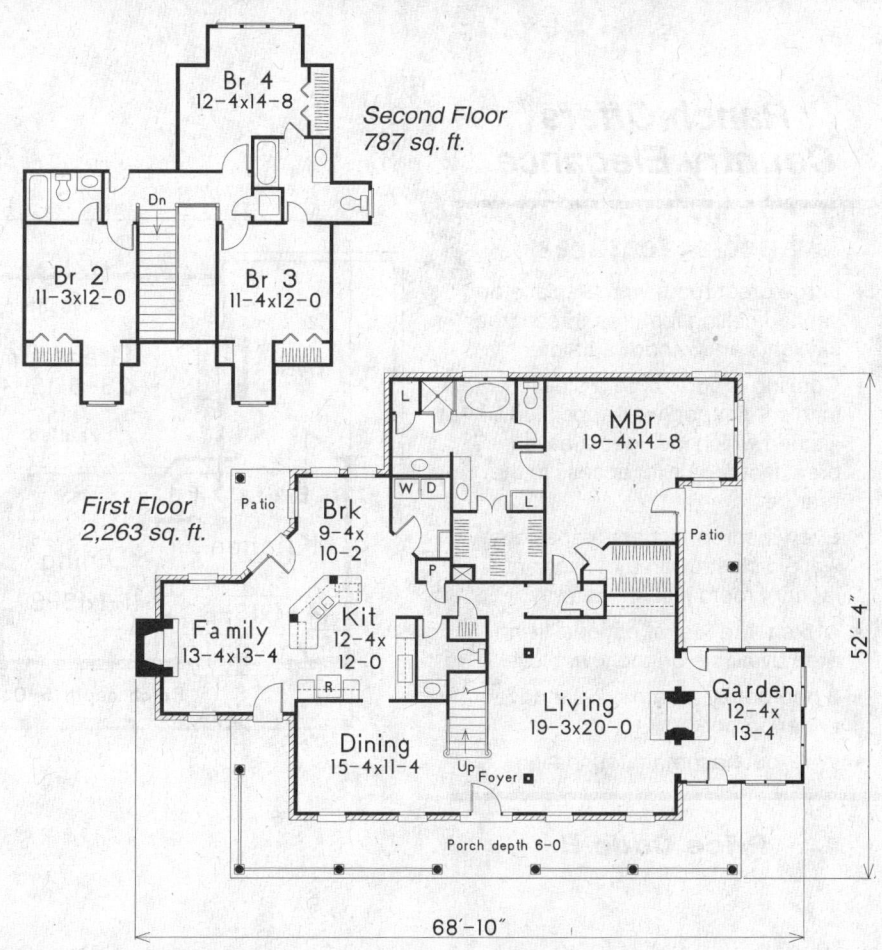

TO ORDER BLUEPRINTS USE THE FORM ON PAGE 15 OR CALL TOLL-FREE 1-877-671-6036
View thousands more home plans online at www.familyhandyman.com/homeplans

Plan #718-007D-0085

1,787 total square feet of living area

Ranch Offers Country Elegance

Special features

- Large great room with fireplace and vaulted ceiling features three large skylights and windows galore
- Cooking is sure to be a pleasure in this L-shaped well-appointed kitchen which includes a bayed breakfast area with access to the rear deck
- Every bedroom offers a spacious walk-in closet with a convenient laundry room just steps away
- 415 square feet of optional living area available on the lower level
- 3 bedrooms, 2 baths, 2-car drive under garage
- Walk-out basement foundation

Price Code B

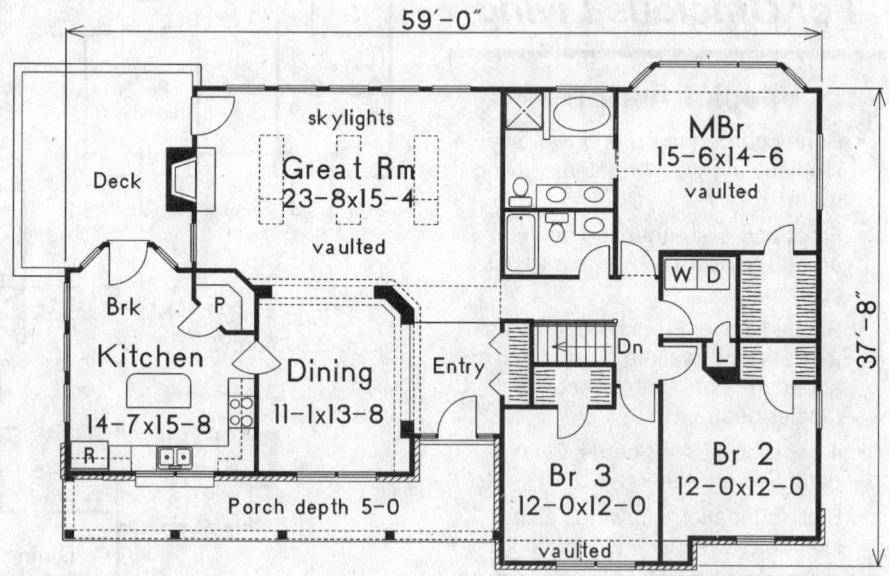

TO ORDER BLUEPRINTS USE THE FORM ON PAGE 15 OR CALL TOLL-FREE 1-877-671-6036
View thousands more home plans online at www.familyhandyman.com/homeplans

Plan #718-058D-0032

1,879 total square feet of living area

Charming Wrap-Around Porch

Special features

- Open floor plan on both floors makes home appear larger
- Loft area overlooks great room or can become an optional fourth bedroom
- Large storage in rear of home has access from exterior
- 3 bedrooms, 2 baths
- Crawl space foundation

Price Code C

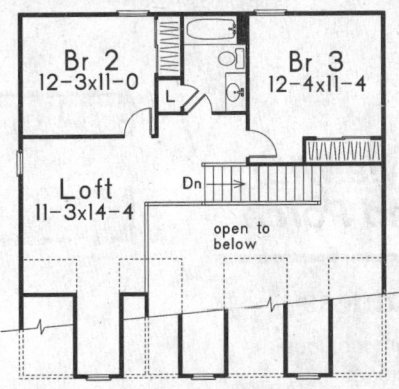

Second Floor 565 sq. ft.

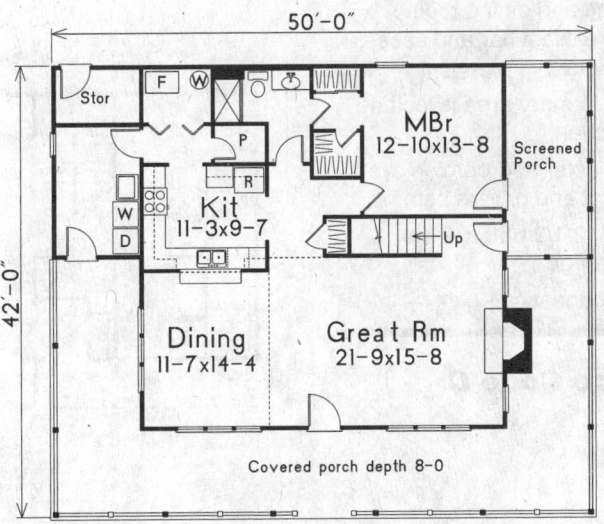

First Floor 1,314 sq. ft.

TO ORDER BLUEPRINTS USE THE FORM ON PAGE 15 OR CALL TOLL-FREE 1-877-671-6036

View thousands more home plans online at www.familyhandyman.com/homeplans

Plan #718-040D-0027

1,597 total square feet of living area

Country Style With Wrap-Around Porch

Special features

- Spacious family room includes a fireplace and coat closet
- Open kitchen and dining room provide a breakfast bar and access to the outdoors
- Convenient laundry area is located near the kitchen
- Secluded master bedroom enjoys a walk-in closet and private bath
- 4 bedrooms, 2 1/2 baths, 2-car detached garage
- Basement foundation

Price Code C

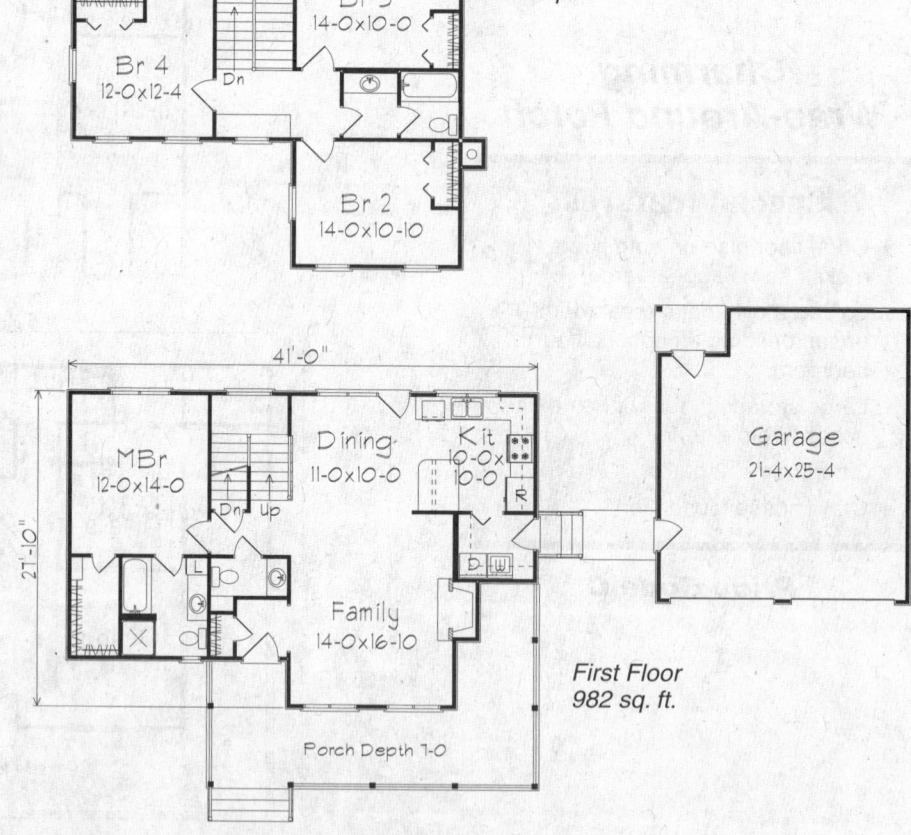

Second Floor 615 sq. ft.

Br 3 14-0x10-0
Br 4 12-0x12-4
Br 2 14-0x10-10

First Floor 982 sq. ft.

41'-0"
27'-10"
MBr 12-0x14-0
Dining 11-0x10-0
Kit 10-0x10-0
Family 14-0x16-10
Garage 21-4x25-4
Porch Depth 7-0

TO ORDER BLUEPRINTS USE THE FORM ON PAGE 15 OR CALL TOLL-FREE 1-877-671-6036
View thousands more home plans online at www.familyhandyman.com/HOMEPLANS

Plan #718-035D-0028

1,779 total square feet of living area

Elaborate Dining Room

Special features

- Well-designed floor plan has a vaulted family room with fireplace and access to the outdoors
- Decorative columns separate the dining area from the foyer
- A vaulted ceiling adds spaciousness in the master bath that also features a walk-in closet
- 3 bedrooms, 2 baths, 2-car garage
- Walk-out basement, slab or crawl space foundation, please specify when ordering

Price Code B

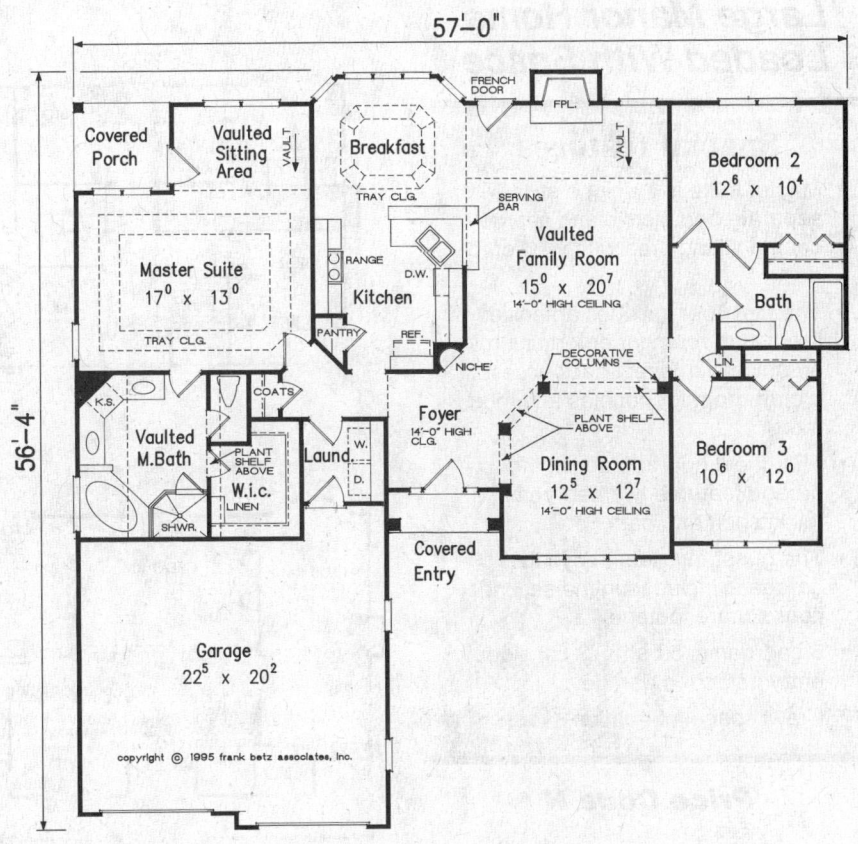

TO ORDER BLUEPRINTS USE THE FORM ON PAGE 15 OR CALL TOLL-FREE 1-877-671-6036
View thousands more home plans online at www.familyhandyman.com/homeplans

Plan #718-011D-0035

6,088 total square feet of living area

Large Manor Home Loaded With Space

Special features

- Master suite is a unique style with separate bed alcove and a large central sitting area with view onto deck
- The first floor includes amenities like a club room for entertaining, an office with direct deck access, a craft room for hobbies and much more
- The guest quarters above the garage features two bedrooms, a full kitchen and bath
- The guest quarters above the garage is included in the second floor square footage
- 6 bedrooms, 5 baths, 3-car side entry detached garage
- Crawl space foundation

Price Code H

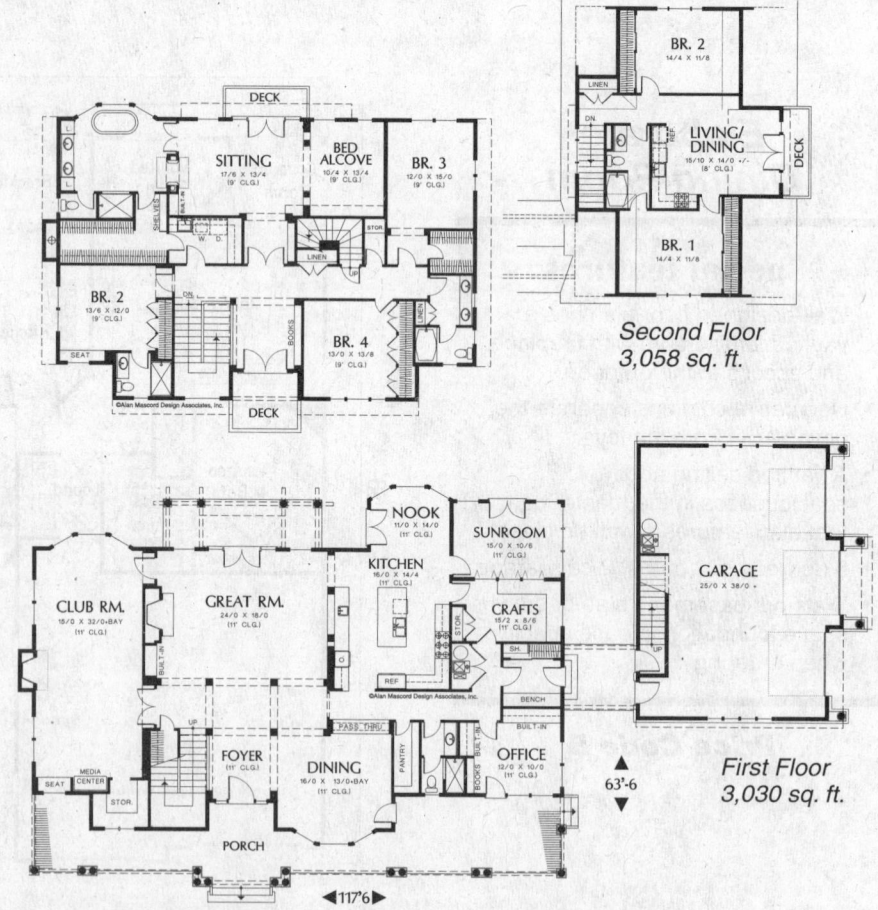

TO ORDER BLUEPRINTS USE THE FORM ON PAGE 15 OR CALL TOLL-FREE 1-877-671-6036
View thousands more home plans online at www.familyhandyman.com/homeplans

Plan #718-037D-0013

2,213 total square feet of living area

Outdoor Living Area Created By Veranda

Special features

- Master bedroom features a full bath with separate vanities, large walk-in closet and access to the veranda
- Living room is enhanced by a fireplace, bay window and columns framing the gallery
- 9' ceilings throughout home add to open feeling
- 4 bedrooms, 2 1/2 baths, 2-car side entry garage
- Slab foundation

Price Code E

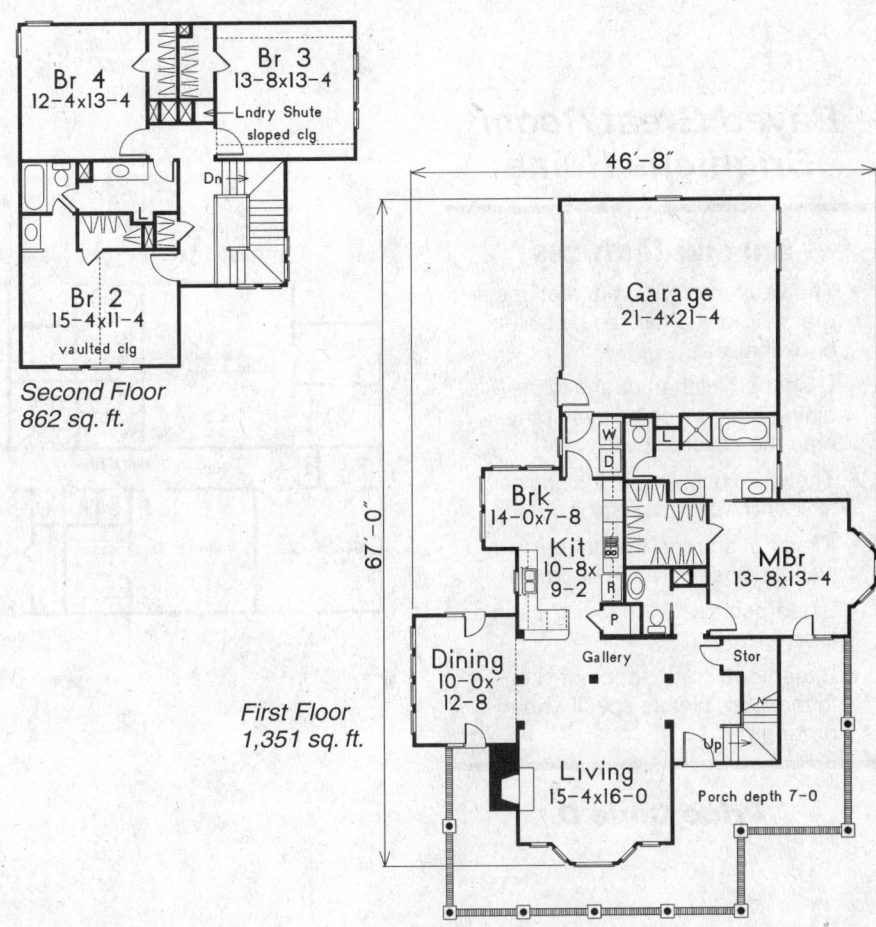

Second Floor 862 sq. ft.

First Floor 1,351 sq. ft.

TO ORDER BLUEPRINTS USE THE FORM ON PAGE 15 OR CALL TOLL-FREE 1-877-671-6036
View thousands more home plans online at www.familyhandyman.com/homeplans

Plan #718-077D-0003

1,896 total square feet of living area

Bayed Great Room Brightens Home

Special features

- The vaulted great room features a grand fireplace flanked by built-in bookshelves
- U-shaped kitchen opens to the dining area which enjoys access onto the covered porch
- The large utility room includes a sink and walk-in pantry
- Plenty of storage throughout with a walk-in closet in each bedroom
- 3 bedrooms, 2 1/2 baths, 2-car side entry garage
- Basement, crawl space or slab foundation, please specify when ordering

Price Code D

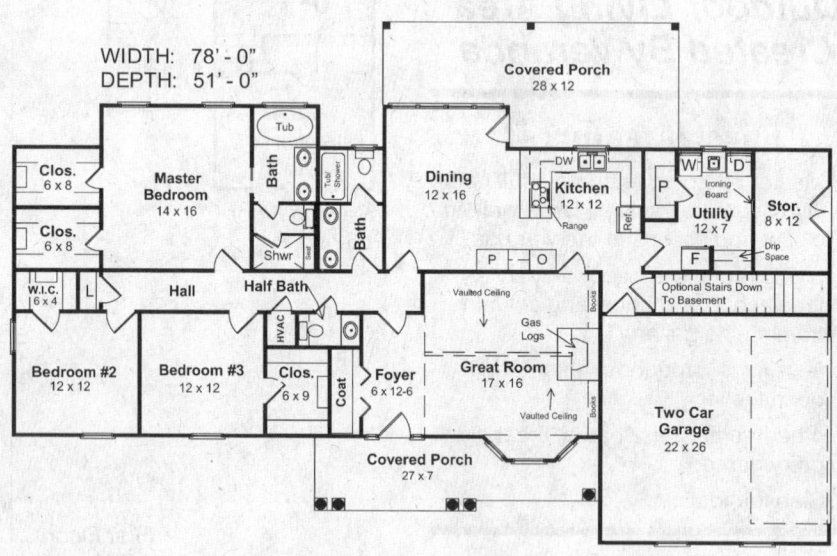

Plan #718-006D-0004

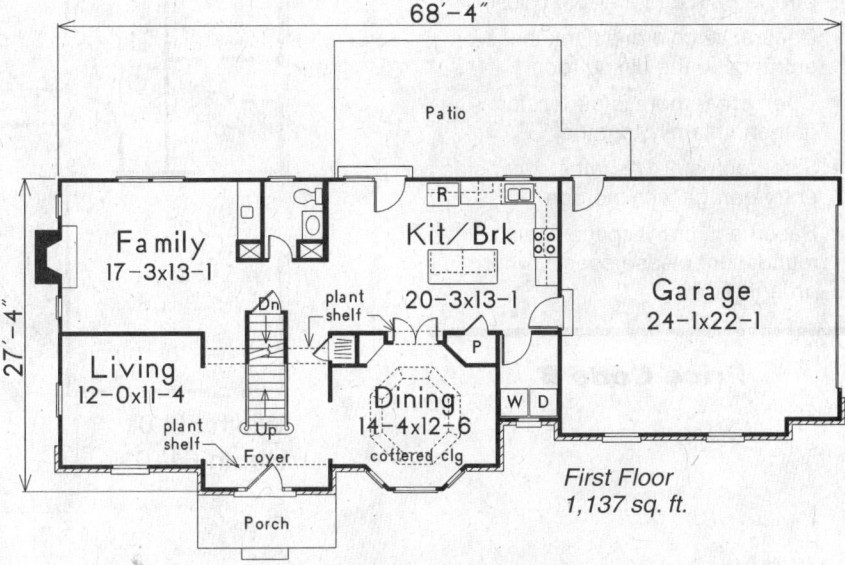

1,996 total square feet of living area

Blends Open And Private Living Areas

Special features

- Dining area features an octagon-shaped coffered ceiling and built-in china cabinet
- Both the master bath and second floor bath have cheerful skylights
- Family room includes a wet bar and fireplace flanked by attractive quarter round windows
- 9' ceilings throughout the first floor with plant shelving in foyer and dining area
- 3 bedrooms, 2 1/2 baths, 2-car side entry garage
- Basement foundation, drawings also include crawl space and slab foundations

Price Code C

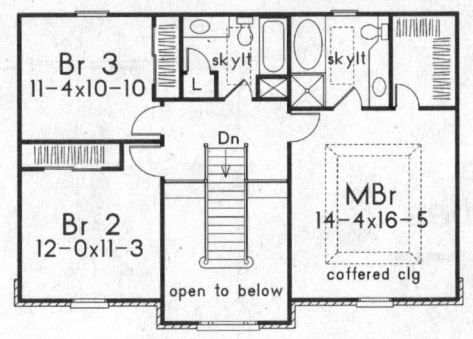

Second Floor 859 sq. ft.

First Floor 1,137 sq. ft.

TO ORDER BLUEPRINTS USE THE FORM ON PAGE 15 OR CALL TOLL-FREE 1-877-671-6036
View thousands more home plans online at www.familyhandyman.com/HOMEPLANS

Plan #718-067D-0004

1,698 total square feet of living area

Stunning Triple Dormers And Arches

Special features

- Vaulted master bedroom has a private bath and a walk-in closet
- Decorative columns flank the entrance to the dining room
- Open great room is perfect for gathering family together
- 3 bedrooms, 2 1/2 baths, 2-car side entry garage with storage
- Basement, crawl space or slab foundation, please specify when ordering

Price Code B

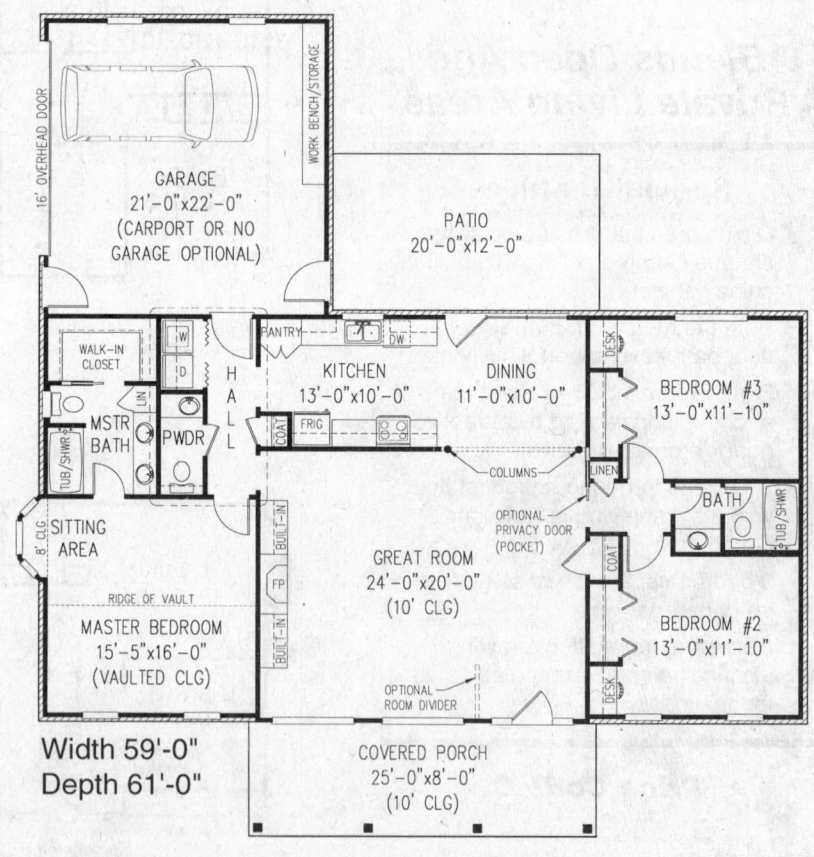

Width 59'-0"
Depth 61'-0"

TO ORDER BLUEPRINTS USE THE FORM ON PAGE 15 OR CALL TOLL-FREE 1-877-671-6036
View thousands more home plans online at www.familyhandyman.com/homeplans

Plan #718-001D-0031

1,501 total square feet of living area

Country-Style Home With Large Front Porch

Special features

- Spacious kitchen with dining area is open to the outdoors
- Convenient utility room is adjacent to garage
- Master bedroom features a private bath, dressing area and access to the large covered porch
- Large family room creates openness
- 3 bedrooms, 2 baths, 2-car side entry garage
- Basement foundation, drawings also include crawl space and slab foundations

Price Code B

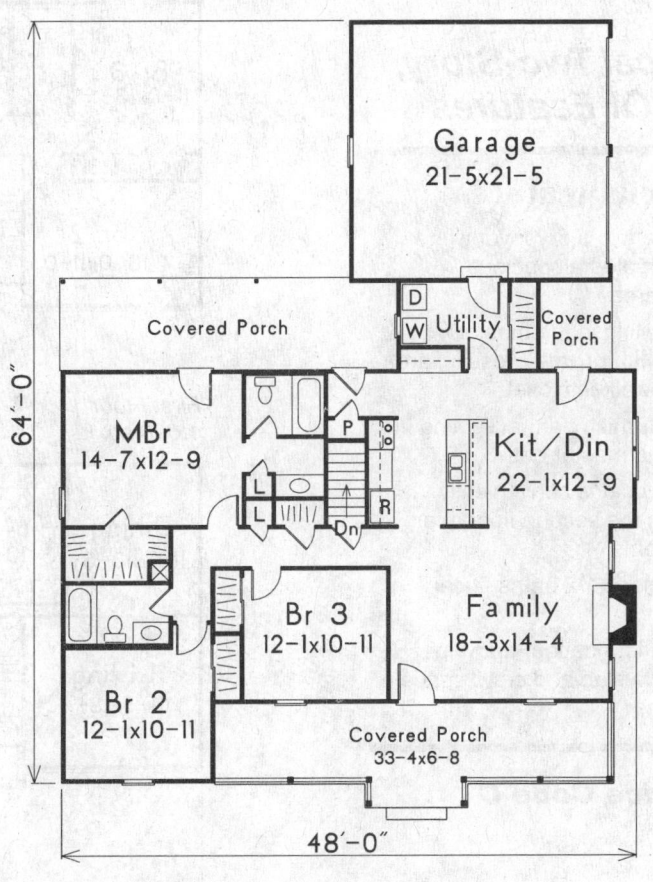

TO ORDER BLUEPRINTS USE THE FORM ON PAGE 15 OR CALL TOLL-FREE 1-877-671-6036
View thousands more home plans online at www.familyhandyman.com/HOMEPLANS

Plan #718-003D-0001

2,058 total square feet of living area

Practical Two-Story, Full Of Features

Special features

- Handsome two-story foyer with balcony creates a spacious entrance area
- Vaulted ceiling in the master bedroom with private dressing area and large walk-in closet
- Skylights furnish natural lighting in the hall and master bath
- Laundry closet is conveniently located on the second floor near the bedrooms
- 3 bedrooms, 2 1/2 baths, 2-car garage
- Basement foundation, drawings also include slab and crawl space foundations

Price Code C

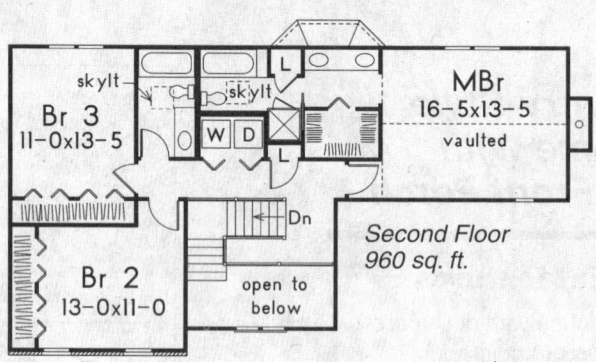

Second Floor 960 sq. ft.

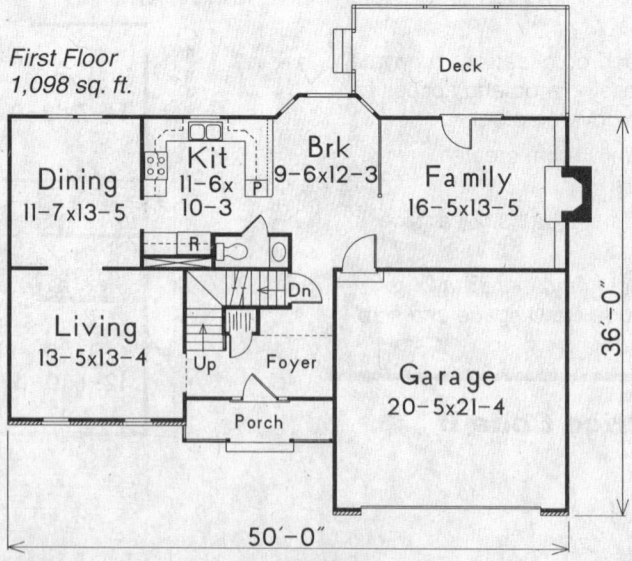

First Floor 1,098 sq. ft.

TO ORDER BLUEPRINTS USE THE FORM ON PAGE 15 OR CALL TOLL-FREE 1-877-671-6036
View thousands more home plans online at www.familyhandyman.com/homeplans

Plan #718-055D-0118

2,789 total square feet of living area

Spacious Design With A Luxurious Appeal

Special features

- Master bedroom with large walk-in closets has a glass shower and whirlpool tub
- Great room has a sunny wall of windows creating a cheerful atmosphere
- Second floor includes bonus room with 286 square feet of living area
- 4 bedrooms, 3 baths, 2-car side entry garage
- Walk-out basement, basement, crawl space or slab foundation, please specify when ordering

Price Code E

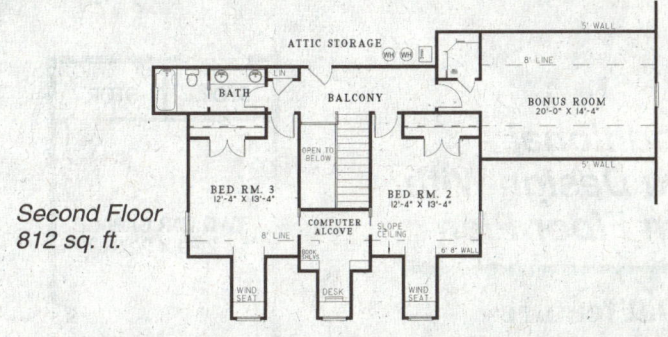

Second Floor
812 sq. ft.

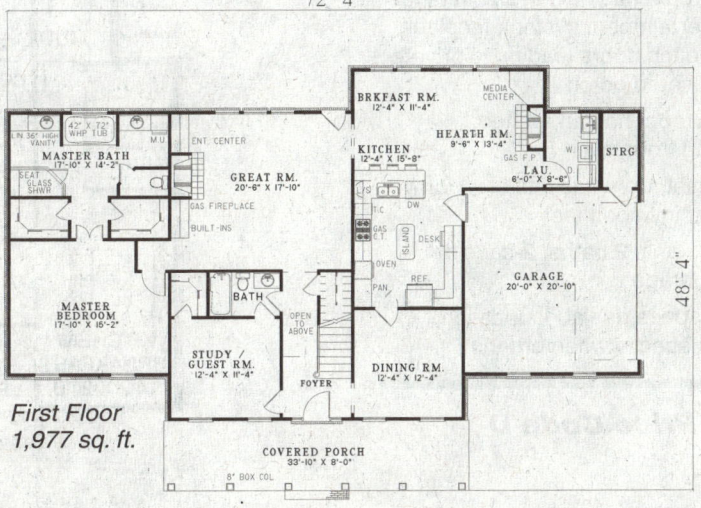

First Floor
1,977 sq. ft.

TO ORDER BLUEPRINTS USE THE FORM ON PAGE 15 OR CALL TOLL-FREE 1-877-671-6036
View thousands more home plans online at www.familyhandyman.com/HOMEPLANS

Plan #718-028D-0010

2,214 total square feet of living area

Traditional Southern Design With Modern Floor Plan

Special features

- Great room has built-in cabinets for an entertainment system, fireplace and French doors leading to private rear covered porch
- Dining room has an arched opening from foyer
- Breakfast room has lots of windows for a sunny open feel
- 3 bedrooms, 2 baths, 2-car side entry garage
- Crawl space or slab foundation, please specify when ordering

Price Code D

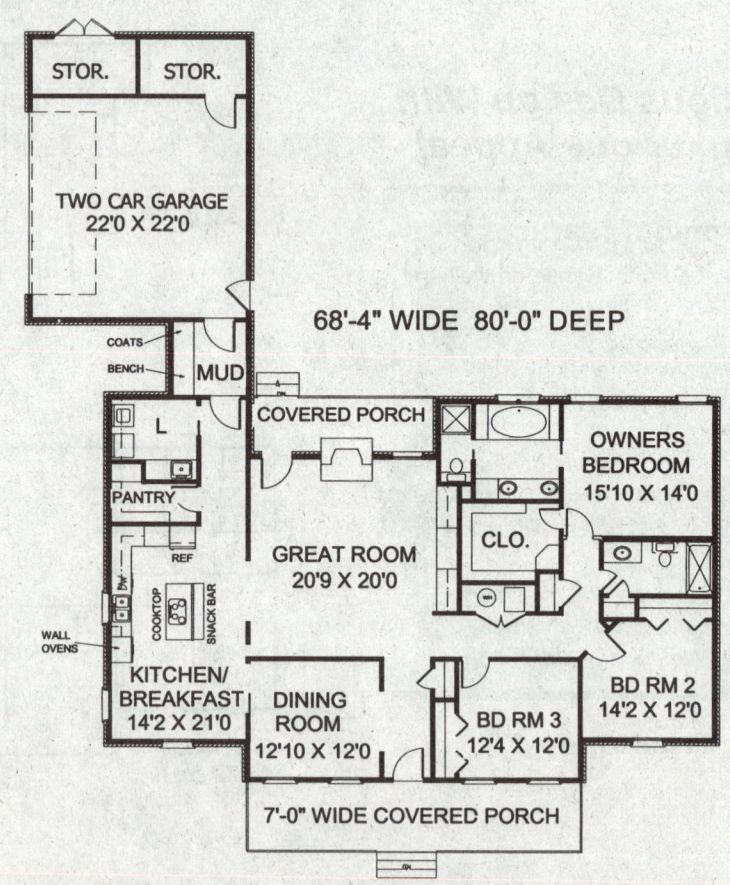

TO ORDER BLUEPRINTS USE THE FORM ON PAGE 15 OR CALL TOLL-FREE 1-877-671-6036
View thousands more home plans online at www.familyhandyman.com/homeplans

Plan #718-017D-0006

3,006 total square feet of living area

Third Floor All-Purpose Room

Special features

- Energy efficient home with 2" x 6" exterior walls
- Large all-purpose room and bath on third floor
- Efficient U-shaped kitchen includes a pantry and adjacent planning desk
- 4 bedrooms, 3 1/2 baths, 2-car side entry garage
- Basement foundation, drawings also include slab foundation

Price Code E

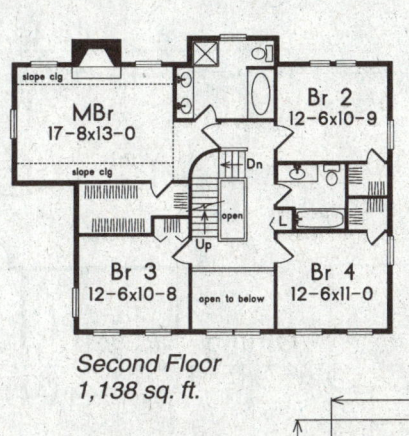

Second Floor 1,138 sq. ft.

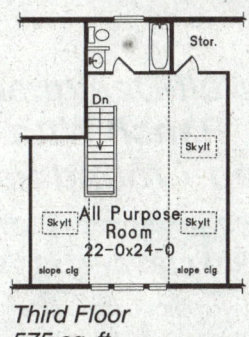

Third Floor 575 sq. ft.

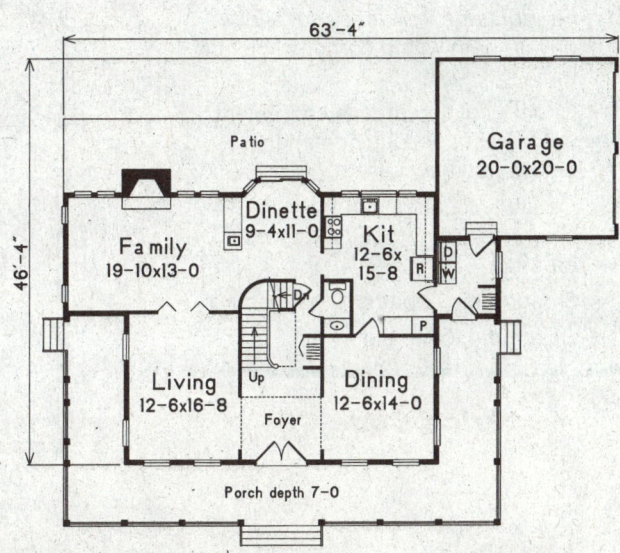

First Floor 1,293 sq. ft.

TO ORDER BLUEPRINTS USE THE FORM ON PAGE 15 OR CALL TOLL-FREE 1-877-671-6036
View thousands more home plans online at www.familyhandyman.com/HOMEPLANS

Plan #718-004D-0002

1,823 total square feet of living area

Well-Designed Ranch With Wrap-Around Porch

Special features

- Vaulted living room is spacious and easily accesses the dining area
- The master bedroom boasts a tray ceiling, large walk-in closet and a private bath with a corner whirlpool tub
- Cheerful dining area is convenient to the U-shaped kitchen and also enjoys patio access
- Centrally located laundry room connects the garage to the living areas
- 3 bedrooms, 2 baths, 2-car garage
- Basement foundation

Price Code C

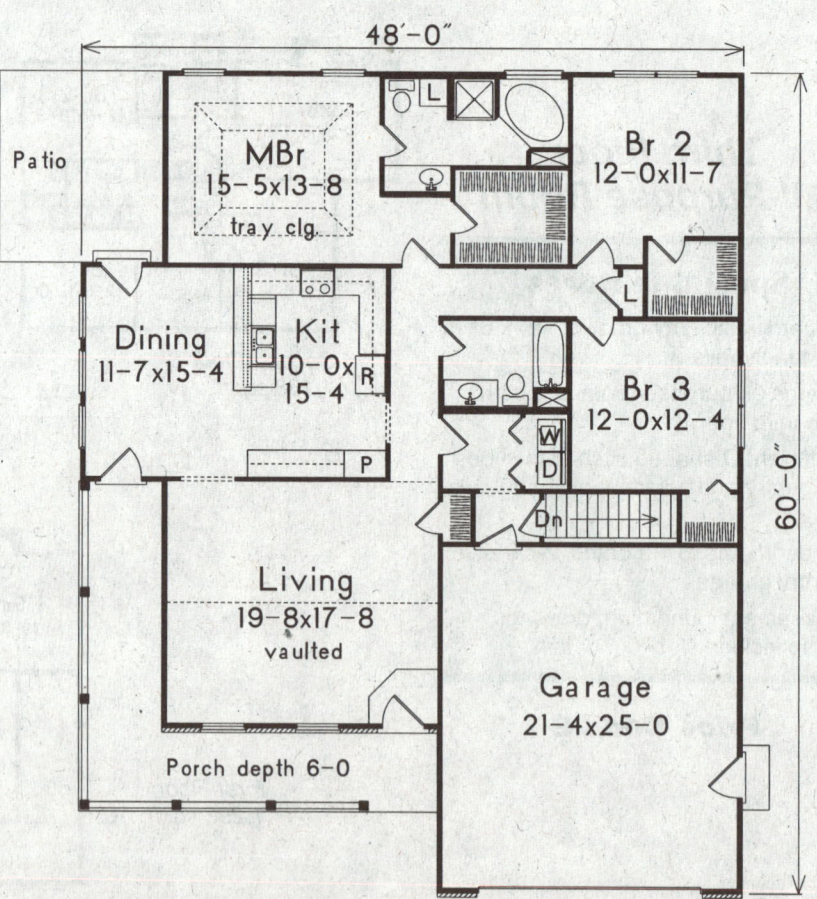

TO ORDER BLUEPRINTS USE THE FORM ON PAGE 15 OR CALL TOLL-FREE 1-877-671-6036
View thousands more home plans online at www.familyhandyman.com/homeplans

Plan #718-056D-0008

1,821 total square feet of living area

Great-Looking Gables Add Style

Special features

- 9' ceilings throughout the first floor
- Master suite is secluded for privacy and has a spacious bath
- Sunny breakfast room features a bay window
- Bonus room on the second floor has an additional 191 square feet of living area
- 3 bedrooms, 2 baths, 2-car side entry garage
- Basement or slab foundation, please specify when ordering

Price Code E

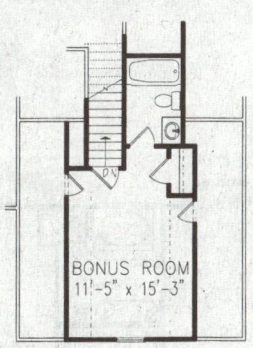

Optional Second Floor

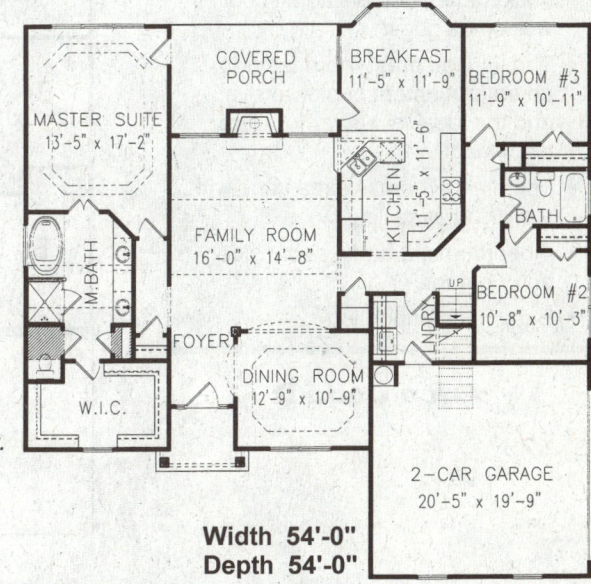

First Floor 1,821 sq. ft.

Width 54'-0"
Depth 54'-0"

TO ORDER BLUEPRINTS USE THE FORM ON PAGE 15 OR CALL TOLL-FREE 1-877-671-6036
View thousands more home plans online at www.familyhandyman.com/HOMEPLANS

Plan #718-007D-0062

2,483 total square feet of living area

Classic Elegance

Special features

- A large entry porch with open brick arches and palladian door welcomes guests
- The vaulted great room features an entertainment center alcove and the ideal layout for furniture placement
- The dining room is extra large with a stylish tray ceiling
- 4 bedrooms, 2 baths, 2-car side entry garage
- Basement foundation

Price Code D

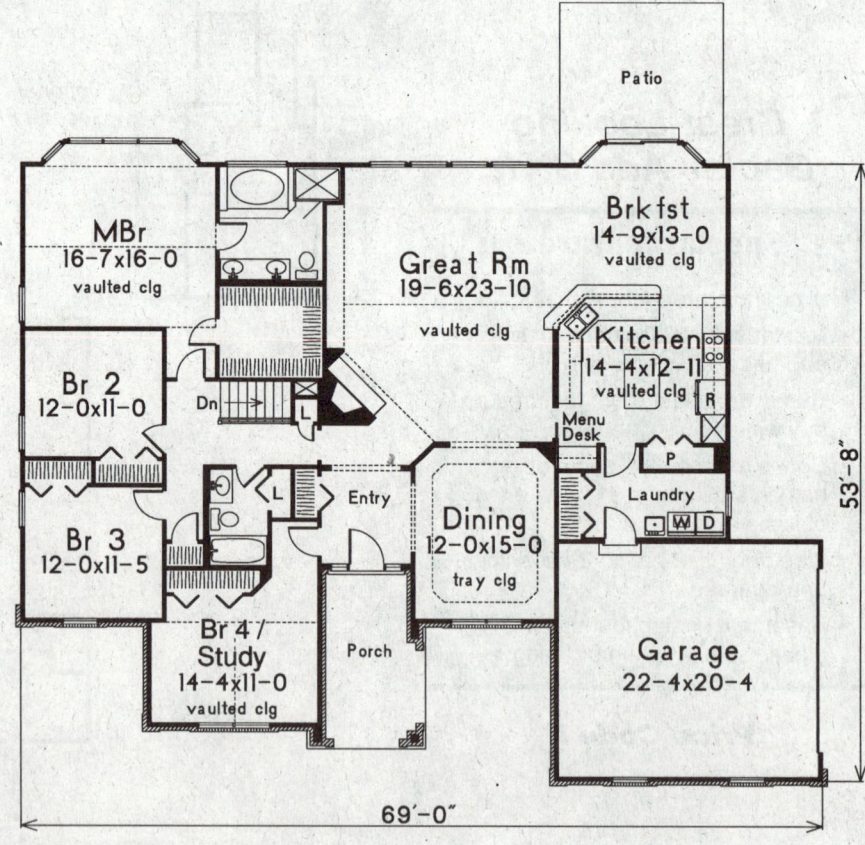

TO ORDER BLUEPRINTS USE THE FORM ON PAGE 15 OR CALL TOLL-FREE 1-877-671-6036
View thousands more home plans online at www.familyhandyman.com/homeplans

Plan #718-067D-0010

2,431 total square feet of living area

Optimum Style For Family Living

Special features

- Second floor includes a wonderful casual family room with corner fireplace and reading nook
- The great room, living and dining areas all combine to create one large space ideal for entertaining or family gatherings
- Built-in pantry in breakfast area
- Plans include a three bedroom option that has a larger second floor family room and a two-story foyer
- 4 bedrooms, 2 1/2 baths, 2-car garage with shop/storage area
- Basement, crawl space or slab foundation, please specify when ordering

Price Code D

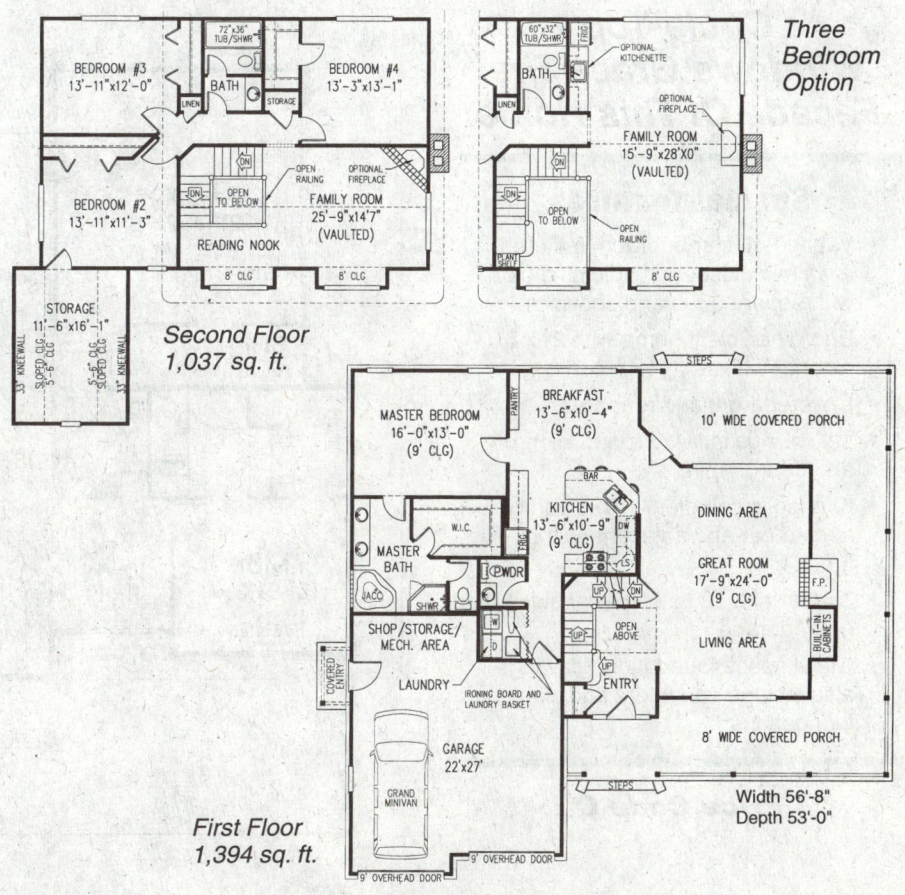

TO ORDER BLUEPRINTS USE THE FORM ON PAGE 15 OR CALL TOLL-FREE 1-877-671-6036
View thousands more home plans online at www.familyhandyman.com/HOMEPLANS

Plan #718-021D-0012

1,672 total square feet of living area

Circle-Top Windows Grace The Facade Of This Home

Special features

- Vaulted master bedroom features a walk-in closet and adjoining bath with separate tub and shower
- Energy efficient home with 2" x 6" exterior walls
- Covered front and rear porches
- 12' ceilings in living room, kitchen and bedroom #2
- Kitchen is complete with a pantry, angled bar and adjacent eating area
- 3 bedrooms, 2 baths, 2-car side entry garage
- Crawl space foundation, drawings also include basement and slab foundations

Price Code C

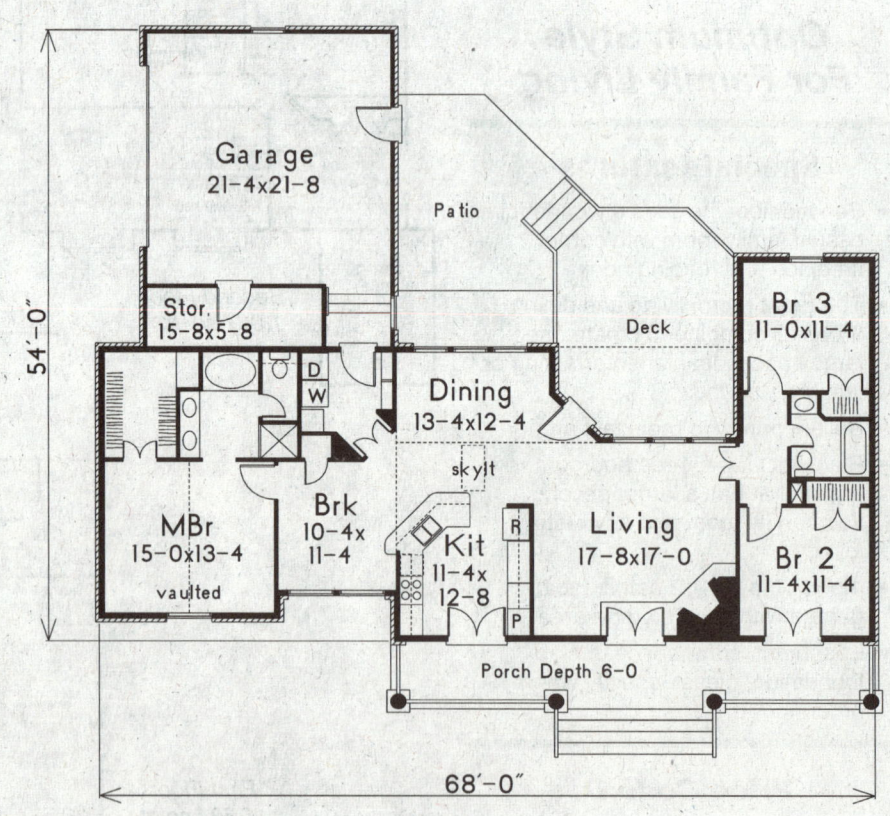

TO ORDER BLUEPRINTS USE THE FORM ON PAGE 15 OR CALL TOLL-FREE 1-877-671-6036
View thousands more home plans online at www.familyhandyman.com/homeplans

Plan #718-001D-0016

2,847 total square feet of living area

Compact Design Offers Privacy

Special features

- Secluded first floor master bedroom includes an oversized window and a large walk-in closet
- Extensive attic storage and closet space
- Spacious second floor bedrooms, two of which share a private bath
- Great starter home with option to finish the second floor as needed
- 4 bedrooms, 3 1/2 baths, 2-car garage
- Basement foundation, drawings also include slab and crawl space foundations

Price Code E

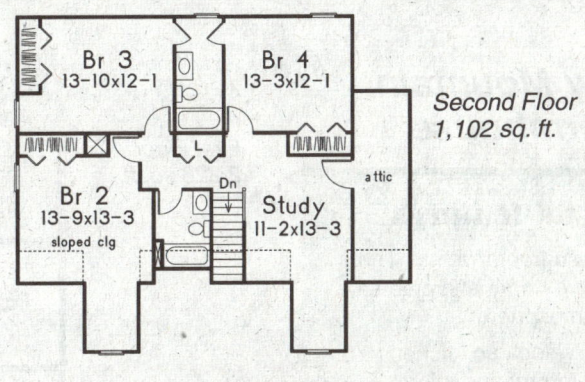

Second Floor 1,102 sq. ft.

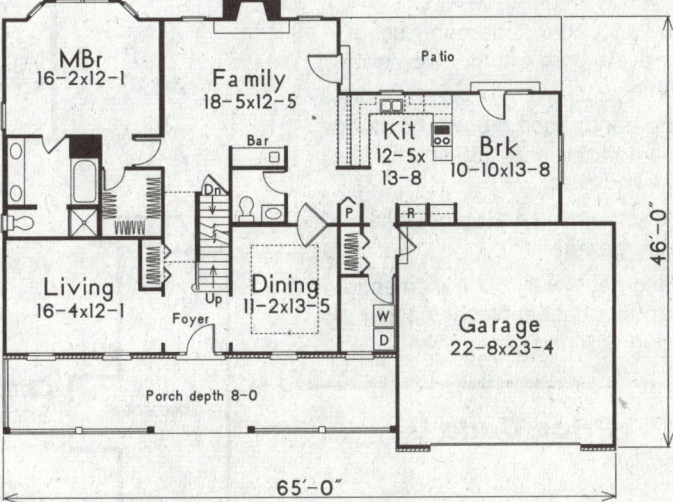

First Floor 1,745 sq. ft.

TO ORDER BLUEPRINTS USE THE FORM ON PAGE 15 OR CALL TOLL-FREE 1-877-671-6036
View thousands more home plans online at www.familyhandyman.com/HOMEPLANS

Plan #718-047D-0077

2,326 total square feet of living area

Cozy Mountain Farmhouse

Special features

- A glorious sunroom with skylights brightens the home and creates a relaxing atmosphere
- The centrally located kitchen serves the formal and informal dining areas with ease
- The secondary bedrooms share a private bath with double-bowl vanity
- The bonus room above the garage has an additional 358 square feet of living area
- 3 bedrooms, 2 1/2 baths, 2-car side entry garage
- Basement, walk-out basement or slab foundation, please specify when ordering

Price Code D

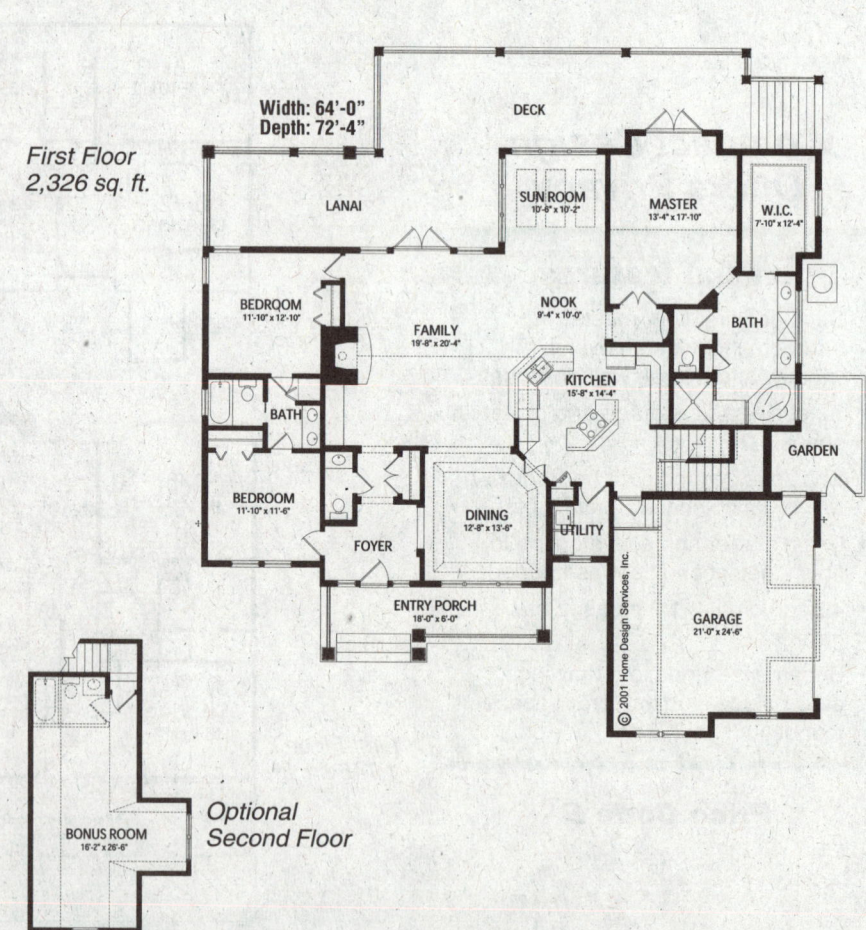

TO ORDER BLUEPRINTS USE THE FORM ON PAGE 15 OR CALL TOLL-FREE 1-877-671-6036
View thousands more home plans online at www.familyhandyman.com/homeplans

Plan #718-028D-0049

2,214 total square feet of living area

Modern Floor Plan

Special features

- Great room features built-in cabinets for an entertainment center and storage and French-door access onto the rear porch
- The kitchen and breakfast area offer a large cooktop island with snack bar, built-in wall oven and easy access to a large walk-in pantry
- The laundry area has plenty of cabinets and drawers for storage and connects to the mud room which has a built-in bench and a coat closet
- The master bedroom enjoys a large walk-in closet, whirlpool tub and double-bowl vanity
- 3 bedrooms, 2 baths, 2-car side entry garage
- Slab or crawl space foundation, please specify when ordering

Price Code D

TO ORDER BLUEPRINTS USE THE FORM ON PAGE 15 OR CALL TOLL-FREE 1-877-671-6036
View thousands more home plans online at www.familyhandyman.com/homeplans

Plan #718-011D-0006

1,873 total square feet of living area

Three-Car Garage With The Look Of A Two-Car Garage

Special features

- Sunny master bedroom has three large windows creating a cheerful feel
- U-shaped kitchen is open to a center island that looks beyond into the dining room
- Cozy den in the front of the home includes a large closet for storage
- 3 bedrooms, 2 baths, 3-car garage
- Crawl space foundation

Price Code D

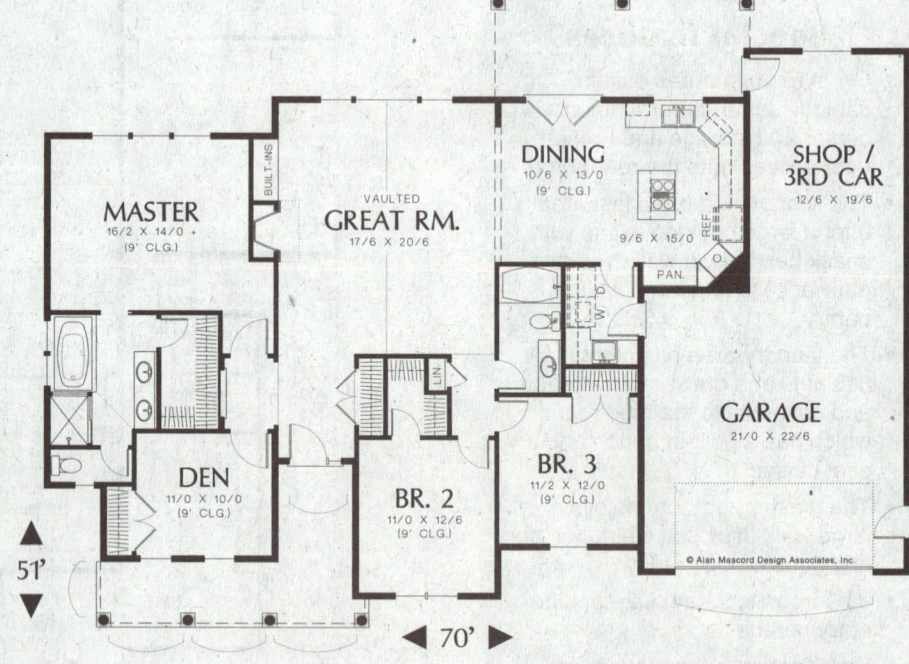

TO ORDER BLUEPRINTS USE THE FORM ON PAGE 15 OR CALL TOLL-FREE 1-877-671-6036
View thousands more home plans online at www.familyhandyman.com/homeplans

Plan #718-040D-0019

1,854 total square feet of living area

Vaulted Ceiling Adds Spaciousness

Special features

- Front entrance is enhanced by arched transom windows and rustic stone
- Isolated master bedroom includes a dressing area and walk-in closet
- Family room features a high sloped ceiling and large fireplace
- Breakfast area accesses covered rear porch
- 3 bedrooms, 2 1/2 baths, 2-car side entry garage
- Basement foundation

Price Code D

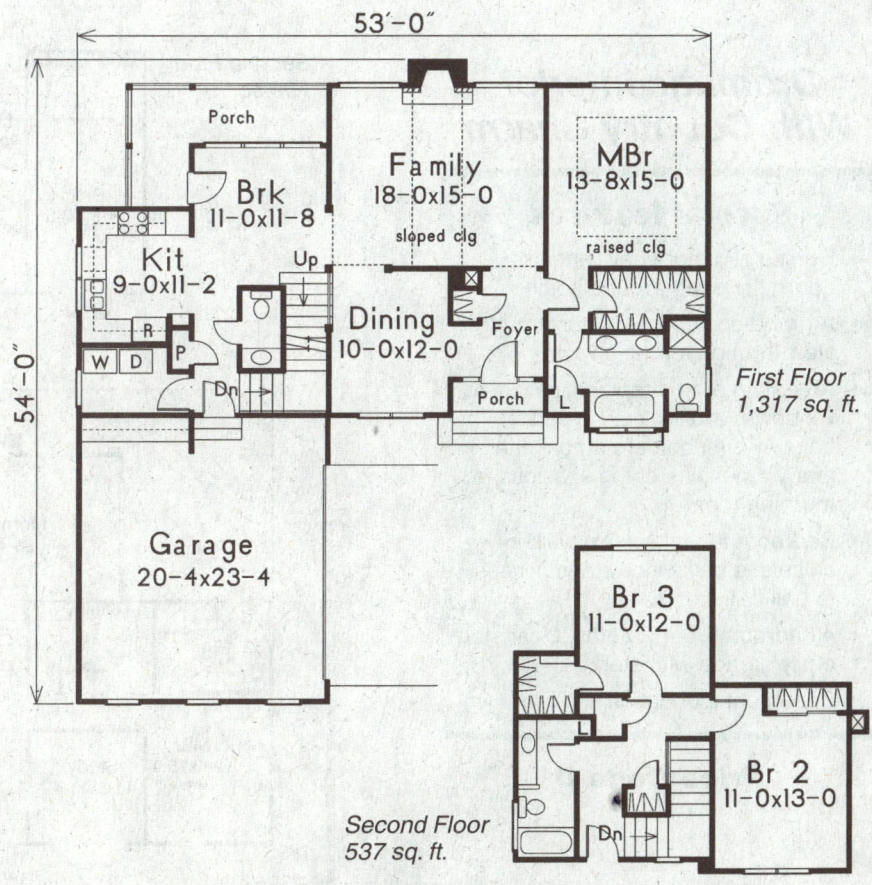

TO ORDER BLUEPRINTS USE THE FORM ON PAGE 15 OR CALL TOLL-FREE 1-877-671-6036
View thousands more home plans online at www.familyhandyman.com/HOMEPLANS

Plan #718-007D-0100

2,409 total square feet of living area

Dramatic Interior With Country Charm

Special features

- Double two-story bay windows adorn the wrap-around porch
- A grand-scale foyer features a 40' view through morning room
- An eating area, fireplace, palladian windows, vaulted ceiling and balcony overlook are among the many amenities of the spacious morning room
- Bedroom #2 enjoys two walk-in closets, a bay window and access to hall bath
- 4 bedrooms, 2 1/2 baths, 2-car side entry garage with storage
- Basement foundation

Price Code D

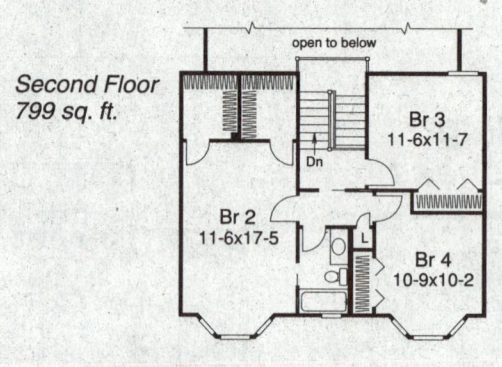

Second Floor 799 sq. ft.

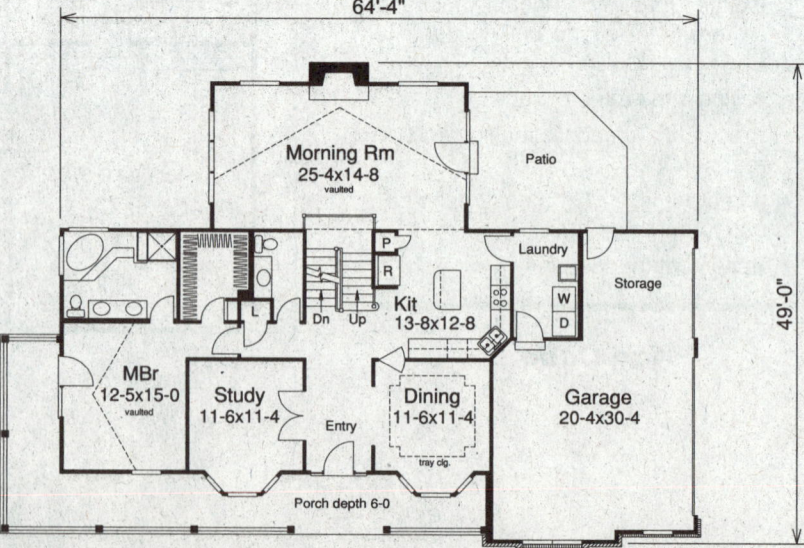

First Floor 1,610 sq. ft.

TO ORDER BLUEPRINTS USE THE FORM ON PAGE 15 OR CALL TOLL-FREE 1-877-671-6036
View thousands more home plans online at www.familyhandyman.com/homeplans

The Family Handyman

Plan #718-001D-0067

1,285 total square feet of living area

Layout Creates Large Open Living Area

Special features

- Accommodating home with ranch-style porch
- Large storage area on back of home
- Master bedroom includes dressing area, private bath and built-in bookcase
- Kitchen features pantry, breakfast bar and complete view to the dining room
- 3 bedrooms, 2 baths
- Crawl space foundation, drawings also include basement and slab foundations

Price Code B

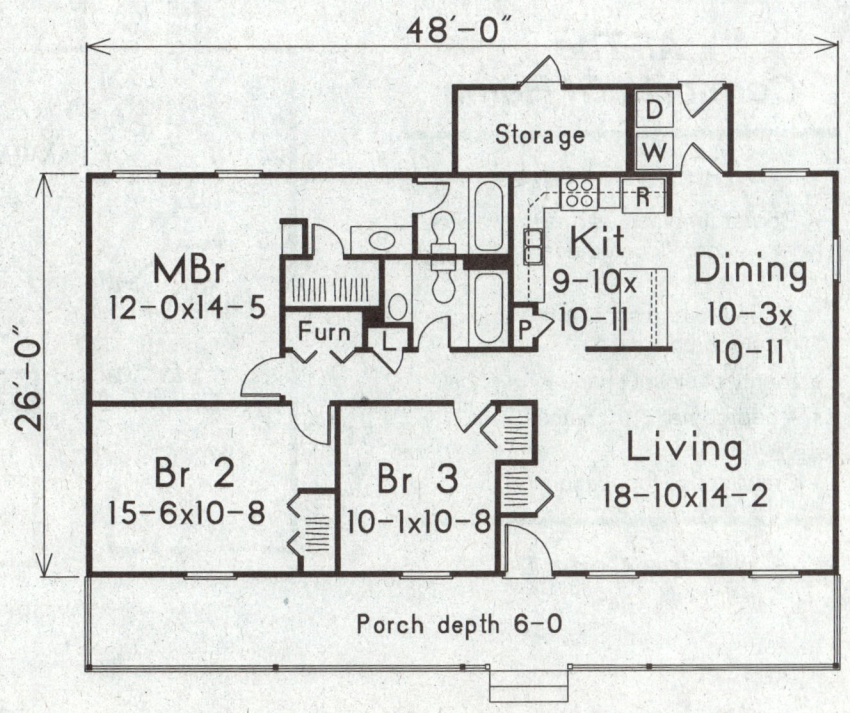

TO ORDER BLUEPRINTS USE THE FORM ON PAGE 15 OR CALL TOLL-FREE 1-877-671-6036
View thousands more home plans online at www.familyhandyman.com/HOMEPLANS

Plan #718-011D-0004

1,997 total square feet of living area

All The Comforts Of Home

Special features

- Corner fireplace warms the vaulted family room located near the kitchen
- A spa tub and shower enhance the master bath
- Plenty of closet space throughout
- 4 bedrooms, 2 1/2 baths, 3-car garage
- Crawl space foundation

Price Code D

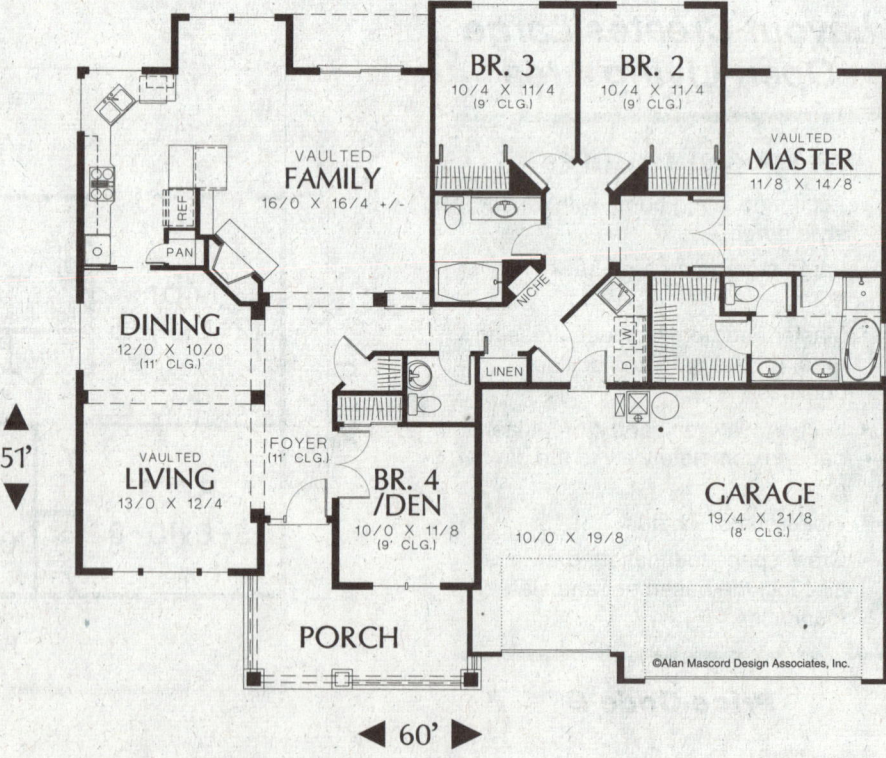

TO ORDER BLUEPRINTS USE THE FORM ON PAGE 15 OR CALL TOLL-FREE 1-877-671-6036
View thousands more home plans online at www.familyhandyman.com/homeplans

Plan #718-055D-0035

3,059 total square feet of living area

Private Guest Quarters On Lower Level

Special features

- Covered porches surround the exterior of this home
- Laundry area includes hobby area connected to the garage
- Bedroom #2 has a bayed sitting area making it also ideal as a study
- 4 bedrooms, 4 baths, 2-car side entry garage
- Basement foundation

Price Code E

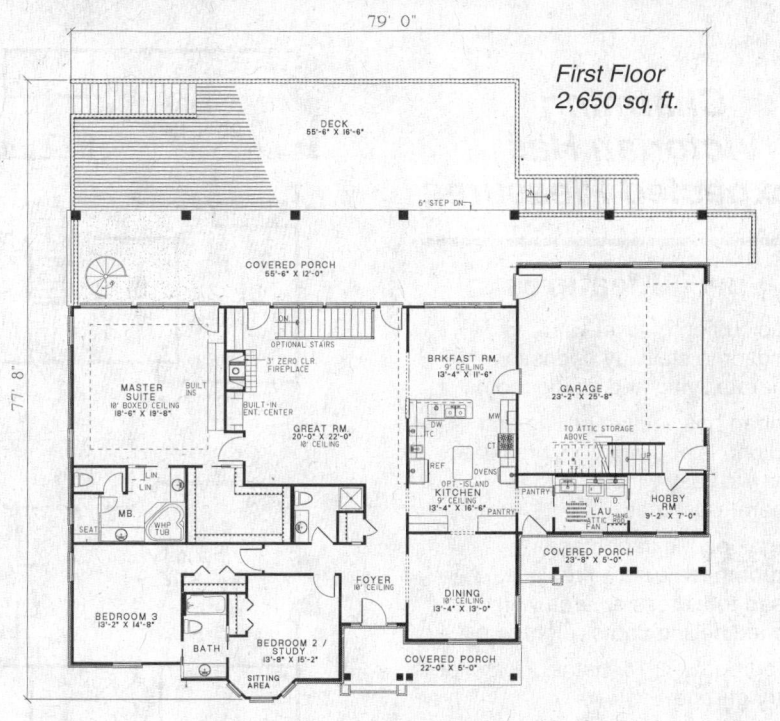

First Floor 2,650 sq. ft.

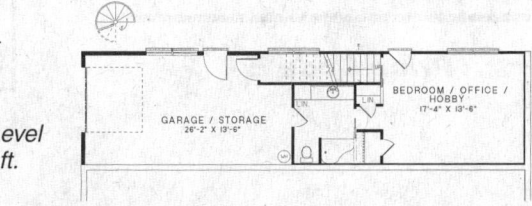

Lower Level 409 sq. ft.

TO ORDER BLUEPRINTS USE THE FORM ON PAGE 15 OR CALL TOLL-FREE 1-877-671-6036
View thousands more home plans online at www.familyhandyman.com/homeplans

Plan #718-001D-0008

2,935 total square feet of living area

Charming Victorian Has Unexpected Pleasures

Special features

- Gracious entry foyer with handsome stairway opens to separate living and dining rooms
- Kitchen has vaulted ceiling and skylight, island worktop, breakfast area with bay window and two separate pantries
- Large second floor master bedroom features a fireplace, raised tub, dressing area with vaulted ceiling and skylight
- 4 bedrooms, 2 1/2 baths, 2-car side entry garage
- Basement foundation

Price Code E

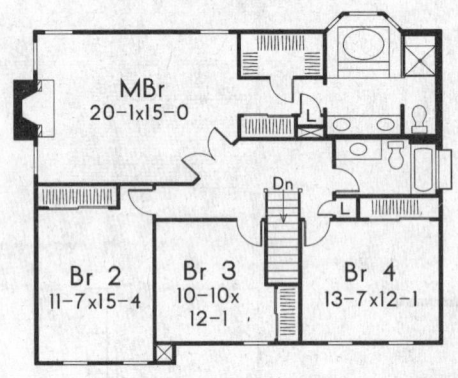

Second Floor 1,320 sq. ft.

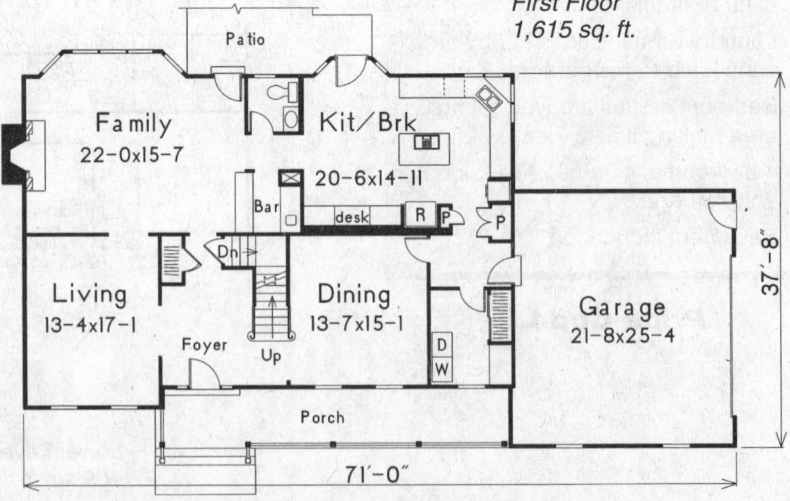

First Floor 1,615 sq. ft.

Plan #718-060D-0005

1,742 total square feet of living area

Raised Plantation Style Home Is Great For All Ages

Special features

- Open formal entry with columns accesses the dining area and great room
- Kitchen has an eating bar overlooking the bayed breakfast room with separate laundry room and half bath
- Master bath has a step-up tub with windows on two sides, separate shower and huge walk-in closet
- Large master suite has a coffered ceiling
- 3 bedrooms, 2 1/2 baths, 2-car side entry garage with storage
- Slab or crawl space foundation, please specify when ordering

Price Code B

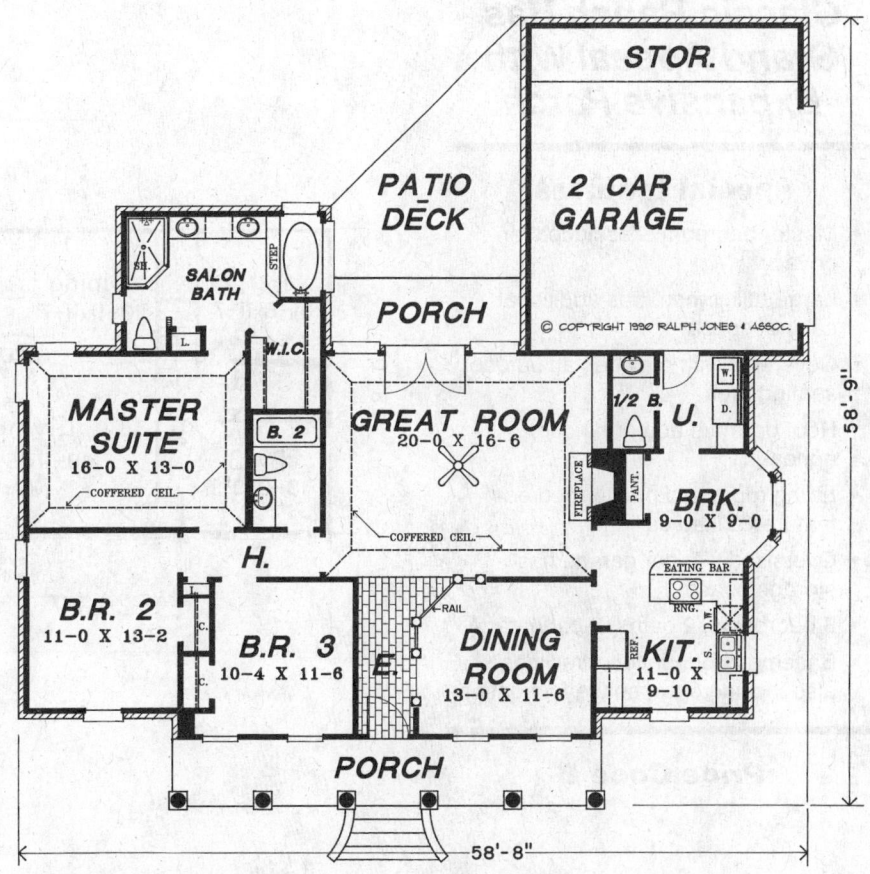

TO ORDER BLUEPRINTS USE THE FORM ON PAGE 15 OR CALL TOLL-FREE 1-877-671-6036
View thousands more home plans online at www.familyhandyman.com/homeplans

Plan #718-005D-0001

1,400 total square feet of living area

Classic Ranch Has Grand Appeal With Expansive Porch

Special features

- Master bedroom is secluded for privacy
- Large utility room has additional cabinet space
- Covered porch provides an outdoor seating area
- Roof dormers add great curb appeal
- Living room and master bedroom feature vaulted ceilings
- Oversized two-car garage has storage space
- 3 bedrooms, 2 baths, 2-car garage
- Basement foundation, drawings also include crawl space foundation

Price Code B

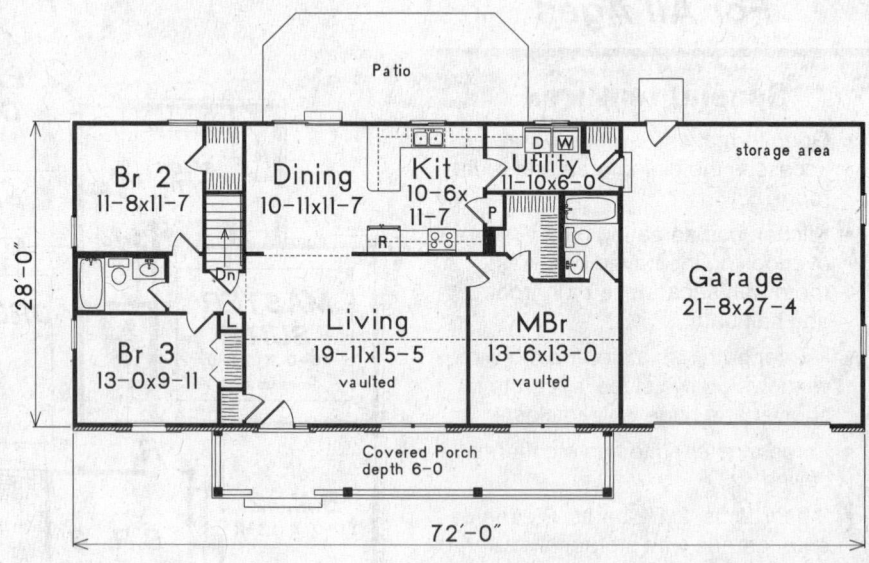

TO ORDER BLUEPRINTS USE THE FORM ON PAGE 15 OR CALL TOLL-FREE 1-877-671-6036
View thousands more home plans online at www.familyhandyman.com/homeplans

Plan #718-077D-0006

2,307 total square feet of living area

Wonderful Open Great Room

Special features

- The bayed breakfast area warms the home with natural light
- The spacious master bedroom boasts two walk-in closets, private bath and a bonus area ideal for an office or nursery
- The vaulted great room includes a grand fireplace, built-in shelves and a double-door entry onto the covered porch
- 3 bedrooms, 2 1/2 baths, 2-car side entry garage
- Basement, crawl space or slab foundation, please specify when ordering

Price Code D

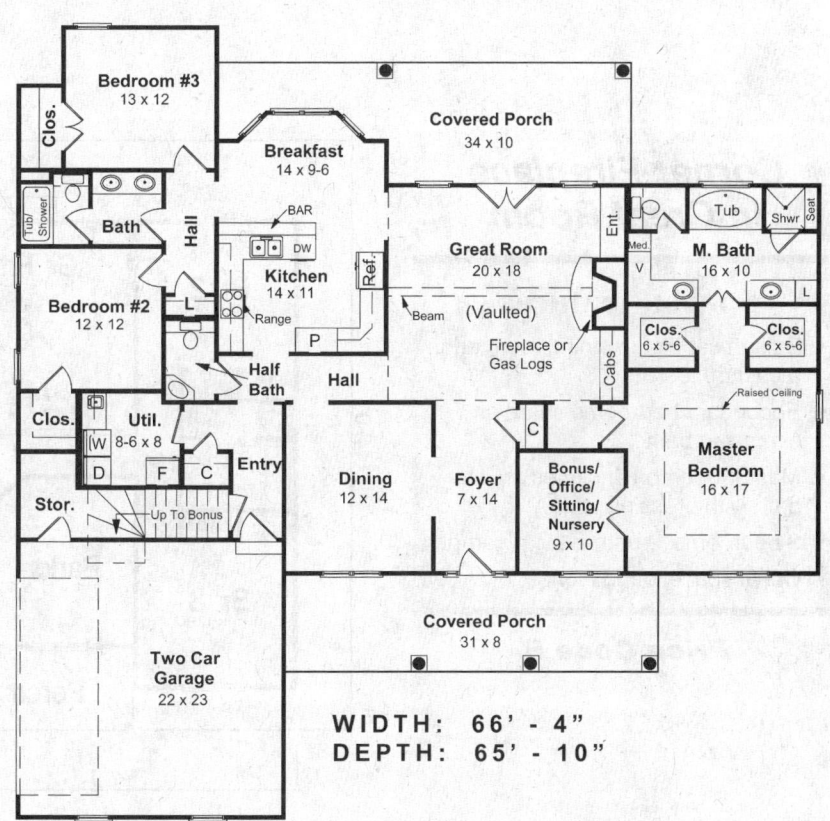

WIDTH: 66' - 4"
DEPTH: 65' - 10"

TO ORDER BLUEPRINTS USE THE FORM ON PAGE 15 OR CALL TOLL-FREE 1-877-671-6036
View thousands more home plans online at www.familyhandyman.com/HOMEPLANS

Plan #718-038D-0040

1,642 total square feet of living area

Corner Fireplace In Great Room

Special features

- Built-in cabinet in dining room adds a custom feel
- Secondary bedrooms share an oversized bath
- Master bedroom includes private bath with dressing table
- 3 bedrooms, 2 baths, 2-car garage
- Crawl space foundation

Price Code B

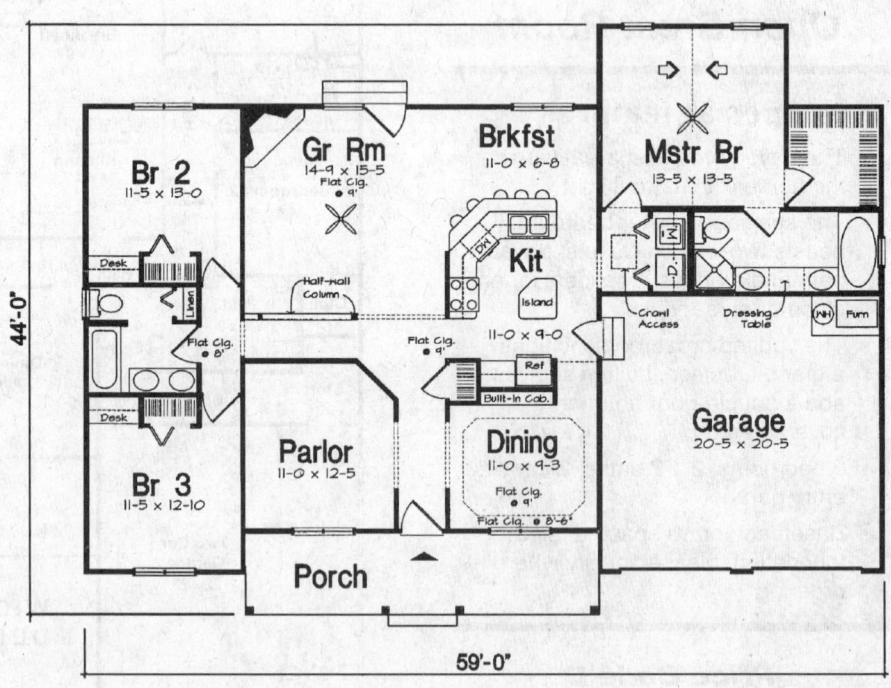

TO ORDER BLUEPRINTS USE THE FORM ON PAGE 15 OR CALL TOLL-FREE 1-877-671-6036
View thousands more home plans online at www.familyhandyman.com/HOMEPLANS

Plan #718-007D-0103

1,231 total square feet of living area

Atrium Living For Views On A Narrow Lot

Special features

- Dutch gables and stone accents provide an enchanting appearance
- The spacious living room offers a masonry fireplace, atrium with window wall and is open to a dining area with bay window
- Kitchen has a breakfast counter, lots of cabinet space and glass sliding doors to a balcony
- 380 square feet of optional living area on the lower level
- 2 bedrooms, 2 baths, 1-car drive under garage
- Walk-out basement foundation

Price Code A

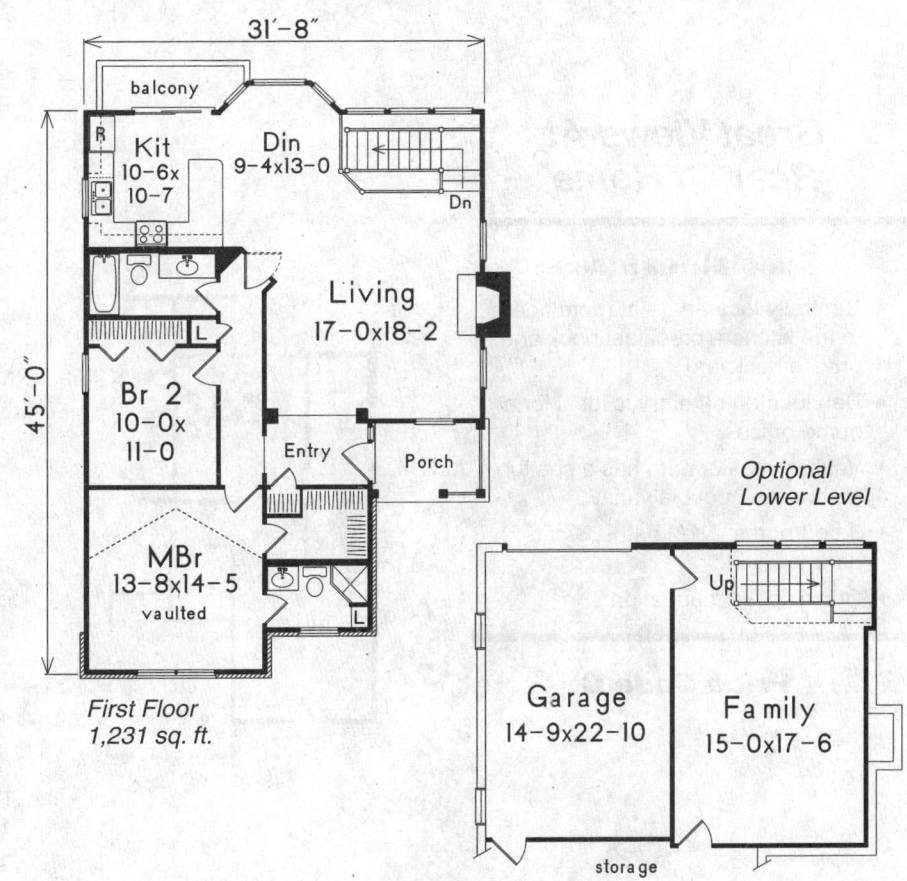

TO ORDER BLUEPRINTS USE THE FORM ON PAGE 15 OR CALL TOLL-FREE 1-877-671-6036
View thousands more home plans online at www.familyhandyman.com/HOMEPLANS

Plan #718-011D-0010

2,197 total square feet of living area

Great Views At Rear Of Home

Special features

- Centrally located great room opens to the kitchen, breakfast nook and private backyard
- Den located off entry is ideal for a home office
- Vaulted master bath has a spa tub, shower and double vanity
- 3 bedrooms, 2 1/2 baths, 3-car garage
- Crawl space foundation

Price Code C

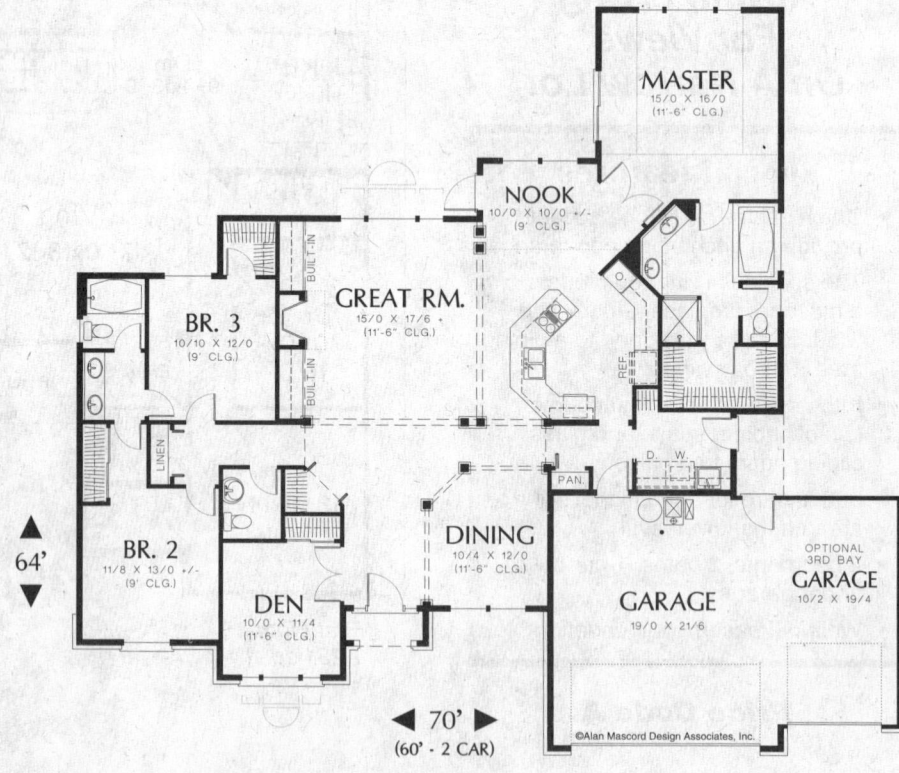

TO ORDER BLUEPRINTS USE THE FORM ON PAGE 15 OR CALL TOLL-FREE 1-877-671-6036
View thousands more home plans online at www.familyhandyman.com/HOMEPLANS

Plan #718-007D-0008

2,452 total square feet of living area

Charming Design Features Home Office

Special features

- Cheery and spacious home office room with private entrance and bath, two closets, vaulted ceiling and transomed window is perfect shown as a home office or a fourth bedroom
- Delightful great room features a vaulted ceiling, fireplace, extra storage closets and patio doors to sundeck
- Extra-large kitchen features walk-in pantry, cooktop island and bay window
- Vaulted master bedroom includes transomed windows, walk-in closet and luxurious bath
- 3 bedrooms, 2 1/2 baths, 3-car garage
- Basement foundation

Price Code D

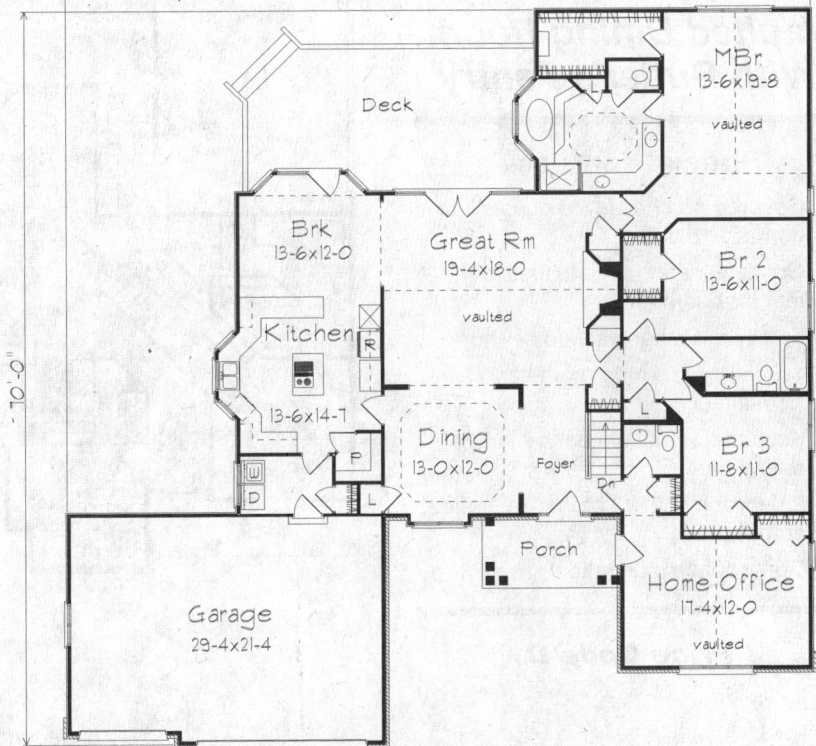

TO ORDER BLUEPRINTS USE THE FORM ON PAGE 15 OR CALL TOLL-FREE 1-877-671-6036
View thousands more home plans online at www.familyhandyman.com/HOMEPLANS

Plan #718-043D-0011

2,422 total square feet of living area

Vaulted Dining Room With Butler's Pantry

Special features

- Covered porches invite guests into home
- Convenient and private first floor master bedroom
- Family room has vaulted ceiling
- 10' ceiling in dining room has a formal feel
- Kitchen has walk-in pantry and eating bar
- 3 bedrooms, 2 1/2 baths, 3-car side entry garage
- Crawl space foundation

Price Code D

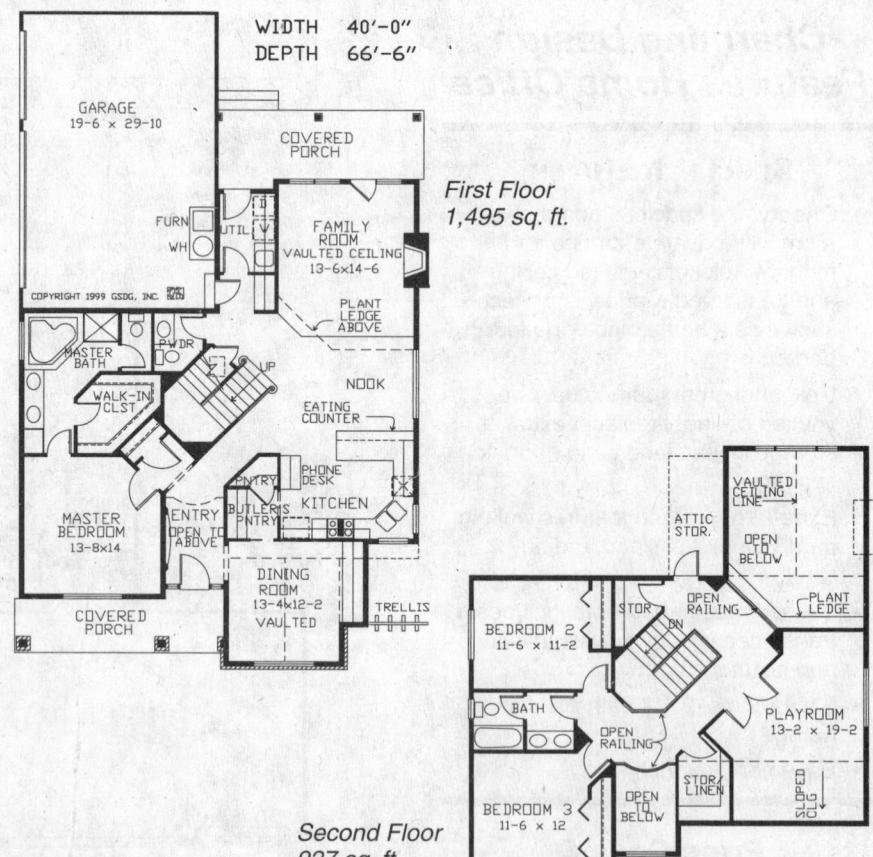

WIDTH 40'-0"
DEPTH 66'-6"

First Floor
1,495 sq. ft.

Second Floor
927 sq. ft.

TO ORDER BLUEPRINTS USE THE FORM ON PAGE 15 OR CALL TOLL-FREE 1-877-671-6036
View thousands more home plans online at www.familyhandyman.com/homeplans

Plan #718-013D-0022

1,992 total square feet of living area

Triple Dormers Create Terrific Curb Appeal

Special features

- Interesting angled walls add drama to many of the living areas including the family room, master bedroom and breakfast area
- Covered porch includes a spa and the outdoor kitchen with sink, refrigerator and cooktop
- Enter the majestic master bath to find a dramatic corner oversized tub
- 4 bedrooms, 3 baths, 2-car side entry garage
- Basement, crawl space or slab foundation, please specify when ordering

Price Code C

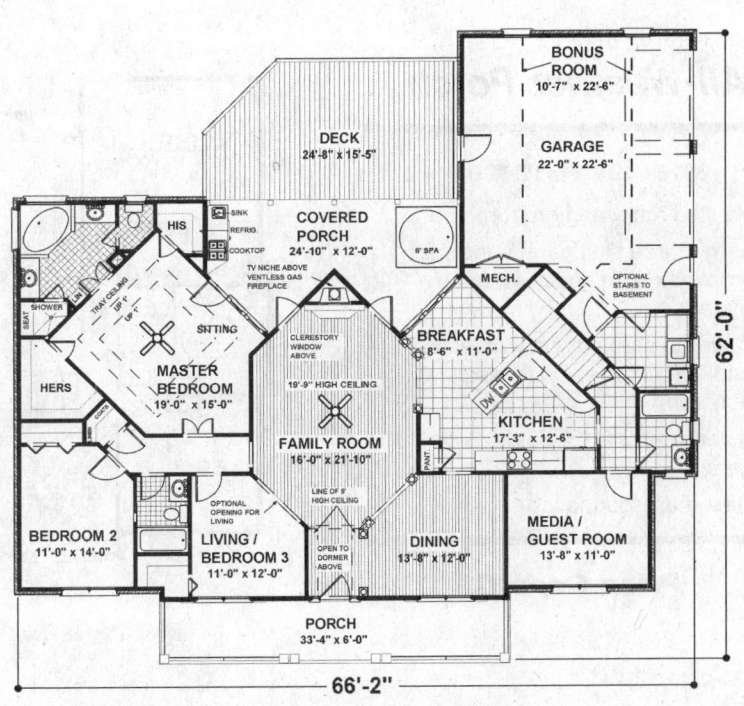

TO ORDER BLUEPRINTS USE THE FORM ON PAGE 15 OR CALL TOLL-FREE 1-877-671-6036
View thousands more home plans online at www.familyhandyman.com/HOMEPLANS

Plan #718-051D-0055

1,907 total square feet of living area

All-Weather Porch

Special features

- Vaulted entry and great room
- Large three stall garage includes ample storage space for hobby materials
- Covered porch directly off eating nook provides easy access to the outdoors
- 3 bedrooms, 2 1/2 baths, 3-car garage
- Basement foundation

Price Code C

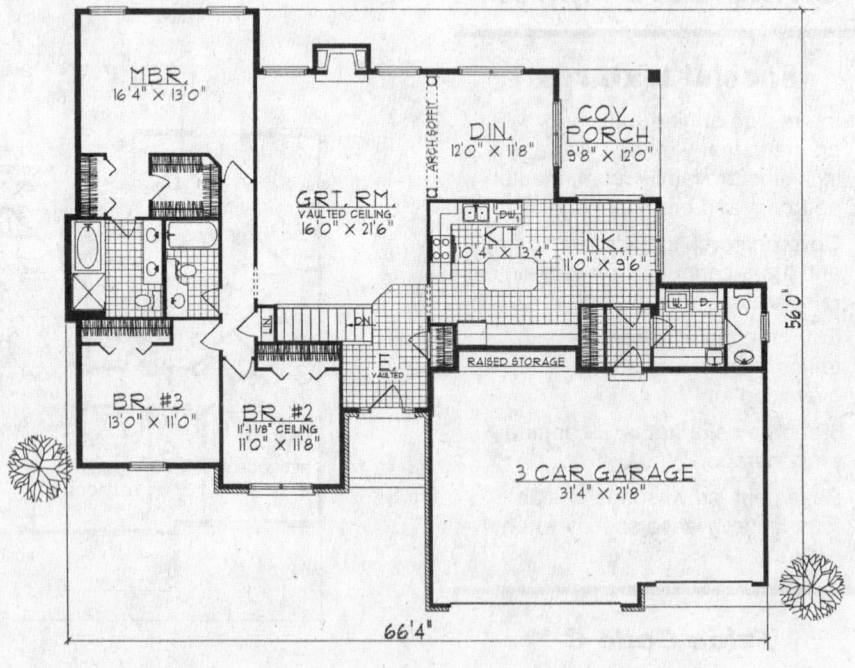

TO ORDER BLUEPRINTS USE THE FORM ON PAGE 15 OR CALL TOLL-FREE 1-877-671-6036
View thousands more home plans online at www.familyhandyman.com/HOMEPLANS

Plan #718-007D-0048

2,758 total square feet of living area

Excellent Ranch For Country Setting

Special features

- Vaulted great room excels with fireplace, wet bar, plant shelves and skylights
- Fabulous master bedroom enjoys a fireplace, large bath, walk-in closet and vaulted ceiling
- Trendsetting kitchen and breakfast area adjoins the spacious screened porch
- Convenient office near kitchen is perfect for computer room, hobby enthusiast or fifth bedroom
- 4 bedrooms, 2 1/2 baths, 3-car side entry garage
- Basement foundation

Price Code E

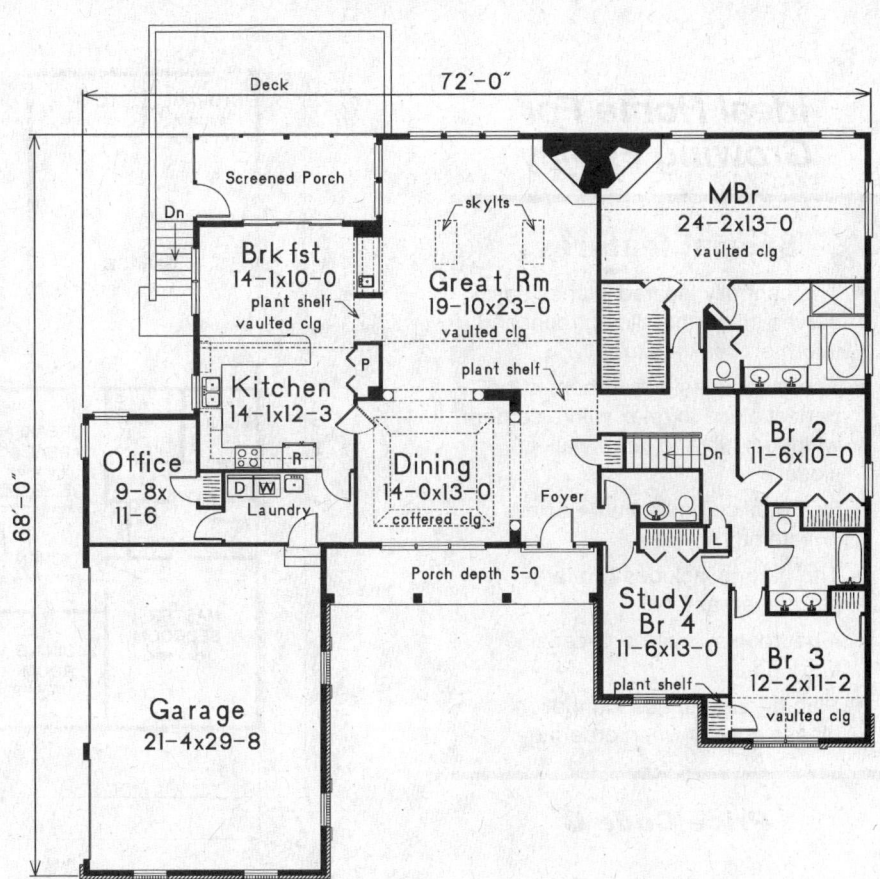

TO ORDER BLUEPRINTS USE THE FORM ON PAGE 15 OR CALL TOLL-FREE 1-877-671-6036
View thousands more home plans online at www.familyhandyman.com/HOMEPLANS

Plan #718-028D-0030

1,856 total square feet of living area

Ideal Home For Growing Family

Special features

- The centrally located kitchen easily serves the formal dining room and informal breakfast area
- The grand master bedroom is the perfect place to relax with a corner whirlpool tub and large walk-in closet
- Home office/bedroom #4 enjoys a private bath
- The garage includes two large storage areas
- 4 bedrooms, 3 baths, 2-car side entry garage
- Slab or crawl space foundation, please specify when ordering

Price Code C

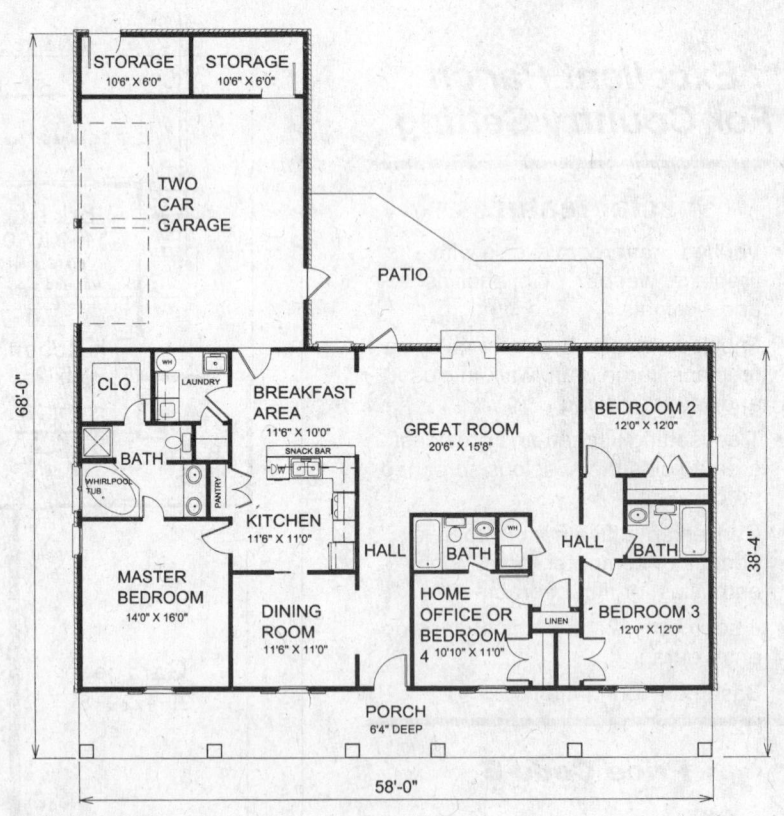

TO ORDER BLUEPRINTS USE THE FORM ON PAGE 15 OR CALL TOLL-FREE 1-877-671-6036
View thousands more home plans online at www.familyhandyman.com/HOMEPLANS

Plan #718-021D-0008

1,266 total square feet of living area

Compact, Convenient And Charming

Special features

- Narrow frontage is perfect for small lots
- Energy efficient home with 2" x 6" exterior walls
- Prominent central hall provides a convenient connection for all main rooms
- Design incorporates full-size master bedroom complete with dressing room, bath and walk-in closet
- Angled kitchen includes handy laundry facilities and is adjacent to an oversized storage area
- 3 bedrooms, 2 baths, 2-car rear entry garage
- Crawl space foundation, drawings also include slab foundation

Price Code A

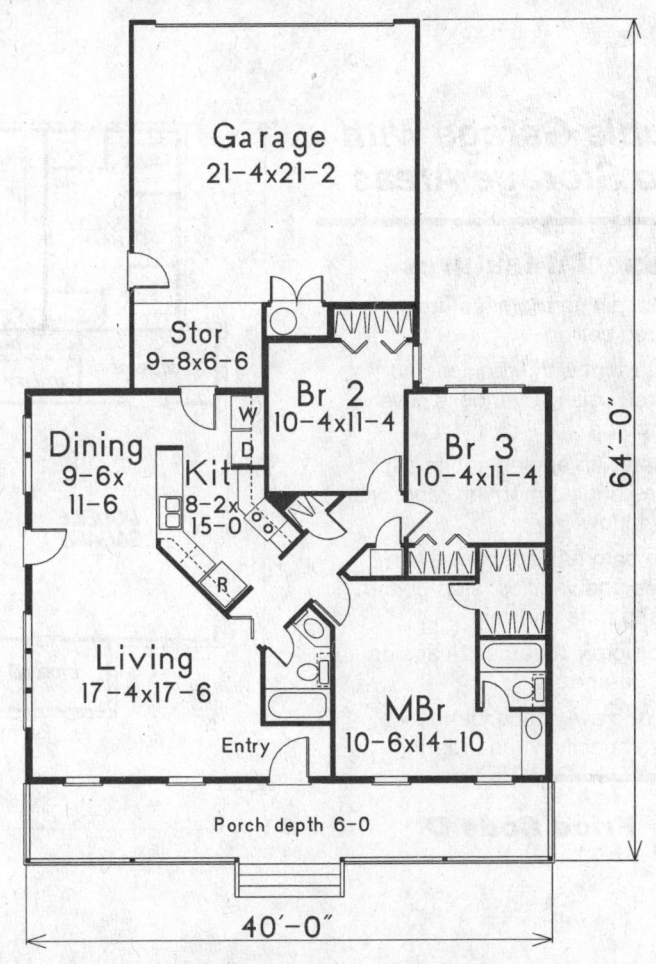

TO ORDER BLUEPRINTS USE THE FORM ON PAGE 15 OR CALL TOLL-FREE 1-877-671-6036
View thousands more home plans online at www.familyhandyman.com/homeplans

Plan #718-060D-0008

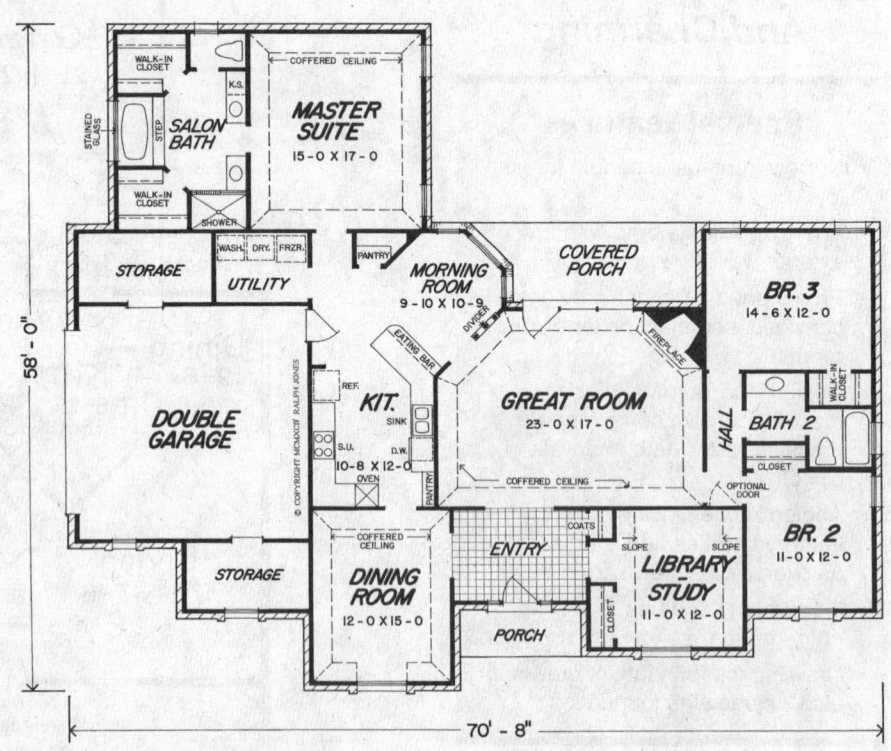

2,281 total square feet of living area

Double Garage With Two Storage Areas

Special features

- Formal dining room features a coffered ceiling
- Great room with fireplace and coffered ceiling overlooks covered back porch
- Kitchen with angled eating bar adjoins angled morning room with bay window
- Salon bath has double walk-in closets and vanities, step-up tub and separate shower
- 3 bedrooms, 2 baths, 2-car side entry garage
- Slab or crawl space foundation, please specify when ordering

Price Code D

TO ORDER BLUEPRINTS USE THE FORM ON PAGE 15 OR CALL TOLL-FREE 1-877-671-6036
View thousands more home plans online at www.familyhandyman.com/HOMEPLANS

Plan #718-001D-0066

2,511 total square feet of living area

Impressive Exterior, Spacious Interior

Special features

- Kitchen, breakfast and living rooms feature tray ceilings
- Various architectural elements combine to create an impressive exterior
- Master bedroom includes large walk-in closet, oversized bay window and private bath with shower and tub
- Large utility room has a convenient workspace
- 4 bedrooms, 2 1/2 baths, 3-car side entry garage
- Basement foundation, drawings also include crawl space and slab foundations

Price Code D

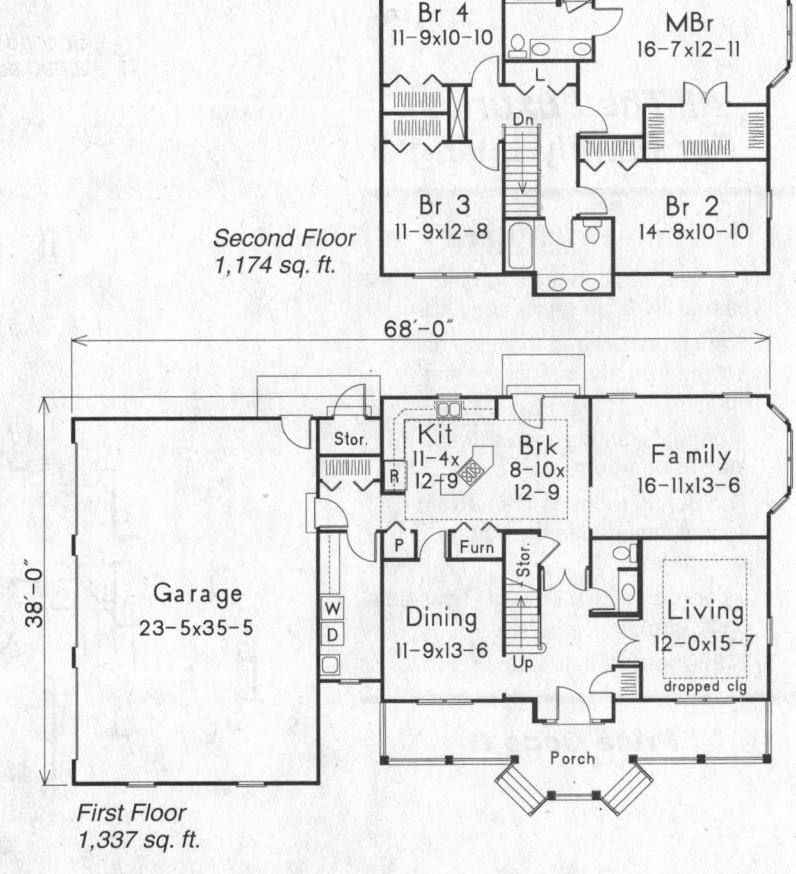

Second Floor 1,174 sq. ft.

First Floor 1,337 sq. ft.

TO ORDER BLUEPRINTS USE THE FORM ON PAGE 15 OR CALL TOLL-FREE 1-877-671-6036
View thousands more home plans online at www.familyhandyman.com/homeplans

Plan #718-071D-0008

4,100 total square feet of living area

All The Luxuries For Family Living

Special features

- Family room connects to other casual living areas for convenience
- French doors keep the cozy den private from the rest of the first floor
- A beautiful sitting area extends the master bedroom
- The bonus room on the second floor is included in the square footage
- 4 bedrooms, 3 1/2 baths, 3-car side entry garage
- Crawl space foundation

Price Code G

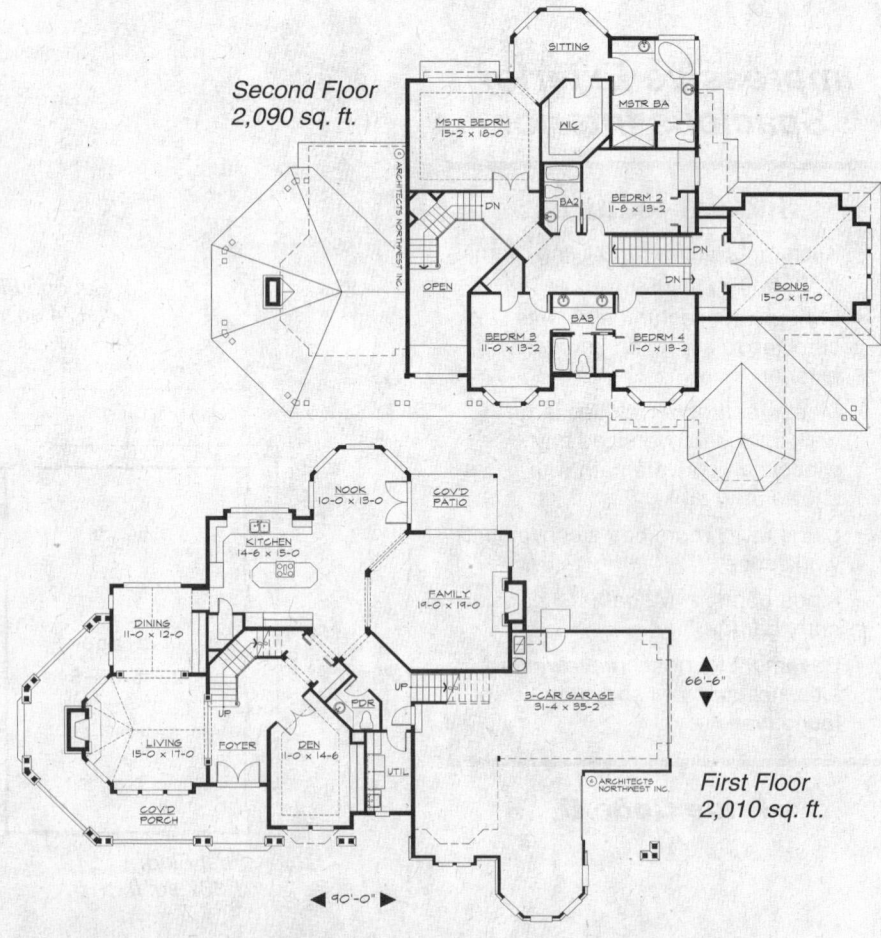

TO ORDER BLUEPRINTS USE THE FORM ON PAGE 15 OR CALL TOLL-FREE 1-877-671-6036
View thousands more home plans online at www.familyhandyman.com/HOMEPLANS

Plan #718-007D-0118

1,991 total square feet of living area

Impressive Home For Country Living

Special features

- A large porch with roof dormers and flanking stonework creates a distinctive country appeal
- The highly functional U-shaped kitchen is open to the dining and living rooms defined by a colonnade
- Large bay windows are enjoyed by both the living room and master bedroom
- Every bedroom features spacious walk-in closets and its own private bath
- 3 bedrooms, 3 1/2 baths, 2-car side entry garage
- Basement foundation

Price Code C

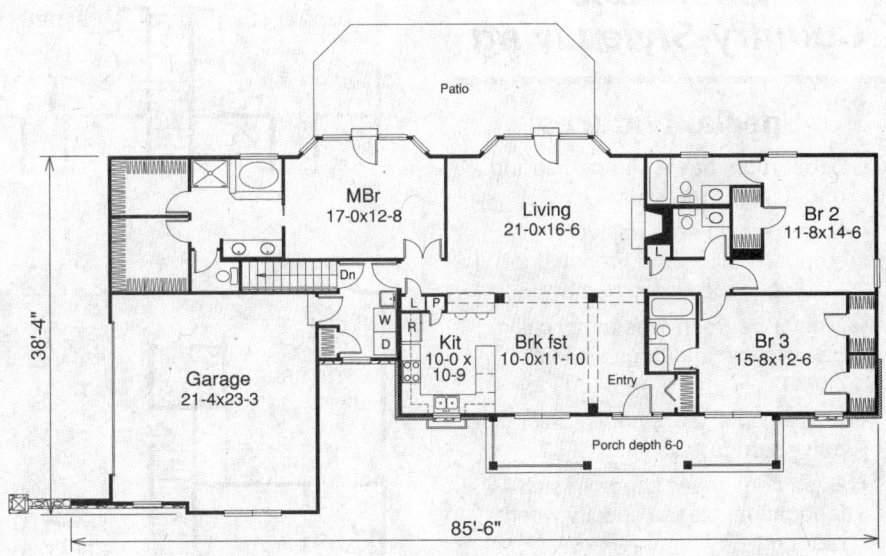

TO ORDER BLUEPRINTS USE THE FORM ON PAGE 15 OR CALL TOLL-FREE 1-877-671-6036
View thousands more home plans online at www.familyhandyman.com/HOMEPLANS

The Family Handyman

Plan #718-016D-0051

1,945 total square feet of living area

Affordable Country-Style Living

Special features
- Great room has a stepped ceiling and a fireplace
- Bayed dining area enjoys a stepped ceiling and French door leading to a covered porch
- Master bedroom has a tray ceiling, bay window and large walk-in closet
- 3 bedrooms, 2 1/2 baths, 2-car side entry garage
- Basement, crawl space or slab foundation, please specify when ordering

Price Code D

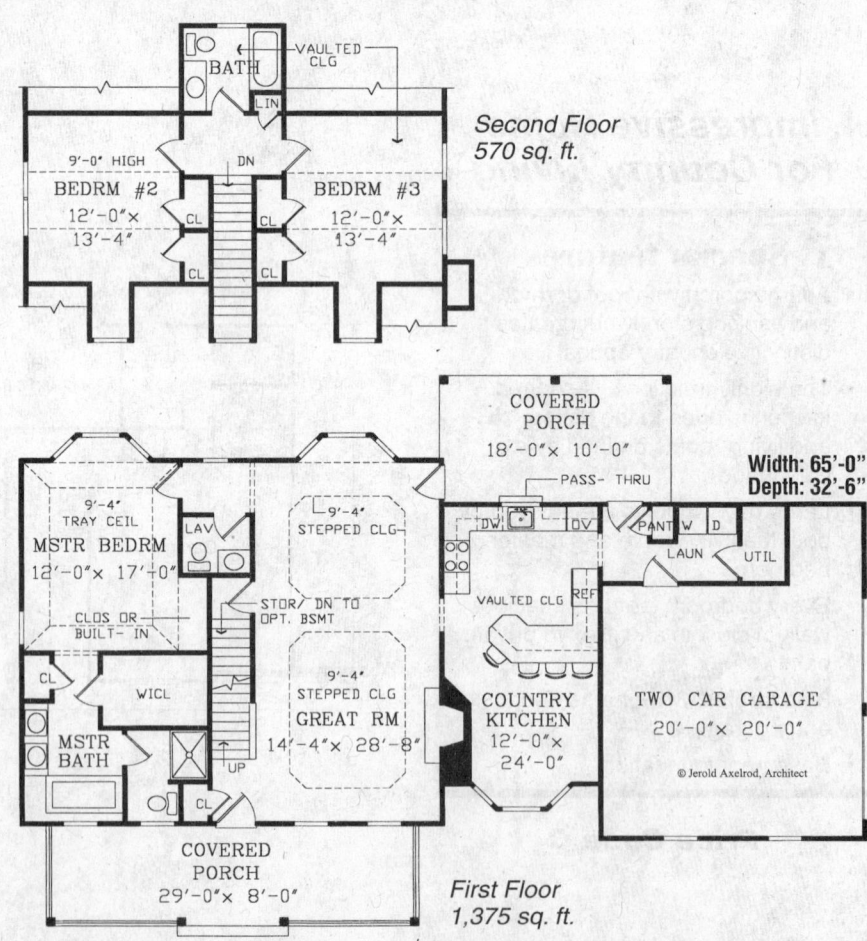

Width: 65'-0"
Depth: 32'-6"

Second Floor 570 sq. ft.

First Floor 1,375 sq. ft.

TO ORDER BLUEPRINTS USE THE FORM ON PAGE 15 OR CALL TOLL-FREE 1-877-671-6036
View thousands more home plans online at www.familyhandyman.com/HOMEPLANS

Plan #718-047D-0024

1,786 total square feet of living area

Front Porch Creates Cozy Feeling

Special features

- Galley-style kitchen is compact, but efficient
- Bay-shaped dining area is flooded with sunlight
- Living room is the center of this home making it an ideal gathering place
- Optional second floor has an additional 262 square feet of living area
- 3 bedrooms, 2 baths, 2-car garage
- Slab foundation

Price Code B

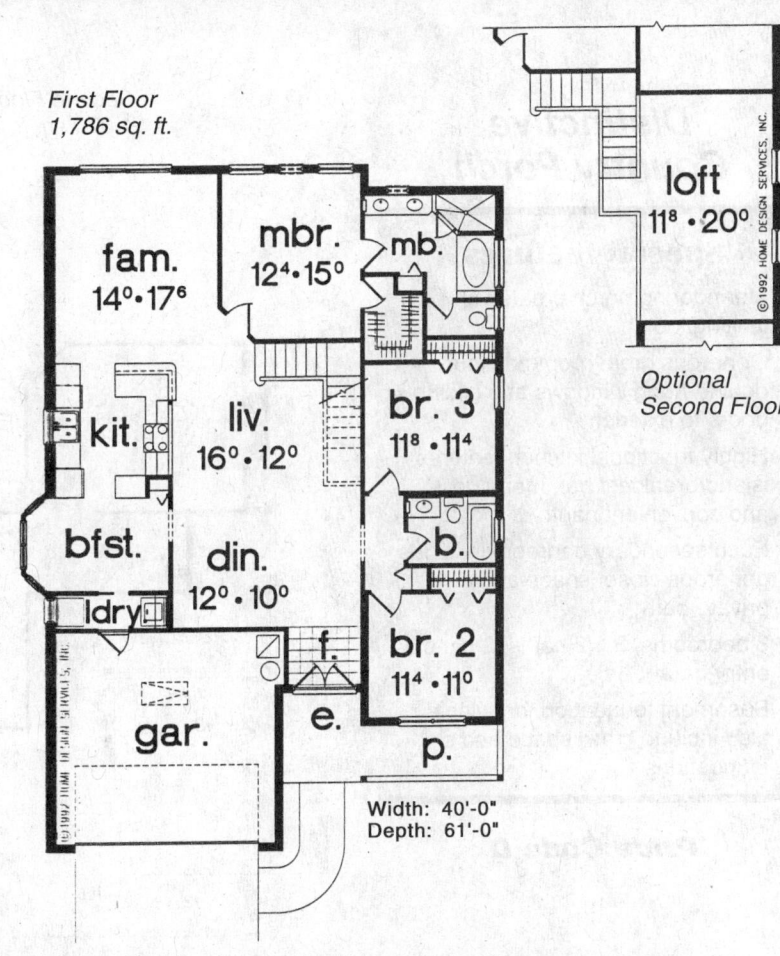

TO ORDER BLUEPRINTS USE THE FORM ON PAGE 15 OR CALL TOLL-FREE 1-877-671-6036
View thousands more home plans online at www.familyhandyman.com/homeplans

Plan #718-007D-0011

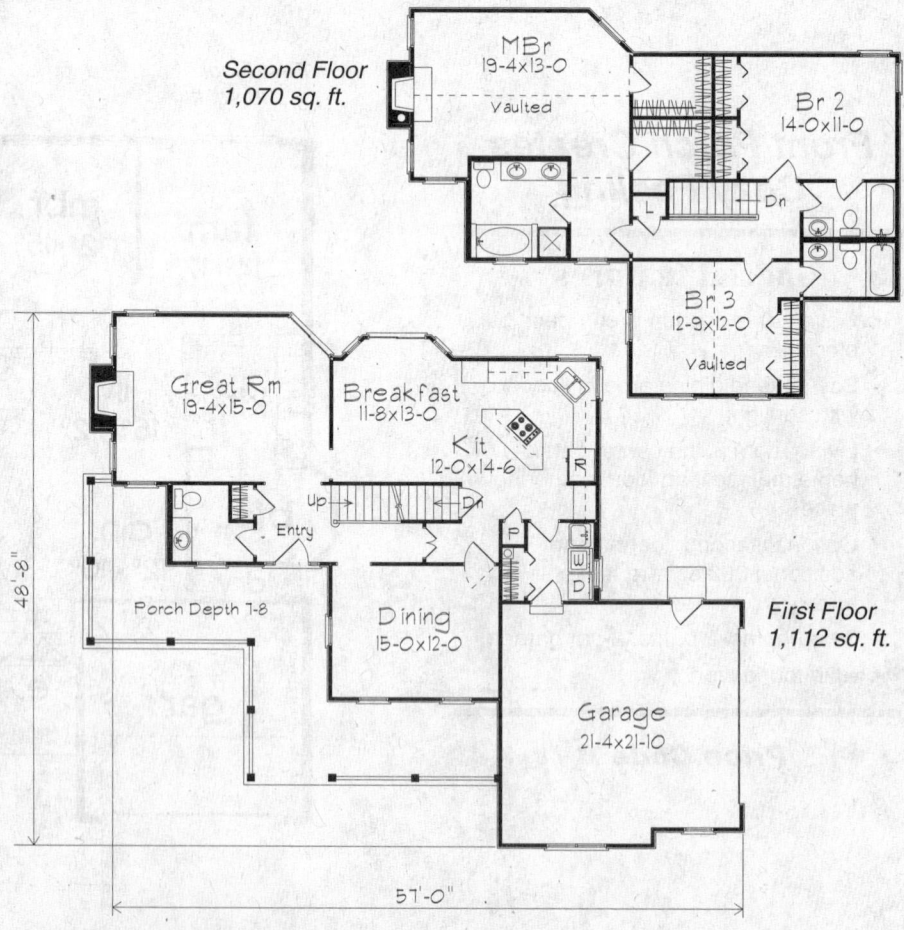

2,182 total square feet of living area

Distinctive Country Porch

Special features

- Meandering porch creates an inviting look
- Generous great room has four double-hung windows and gliding doors to exterior
- Highly functional kitchen features island/breakfast bar, menu desk and convenient pantry
- Each secondary bedroom includes generous closet space and a private bath
- 3 bedrooms, 3 1/2 baths, 2-car side entry garage
- Basement foundation, drawings also include crawl space and slab foundations

Price Code D

Plan #718-051D-0124

2,236 total square feet of living area

Porch Adds Country Charm

Special features

- The family room features double-door access into the formal living room and a grand fireplace flanked by windows
- All bedrooms are located on the second floor for privacy and enjoy walk-in closets
- The centrally located kitchen serves the charming nook and formal dining room with ease
- 4 bedrooms, 2 1/2 baths, 3-car side entry garage
- Basement foundation

Price Code E

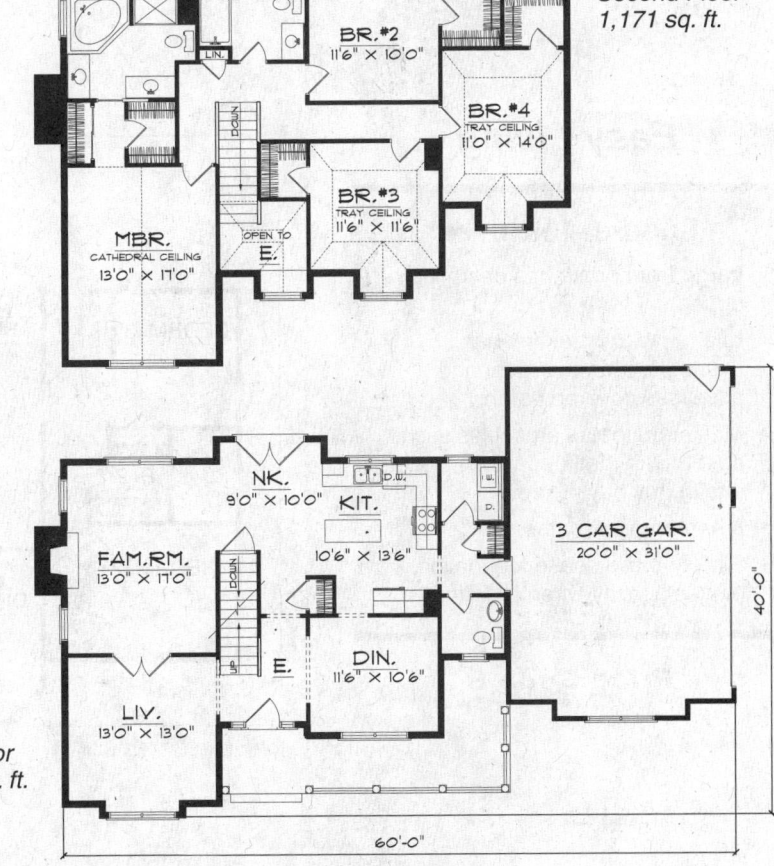

Second Floor 1,171 sq. ft.

First Floor 1,065 sq. ft.

TO ORDER BLUEPRINTS USE THE FORM ON PAGE 15 OR CALL TOLL-FREE 1-877-671-6036
View thousands more home plans online at www.familyhandyman.com/homeplans

Plan #718-030D-0003

1,753 total square feet of living area

Easy Living

Special features

- Large front porch has charming appeal
- Kitchen with breakfast bar overlooks morning room and accesses covered porch
- Master suite has amenities such as a private bath, spacious closets and sunny bay window
- 3 bedrooms, 2 baths
- Slab or crawl space foundation, please specify when ordering

Price Code B

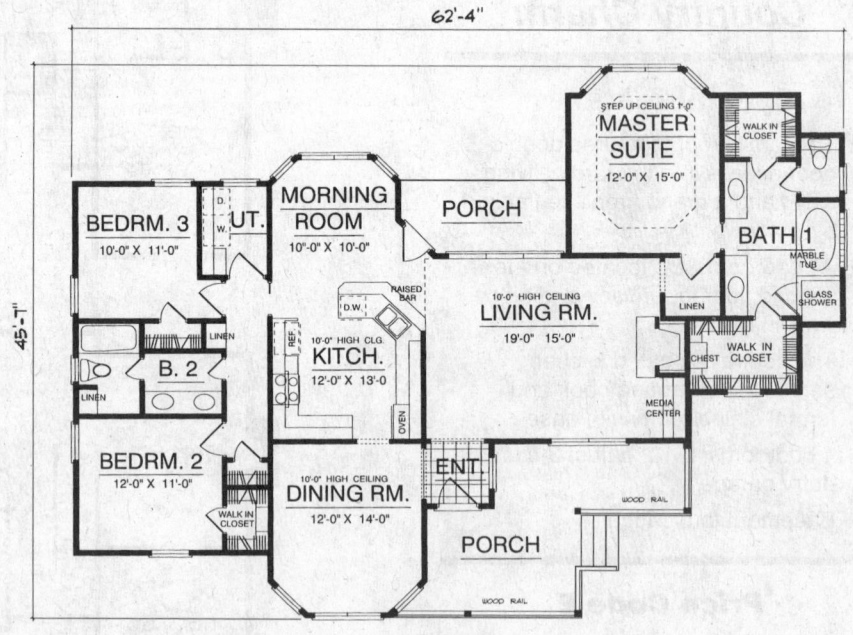

TO ORDER BLUEPRINTS USE THE FORM ON PAGE 15 OR CALL TOLL-FREE 1-877-671-6036
View thousands more home plans online at www.familyhandyman.com/HOMEPLANS

Plan #718-029D-0002

1,619 total square feet of living area

Country-Style Porch Adds Charm

Special features
- Private second floor bedroom and bath
- Kitchen features a snack bar and adjacent dining area
- Master bedroom has a private bath
- Centrally located washer and dryer
- 3 bedrooms, 3 baths
- Basement foundation, drawings also include crawl space and slab foundations

Price Code B

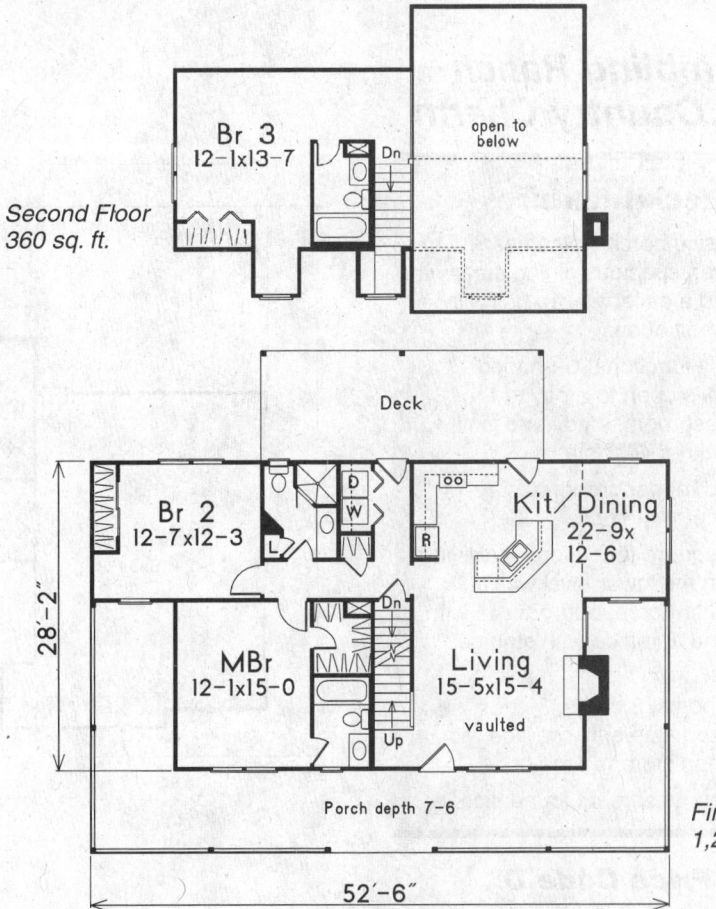

TO ORDER BLUEPRINTS USE THE FORM ON PAGE 15 OR CALL TOLL-FREE 1-877-671-6036
View thousands more home plans online at www.familyhandyman.com/homeplans

Plan #718-007D-0078

2,514 total square feet of living area

Rambling Ranch With Country Charm

Special features

- Expansive porch welcomes you to the foyer, spacious dining area with bay and a gallery-sized hall with plant shelf above
- A highly functional U-shaped kitchen is open to a bayed breakfast room, study and family room with a 46' vista
- Vaulted rear sunroom has a fireplace
- 1,509 square feet of optional living area on the lower level with a recreation room, bedroom #4 with bath and an office with storage closet
- 3 bedrooms, 2 baths, 3-car oversized side entry garage with workshop/storage area
- Walk-out basement foundation

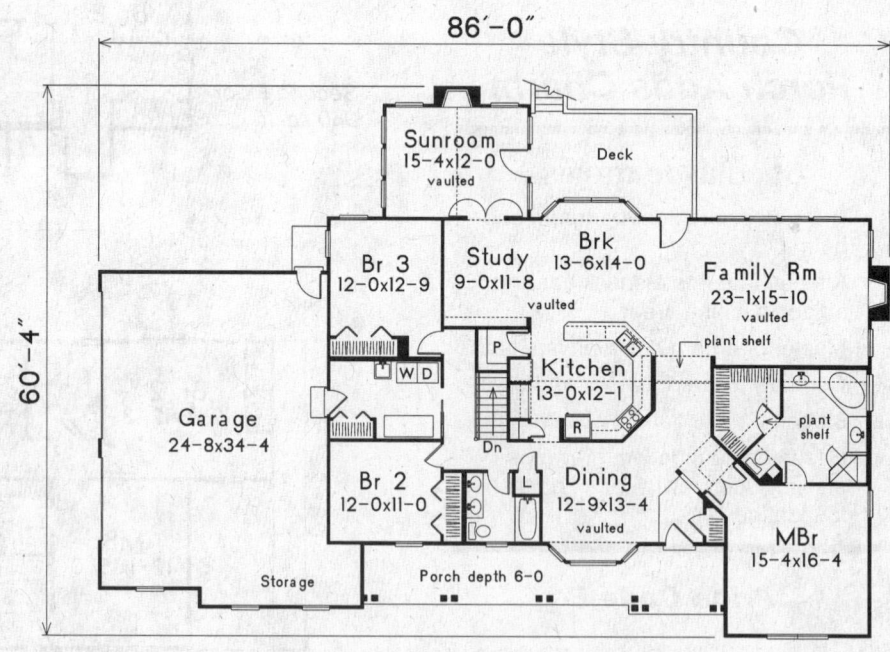

Price Code D

TO ORDER BLUEPRINTS USE THE FORM ON PAGE 15 OR CALL TOLL-FREE 1-877-671-6036
View thousands more home plans online at www.familyhandyman.com/HOMEPLANS

Plan #718-055D-0089

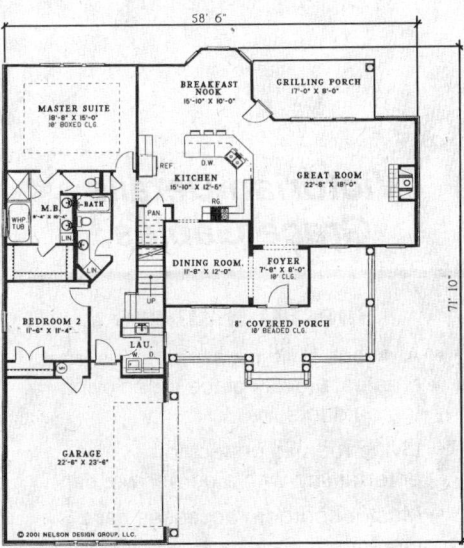

2,635 total square feet of living area

Charming Porch Is A Focal Point

Special features

- Formal dining room accesses kitchen
- Breakfast room has bay window and access to rear grilling porch
- Lots of storage space throughout
- 4 bedrooms, 3 baths, 2-car side entry garage
- Slab or crawl space foundation, please specify when ordering

Price Code E

First Floor 1,992 sq. ft.

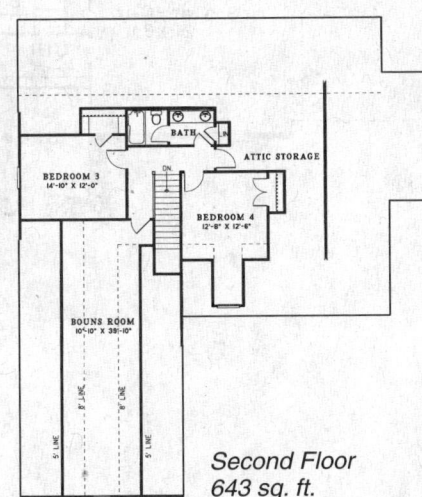

Second Floor 643 sq. ft.

TO ORDER BLUEPRINTS USE THE FORM ON PAGE 15 OR CALL TOLL-FREE 1-877-671-6036
View thousands more home plans online at www.familyhandyman.com/homeplans

Plan #718-036D-0001

2,267 total square feet of living area

Victorian Details
Grace Gables

Special features
- A unique built-in gazebo in the front creates a lovely place for enjoying the outdoors
- Living room is perfect for entertaining with a corner wet bar
- Master bedroom accesses patio directly
- 3 bedrooms, 3 baths, 3-car side entry garage
- Slab foundation

Price Code D

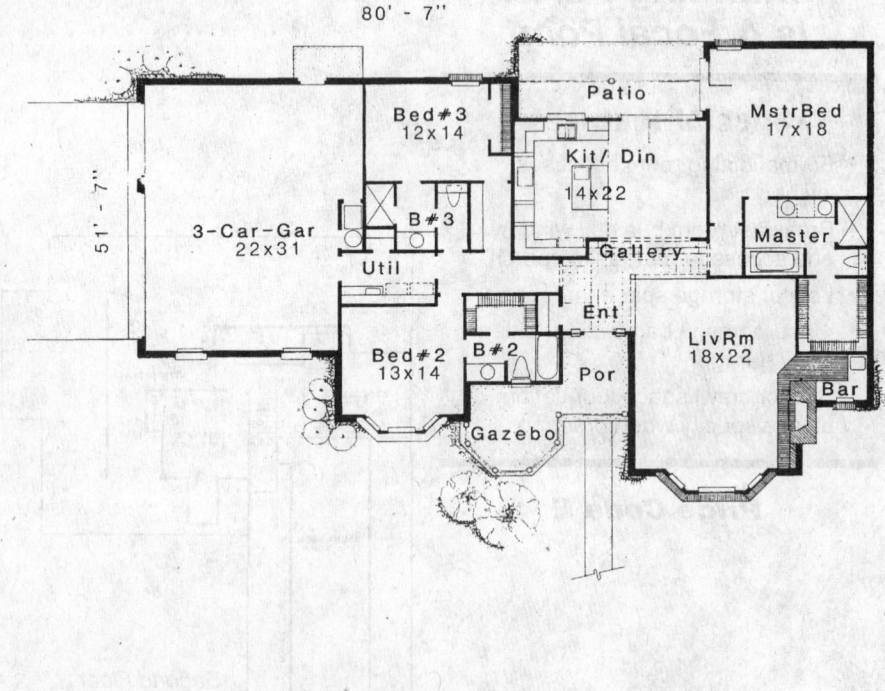

TO ORDER BLUEPRINTS USE THE FORM ON PAGE 15 OR CALL TOLL-FREE 1-877-671-6036
View thousands more home plans online at www.familyhandyman.com/HOMEPLANS

Plan #718-017D-0007

1,567 total square feet of living area

Pillared Front Porch Generates Charm And Warmth

Special features

- Living room flows into the dining room shaped by an angled pass-through into the kitchen
- Cheerful, windowed dining area
- Future area available on the second floor has an additional 338 square feet of living area
- Master bedroom is separated from other bedrooms for privacy
- 3 bedrooms, 2 baths, 2-car side entry garage
- Partial basement/crawl space foundation, drawings also include slab foundation

Price Code C

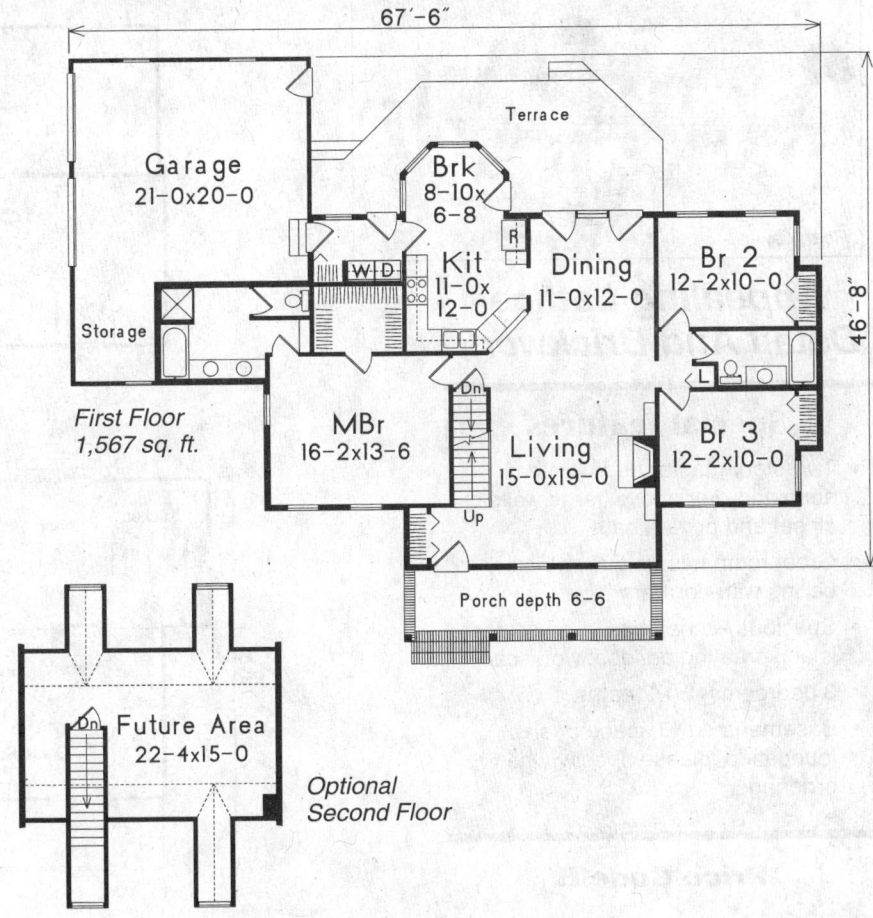

TO ORDER BLUEPRINTS USE THE FORM ON PAGE 15 OR CALL TOLL-FREE 1-877-671-6036
View thousands more home plans online at www.familyhandyman.com/homeplans

Plan #718-038D-0054

1,560 total square feet of living area

Rear View

Appealing Lattice Detail And Brickwork

Special features

- Two-story master bedroom has sunny dormer above, large walk-in closet and private bath
- Great room has unique two-story ceiling with dormers
- Spacious kitchen has large center island creating an ideal workspace
- 3 bedrooms, 2 1/2 baths
- Basement, crawl space or slab foundation, please specify when ordering

Price Code B

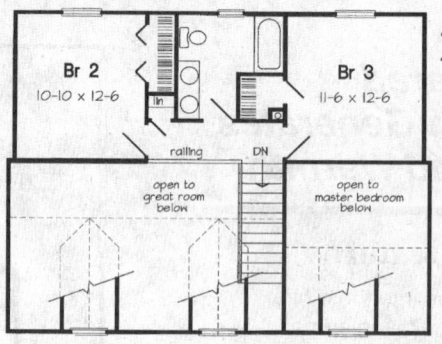

Second Floor 499 sq. ft.

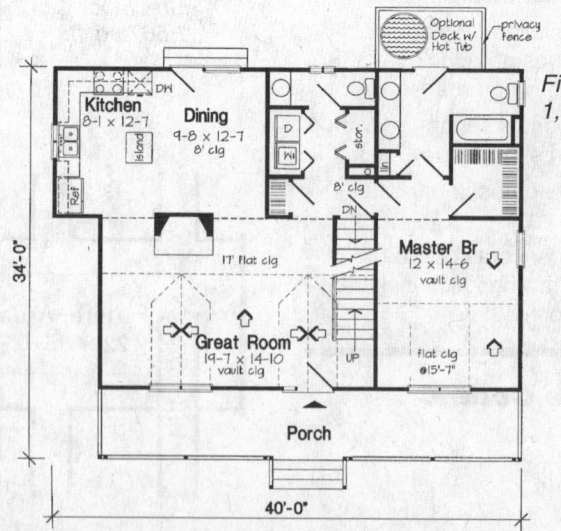

First Floor 1,061 sq. ft.

TO ORDER BLUEPRINTS USE THE FORM ON PAGE 15 OR CALL TOLL-FREE 1-877-671-6036

View thousands more home plans online at www.familyhandyman.com/homeplans

Plan #718-056D-0027

1,580 total square feet of living area

Double-Gabled Ranch Cottage

Special features

- Dining room has columns which maintain an open feeling
- Sunny breakfast room is located off the kitchen
- 9' ceilings throughout the first floor
- Optional second floor has an additional 336 square feet of living area
- 2 bedrooms, 2 baths, 3-car side entry garage
- Slab foundation

Price Code E

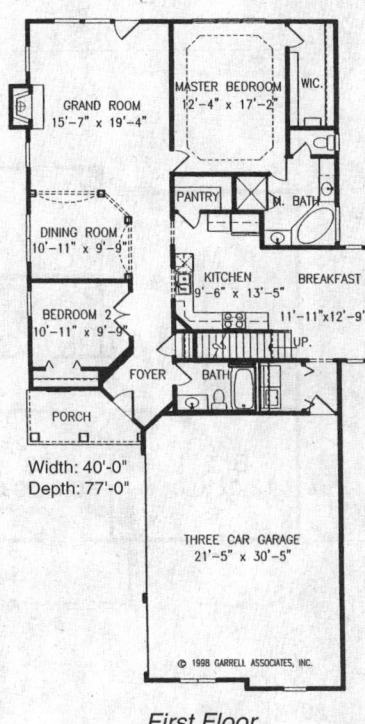

First Floor
1,580 sq. ft.

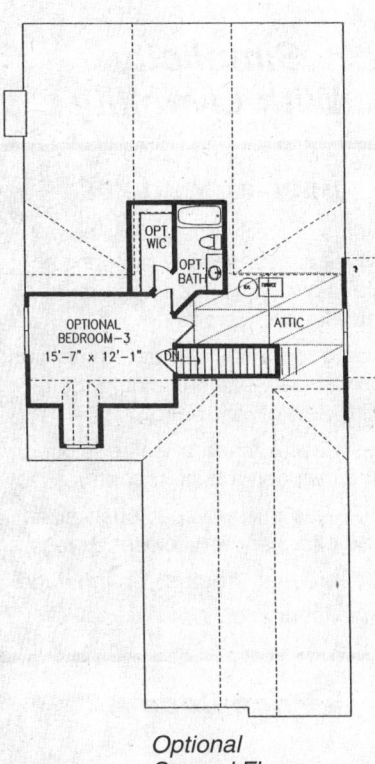

Optional
Second Floor

TO ORDER BLUEPRINTS USE THE FORM ON PAGE 15 OR CALL TOLL-FREE 1-877-671-6036
View thousands more home plans online at www.familyhandyman.com/HOMEPLANS

Plan #718-007D-0126

1,365 total square feet of living area

Simplicity With Livability

Special features

- Home is easily adaptable for physical accessibility featuring no stairs and extra-wide hall baths, laundry and garage
- Living room has separate entry and opens to a spacious dining room with view of rear patio
- L-shaped kitchen is well-equipped and includes a built-in pantry
- All bedrooms are spaciously sized and offer generous closet storage
- 3 bedrooms, 2 baths, 1-car garage
- Slab foundation

Price Code A

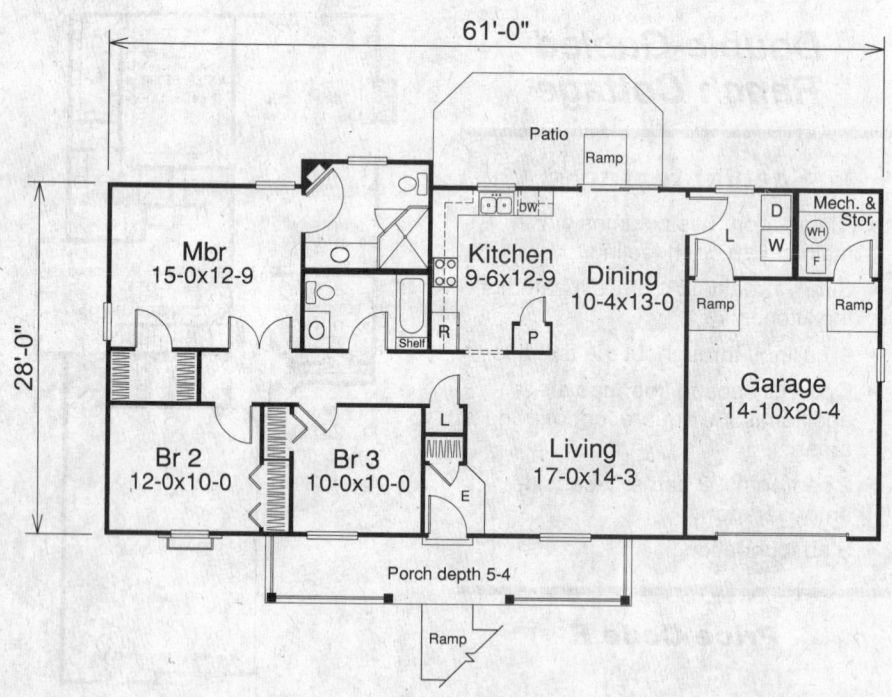

TO ORDER BLUEPRINTS USE THE FORM ON PAGE 15 OR CALL TOLL-FREE 1-877-671-6036
View thousands more home plans online at www.familyhandyman.com/homeplans

Plan #718-052D-0089

2,911 total square feet of living area

Dormers Enhance This Country-Style Home

Special features

- Wrap-around porch with double columns
- Optional living area and bedroom above two-car garage has 512 square feet of living area
- Beautiful master bath with corner tub, separate shower and large walk-in closet
- Large sundeck offers a great area to relax
- 3 bedrooms, 2 1/2 baths, 2-car side entry garage
- Partial basement/crawl space foundation

Price Code E

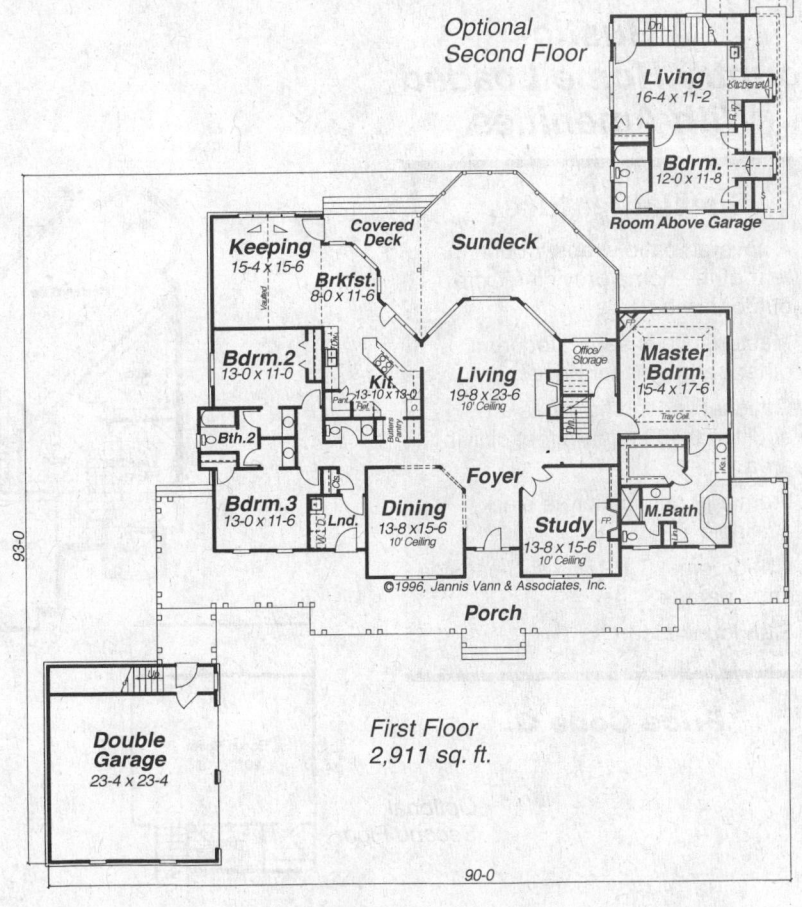

TO ORDER BLUEPRINTS USE THE FORM ON PAGE 15 OR CALL TOLL-FREE 1-877-671-6036
View thousands more home plans online at www.familyhandyman.com/homeplans

Plan #718-047D-0062

3,359 total square feet of living area

A Rustic Country Home Loaded With Amenities

Special features

- A covered patio wraps around the rear of the home providing extra outdoor living area
- Master suite is separated from other bedrooms for privacy
- Optional second floor has an additional 459 square feet of living area
- Framing - only concrete block available
- 4 bedrooms, 3 1/2 baths, 3-car side entry garage
- Slab foundation

Price Code G

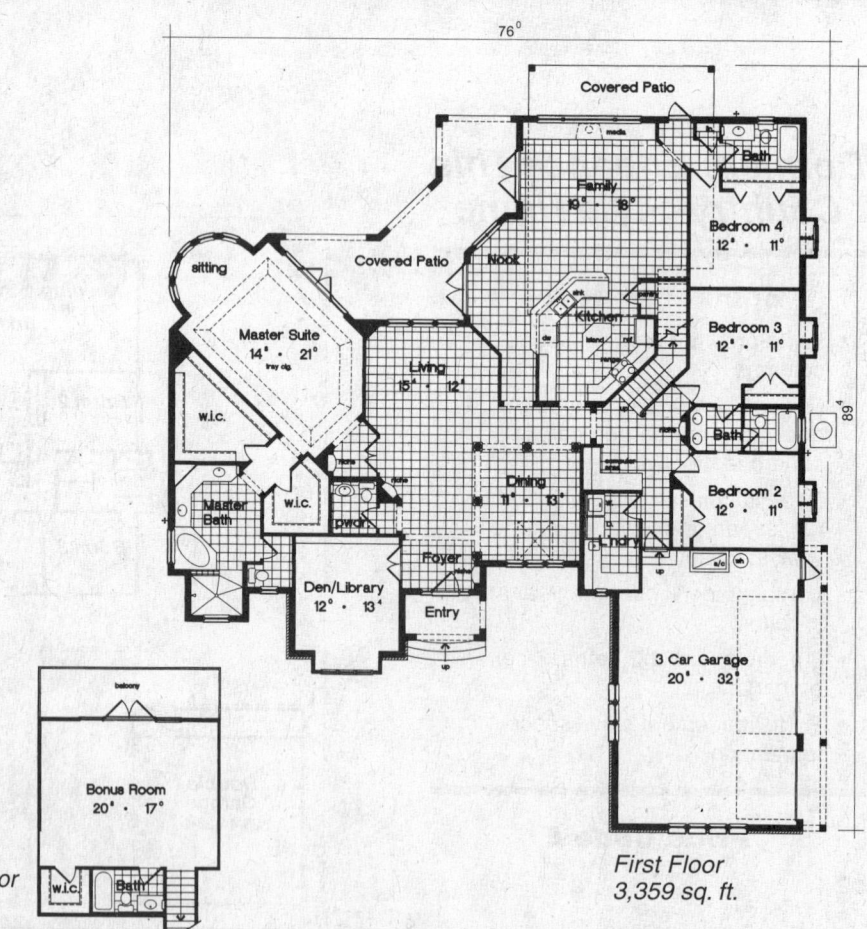

TO ORDER BLUEPRINTS USE THE FORM ON PAGE 15 OR CALL TOLL-FREE 1-877-671-6036
View thousands more home plans online at www.familyhandyman.com/homeplans

Plan #718-007D-0064

2,967 total square feet of living area

Picture Perfect For A Country Setting

Special features

- An exterior with charm graced with country porch and multiple arched projected box windows
- Dining area is oversized and adjoins a fully equipped kitchen with walk-in pantry
- Two bay windows light up the enormous informal living area to the rear
- 4 bedrooms, 3 1/2 baths, 3-car side entry garage
- Basement foundation

Price Code E

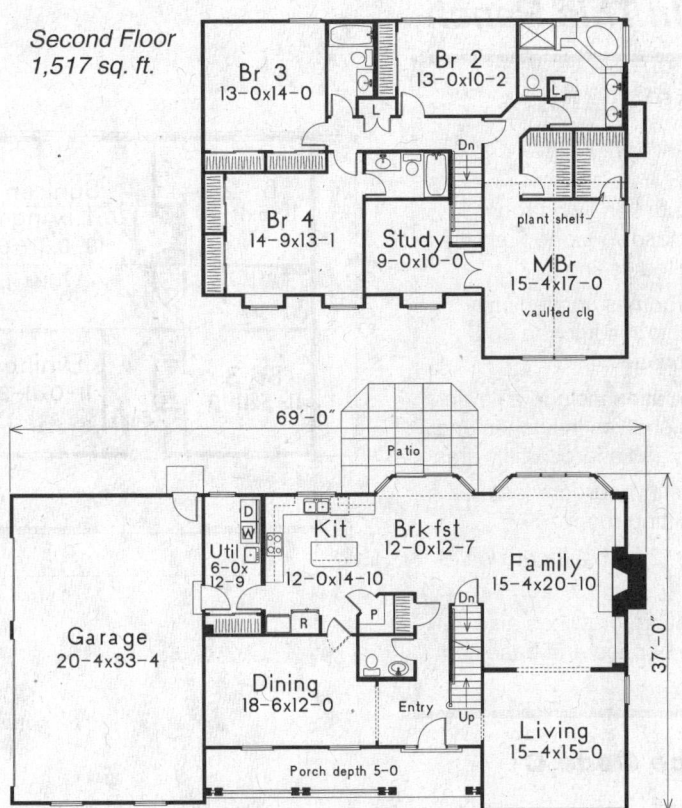

TO ORDER BLUEPRINTS USE THE FORM ON PAGE 15 OR CALL TOLL-FREE 1-877-671-6036
View thousands more home plans online at www.familyhandyman.com/HOMEPLANS

Plan #718-021D-0006

1,600 total square feet of living area

Charming Country Styling In This Ranch

Special features

- Energy efficient home with 2" x 6" exterior walls
- Impressive sunken living room features a massive stone fireplace and 16' vaulted ceiling
- The dining room is conveniently located next to the kitchen and divided for privacy
- Special amenities include a sewing room, glass shelves in kitchen and master bath and a large utility area
- Sunken master bedroom features a distinctive sitting room
- 3 bedrooms, 2 baths, 2-car side entry garage
- Slab foundation, drawings also include crawl space and basement foundations

Price Code C

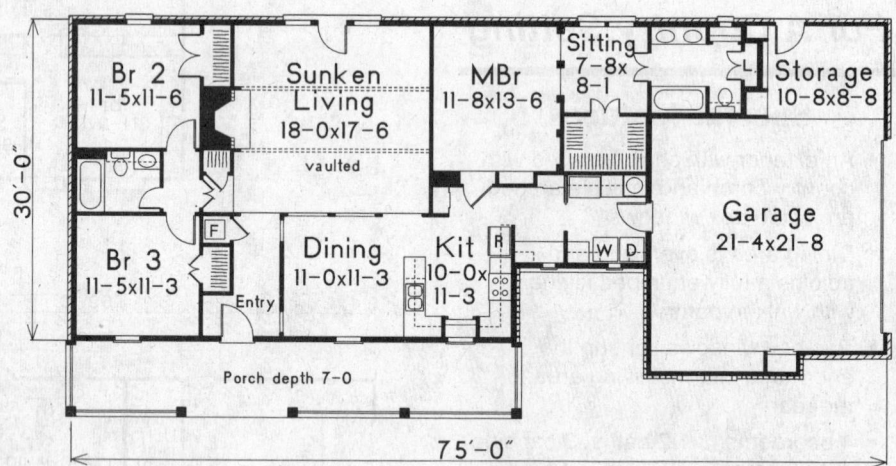

TO ORDER BLUEPRINTS USE THE FORM ON PAGE 15 OR CALL TOLL-FREE 1-877-671-6036
View thousands more home plans online at www.familyhandyman.com/homeplans

Plan #718-055D-0103

2,716 total square feet of living area

Amenity-Full Master Bath

Special features

- Master suite has lots of privacy from other bedrooms
- 10' ceiling in formal dining room makes an impression
- Bonus room on the second floor has an additional 438 square feet of living area
- 4 bedrooms, 4 baths, 2-car side entry garage
- Crawl space or slab foundation, please specify when ordering

Price Code E

First Floor
2,716 sq. ft.

Optional Second Floor

Plan #718-007D-0157

1,599 total square feet of living area

Inviting Ranch

Special features

- Spacious entry leads to the great room featuring a vaulted ceiling, fireplace and an octagon-shaped dining area with views to the covered patio
- The kitchen enjoys a snack counter open to the dining area, a breakfast area with bay window and a built-in pantry
- Master bedroom has a sitting area, large walk-in closet and a luxury bath
- The laundry room has a convenient half bath and access to the garage with storage area
- 4 bedrooms, 2 1/2 baths, 2-car garage
- Basement foundation

Price Code B

TO ORDER BLUEPRINTS USE THE FORM ON PAGE 15 OR CALL TOLL-FREE 1-877-671-6036
View thousands more home plans online at www.familyhandyman.com/HOMEPLANS

Plan #718-062D-0043

2,750 total square feet of living area

Victorian Accents Create A Custom Feel

Special features

- Spacious dining room is connected to the kitchen for ease and also has access onto the wrap-around porch
- A double-door entry leads into the master bedroom enhanced with a spacious walk-in closet and a private bath with whirlpool tub
- Secluded den is an ideal place for a home office
- 4 bedrooms, 2 1/2 baths, 2-car side entry garage
- Basement or crawl space foundation, please specify when ordering

Price Code E

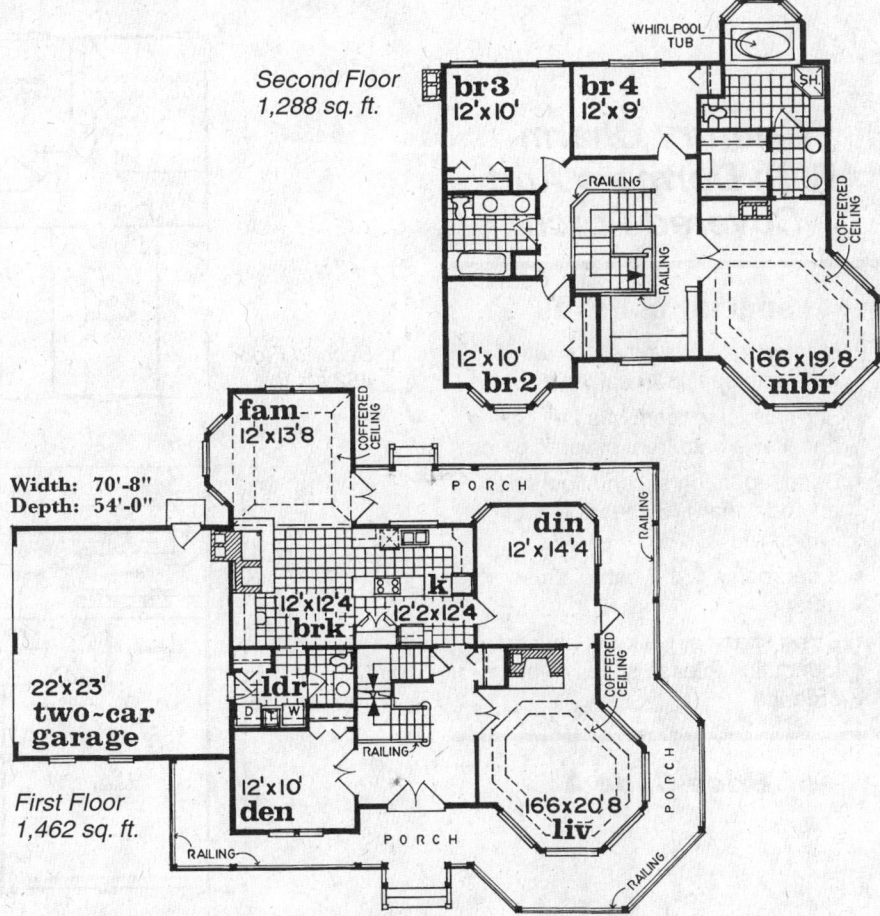

Width: 70'-8"
Depth: 54'-0"

Second Floor 1,288 sq. ft.

First Floor 1,462 sq. ft.

TO ORDER BLUEPRINTS USE THE FORM ON PAGE 15 OR CALL TOLL-FREE 1-877-671-6036
View thousands more home plans online at www.familyhandyman.com/homeplans

Plan #718-035D-0013

1,497 total square feet of living area

Country Charm With Dormers And Covered Porch

Special features

- Master suite has private luxurious bath with spacious walk-in closet
- Formal dining room has tray ceiling and views onto front covered porch
- Bonus room on second floor has an additional 175 square feet of living area
- 3 bedrooms, 2 1/2 baths, 2-car garage
- Crawl space or walk-out basement foundation, please specify when ordering

Price Code A

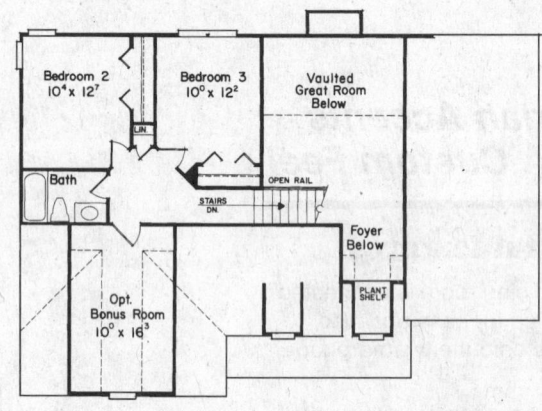

Second Floor 432 sq. ft.

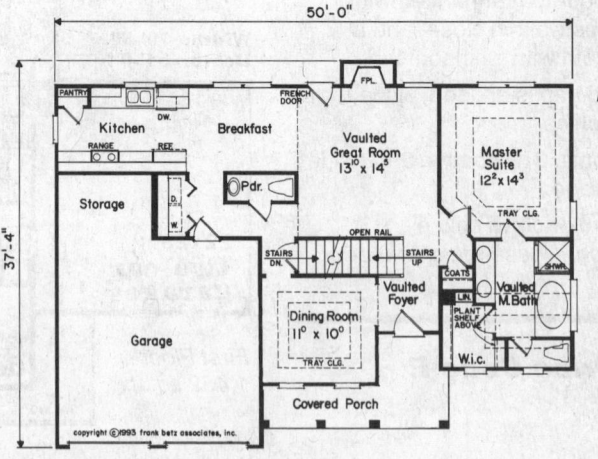

First Floor 1,065 sq. ft.

TO ORDER BLUEPRINTS USE THE FORM ON PAGE 15 OR CALL TOLL-FREE 1-877-671-6036
View thousands more home plans online at www.familyhandyman.com/homeplans

Plan #718-007D-0137

1,568 total square feet of living area

Country Lodge With Screened Porch And Fireplace

Special features

- Multiple entrances from three porches
- The lodge-like great room features a vaulted ceiling, stone fireplace, step-up entrance foyer and opens to a huge screened porch
- The kitchen has an island and peninsula, a convenient laundry room and adjoins the dining area
- The master bedroom has two walk-in closets, a luxury bath and access to the screened porch and patio
- 2 bedrooms, 2 baths, 3-car side entry garage
- Crawl space foundation

Price Code B

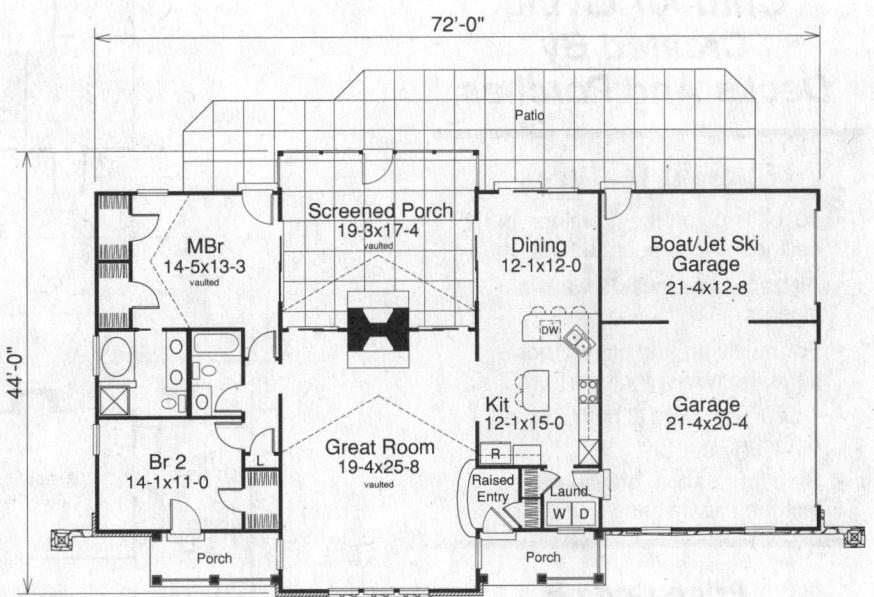

TO ORDER BLUEPRINTS USE THE FORM ON PAGE 15 OR CALL TOLL-FREE 1-877-671-6036
View thousands more home plans online at www.familyhandyman.com/HOMEPLANS

Plan #718-023D-0001

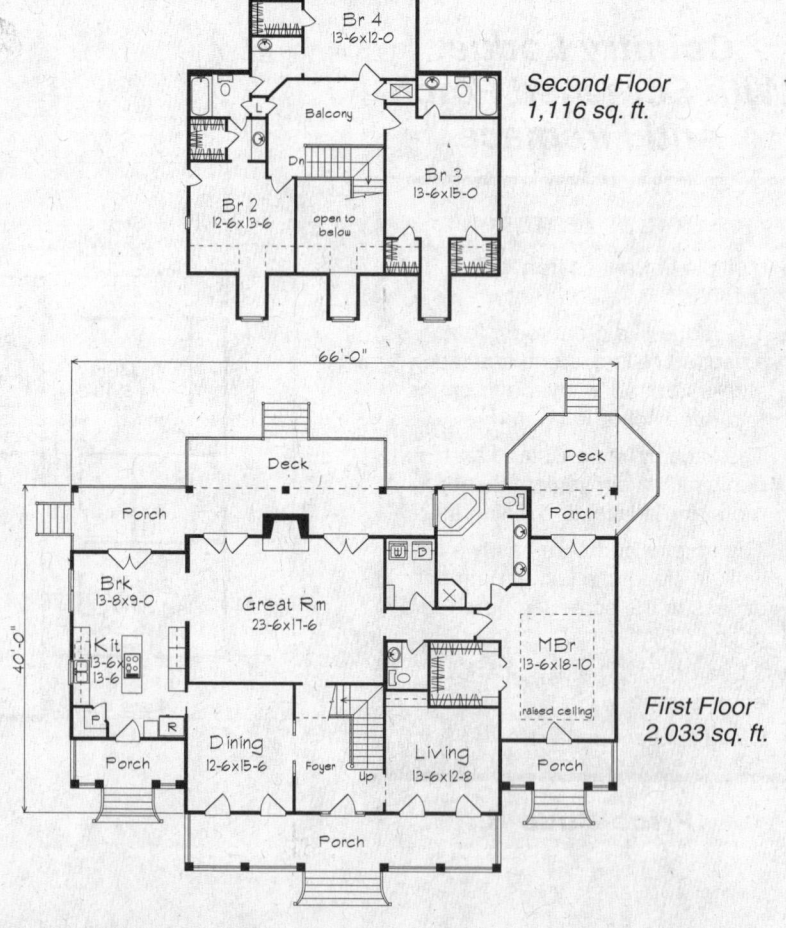

3,149 total square feet of living area

Second Floor 1,116 sq. ft.

First Floor 2,033 sq. ft.

Outdoor Living Created By Decks And Porches

Special features

- 10' ceilings on the first floor and 9' ceilings on the second floor
- All bedrooms include walk-in closets
- Formal living and dining rooms flank the two-story foyer
- 4 bedrooms, 3 1/2 baths, 2-car detached garage
- Slab foundation, drawings also include crawl space foundation

Price Code E

TO ORDER BLUEPRINTS USE THE FORM ON PAGE 15 OR CALL TOLL-FREE 1-877-671-6036
View thousands more home plans online at www.familyhandyman.com/homeplans

Plan #718-037D-0014

2,932 total square feet of living area

Fireplaces Add Warm Cozy Feeling

Special features

- 9' ceilings throughout home
- Rear stairs create convenient access to second floor from living area
- Spacious kitchen has pass-through to the family room, a convenient island and pantry
- Cozy built-in table in breakfast area
- Secluded master bedroom has a luxurious bath and patio access
- 4 bedrooms, 3 1/2 baths, 2-car side entry garage
- Slab foundation

Price Code F

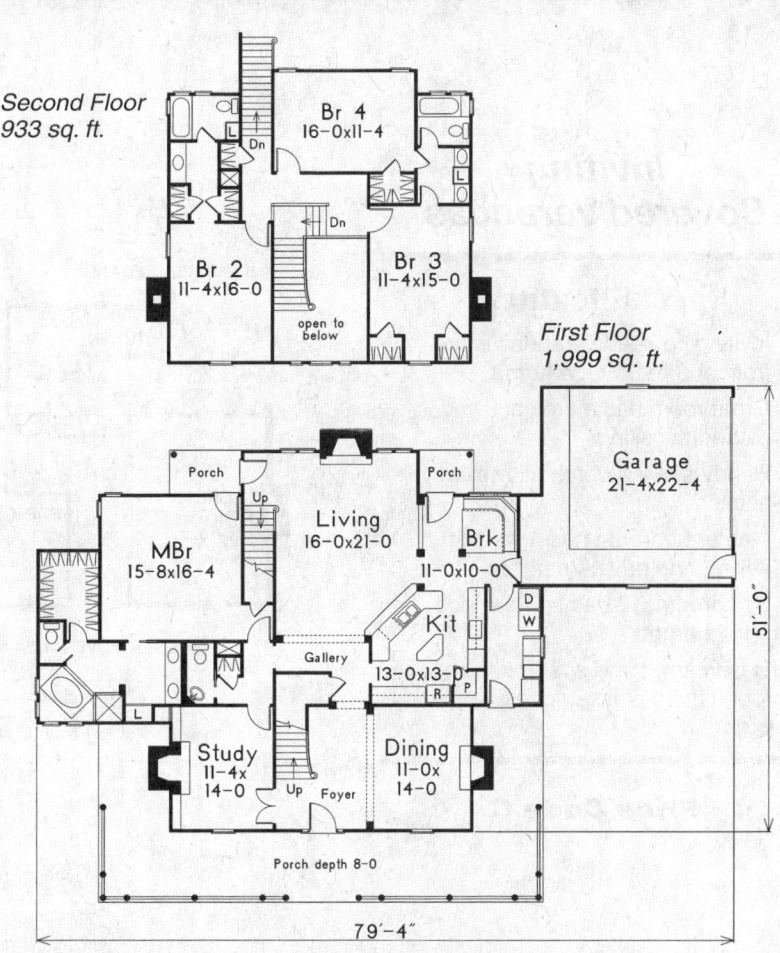

TO ORDER BLUEPRINTS USE THE FORM ON PAGE 15 OR CALL TOLL-FREE 1-877-671-6036
View thousands more home plans online at www.familyhandyman.com/HOMEPLANS

Plan #718-036D-0048

1,830 total square feet of living area

Inviting Covered Verandas

Special features

- Inviting covered verandas in the front and rear of the home
- Great room has a fireplace and cathedral ceiling
- Handy service porch allows easy access
- Master bedroom has a vaulted ceiling and private bath
- 3 bedrooms, 2 baths, 3-car side entry garage
- Basement, crawl space or slab foundation, please specify when ordering

Price Code C

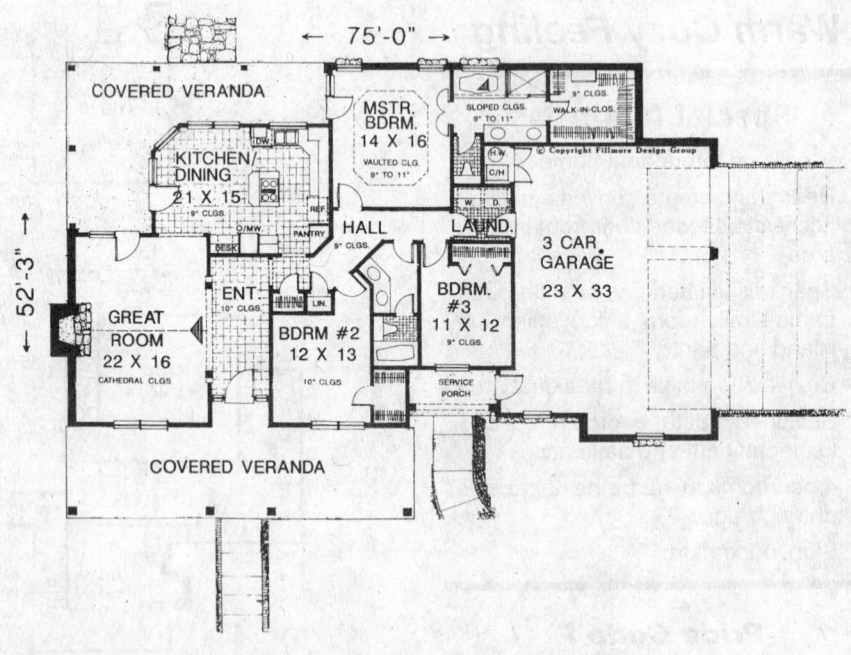

TO ORDER BLUEPRINTS USE THE FORM ON PAGE 15 OR CALL TOLL-FREE 1-877-671-6036
View thousands more home plans online at www.familyhandyman.com/homeplans

Plan #718-047D-0020

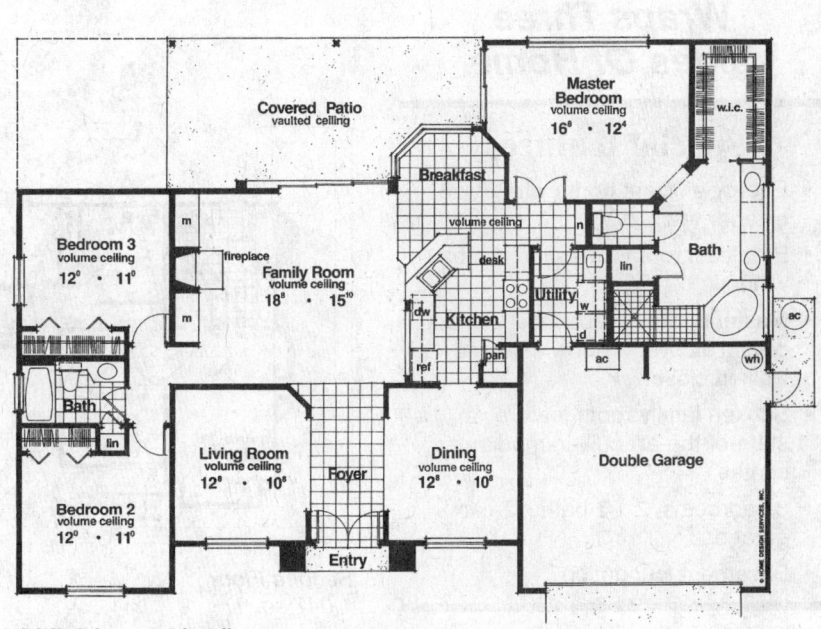

1,783 total square feet of living area

Stately And Functional Family Room

Special features

- Formal living and dining rooms in the front of the home
- Kitchen overlooks breakfast area
- Conveniently located laundry area is near the kitchen and master bedroom
- Plans include a version with 4 bedrooms, 3 baths and an additional 206 square feet of living area
- 3 bedrooms, 2 baths, 2-car garage
- Slab foundation

Price Code B

Width: 60'-0"
Depth: 45'-0"

TO ORDER BLUEPRINTS USE THE FORM ON PAGE 15 OR CALL TOLL-FREE 1-877-671-6036
View thousands more home plans online at www.familyhandyman.com/HOMEPLANS

157

The Family Handyman

Plan #718-062D-0039

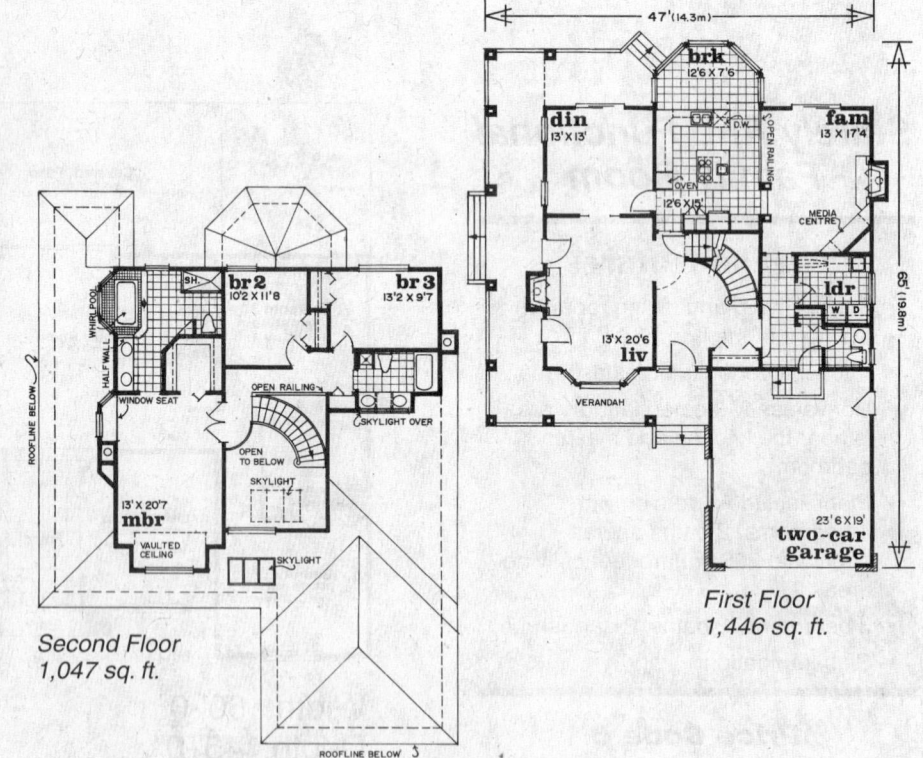

2,493 total square feet of living area

Covered Verandah Wraps Three Sides Of Home

Special features

- Energy efficient home with 2" x 6" exterior walls
- Breakfast room is nestled in a bay window
- Master bedroom boasts a vaulted ceiling alcove, window seat and walk-in closet
- Sunken family room features a state-of-the-art built-in media center
- 3 bedrooms, 2 1/2 baths, 2-car garage
- Basement foundation

Price Code D

Second Floor 1,047 sq. ft.

First Floor 1,446 sq. ft.

TO ORDER BLUEPRINTS USE THE FORM ON PAGE 15 OR CALL TOLL-FREE 1-877-671-6036
View thousands more home plans online at www.familyhandyman.com/HOMEPLANS

Plan #718-039D-0012

1,815 total square feet of living area

Large Built-In Desk

Special features

- Second floor has built-in desk in hall that is ideal as a computer work station or mini office area
- Two doors into the laundry area make it handy from the master bedroom and the rest of the home
- Inviting covered porch
- Lots of counterspace and cabinetry in kitchen
- 3 bedrooms, 2 1/2 baths, 2-car side entry garage
- Basement foundation

Price Code C

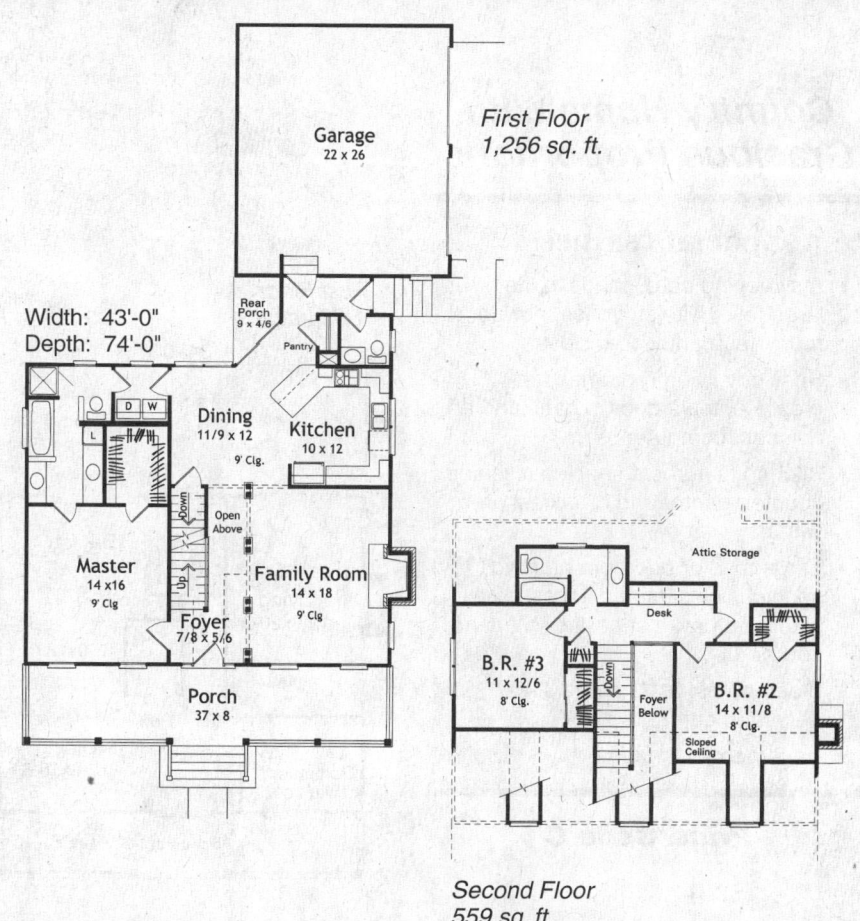

TO ORDER BLUEPRINTS USE THE FORM ON PAGE 15 OR CALL TOLL-FREE 1-877-671-6036
View thousands more home plans online at www.familyhandyman.com/HOMEPLANS

Plan #718-007D-0122

2,054 total square feet of living area

Country Home With Gracious Proportions

Special features

- A sweeping porch leads to the large foyer with staircase, powder room and handy coat closet
- Spacious living room has a fireplace, triple door to patio and an adjacent computer room
- Kitchen features a snack bar, island counter, pantry and breakfast area with bay window
- Large master bedroom has two spacious closets and accesses a luxury bath with separate toilet and corner tub
- 3 bedrooms, 2 1/2 baths, 2-car detached garage
- Basement foundation

Price Code C

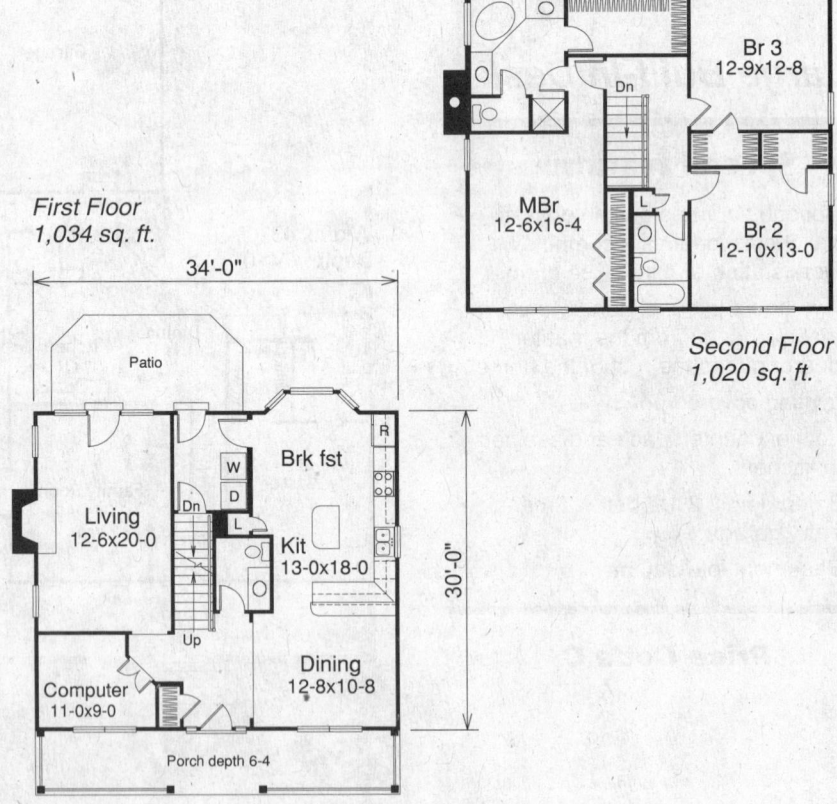

First Floor 1,034 sq. ft.

Second Floor 1,020 sq. ft.

Plan #718-048D-0001

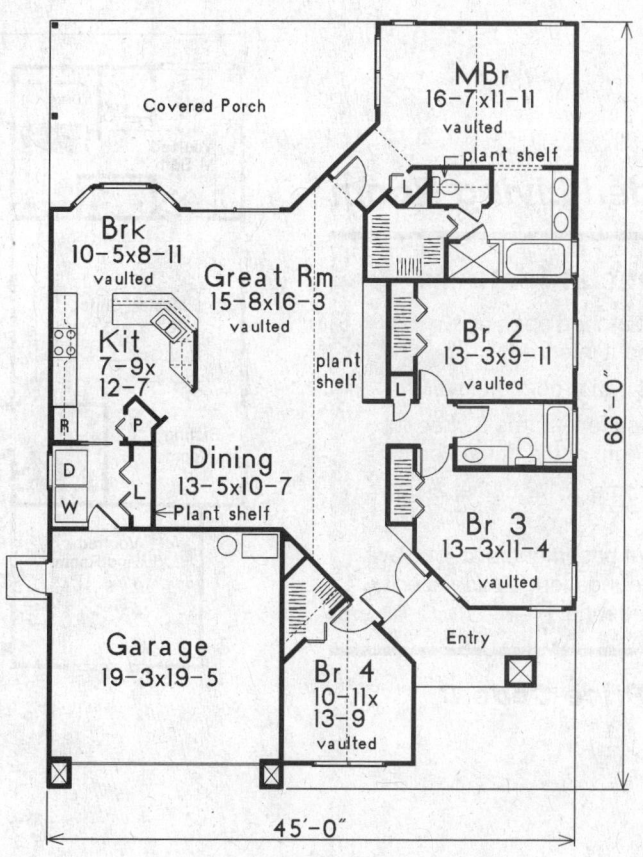

1,865 total square feet of living area

Wonderful Great Room

Special features

- The large foyer opens into an expansive dining area and great room
- Home features vaulted ceilings throughout
- Master bedroom features an angled entry, vaulted ceiling, plant shelf and bath with double vanity, tub and shower
- 4 bedrooms, 2 baths, 2-car garage
- Slab foundation, drawings also include crawl space foundation

Price Code D

TO ORDER BLUEPRINTS USE THE FORM ON PAGE 15 OR CALL TOLL-FREE 1-877-671-6036
View thousands more home plans online at www.familyhandyman.com/HOMEPLANS

Plan #718-035D-0021

1,978 total square feet of living area

Secluded Living Room

Special features

- Elegant arched openings throughout interior
- Vaulted living room off foyer
- Master suite features a cheerful sitting room and a private bath
- 3 bedrooms, 2 1/2 baths, 2-car garage
- Walk-out basement, slab or crawl space foundation, please specify when ordering

Price Code C

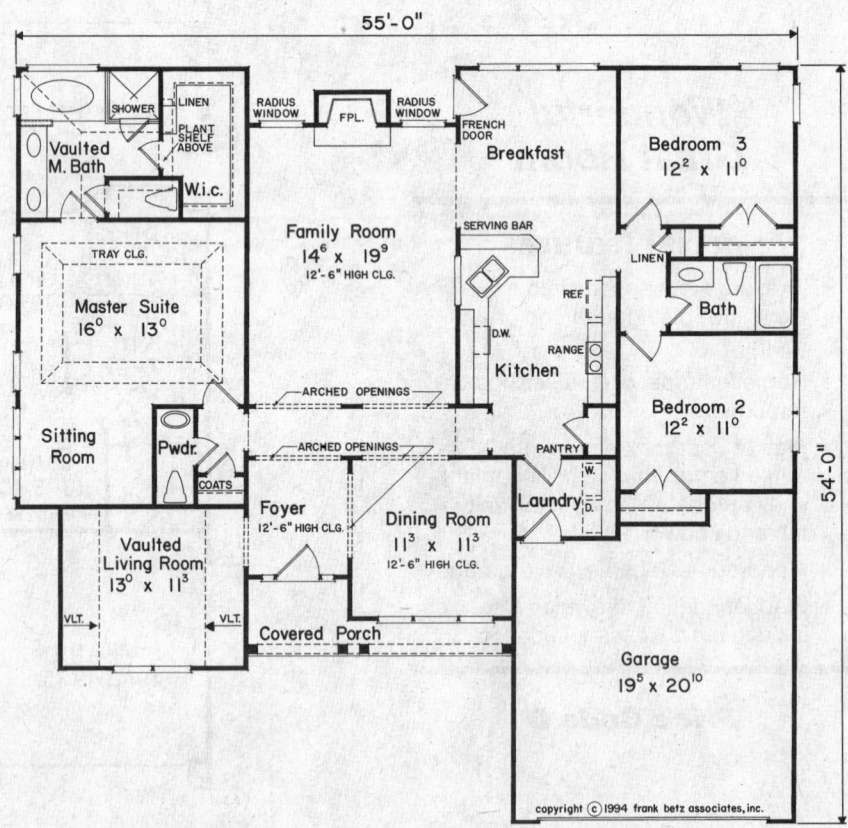

TO ORDER BLUEPRINTS USE THE FORM ON PAGE 15 OR CALL TOLL-FREE 1-877-671-6036
View thousands more home plans online at www.familyhandyman.com/homeplans

Plan #718-007D-0055

2,029 total square feet of living area

Country Home With Front Orientation

Special features

- Stonework, gables, roof dormer and double porches create a country flavor
- Kitchen enjoys extravagant cabinetry and counterspace in a bay, island snack bar, built-in pantry and cheery dining area with multiple tall windows
- Angled stair descends from large entry with wood columns and is open to vaulted great room with corner fireplace
- Master bedroom boasts two walk-in closets, a private bath with double-door entry and a secluded porch
- 4 bedrooms, 2 baths, 2-car side entry garage
- Basement foundation, drawings also include crawl space and slab foundations

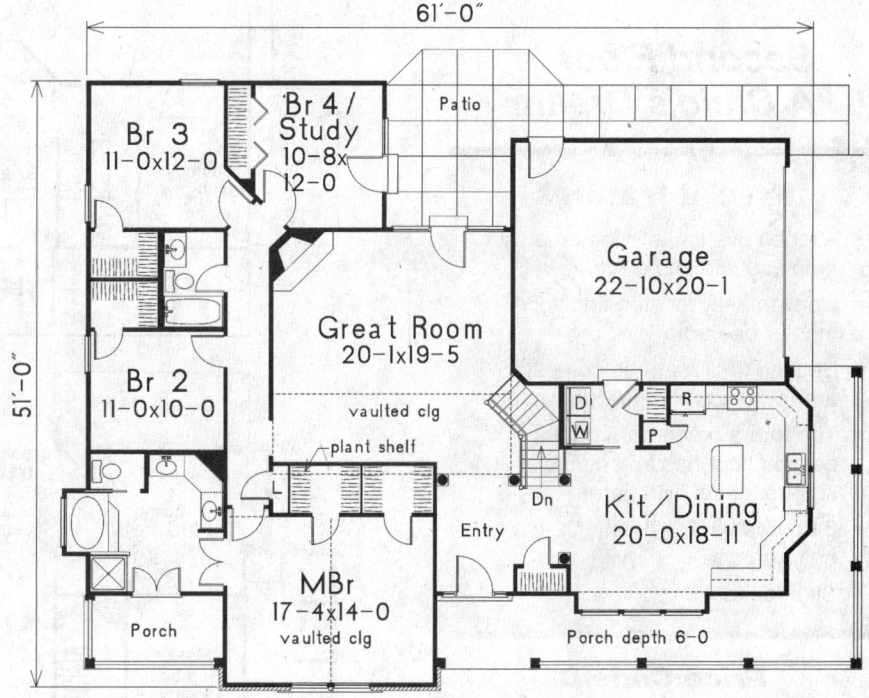

Price Code D

TO ORDER BLUEPRINTS USE THE FORM ON PAGE 15 OR CALL TOLL-FREE 1-877-671-6036
View thousands more home plans online at www.familyhandyman.com/HOMEPLANS

The Family Handyman

Plan #718-024D-0019

2,331 total square feet of living area

Second Floor Is A Child's Dream

Special features

- Kitchen overlooks living area with fireplace and lots of windows
- Conveniently located first floor master bedroom
- Second floor features computer area with future gameroom space
- The future gameroom on the second floor has an additional 264 square feet of living area
- 3 bedrooms, 2 1/2 baths, 2-car side entry garage
- Slab foundation

Price Code D

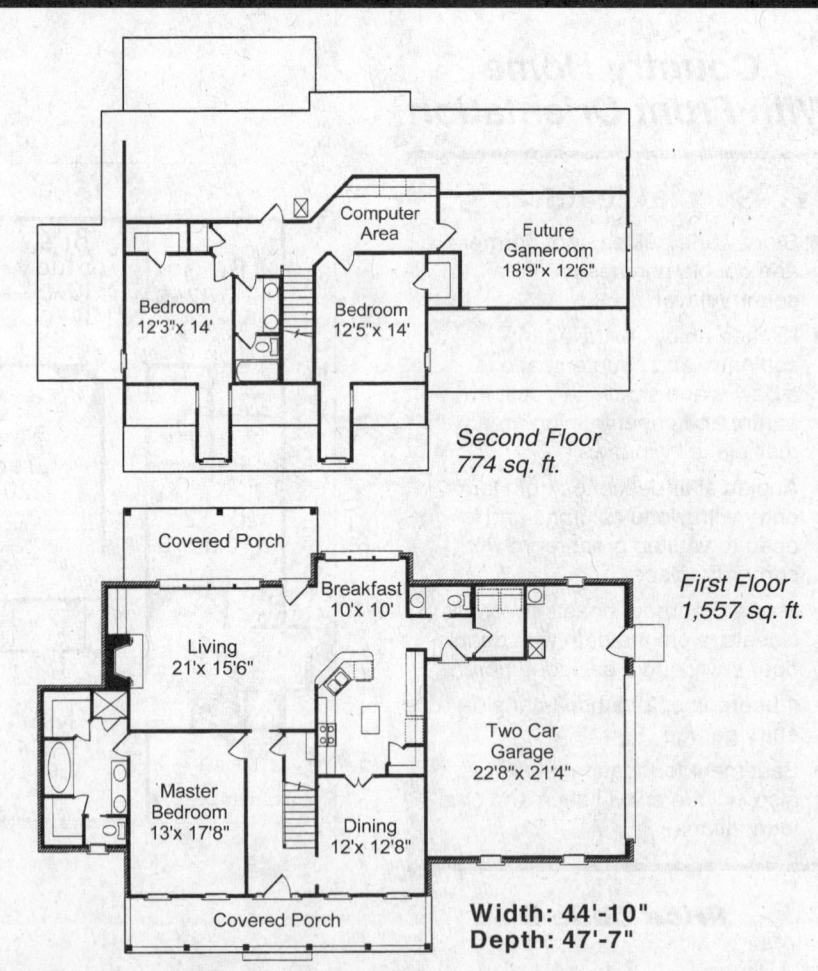

Second Floor 774 sq. ft.

First Floor 1,557 sq. ft.

Width: 44'-10"
Depth: 47'-7"

TO ORDER BLUEPRINTS USE THE FORM ON PAGE 15 OR CALL TOLL-FREE 1-877-671-6036
View thousands more home plans online at www.familyhandyman.com/homeplans

Plan #718-053D-0016

2,216 total square feet of living area

Stately Colonial Features Porch With Overhead Balcony

Special features

- Luxury master bedroom suite features full-windowed bathtub bay, double walk-in closets and access to the front balcony
- Spacious kitchen has enough space for dining
- Second floor laundry facility is centrally located
- 4 bedrooms, 2 1/2 baths, 2-car drive under garage
- Basement foundation

Price Code D

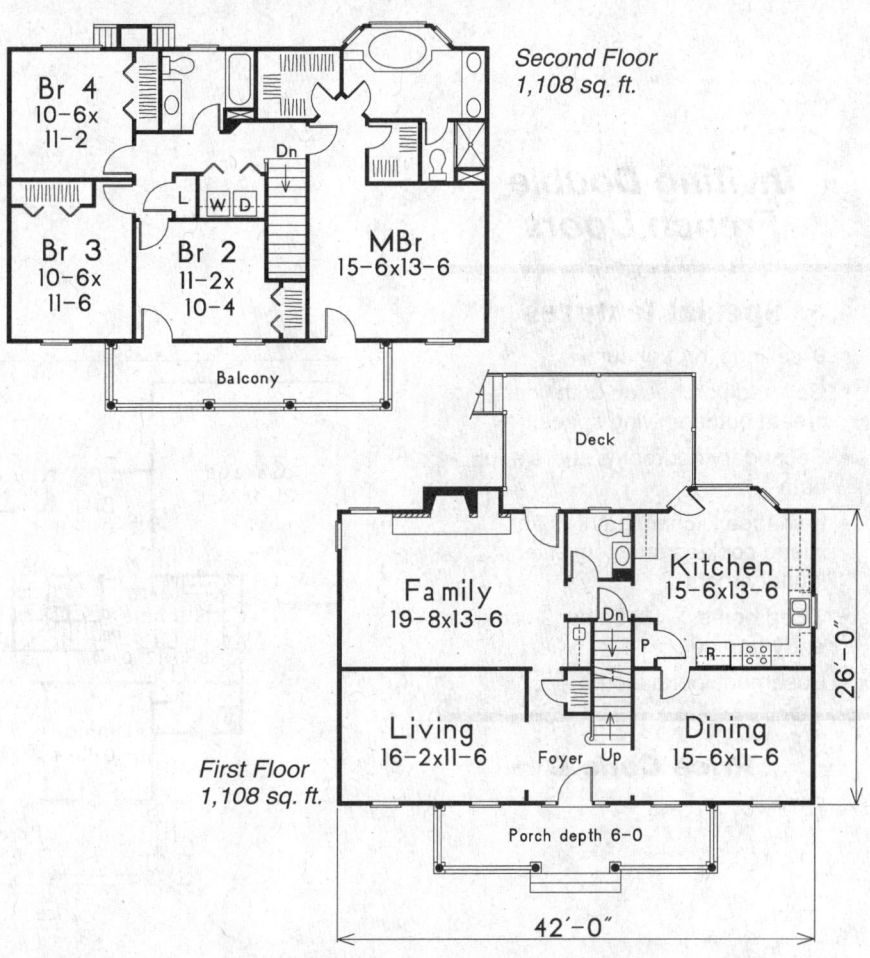

TO ORDER BLUEPRINTS USE THE FORM ON PAGE 15 OR CALL TOLL-FREE 1-877-671-6036
View thousands more home plans online at www.familyhandyman.com/homeplans

Plan #718-040D-0022

2,327 total square feet of living area

Inviting Double French Doors

Special features

- 9' ceilings throughout
- Covered porches on both floors create outdoor living space
- Secondary bedrooms share a full bath
- L-shaped kitchen features an island cooktop and convenient laundry room
- 3 bedrooms, 2 1/2 baths, 2-car side entry garage
- Basement foundation

Price Code D

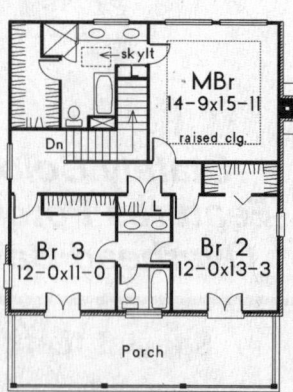

Second Floor
1,011 sq. ft.

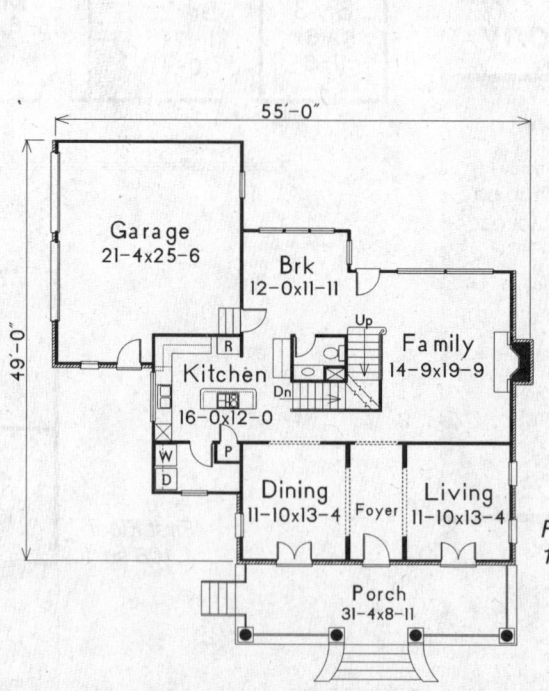

First Floor
1,316 sq. ft.

TO ORDER BLUEPRINTS USE THE FORM ON PAGE 15 OR CALL TOLL-FREE 1-877-671-6036
View thousands more home plans online at www.familyhandyman.com/homeplans

Plan #718-027D-0005

2,135 total square feet of living area

Open Breakfast/Family Room Combination

Special features

- Family room features extra space, an impressive fireplace and full wall of windows that joins the breakfast room creating a spacious entertainment area
- Washer and dryer are conveniently located on the second floor near the bedrooms
- The kitchen features an island counter and pantry
- 4 bedrooms, 2 1/2 baths, 2-car garage
- Basement foundation

Price Code D

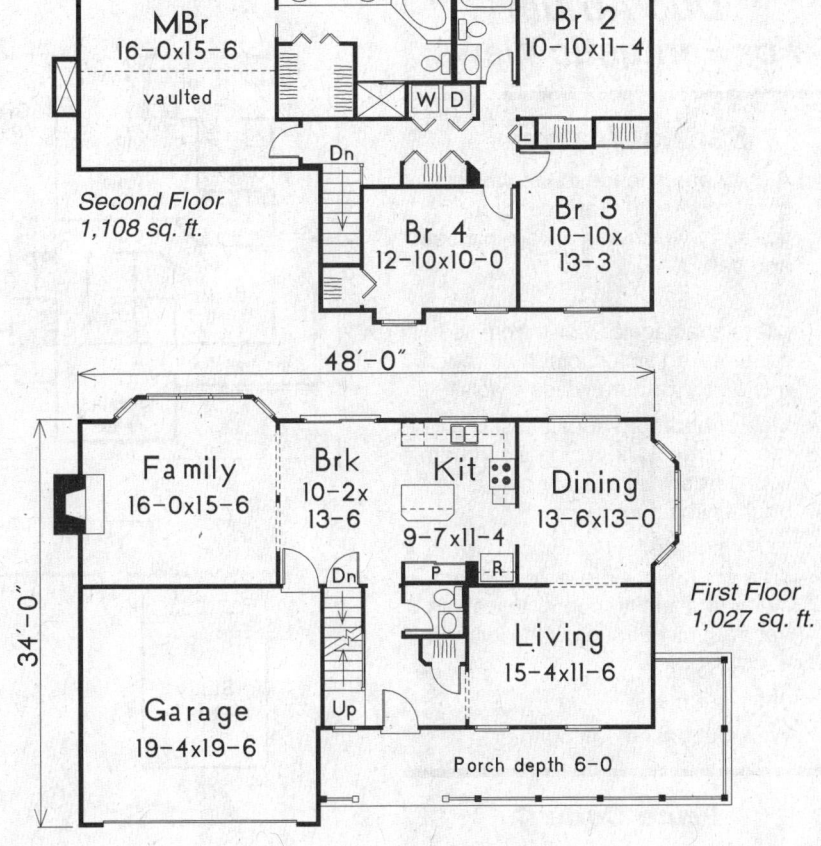

TO ORDER BLUEPRINTS USE THE FORM ON PAGE 15 OR CALL TOLL-FREE 1-877-671-6036
View thousands more home plans online at www.familyhandyman.com/homeplans

Plan #718-007D-0089

2,125 total square feet of living area

Duo Atrium For Fantastic Views

Special features

- A cozy porch leads to the vaulted great room with fireplace through the entry which has a walk-in closet and bath
- Large and well-arranged kitchen offers spectacular views from its cantilevered sink cabinetry through a two-story atrium window wall
- Master bedroom boasts a sitting room, large walk-in closet and bath with garden tub overhanging a brightly lit atrium
- 1,047 square feet of optional living area on the lower level featuring a study and family room with walk-in bar and full bath below the kitchen
- 3 bedrooms, 2 1/2 baths, 2-car side entry garage
- Walk-out basement foundation

Price Code C

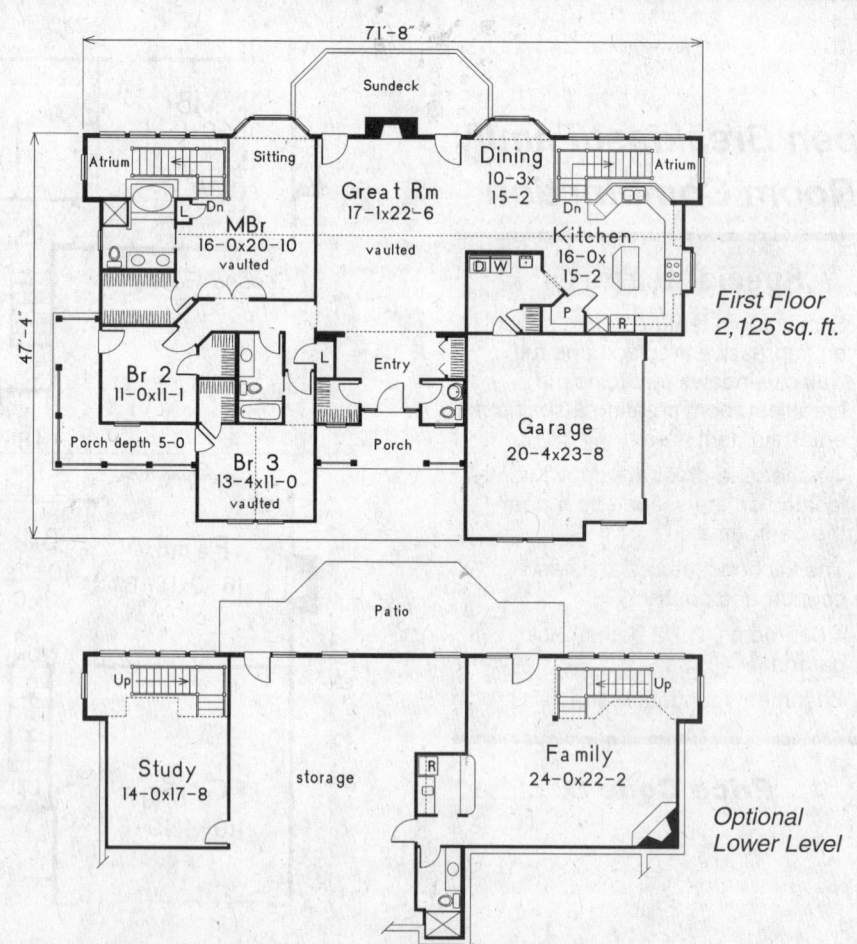

First Floor 2,125 sq. ft.

Optional Lower Level

TO ORDER BLUEPRINTS USE THE FORM ON PAGE 15 OR CALL TOLL-FREE 1-877-671-6036
View thousands more home plans online at www.familyhandyman.com/homeplans

Plan #718-058D-0016

1,558 total square feet of living area

Lovely, Spacious Floor Plan

Special features

- The spacious utility room is located conveniently between the garage and kitchen/dining area
- Bedrooms are separated from the living area by a hallway
- Enormous living area with fireplace and vaulted ceiling opens to the kitchen and dining area
- Master bedroom is enhanced with a large bay window, walk-in closet and private bath
- 3 bedrooms, 2 baths, 2-car garage
- Basement foundation

Price Code B

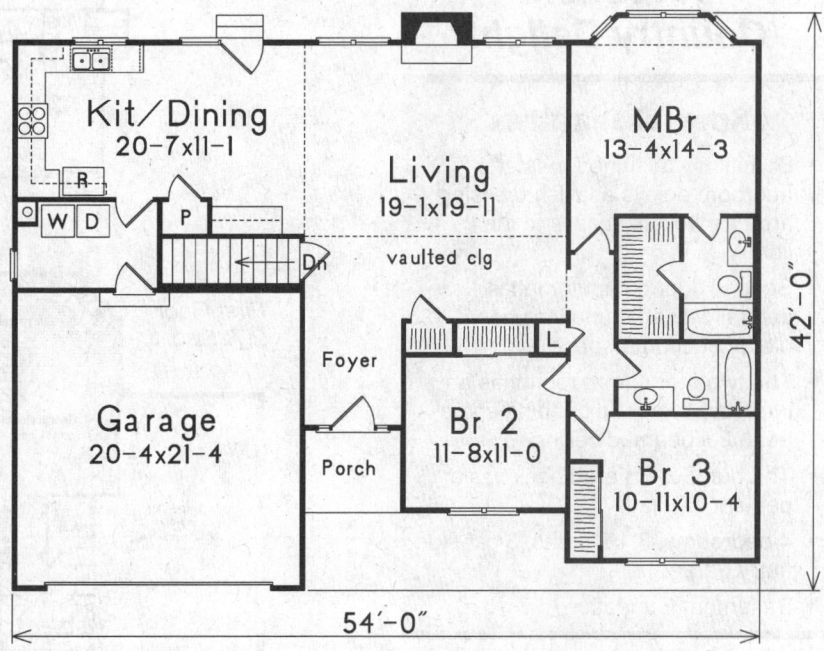

The Family Handyman

Plan #718-065D-0043

3,816 total square feet of living area

A French Country Delight

Special features

- Beautifully designed master bedroom enjoys a lavish dressing area as well as access to the library
- Second floor computer loft is centrally located and includes plenty of counterspace
- The two-story great room has an impressive arched opening and a beautiful beamed ceiling
- The outdoor covered deck has a popular fireplace
- 4 bedrooms, 3 1/2 baths, 3-car side entry garage
- Basement foundation

Price Code F

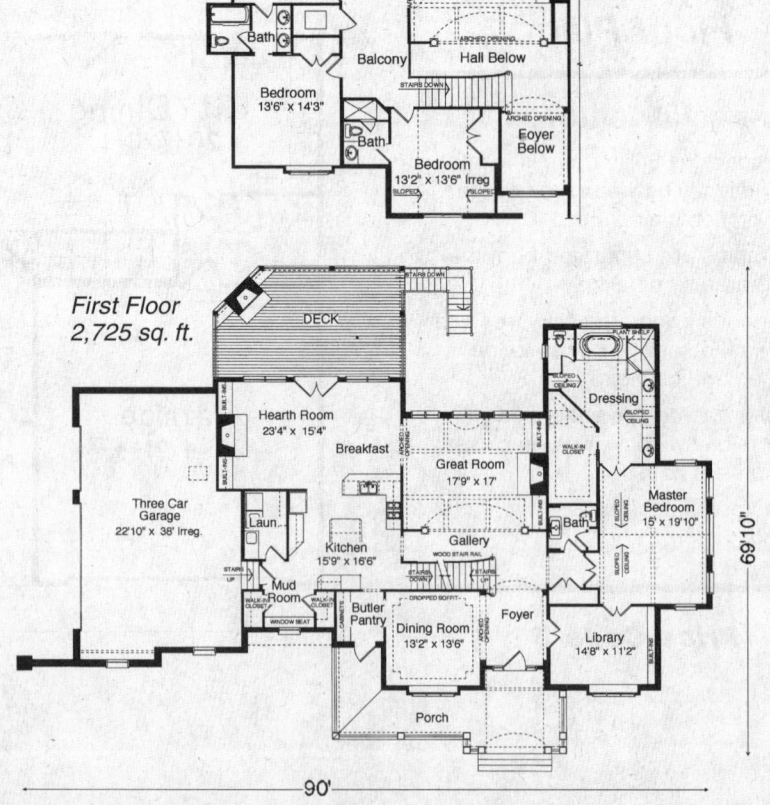

Second Floor 1,091 sq. ft.

First Floor 2,725 sq. ft.

TO ORDER BLUEPRINTS USE THE FORM ON PAGE 15 OR CALL TOLL-FREE 1-877-671-6036
View thousands more home plans online at www.familyhandyman.com/homeplans

Plan #718-037D-0002

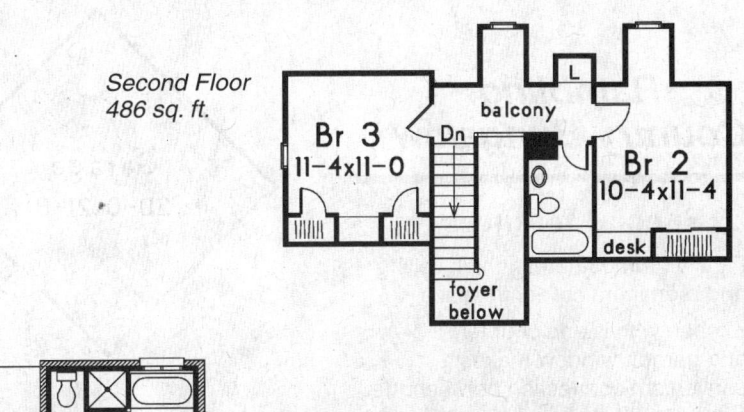

1,816 total square feet of living area

English Cottage With Modern Amenities

Special features

- The living room features a two-way fireplace with nearby window seat
- Wrap-around dining room windows create a sunroom appearance
- Master bedroom has abundant closet and storage
- Rear dormers, closets and desk areas create an interesting and functional second floor
- 3 bedrooms, 2 1/2 baths, 2-car detached garage
- Slab foundation, drawings also include crawl space foundation

Price Code C

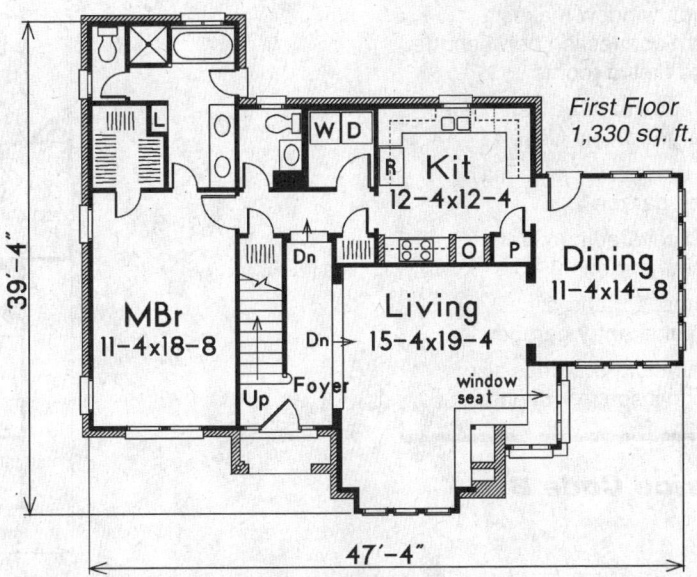

TO ORDER BLUEPRINTS USE THE FORM ON PAGE 15 OR CALL TOLL-FREE 1-877-671-6036

View thousands more home plans online at www.familyhandyman.com/homeplans

Plan #718-040D-0003

1,475 total square feet of living area

Rambling Country Bungalow

Special features

- Family room features a high ceiling and prominent corner fireplace
- Kitchen with island counter and garden window makes a convenient connection between the family and dining rooms
- Hallway leads to three bedrooms all with large walk-in closets
- Covered breezeway joins main house and garage
- Full-width covered porch entry lends a country touch
- 3 bedrooms, 2 baths, 2-car detached side entry garage
- Slab foundation, drawings also include crawl space foundation

Price Code B

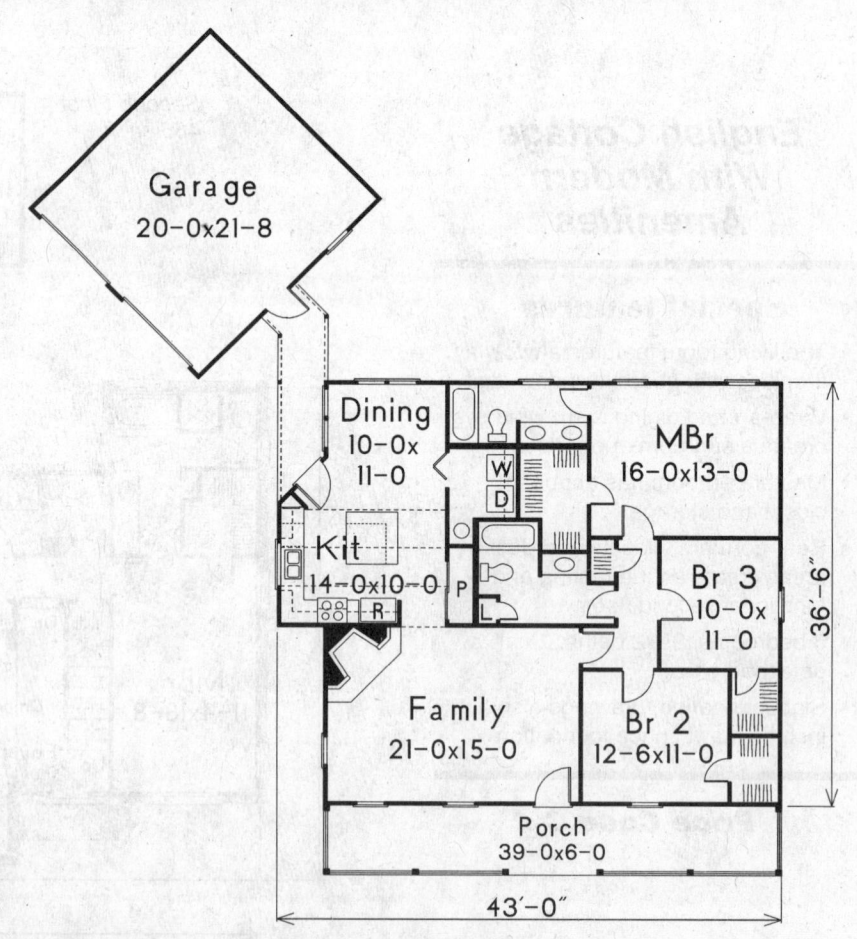

TO ORDER BLUEPRINTS USE THE FORM ON PAGE 15 OR CALL TOLL-FREE 1-877-671-6036
View thousands more home plans online at www.familyhandyman.com/homeplans

Plan #718-062D-0059

1,588 total square feet of living area

Country Accents Make This Home

Special features

- Master bedroom is located on the first floor for convenience
- Cozy great room has a fireplace
- Dining room has access to both the front and rear porches
- Two secondary bedrooms and a bath complete the second floor
- 3 bedrooms, 2 1/2 baths
- Basement or crawl space foundation, please specify when ordering

Price Code B

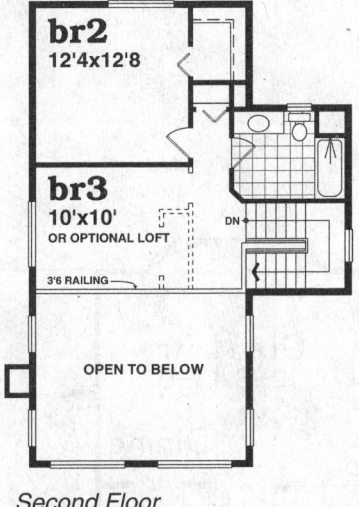

Second Floor 576 sq. ft.

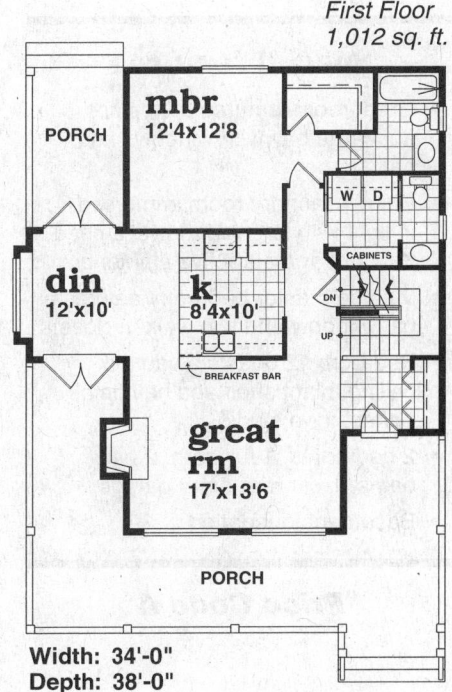

First Floor 1,012 sq. ft.

Width: 34'-0"
Depth: 38'-0"

TO ORDER BLUEPRINTS USE THE FORM ON PAGE 15 OR CALL TOLL-FREE 1-877-671-6036
View thousands more home plans online at www.familyhandyman.com/homeplans

Plan #718-007D-0032

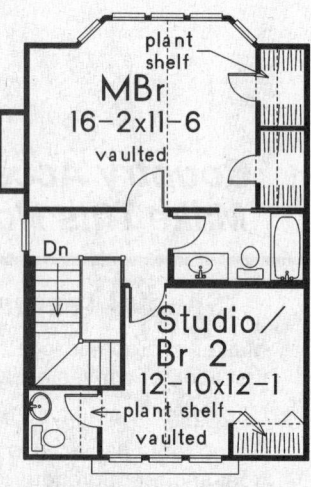

1,294 total square feet of living area

Trendsetting Appeal For A Narrow Lot

Special features

- Great room features a fireplace and large bay with windows and patio doors
- Enjoy a laundry room immersed in light with large windows, arched transom and attractive planter box
- Vaulted master bedroom features a bay window and two walk-in closets
- Bedroom #2 boasts a vaulted ceiling, plant shelf and half bath, perfect for a studio
- 2 bedrooms, 1 full bath, 2 half baths, 1-car rear entry garage
- Basement foundation

Price Code A

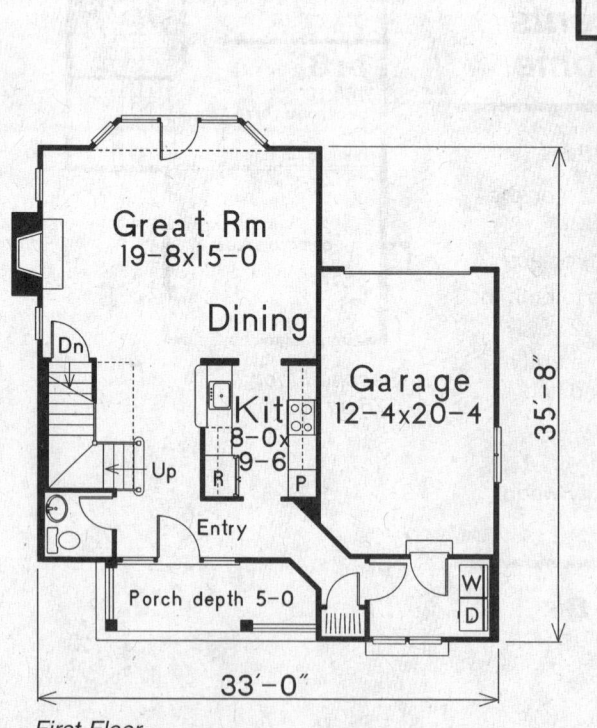

Second Floor
576 sq. ft.

First Floor
718 sq. ft.

Plan #718-053D-0001

1,582 total square feet of living area

Trim Colonial For Practical Living

Special features

- Conservative layout gives privacy to living and dining areas
- Large fireplace and windows enhance the living area
- Rear door in garage is convenient to the garden and kitchen
- Full front porch adds charm
- Dormers add light to the foyer and bedrooms
- 3 bedrooms, 2 1/2 baths, 1-car garage
- Slab foundation, drawings also include crawl space foundation

Price Code B

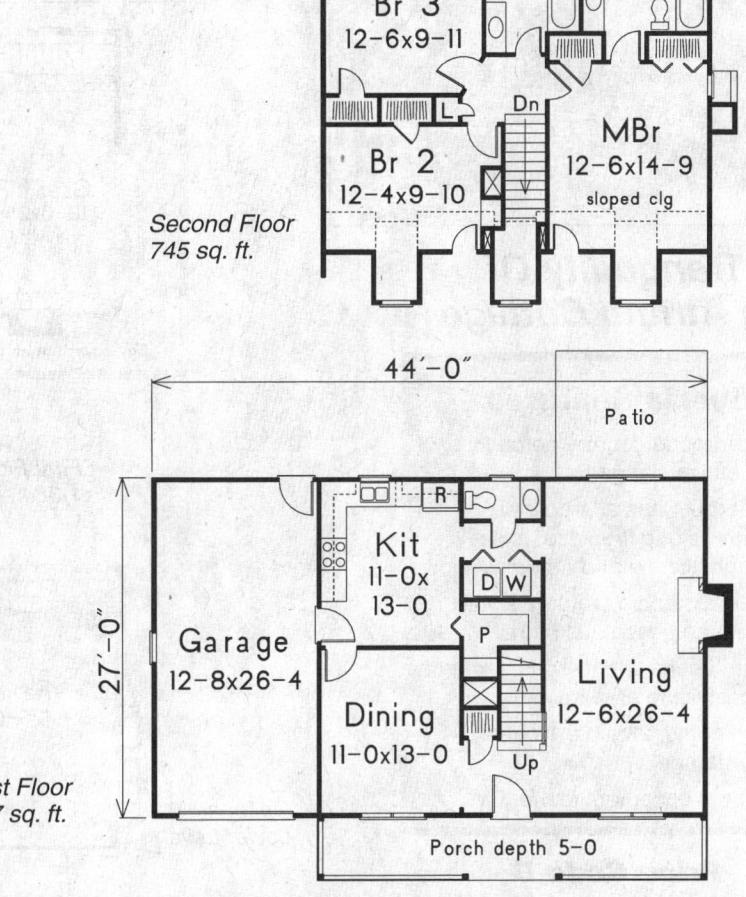

Second Floor 745 sq. ft.

First Floor 837 sq. ft.

TO ORDER BLUEPRINTS USE THE FORM ON PAGE 15 OR CALL TOLL-FREE 1-877-671-6036
View thousands more home plans online at www.familyhandyman.com/homeplans

Plan #718-007D-0068

1,384 total square feet of living area

Rear View

Tranquility Of An Atrium Cottage

Special features

- Wrap-around country porch for peaceful evenings
- Great room has a large bay window, stone fireplace, pass-through kitchen and atrium window
- Master bedroom features a walk-in closet and a fabulous bath
- Atrium opens to 611 square feet of optional living area below
- 2 bedrooms, 2 baths, 1-car side entry garage
- Walk-out basement foundation

Price Code B

First Floor 1,384 sq. ft.

Optional Lower Level

176 **TO ORDER BLUEPRINTS USE THE FORM ON PAGE 15 OR CALL TOLL-FREE 1-877-671-6036**
View thousands more home plans online at www.familyhandyman.com/homeplans

Plan #718-037D-0007

2,282 total square feet of living area

Open Format For Easy Living

Special features

- Living and dining rooms combine to create a large, convenient entertaining area that includes a fireplace
- Comfortable veranda allows access from secondary bedrooms
- Second floor game room overlooks foyer and includes a full bath
- Kitchen and breakfast areas are surrounded by mullioned windows
- 3 bedrooms, 3 baths, 2-car detached garage
- Slab foundation, drawings also include crawl space foundation

Price Code D

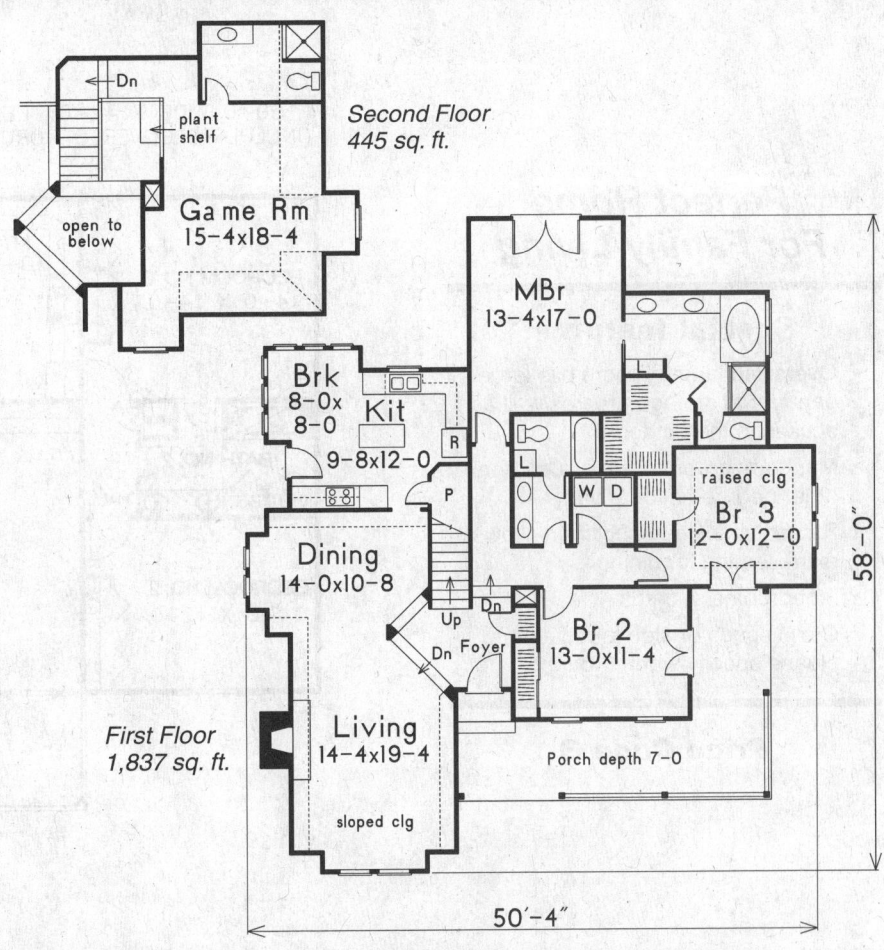

TO ORDER BLUEPRINTS USE THE FORM ON PAGE 15 OR CALL TOLL-FREE 1-877-671-6036
View thousands more home plans online at www.familyhandyman.com/homeplans

Plan #718-028D-0006

1,700 total square feet of living area

Perfect Home For Family Living

Special features

- Oversized laundry room has large pantry and storage area as well as access to the outdoors
- Master bedroom is separated from other bedrooms for privacy
- Raised snack bar in kitchen allows extra seating for dining
- 3 bedrooms, 2 baths
- Crawl space or slab foundation, please specify when ordering

Price Code B

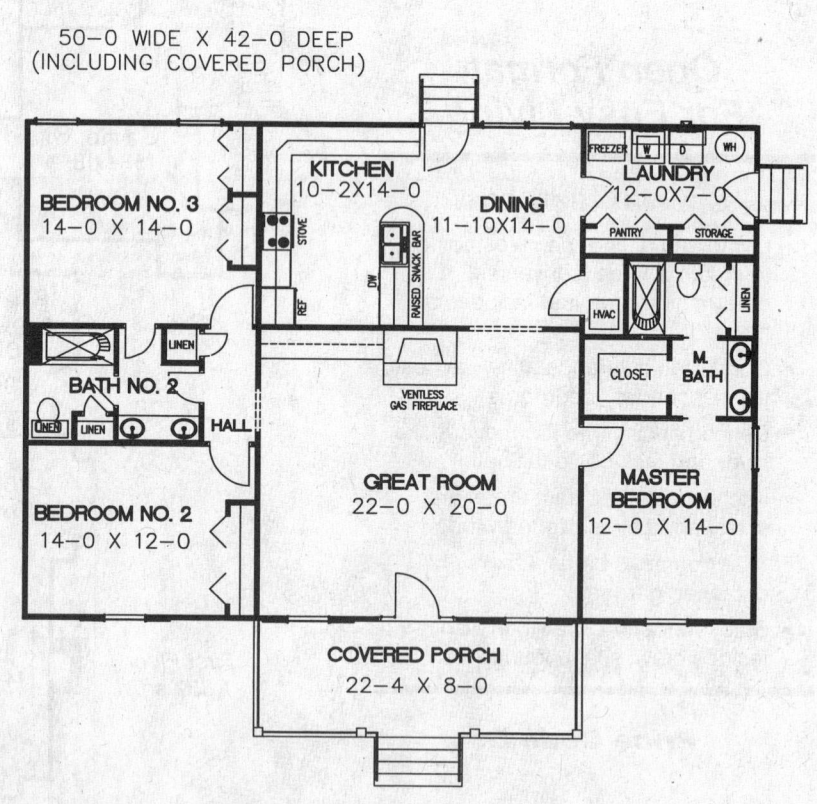

Plan #718-055D-0016

2,698 total square feet of living area

Cozy Covered Porches

Special features

- Great room feels spacious with a vaulted ceiling and windows overlooking the covered porch
- Master bath has a glass shower and whirlpool tub
- Laundry area includes counterspace and a sink
- 4 bedrooms, 3 baths, 2-car side entry garage
- Crawl space or slab foundation, please specify when ordering

Price Code E

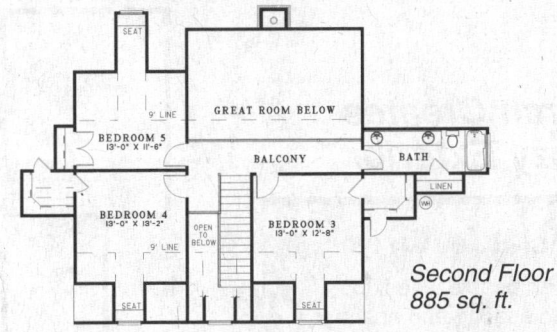

Second Floor 885 sq. ft.

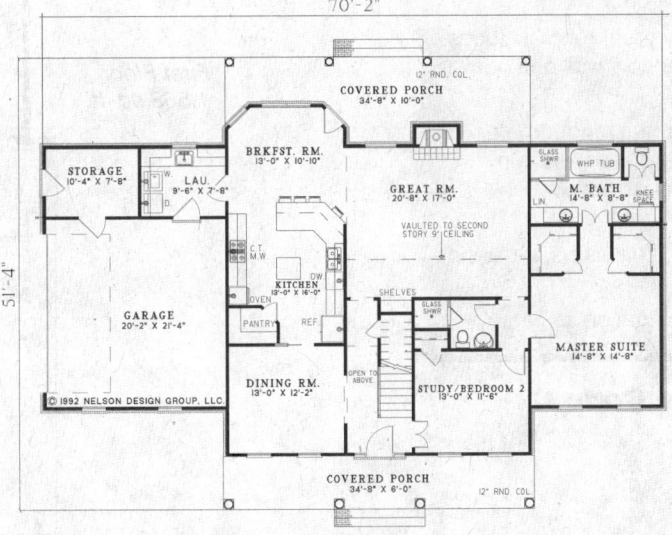

First Floor 1,813 sq. ft.

TO ORDER BLUEPRINTS USE THE FORM ON PAGE 15 OR CALL TOLL-FREE 1-877-671-6036
View thousands more home plans online at www.familyhandyman.com/homeplans

Plan #718-051D-0011

2,155 total square feet of living area

Porch Creates Cozy Exterior

Special features

- The kitchen boasts a cooktop island with seating and opens to the nook which features access to the screened porch
- The two-story great room includes an elegant window wall and fireplace
- The spacious master bedroom features a tray ceiling, walk-in closet and private bath with a relaxing whirlpool tub
- 4 bedrooms, 2 1/2 baths, 2-car side entry garage
- Basement foundation

Price Code C

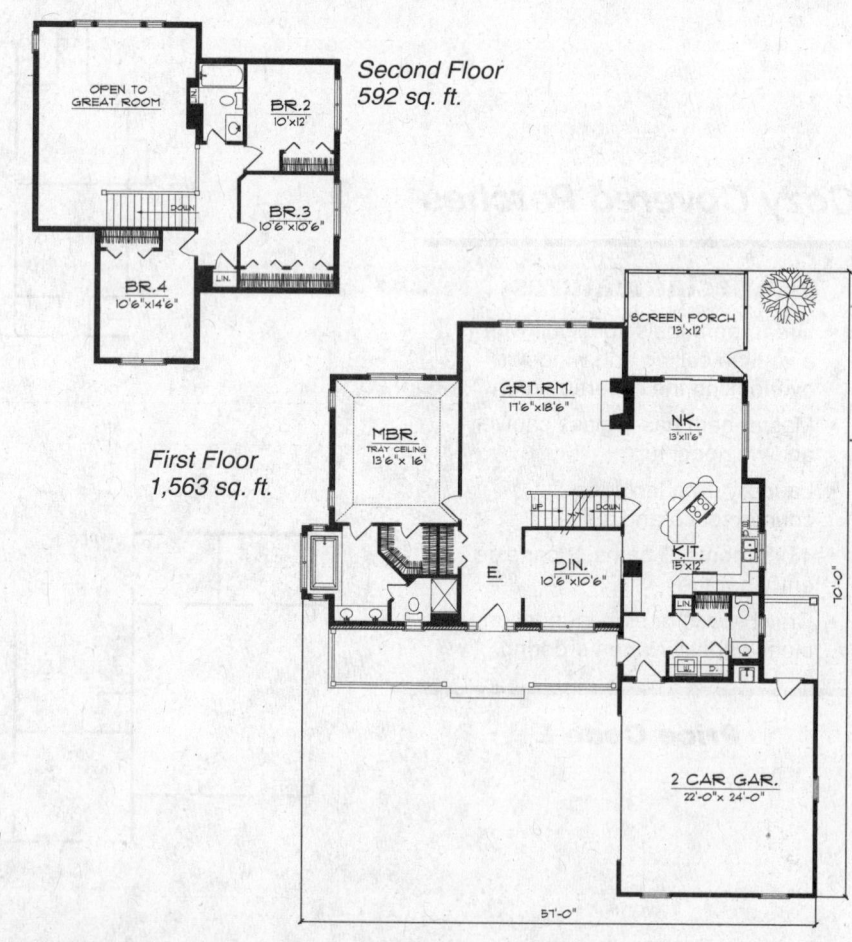

Second Floor 592 sq. ft.

First Floor 1,563 sq. ft.

TO ORDER BLUEPRINTS USE THE FORM ON PAGE 15 OR CALL TOLL-FREE 1-877-671-6036
View thousands more home plans online at www.familyhandyman.com/HOMEPLANS

Plan #718-058D-0038

1,680 total square feet of living area

Open Floor Plan With Extra Amenities

Special features

- Compact and efficient layout in an affordable package
- Second floor has three bedrooms all with oversized closets
- All bedrooms are on the second floor for privacy
- 3 bedrooms, 2 1/2 baths, 2-car garage
- Basement foundation

Price Code B

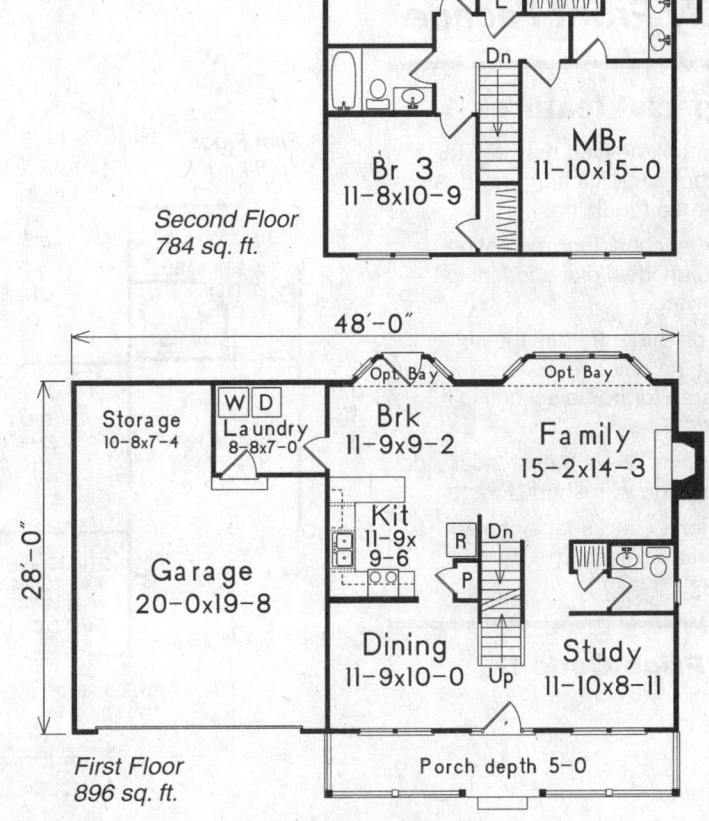

TO ORDER BLUEPRINTS USE THE FORM ON PAGE 15 OR CALL TOLL-FREE 1-877-671-6036
View thousands more home plans online at www.familyhandyman.com/HOMEPLANS

Plan #718-067D-0008

2,327 total square feet of living area

Stately Front Facade

Special features

- Bayed nook nestled between the great room and kitchen provides ample area for dining
- Vaulted second floor recreation room is an ideal place for casual family living
- Room off the entry has the ability to become an office, guest bedroom or an area for home schooling if needed
- 4 bedrooms, 2 1/2 baths, 2-car side entry garage with shop/storage
- Basement, crawl space or slab foundation, please specify when ordering

Price Code D

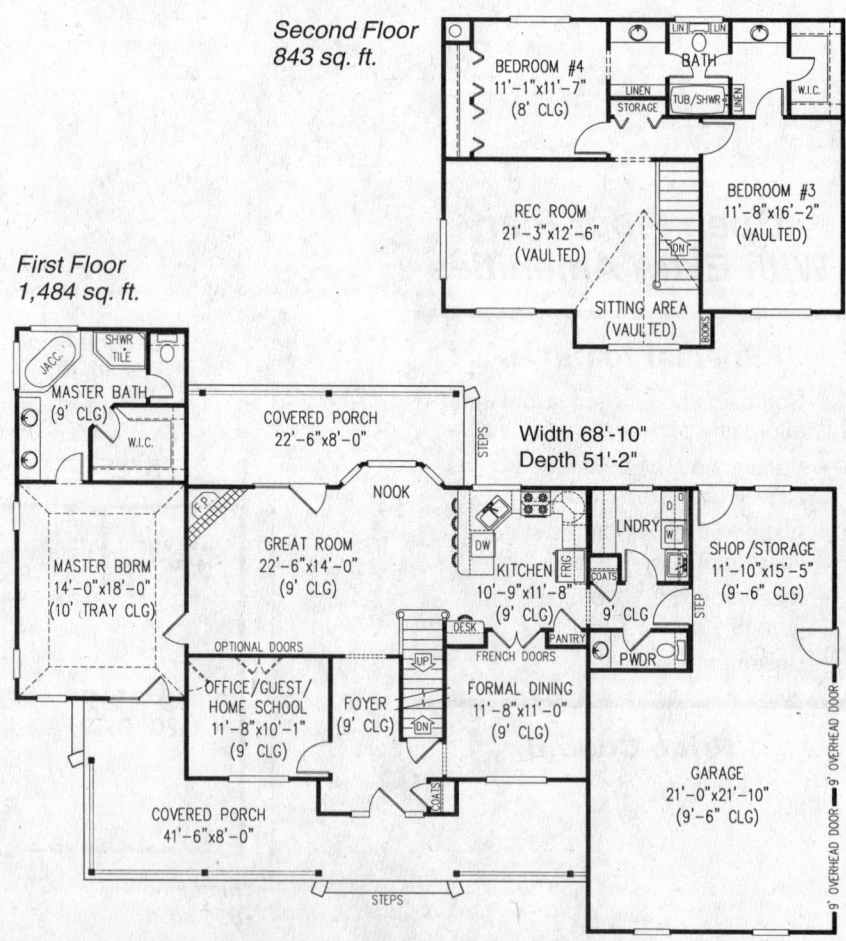

Second Floor 843 sq. ft.
First Floor 1,484 sq. ft.
Width 68'-10"
Depth 51'-2"

TO ORDER BLUEPRINTS USE THE FORM ON PAGE 15 OR CALL TOLL-FREE 1-877-671-6036
View thousands more home plans online at www.familyhandyman.com/HOMEPLANS

Plan #718-007D-0112

1,062 total square feet of living area

Excellent Home For A Small Family

Special features

- Handsome appeal created by triple-gable facade
- An efficient U-shaped kitchen features a snack bar and breakfast room and is open to living room with bay window
- Both the master bedroom, with its own private bath, and bedroom #2/study enjoy access to rear patio
- 3 bedrooms, 2 baths, 2-car garage
- Basement foundation

Price Code AA

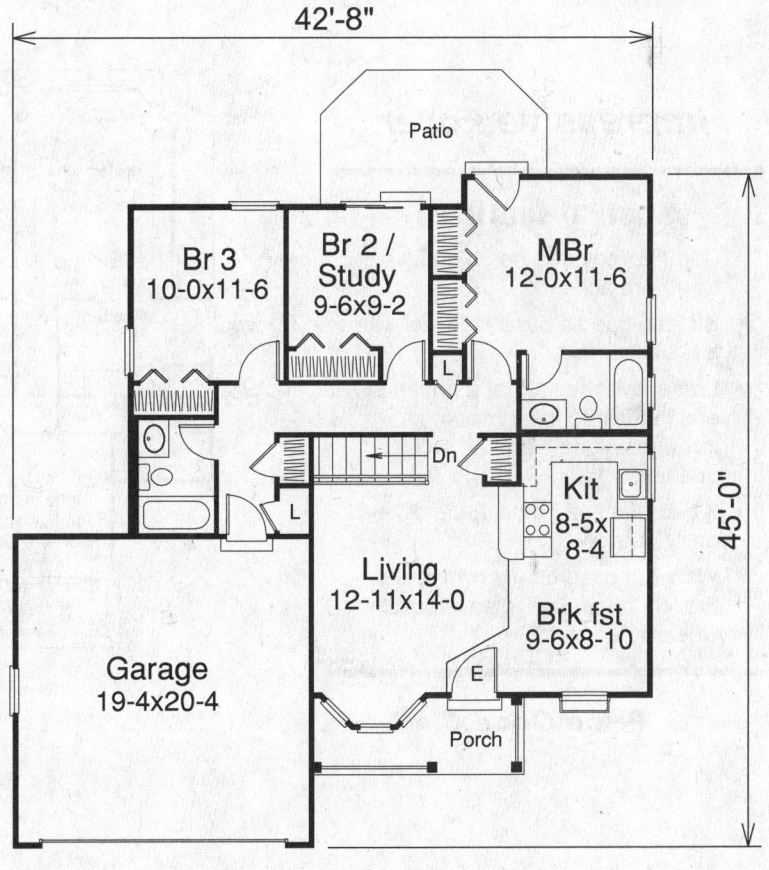

TO ORDER BLUEPRINTS USE THE FORM ON PAGE 15 OR CALL TOLL-FREE 1-877-671-6036
View thousands more home plans online at www.familyhandyman.com/homeplans

Plan #718-035D-0032

1,856 total square feet of living area

Impressive Foyer

Special features

- Beautiful covered porch creates a Southern accent
- Kitchen has an organized feel with lots of cabinetry
- Large foyer has a grand entrance and leads into the family room through columns and an arched opening
- 3 bedrooms, 2 baths, 2-car side entry garage
- Walk-out basement, crawl space or slab foundation, please specify when ordering

Price Code C

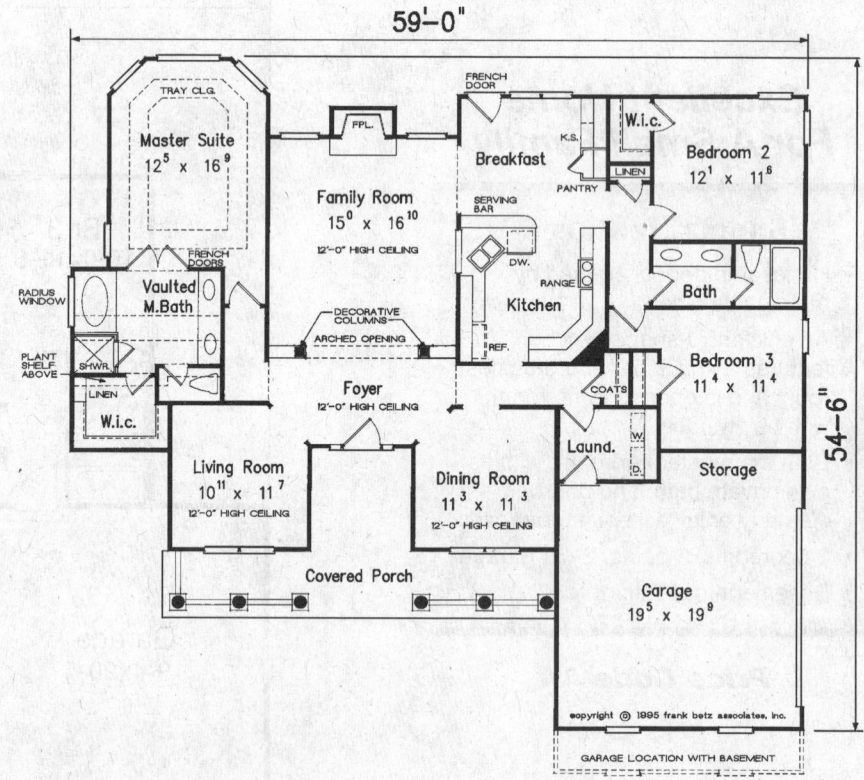

TO ORDER BLUEPRINTS USE THE FORM ON PAGE 15 OR CALL TOLL-FREE 1-877-671-6036
View thousands more home plans online at www.familyhandyman.com/HOMEPLANS

Plan #718-043D-0003

1,890 total square feet of living area

Formal Living And Dining Rooms

Special features

- Inviting covered porch
- Vaulted ceilings in the living, dining and family rooms
- Kitchen is open to the family room and nook
- Large walk-in pantry in the kitchen
- Arch accented master bath has a spa tub, double sinks and walk-in closet
- 3 bedrooms, 2 baths, 2-car garage
- Crawl space foundation

Price Code C

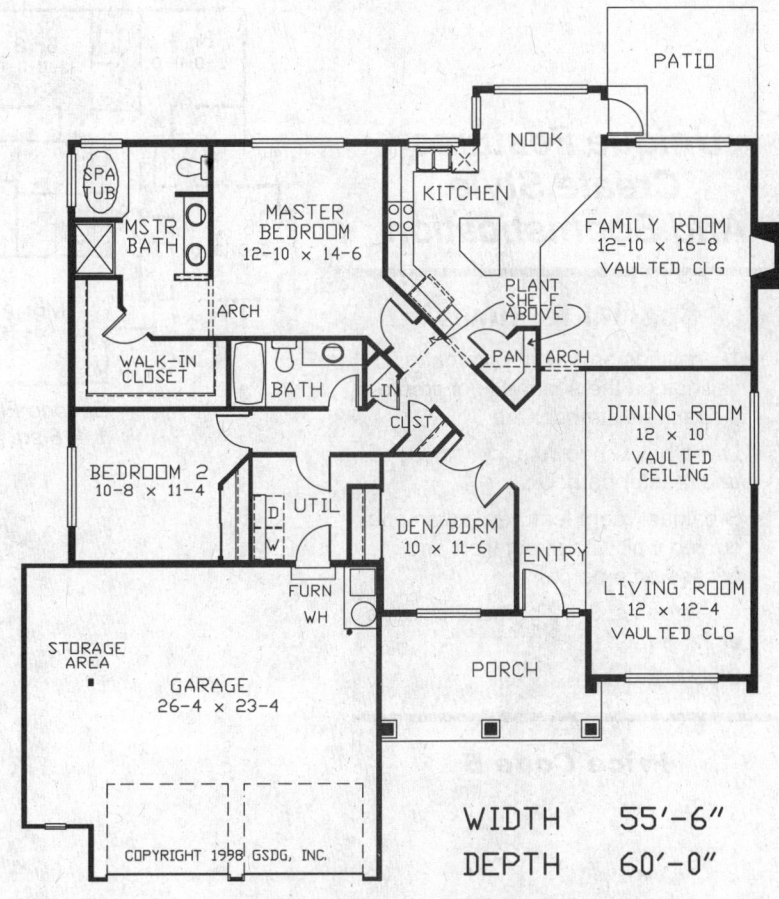

WIDTH 55'-6"
DEPTH 60'-0"

TO ORDER BLUEPRINTS USE THE FORM ON PAGE 15 OR CALL TOLL-FREE 1-877-671-6036
View thousands more home plans online at www.familyhandyman.com/HOMEPLANS

Plan #718-037D-0015

2,772 total square feet of living area

Unique Features Create Style And Sophistication

Special features

- 10' ceilings on the first floor and 9' ceilings on the second floor create a spacious atmosphere
- Large bay windows accent study and master bath
- Breakfast room features a dramatic curved wall with direct view and access onto porch
- 4 bedrooms, 3 1/2 baths, 2-car side entry garage
- Slab foundation

Price Code E

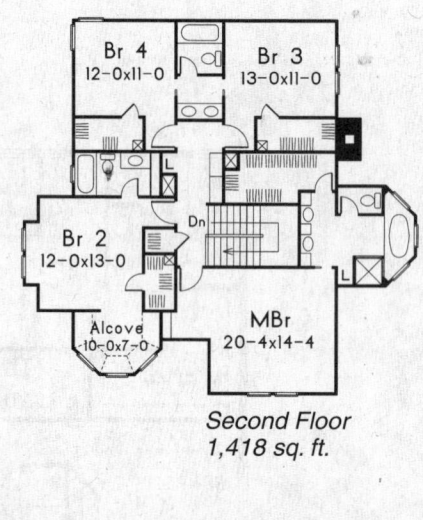

Second Floor 1,418 sq. ft.

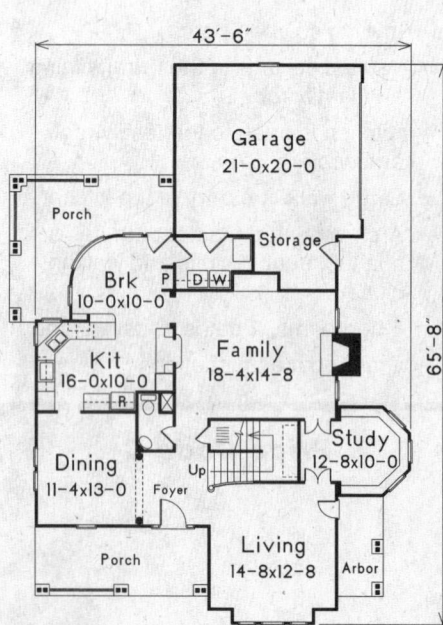

First Floor 1,354 sq. ft.

TO ORDER BLUEPRINTS USE THE FORM ON PAGE 15 OR CALL TOLL-FREE 1-877-671-6036
View thousands more home plans online at www.familyhandyman.com/homeplans

Plan #718-011D-0042

2,561 total square feet of living area

Sophisticated Southern Style

Special features

- Sunny vaulted breakfast nook
- Dormers are a charming touch in the second floor bedrooms
- Columns throughout the first floor help separate rooms while creating a feeling of openness
- Bonus room on the second floor has an additional 232 square feet of living area
- 4 bedrooms, 2 1/2 baths, 2-car side entry garage
- Crawl space foundation

Price Code F

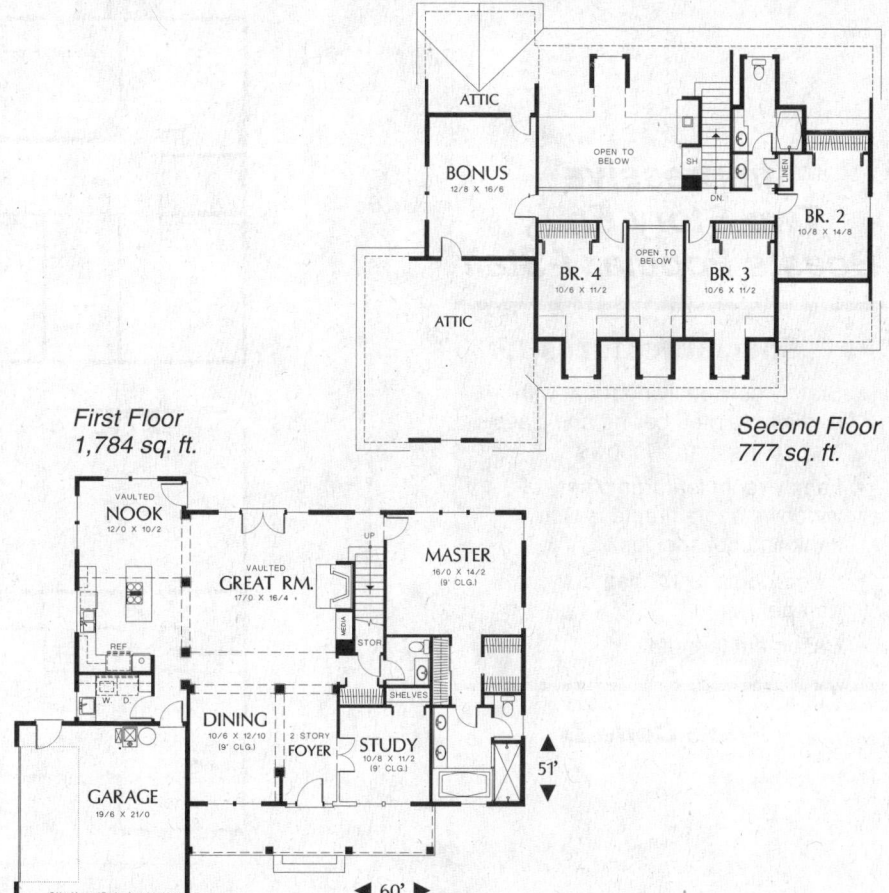

First Floor 1,784 sq. ft.

Second Floor 777 sq. ft.

TO ORDER BLUEPRINTS USE THE FORM ON PAGE 15 OR CALL TOLL-FREE 1-877-671-6036
View thousands more home plans online at www.familyhandyman.com/HOMEPLANS

Plan #718-007D-0005

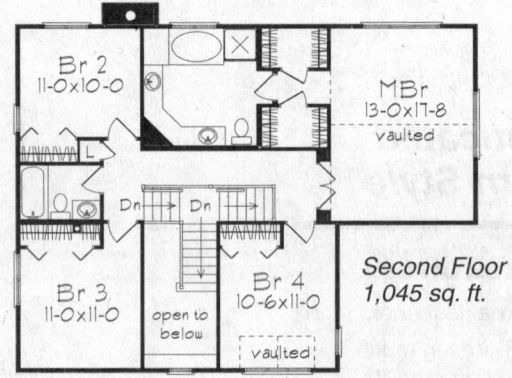

2,336 total square feet of living area

Impressive Two-Story Entry Boasts Popular T-Stair

Special features

- Stately sunken living room with partially vaulted ceiling and classic arched transom windows
- Family room features plenty of windows and a fireplace with flanking bookshelves
- 4 bedrooms, 2 1/2 baths, 2-car garage
- Basement foundation

Price Code D

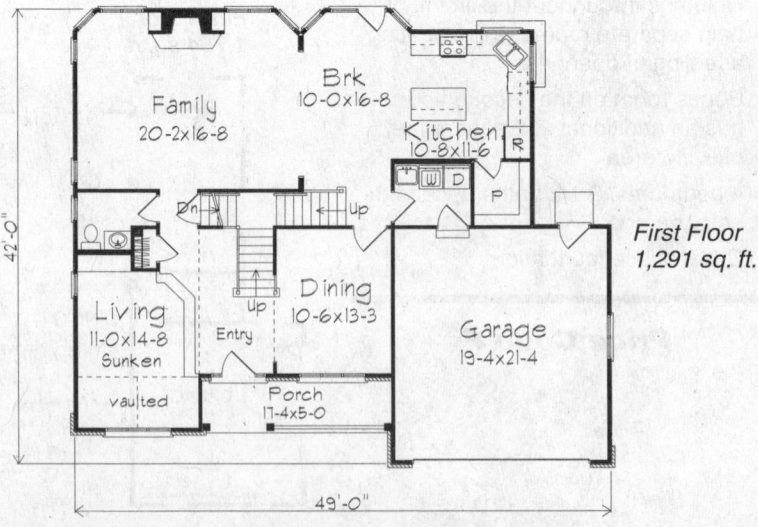

Second Floor 1,045 sq. ft.

First Floor 1,291 sq. ft.

TO ORDER BLUEPRINTS USE THE FORM ON PAGE 15 OR CALL TOLL-FREE 1-877-671-6036
View thousands more home plans online at www.familyhandyman.com/HOMEPLANS

Plan #718-056D-0003

2,272 total square feet of living area

A Cozy Ranch With Rustic Touches

Special features

- 10' ceilings throughout the first floor and 9' ceilings on the second floor
- Lots of storage area on the second floor
- First floor master bedroom has a lovely sitting area with an arched entry
- Second floor bedrooms share a Jack and Jill bath
- 3 bedrooms, 2 1/2 baths, 2-car rear entry garage
- Slab foundation

Price Code G

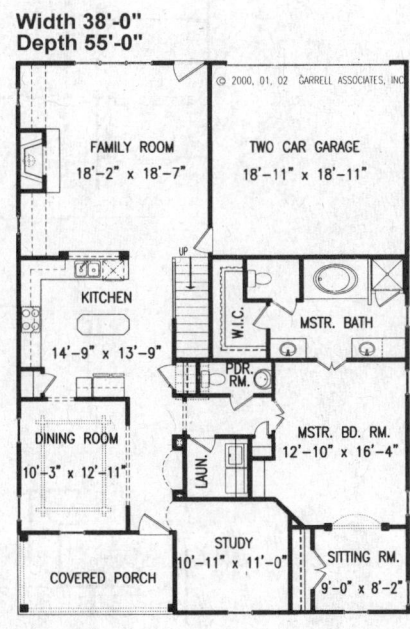

First Floor
1,587 sq. ft.

Width 38'-0"
Depth 55'-0"

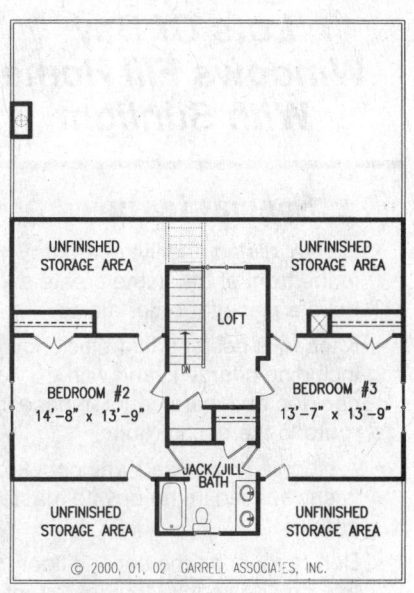

Second Floor
685 sq. ft.

TO ORDER BLUEPRINTS USE THE FORM ON PAGE 15 OR CALL TOLL-FREE 1-877-671-6036
View thousands more home plans online at www.familyhandyman.com/HOMEPLANS

Plan #718-071D-0003

2,890 total square feet of living area

Lots Of Bay Windows Fill Home With Sunlight

Special features

- Formal dining and living rooms in the front of the home create a private place for entertaining
- Kitchen is designed for efficiency including a large island with cooktop and extra counterspace in route to the dining room
- A stunning oversized whirlpool tub is showcased in the private master bath
- Bonus room on the second floor has an additional 240 square feet of living area
- 3 bedrooms, 2 1/2 baths, 3-car side entry garage
- Crawl space foundation

Price Code E

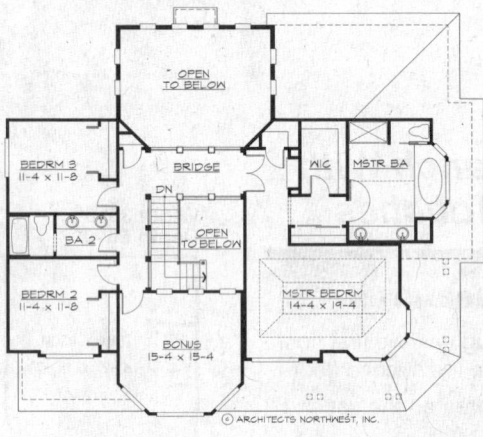

Second Floor
1,260 sq. ft.

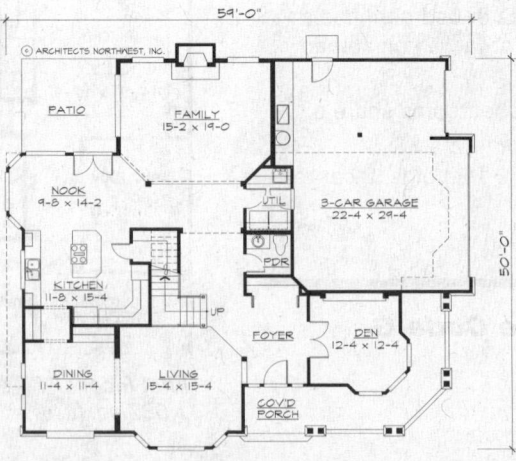

First Floor
1,630 sq. ft.

TO ORDER BLUEPRINTS USE THE FORM ON PAGE 15 OR CALL TOLL-FREE 1-877-671-6036
View thousands more home plans online at www.familyhandyman.com/homeplans

Plan #718-003D-0002

1,676 total square feet of living area

Vaulted Ceilings Add Light And Dimension

Special features

- The living area skylights and large breakfast room with bay window provide plenty of sunlight
- The master bedroom has a walk-in closet and both the secondary bedrooms have large closets
- Vaulted ceilings, plant shelving and a fireplace provide a quality living area
- 3 bedrooms, 2 baths, 2-car garage
- Basement foundation, drawings also include crawl space and slab foundations

Price Code B

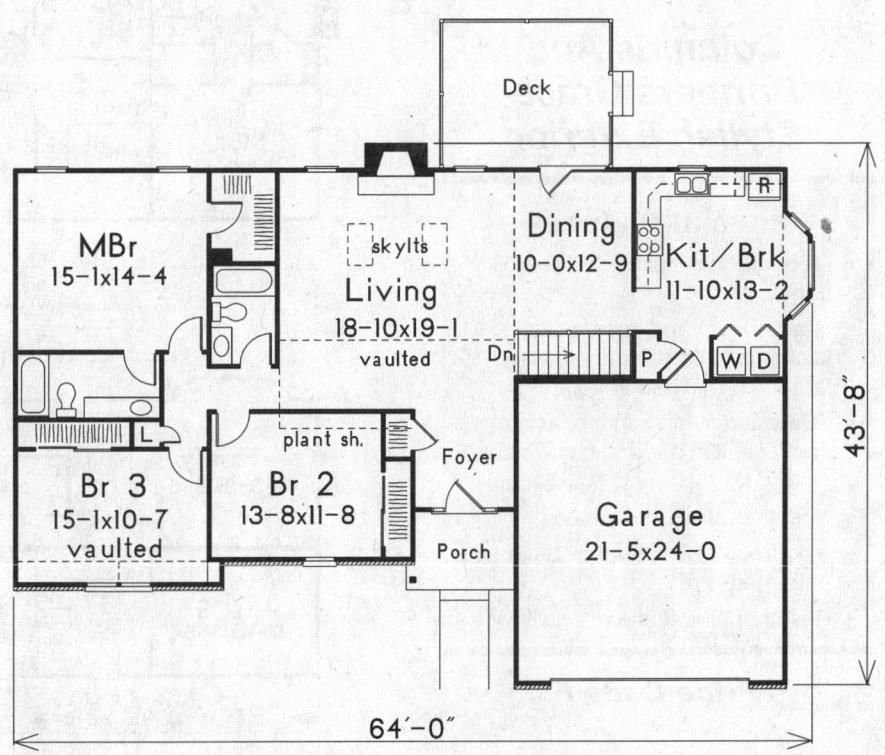

Plan #718-001D-0037

3,216 total square feet of living area

Columns And Dormers Grace Stylish Exterior

Special features

- All bedrooms include private full baths
- Hearth room and combination kitchen/breakfast area create a large informal gathering area
- Oversized family room boasts a fireplace, wet bar and bay window
- Master bedroom has two walk-in closets and a luxurious bath
- 4 bedrooms, 4 1/2 baths, 3-car side entry garage
- Basement foundation

Price Code F

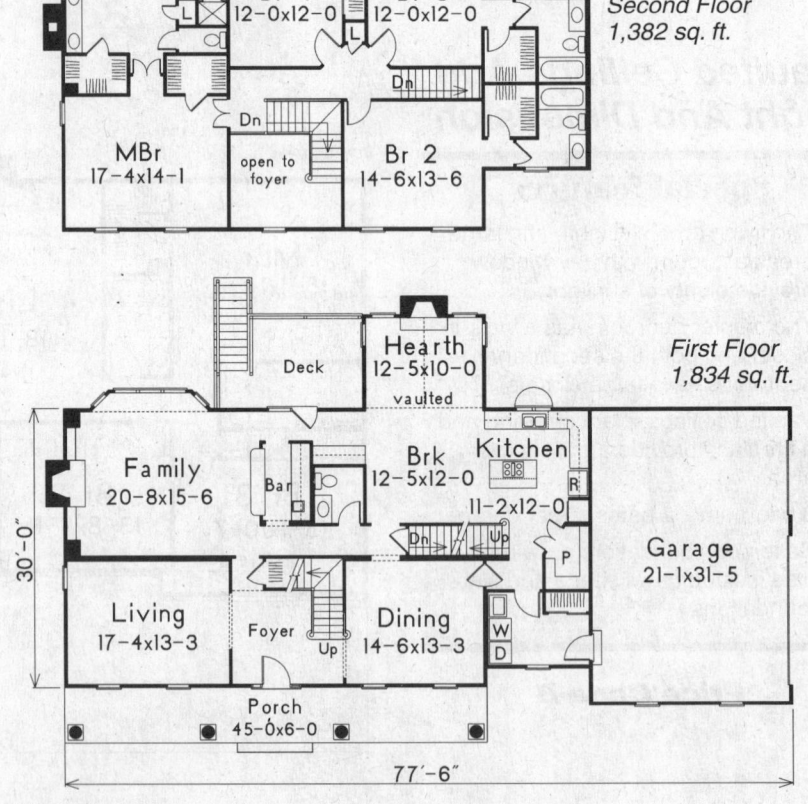

Second Floor 1,382 sq. ft.

First Floor 1,834 sq. ft.

TO ORDER BLUEPRINTS USE THE FORM ON PAGE 15 OR CALL TOLL-FREE 1-877-671-6036
View thousands more home plans online at www.familyhandyman.com/HOMEPLANS

Plan #718-020D-0013

3,012 total square feet of living area

Plenty Of Built-Ins

Special features

- Master bedroom has a sitting area with an entertainment center/library
- Utility room has a sink and includes lots of storage and counterspace
- Future space above garage has an additional 336 square feet of living area
- 4 bedrooms, 3 1/2 baths, 2-car side entry garage
- Crawl space foundation, drawings also include slab and basement foundations

Price Code E

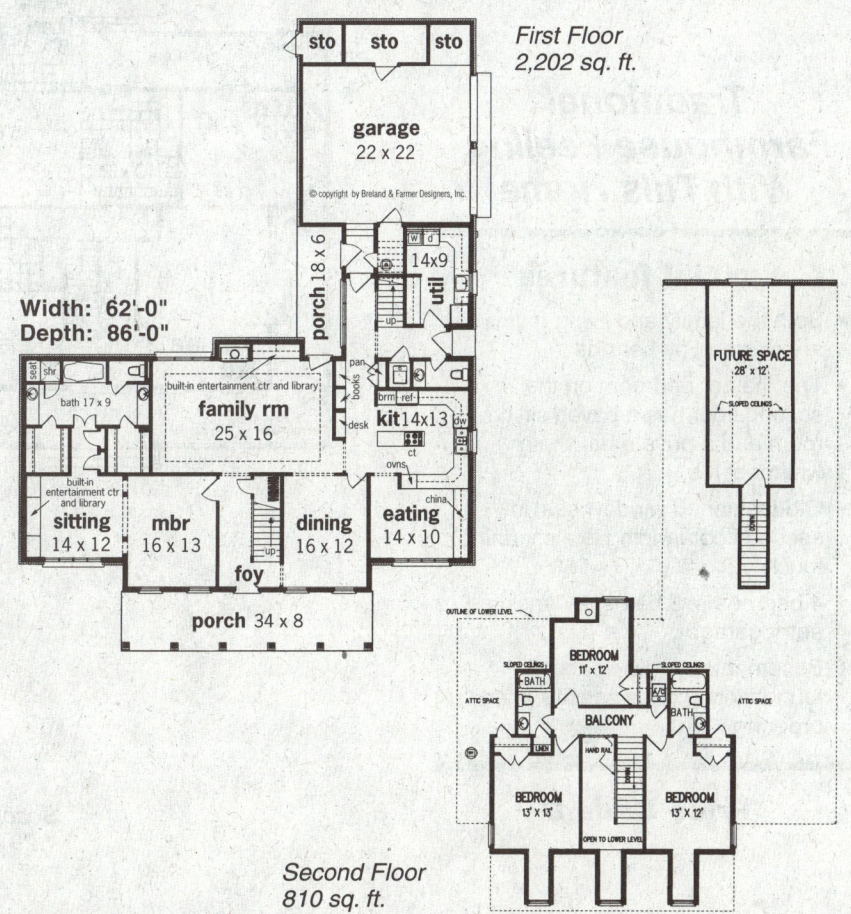

TO ORDER BLUEPRINTS USE THE FORM ON PAGE 15 OR CALL TOLL-FREE 1-877-671-6036
View thousands more home plans online at www.familyhandyman.com/homeplans

Plan #718-062D-0042

2,582 total square feet of living area

Traditional Farmhouse Feeling With This Home

Special features

- Both the family and living rooms are warmed by hearths
- The master bedroom on the second floor has a bayed sitting room and a private bath with whirlpool tub
- Old-fashioned window seat in second floor landing is a charming touch
- 4 bedrooms, 3 baths, 2-car side entry garage
- Basement or crawl space foundation, please specify when ordering

Price Code D

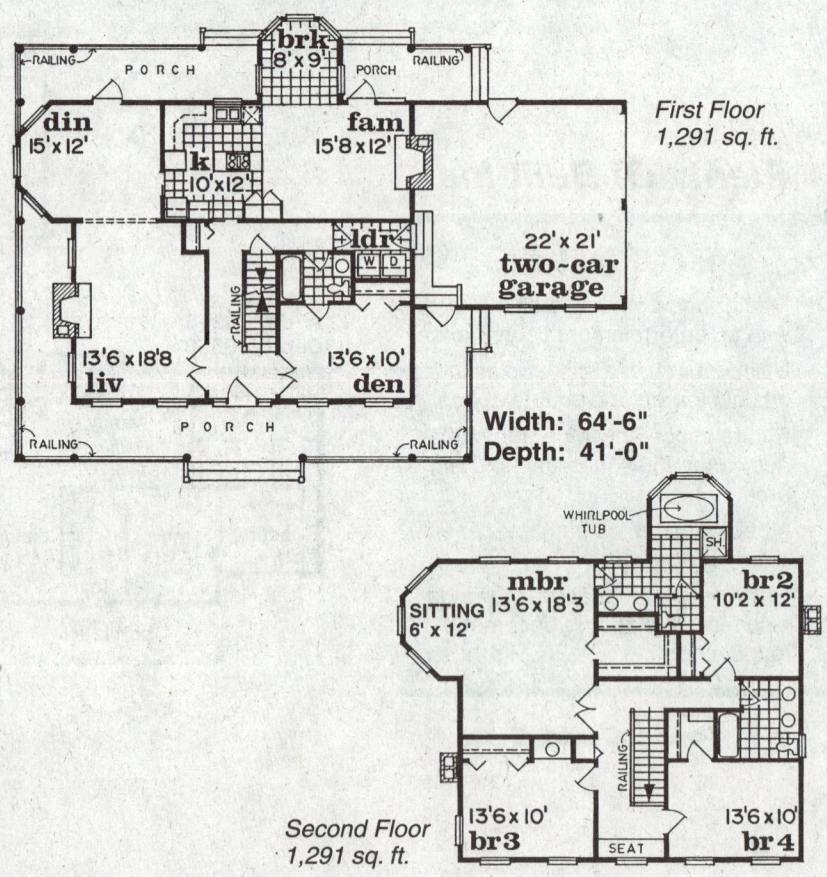

Width: 64'-6"
Depth: 41'-0"

First Floor 1,291 sq. ft.

Second Floor 1,291 sq. ft.

Plan #718-030D-0012

2,143 total square feet of living area

Relaxing Wrap-Around Porch

Special features

- Enter the home into the expansive family room and view the bayed dining area defined by wood columns
- The kitchen includes an island, hutch, extra-large pantry and access to the rear porch
- A study area in a box-bay on the second floor includes built-in bookshelves and a bench with storage
- 4 bedrooms, 3 baths
- Basement, slab or crawl space foundation, please specify when ordering

Price Code C

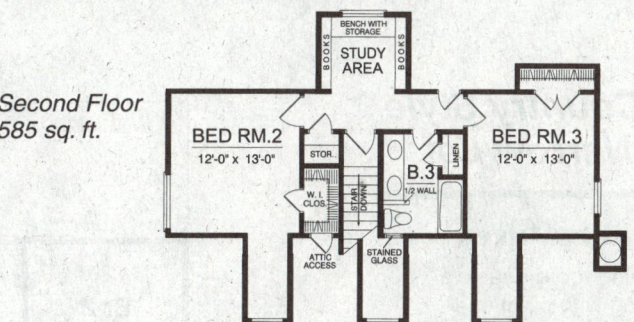

Second Floor 585 sq. ft.

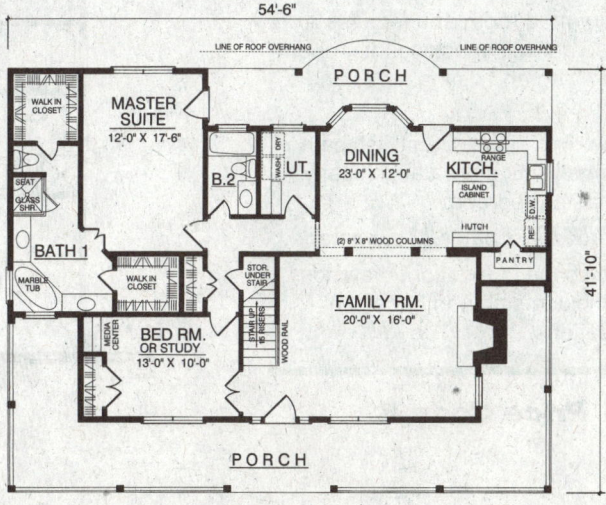

First Floor 1,535 sq. ft.

TO ORDER BLUEPRINTS USE THE FORM ON PAGE 15 OR CALL TOLL-FREE 1-877-671-6036
View thousands more home plans online at www.familyhandyman.com/HOMEPLANS

Plan #718-007D-0162

1,519 total square feet of living area

French Country Style For A Narrow Lot

Special features

- The large living room boasts a vaulted ceiling with plant shelf, fireplace, and opens to the bayed dining area
- The kitchen has an adjoining laundry/mud room and features a vaulted ceiling, snack counter open to the living and dining areas and a built-in pantry
- Two walk-in closets, a stylish bath and small sitting area accompany the master bedroom
- 4 bedrooms, 2 baths, 2-car garage
- Crawl space foundation, drawings also include slab and basement foundations

Price Code B

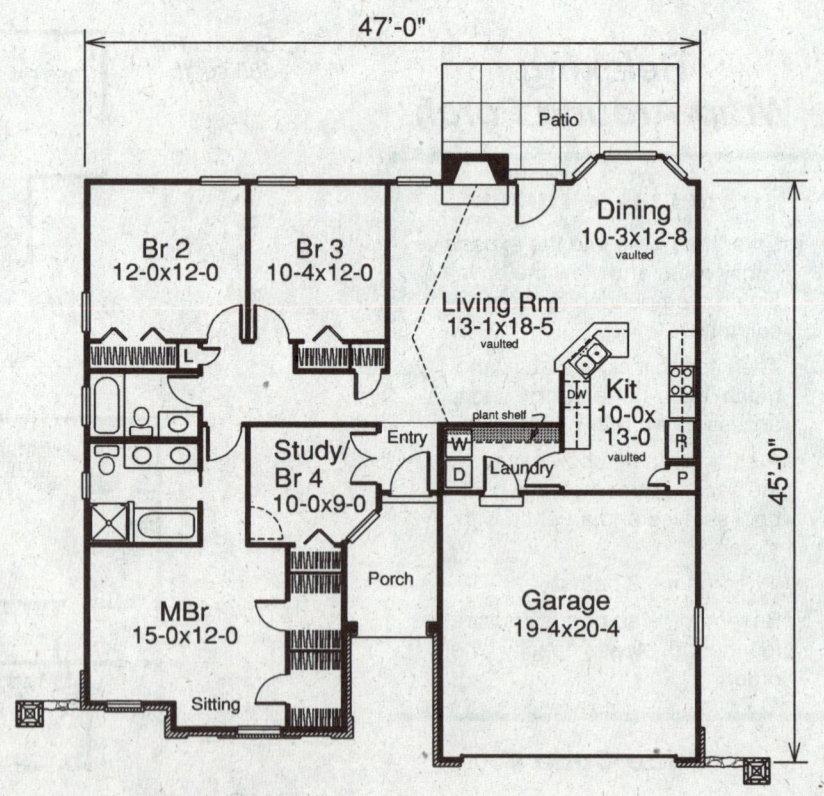

TO ORDER BLUEPRINTS USE THE FORM ON PAGE 15 OR CALL TOLL-FREE 1-877-671-6036
View thousands more home plans online at www.familyhandyman.com/homeplans

Plan #718-053D-0003

1,992 total square feet of living area

Double Bay Window Enhances Front Entry

Special features

- Distinct living, dining and breakfast areas
- Master bedroom boasts a full-end bay window and a cathedral ceiling
- Storage and laundry area are located adjacent to the garage
- Bonus room over the garage for future office or playroom is included in the square footage
- 3 bedrooms, 2 1/2 baths, 2-car garage
- Crawl space foundation, drawings also include basement foundation

Price Code C

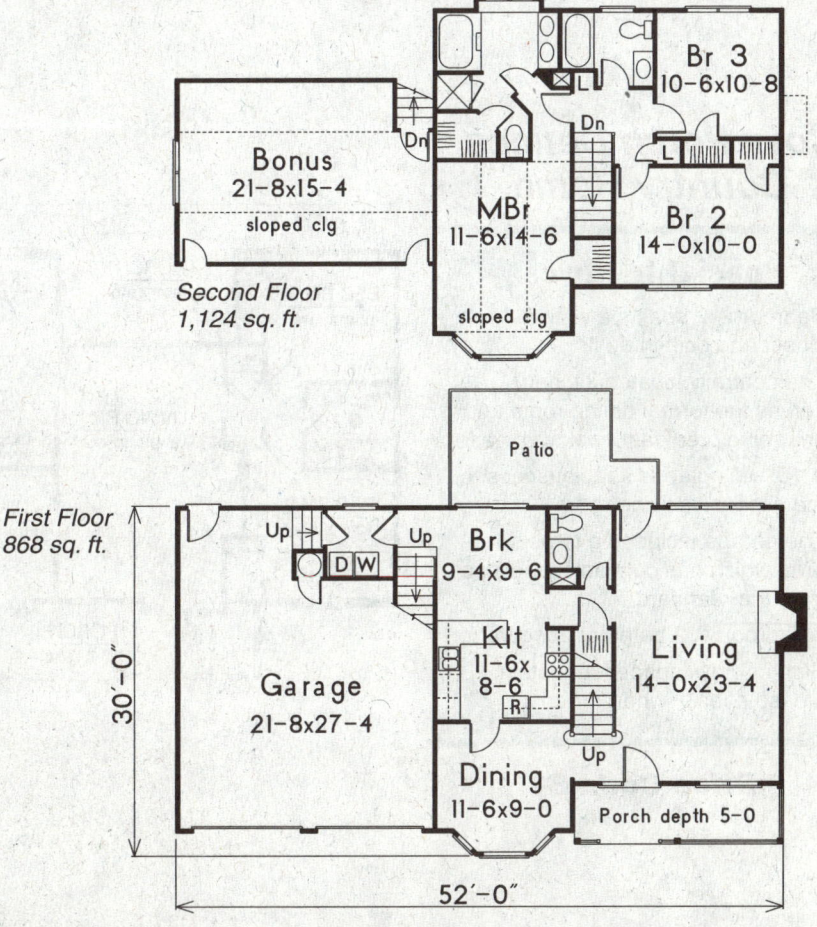

TO ORDER BLUEPRINTS USE THE FORM ON PAGE 15 OR CALL TOLL-FREE 1-877-671-6036
View thousands more home plans online at www.familyhandyman.com/HOMEPLANS

Plan #718-030D-0009

1,772 total square feet of living area

Cozy Porch Defines Country Home

Special features

- Bedroom #2 boasts a walk-in closet and built-in desk
- The centrally located kitchen serves the formal dining room and charming breakfast nook with ease
- A 10' ceiling adds spaciousness to the expansive living room
- The garage includes a large shop area which has convenient access from the rear yard
- 3 bedrooms, 2 baths, 2-car garage
- Slab or crawl space foundation, please specify when ordering

Price Code B

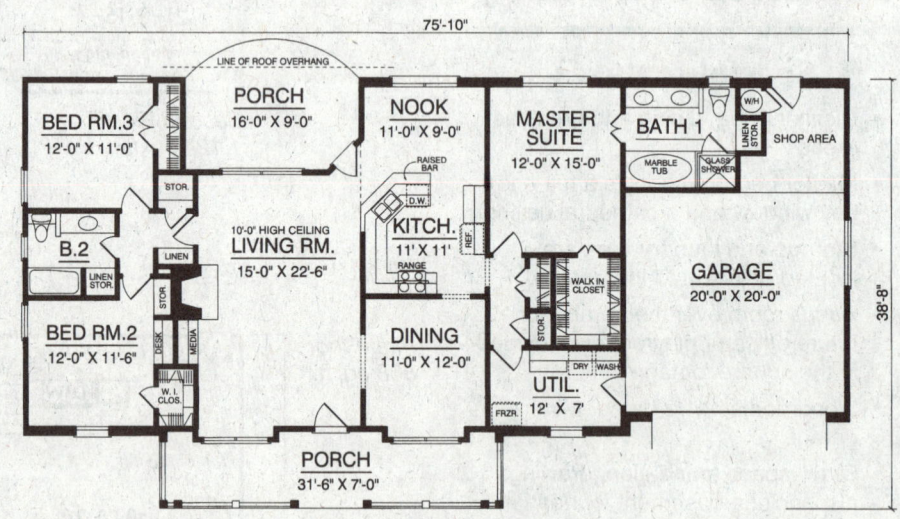

The Family Handyman

Plan #718-007D-0004

2,531 total square feet of living area

Rear View

Exciting Interior

Special features

- Charming porch with dormers leads into vaulted great room with atrium
- Well-designed kitchen and breakfast bar adjoin extra-large laundry/mud room
- Double sinks, tub with window above and plant shelf complete vaulted master bath
- 4 bedrooms, 2 1/2 baths, 2-car side entry garage
- Walk-out basement foundation

Price Code D

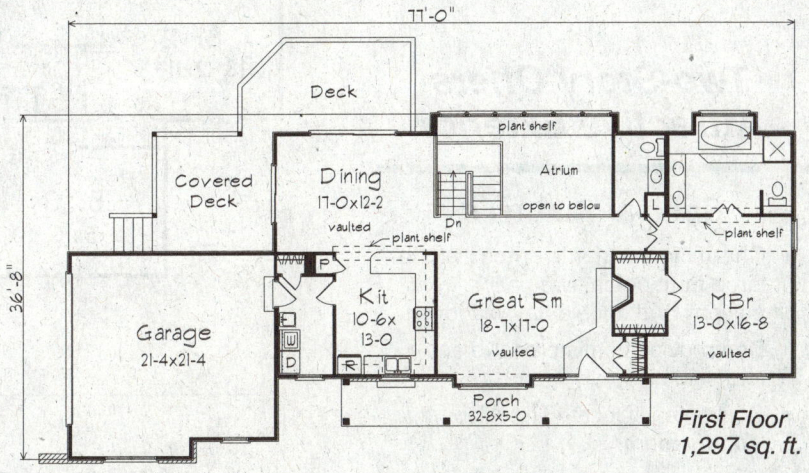
First Floor 1,297 sq. ft.

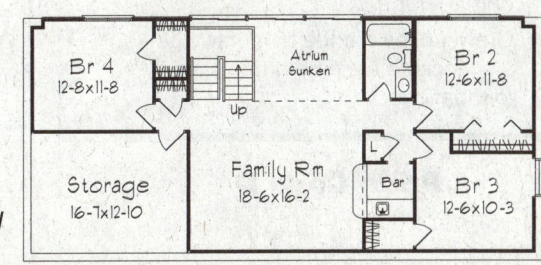
Lower Level 1,234 sq. ft.

TO ORDER BLUEPRINTS USE THE FORM ON PAGE 15 OR CALL TOLL-FREE 1-877-671-6036
View thousands more home plans online at www.familyhandyman.com/HOMEPLANS

Plan #718-001D-0064

2,262 total square feet of living area

Two-Story Offers Attractive Exterior

Special features

- Charming exterior features include large front porch, two patios, front balcony and double bay windows
- Den provides an impressive entry to a sunken family room
- Conveniently located first floor laundry room
- Large master bedroom has a walk-in closet, dressing area and bath
- 3 bedrooms, 2 1/2 baths, 2-car rear entry garage
- Crawl space foundation, drawings also include basement and slab foundations

Price Code D

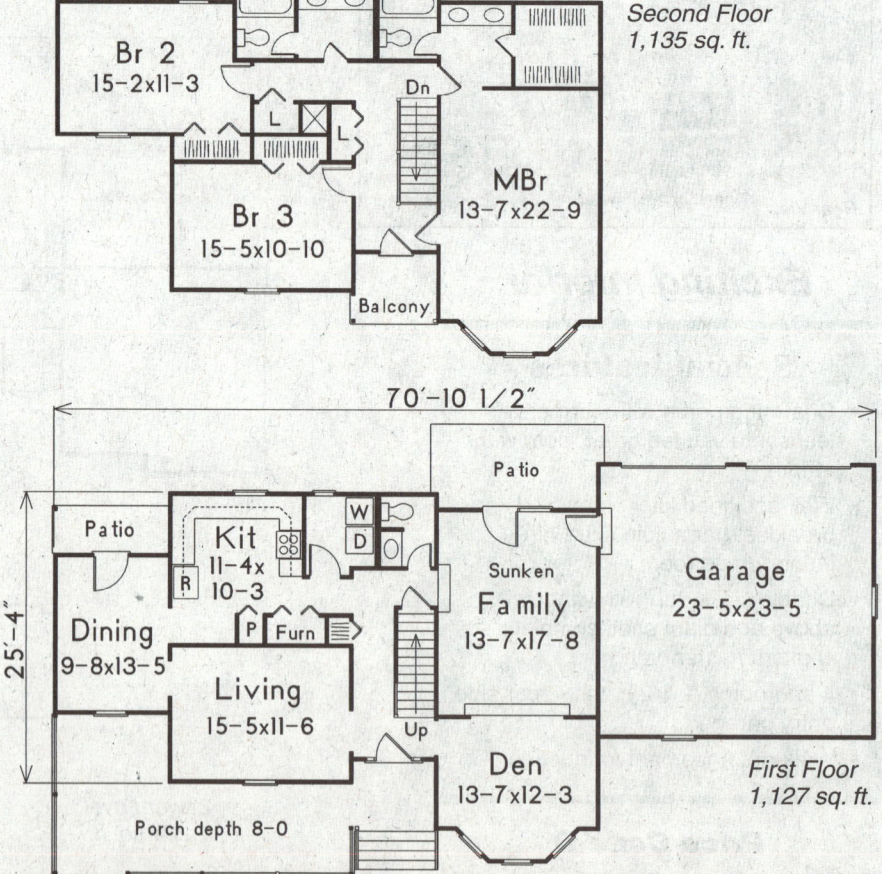

TO ORDER BLUEPRINTS USE THE FORM ON PAGE 15 OR CALL TOLL-FREE 1-877-671-6036
View thousands more home plans online at www.familyhandyman.com/homeplans

Plan #718-007D-0015

2,828 total square feet of living area

Five Bedroom Home Embraces Large Family

Special features

- Popular wrap-around porch gives home country charm
- Secluded, oversized family room with vaulted ceiling and wet bar features many windows
- Any chef would be delighted to cook in this smartly designed kitchen with island and corner windows
- Spectacular master bedroom and bath
- 5 bedrooms, 3 1/2 baths, 2-car side entry garage
- Basement foundation, drawings also include crawl space and slab foundations

Price Code F

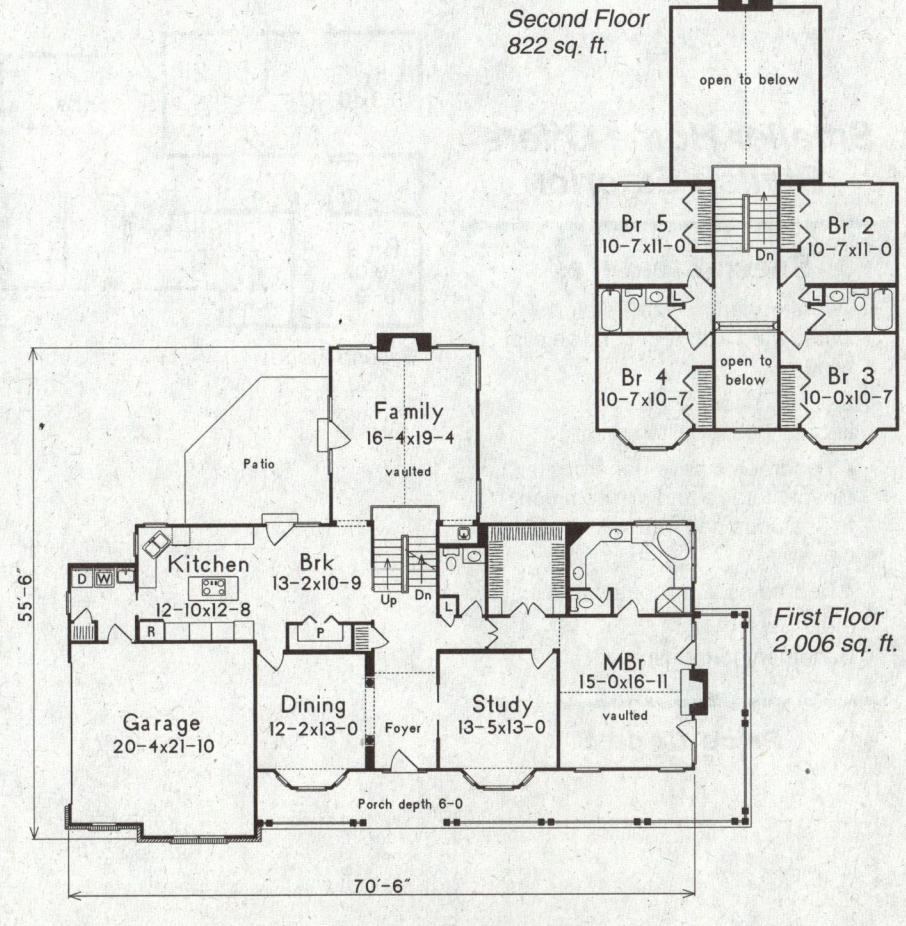

TO ORDER BLUEPRINTS USE THE FORM ON PAGE 15 OR CALL TOLL-FREE 1-877-671-6036
View thousands more home plans online at www.familyhandyman.com/HOMEPLANS

Plan #718-007D-0041

1,700 total square feet of living area

Smaller Home Offers Stylish Exterior

Special features
- Two-story entry with T-stair is illuminated with a decorative oval window
- Skillfully designed U-shaped kitchen has a built-in pantry
- All bedrooms have generous closet storage and are common to spacious hall with walk-in cedar closet
- 4 bedrooms, 2 1/2 baths, 2-car side entry garage
- Basement foundation

Price Code B

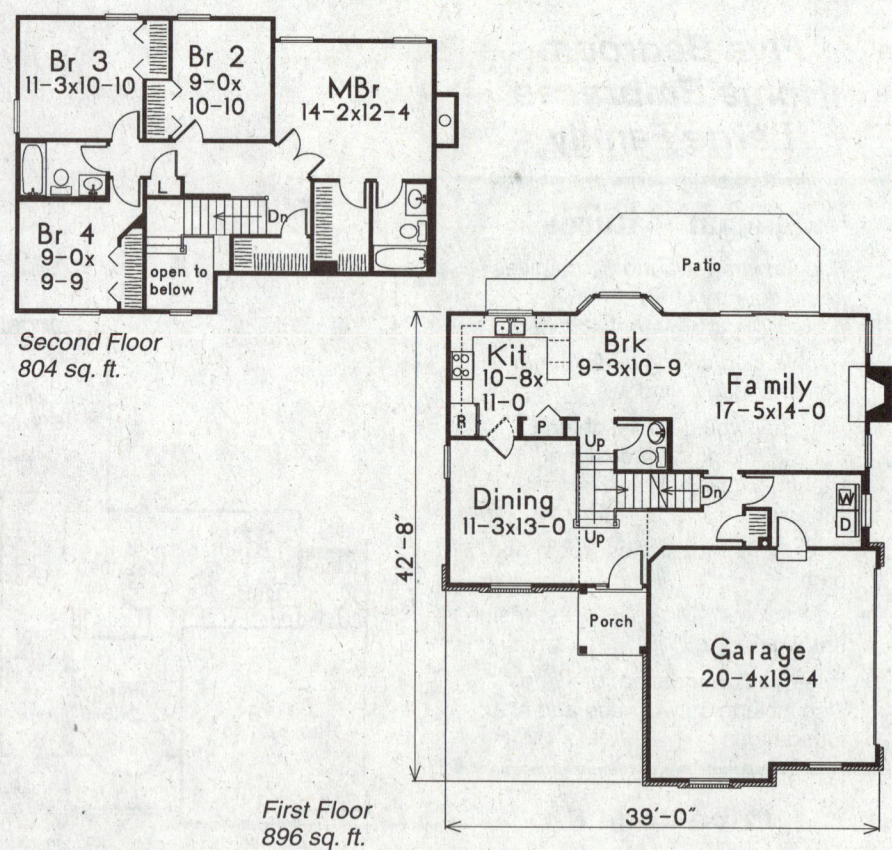

Second Floor
804 sq. ft.

First Floor
896 sq. ft.

Plan #718-011D-0041

3,231 total square feet of living area

Delightful Dormers Add Drama

Special features

- Breakfast nook and kitchen combine creating a large open dining space
- A cozy and private study is convenient to the master bedroom perfect for an office
- Decorative columns enhance the formal dining room
- Bonus room on the second floor is included in the square footage
- 4 bedrooms, 2 1/2 baths, 3-car side entry garage
- Crawl space foundation

Price Code G

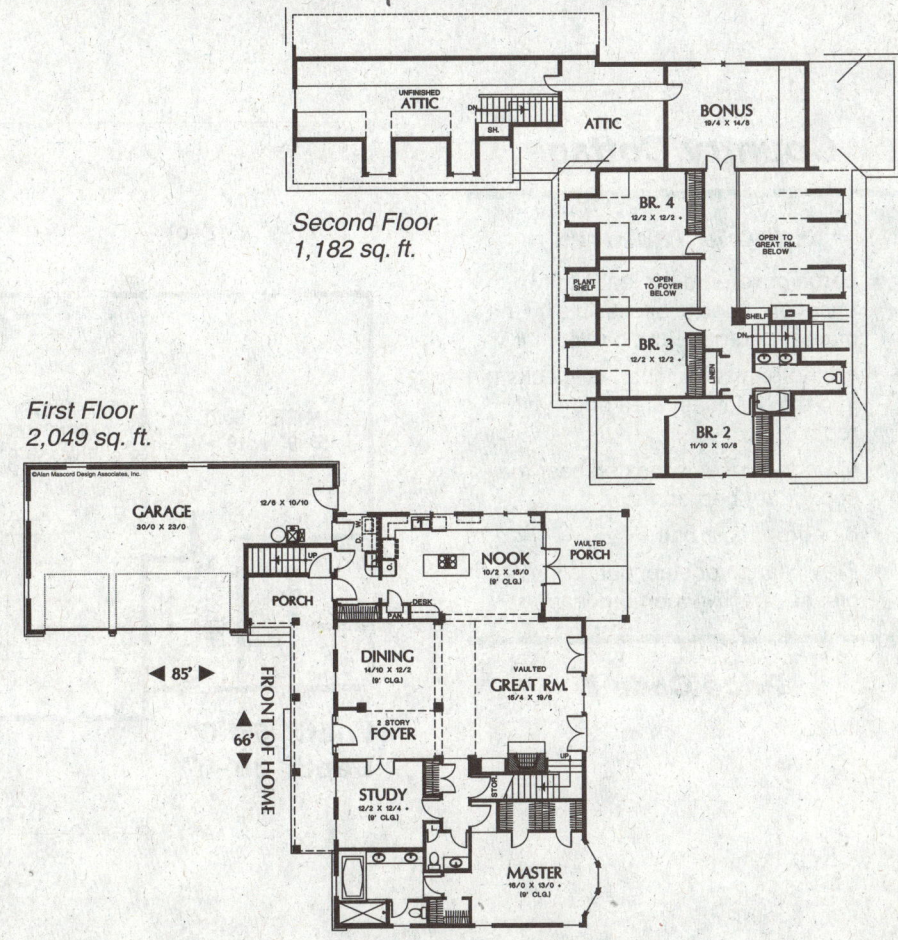

Second Floor 1,182 sq. ft.

First Floor 2,049 sq. ft.

TO ORDER BLUEPRINTS USE THE FORM ON PAGE 15 OR CALL TOLL-FREE 1-877-671-6036
View thousands more home plans online at www.familyhandyman.com/HOMEPLANS

Plan #718-056D-0001

1,624 total square feet of living area

Country Cottage

Special features

- Large covered deck leads to two uncovered decks accessible by the master bedroom and bedroom #3
- Well-organized kitchen overlooks into the breakfast area and family room
- Laundry closet is located near the secondary bedrooms
- 3 bedrooms, 2 baths
- Crawl space or slab foundation, please specify when ordering

Price Code E

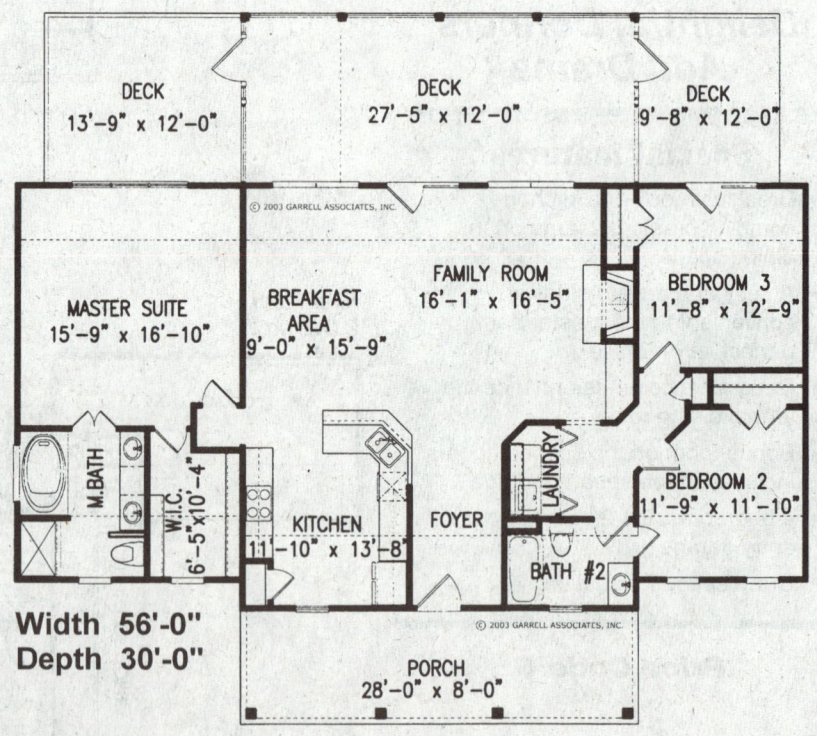

Plan #718-011D-0025

2,287 total square feet of living area

Dramatic U-Shaped Stairs

Special features

- Wrap-around porch creates an inviting feeling
- First floor windows have transom windows above
- Den has see-through fireplace into the family area
- 3 bedrooms, 2 1/2 baths, 2-car side entry garage
- Crawl space foundation

Price Code E

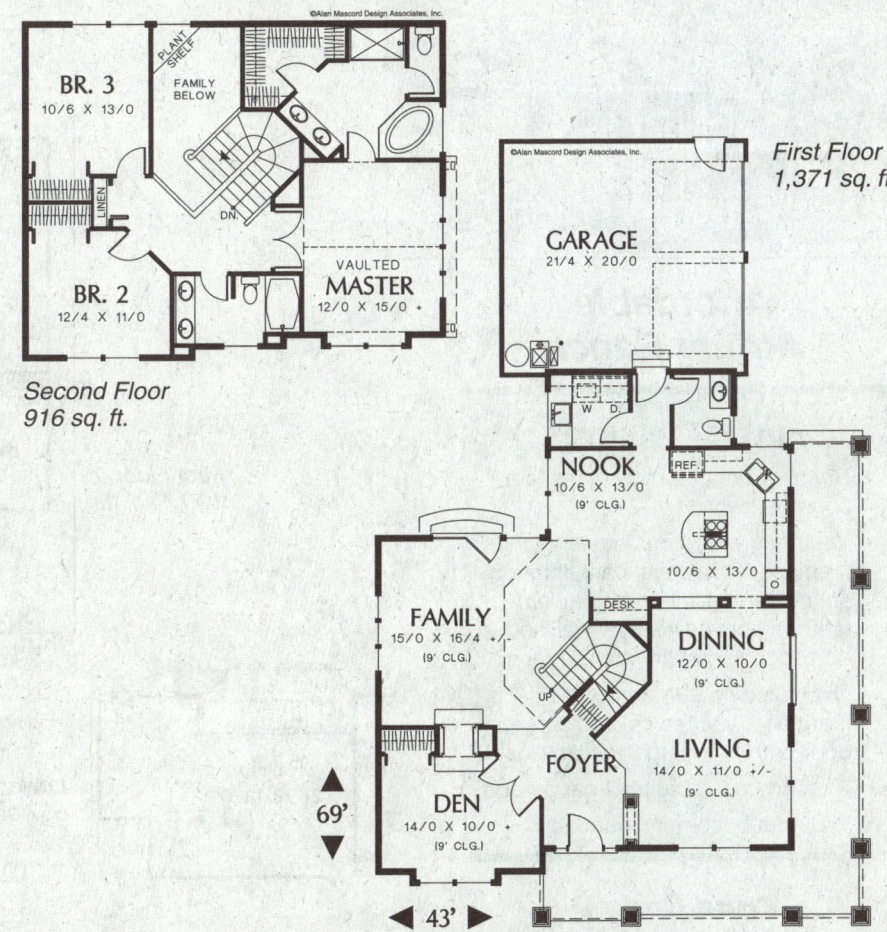

Second Floor 916 sq. ft.

First Floor 1,371 sq. ft.

Plan #718-007D-0053

2,334 total square feet of living area

Rear View

Affordable Atrium Ranch

Special features

- Roomy front porch gives home a country flavor
- Vaulted great room boasts a fireplace, TV alcove, pass-through snack bar to kitchen and atrium featuring bayed window wall and an ascending stair to family room
- Oversized master bedroom features a vaulted ceiling, double-door entry and large walk-in closet
- 3 bedrooms, 2 baths, 2-car garage
- Walk-out basement foundation

First Floor 1,777 sq. ft.

Lower Level 557 sq. ft.

Price Code D

TO ORDER BLUEPRINTS USE THE FORM ON PAGE 15 OR CALL TOLL-FREE 1-877-671-6036
View thousands more home plans online at www.familyhandyman.com/homeplans

Plan #718-013D-0020

1,985 total square feet of living area

Delightful Victorian

Special features

- Cozy family room features a fireplace and double French doors opening onto the porch
- The open kitchen includes a convenient island
- Extraordinary master bedroom has a tray ceiling and a large walk-in closet
- Lovely bayed breakfast area has easy access to the deck
- 3 bedrooms, 2 1/2 baths
- Basement or crawl space foundation, please specify when ordering

Price Code C

First Floor 1,009 sq. ft.

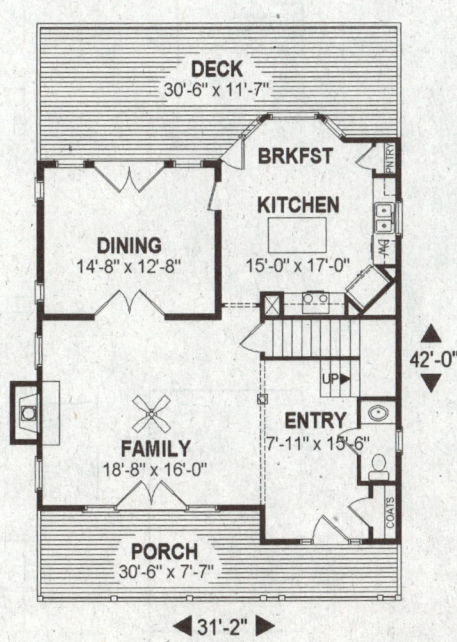

Second Floor 976 sq. ft.

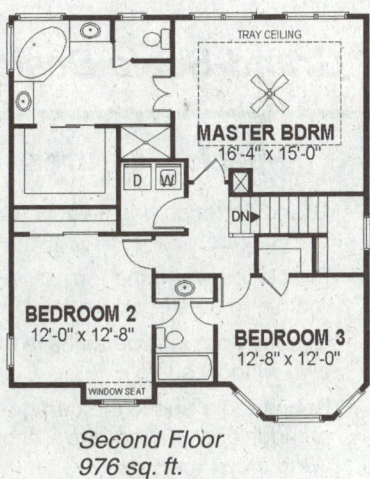

TO ORDER BLUEPRINTS USE THE FORM ON PAGE 15 OR CALL TOLL-FREE 1-877-671-6036
View thousands more home plans online at www.familyhandyman.com/HOMEPLANS

Plan #718-055D-0023

4,237 total square feet of living area

Grand-Scale Design

Special features

- Grand entrance has a vaulted two-story foyer
- Fireplaces warm the formal living room and master bedroom
- Second floor bedrooms have their own window seats
- Bonus room above the garage has an additional 497 square feet of living area
- 4 bedrooms, 3 1/2 baths, 3-car side entry garage
- Basement, crawl space or slab foundation, please specify when ordering

Price Code G

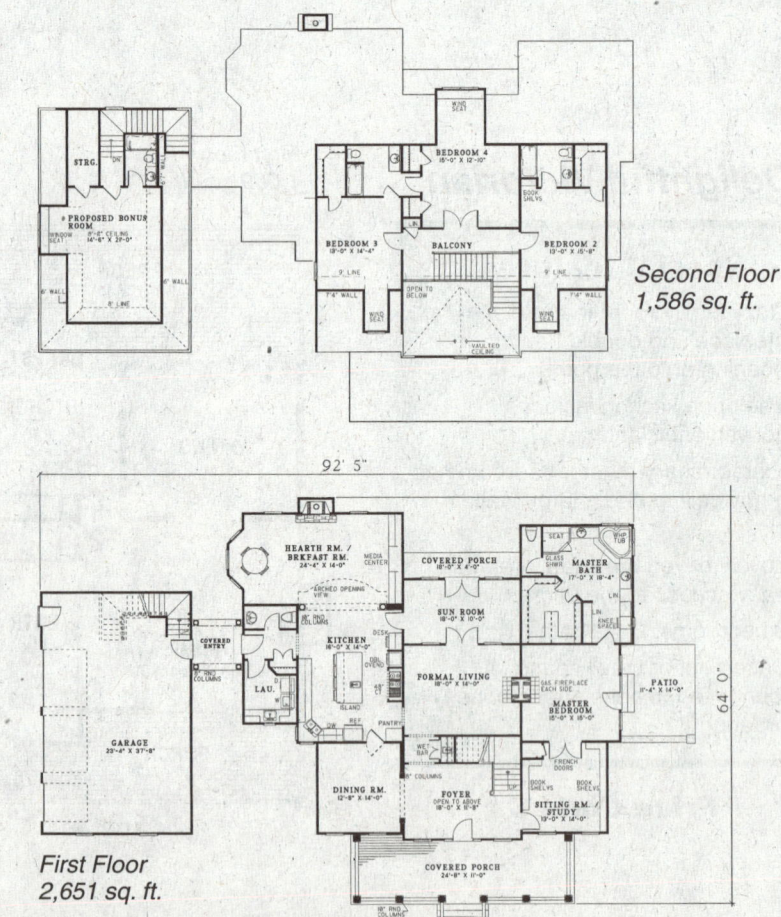

Second Floor 1,586 sq. ft.

First Floor 2,651 sq. ft.

TO ORDER BLUEPRINTS USE THE FORM ON PAGE 15 OR CALL TOLL-FREE 1-877-671-6036
View thousands more home plans online at www.familyhandyman.com/homeplans

Plan #718-006D-0003

1,674 total square feet of living area

Sculptured Roof Line And Facade Add Charm

Special features

- Vaulted great room, dining area and kitchen all enjoy a central fireplace and log bin
- Convenient laundry/mud room is located between the garage and family area with handy stairs to the basement
- Easily expandable screened porch and adjacent patio access the dining area
- Master bedroom features a full bath with tub, separate shower and walk-in closet
- 3 bedrooms, 2 baths, 2-car garage
- Basement foundation, drawings also include crawl space and slab foundations

Price Code B

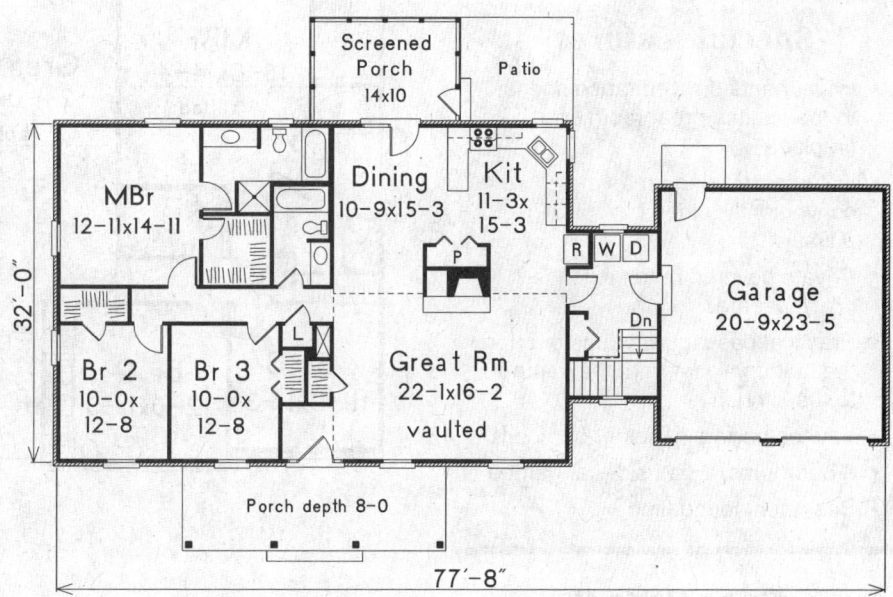

TO ORDER BLUEPRINTS USE THE FORM ON PAGE 15 OR CALL TOLL-FREE 1-877-671-6036
View thousands more home plans online at www.familyhandyman.com/HOMEPLANS

Plan #718-001D-0013

1,882 total square feet of living area

Traditional Exterior, Handsome Accents

Special features

- Wide, handsome entrance opens to the vaulted great room with fireplace
- Living and dining areas are conveniently joined but still allow privacy
- Private covered porch extends breakfast area
- Practical passageway runs through the laundry room from the garage to the kitchen
- Vaulted ceiling in master bedroom
- 3 bedrooms, 2 baths, 2-car garage
- Basement foundation

Price Code D

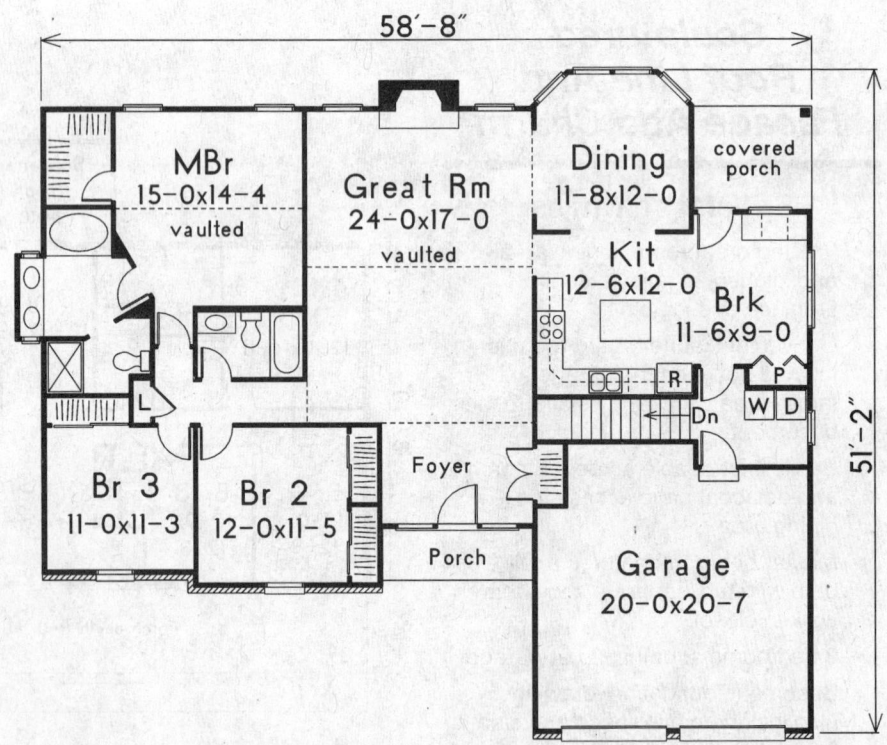

Plan #718-051D-0057

2,229 total square feet of living area

Amenity-Full Ranch

Special features

- Welcoming and expansive front porch
- Dining room has tray ceiling
- Sunny nook with arched soffit creates an inviting entry into this eating space
- 3 bedrooms, 2 baths, 2-car side entry garage
- Basement foundation

Price Code D

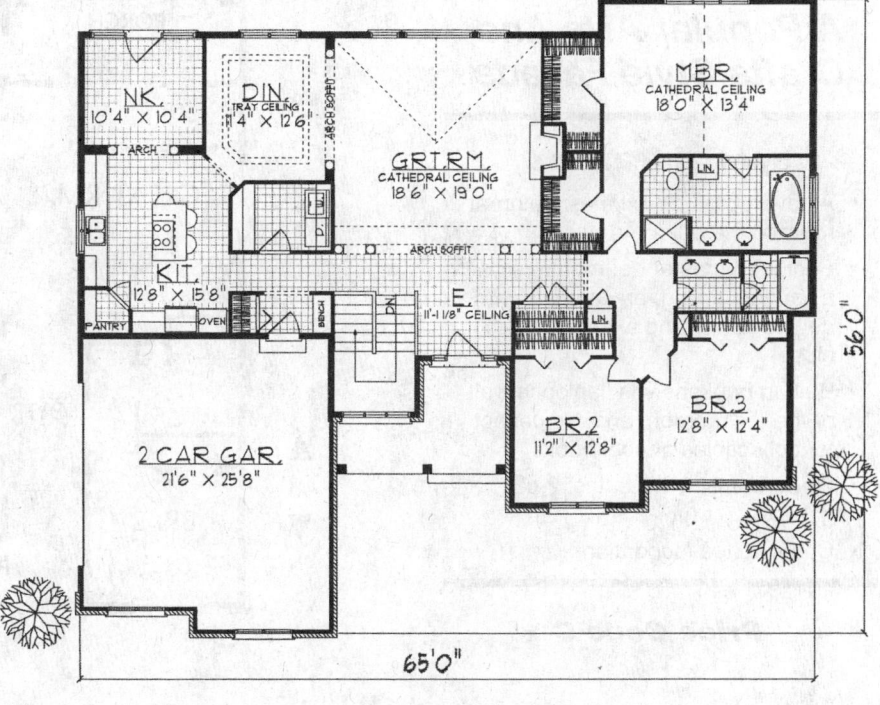

Plan #718-011D-0007

1,580 total square feet of living area

Ranch Has A Popular Arts And Crafts Style Facade

Special features

- A covered porch extends the great room to the outdoors
- Secluded master bedroom enjoys a vaulted ceiling, private bath with double vanity and a large walk-in closet
- Built-in bookshelves flank one wall of the dining room and are perfect for collectibles or cookbooks
- 3 bedrooms, 2 1/2 baths, 2-car garage
- Crawl space foundation

Price Code C

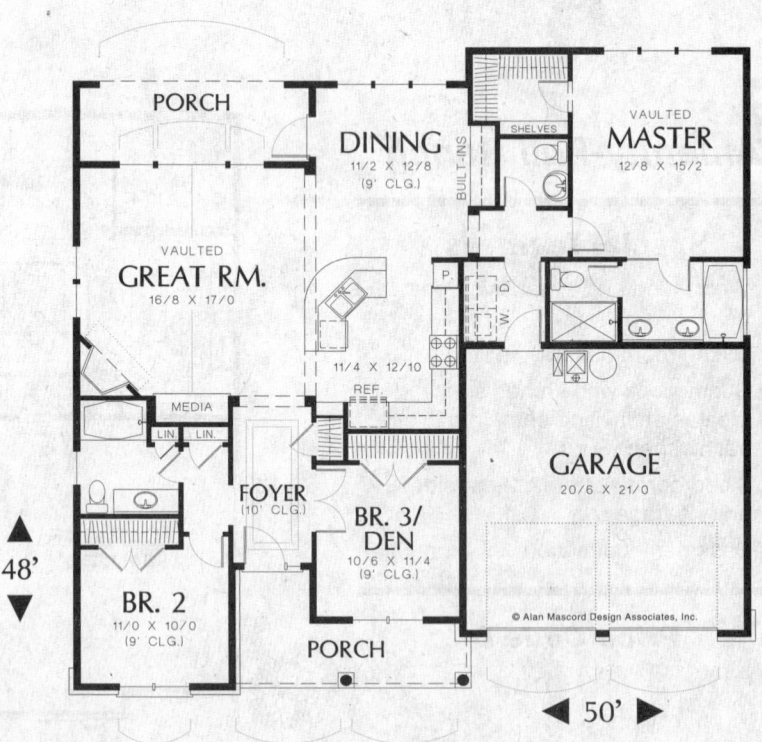

Plan #718-055D-0038

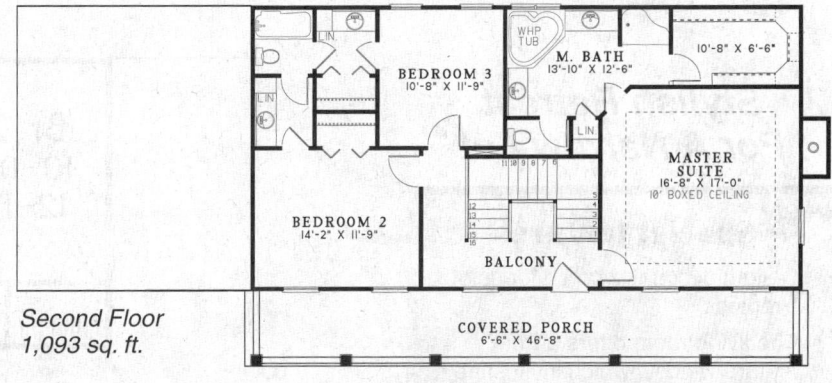

2,247 total square feet of living area

Columned Facade

Special features

- Enormous great room with fireplace extends into a kitchen with center island
- Formal dining area is quiet, yet convenient to kitchen
- All bedrooms are located on the second floor to maintain privacy
- 3 bedrooms, 2 1/2 baths, 2-car side entry garage
- Basement, crawl space or slab foundation, please specify when ordering

Price Code D

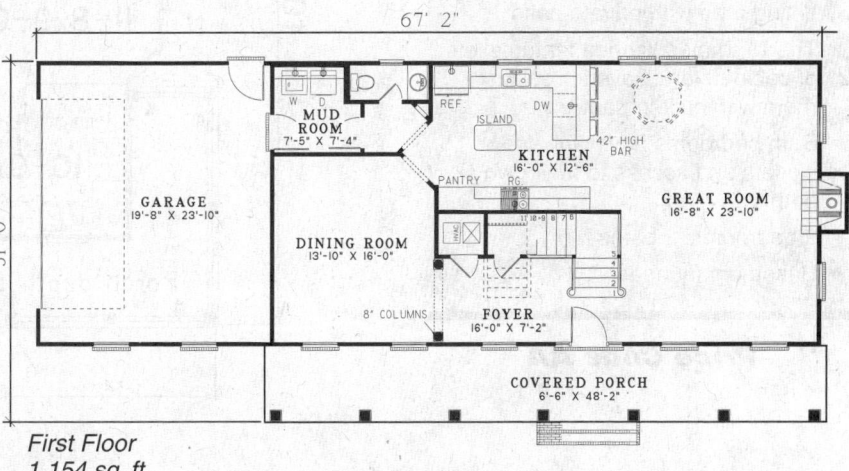

Second Floor 1,093 sq. ft.

First Floor 1,154 sq. ft.

TO ORDER BLUEPRINTS USE THE FORM ON PAGE 15 OR CALL TOLL-FREE 1-877-671-6036
View thousands more home plans online at www.familyhandyman.com/HOMEPLANS

Plan #718-007D-0105

1,084 total square feet of living area

Stylish Retreat For A Narrow Lot

Special features

- Delightful country porch for quiet evenings
- The living room offers a front feature window which invites the sun and includes a fireplace and dining area with private patio
- The U-shaped kitchen features lots of cabinets and bayed breakfast room with built-in pantry
- Both bedrooms have walk-in closets and access to their own bath
- 2 bedrooms, 2 baths
- Basement foundation

Price Code AA

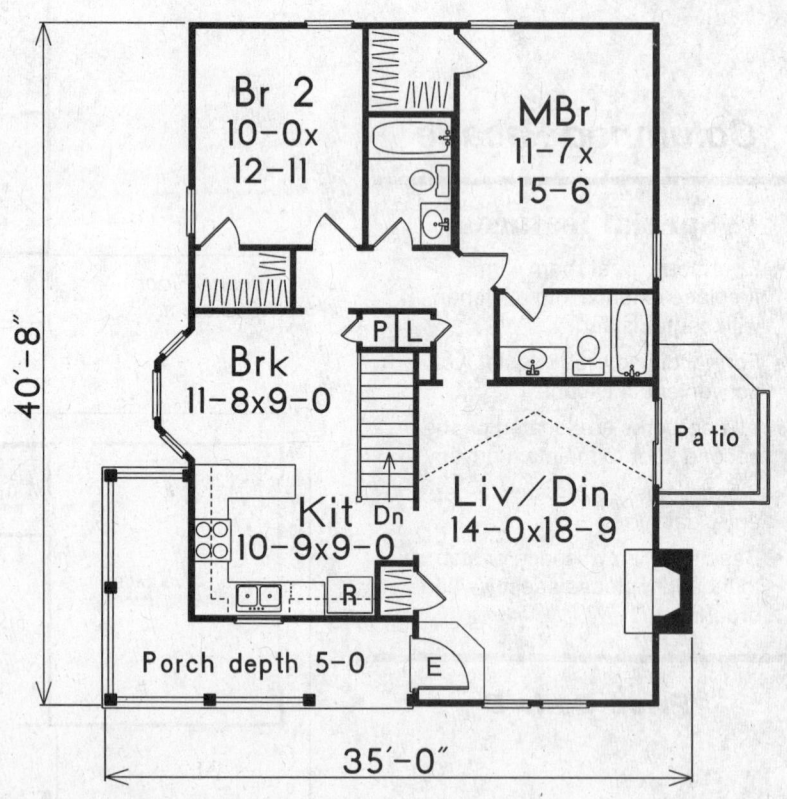

TO ORDER BLUEPRINTS USE THE FORM ON PAGE 15 OR CALL TOLL-FREE 1-877-671-6036
View thousands more home plans online at www.familyhandyman.com/HOMEPLANS

Plan #718-060D-0006

1,945 total square feet of living area

Traditional Elegance

Special features

- Large gathering room with corner fireplace and 12' high ceiling
- Master suite has a coffered ceiling and French door leading to the patio/deck
- Master bath has a cultured marble seat, separate shower and tub
- All bedrooms have walk-in closets
- 3 bedrooms, 2 baths, 2-car side entry garage
- Slab or crawl space foundation, please specify when ordering

Price Code C

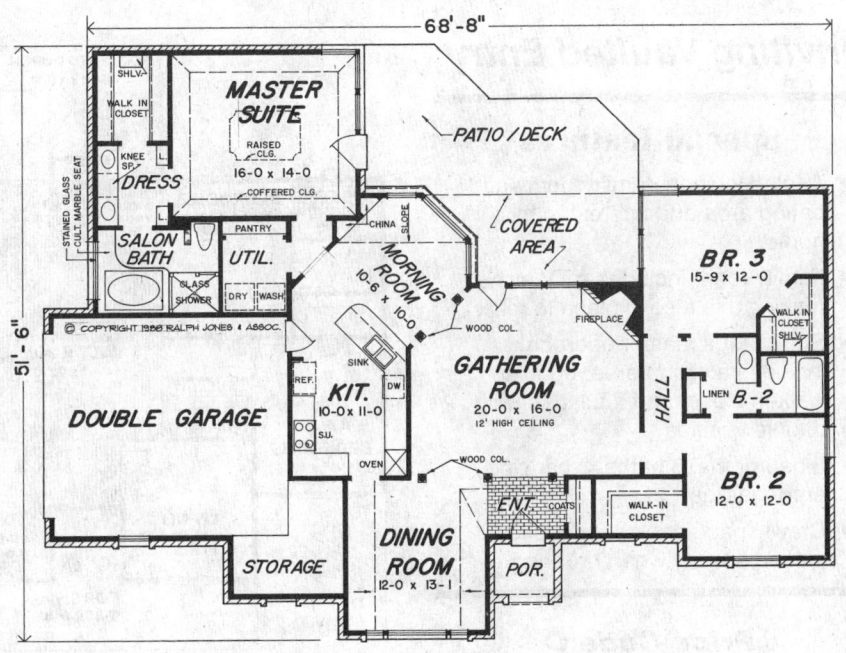

TO ORDER BLUEPRINTS USE THE FORM ON PAGE 15 OR CALL TOLL-FREE 1-877-671-6036
View thousands more home plans online at www.familyhandyman.com/homeplans

Plan #718-013D-0025

2,097 total square feet of living area

Inviting Vaulted Entry

Special features

- Angled kitchen, family room and eating area add interest to this home
- Family room includes a TV niche making this a cozy place to relax
- Sumptuous master bedroom includes a sitting area, double walk-in closet and a full bath with double vanities
- 3 bedrooms, 3 baths, 3-car side entry garage
- Crawl space or slab foundation, please specify when ordering

Price Code C

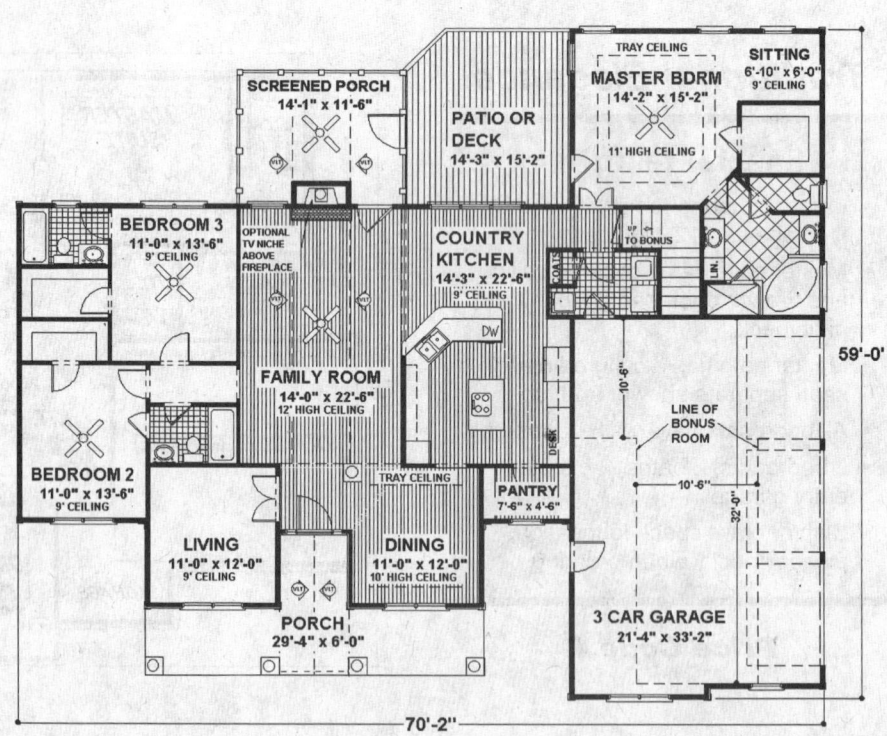

TO ORDER BLUEPRINTS USE THE FORM ON PAGE 15 OR CALL TOLL-FREE 1-877-671-6036
View thousands more home plans online at www.familyhandyman.com/homeplans

Plan #718-007D-0052

2,521 total square feet of living area

Great Looks Accentuated By Elliptical Brick Arches

Special features

- Large living and dining rooms are a plus for formal entertaining or large family gatherings
- Informal kitchen, breakfast and family rooms feature a 37' vista and double bay windows
- Generously sized master bedroom and three secondary bedrooms grace the second floor
- 4 bedrooms, 2 1/2 baths, 2-car garage
- Basement foundation

Price Code D

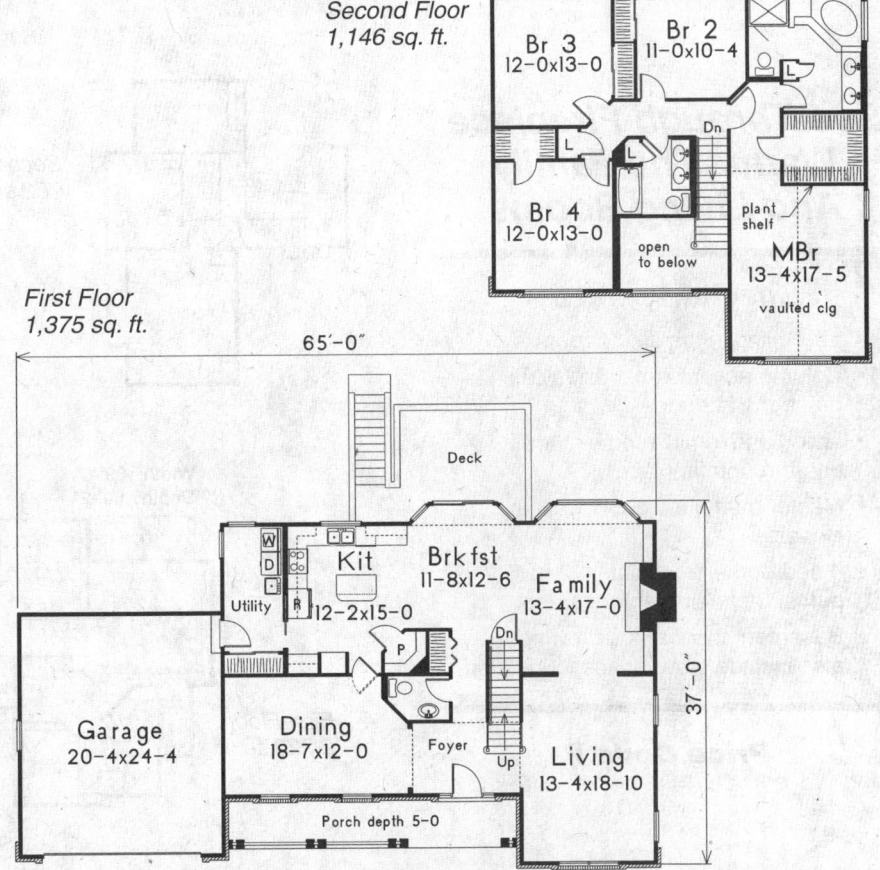

TO ORDER BLUEPRINTS USE THE FORM ON PAGE 15 OR CALL TOLL-FREE 1-877-671-6036
View thousands more home plans online at www.familyhandyman.com/homeplans

Plan #718-043D-0018

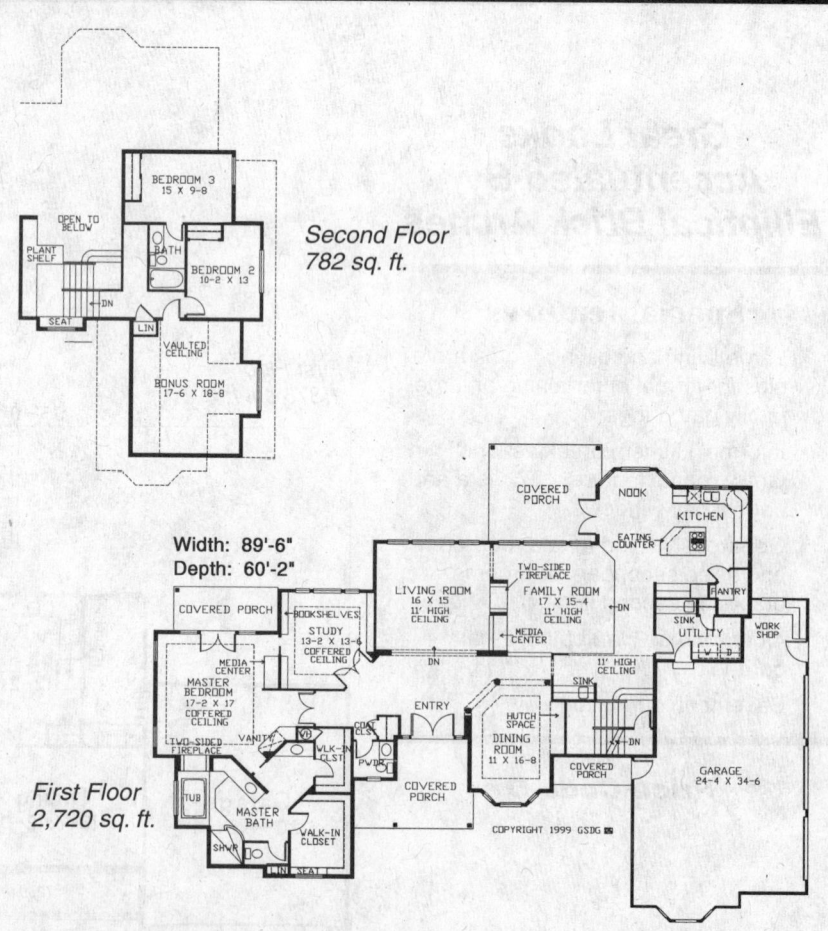

3,502 total square feet of living area

See-Through Fireplace Warms The Family And Living Rooms

Special features

- 12' ceiling in the dining room
- Column accents and display niches grace the interior
- Living and family rooms share a see-through fireplace
- Master bath has double walk-in closets
- 4 bedrooms, 2 full baths, 2 half baths, 3-car side entry garage
- Basement foundation, drawings also include crawl space foundation

Price Code F

Width: 89'-6"
Depth: 60'-2"

Second Floor 782 sq. ft.

First Floor 2,720 sq. ft.

TO ORDER BLUEPRINTS USE THE FORM ON PAGE 15 OR CALL TOLL-FREE 1-877-671-6036
View thousands more home plans online at www.familyhandyman.com/homeplans

Plan #718-007D-0049

1,791 total square feet of living area

Classic Exterior Employs Innovative Planning

Special features

- Vaulted great room and octagon-shaped dining area enjoy the view of the covered patio
- Kitchen features a pass-through to dining area, center island, large walk-in pantry and breakfast room with large bay window
- Master bedroom is vaulted with sitting area
- 4 bedrooms, 2 baths, 2-car garage with storage
- Basement foundation, drawings also include crawl space and slab foundations

Price Code C

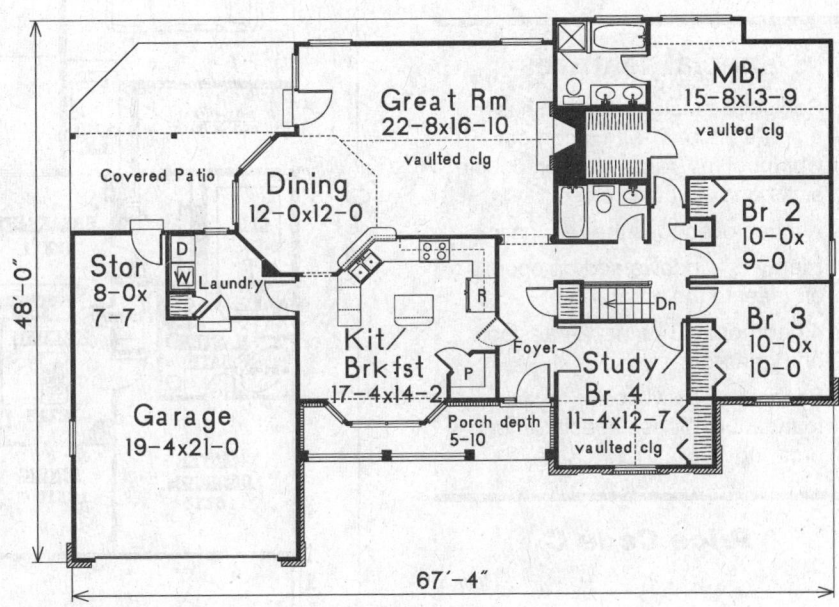

TO ORDER BLUEPRINTS USE THE FORM ON PAGE 15 OR CALL TOLL-FREE 1-877-671-6036
View thousands more home plans online at www.familyhandyman.com/HOMEPLANS

Plan #718-028D-0008

2,156 total square feet of living area

Award-Winning Style With This Design

Special features

- Secluded master bedroom has a spa-style bath with a corner whirlpool tub, large shower, double sinks and a walk-in closet
- Kitchen overlooks the rear patio
- Plenty of windows add an open, airy feel to the great room
- 4 bedrooms, 3 baths, 2-car side entry garage
- Basement, crawl space or slab foundation, please specify when ordering

Price Code C

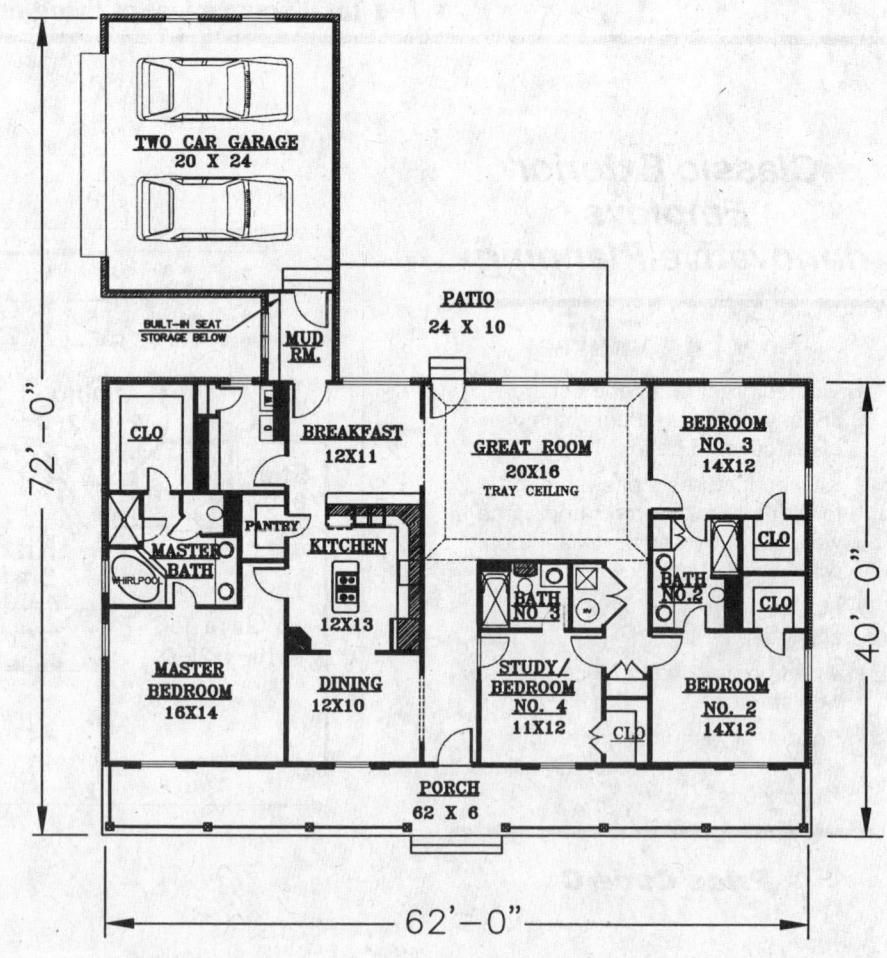

TO ORDER BLUEPRINTS USE THE FORM ON PAGE 15 OR CALL TOLL-FREE 1-877-671-6036
View thousands more home plans online at www.familyhandyman.com/HOMEPLANS

Plan #718-013D-0011

1,643 total square feet of living area

Appealing Charming Porch

Special features

- First floor master bedroom has a private bath, walk-in closet and easy access to the laundry closet
- Comfortable family room features a vaulted ceiling and a cozy fireplace
- Two bedrooms on the second floor share a bath
- 3 bedrooms, 2 1/2 baths, 2-car drive under garage
- Basement or crawl space foundation, please specify when ordering

Price Code B

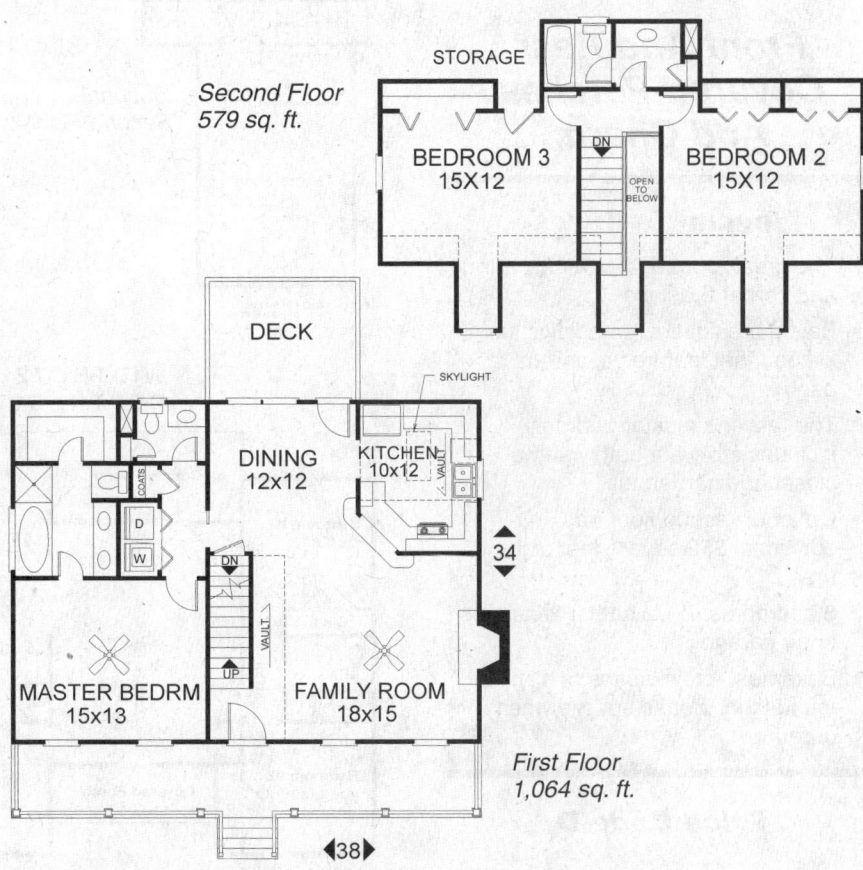

TO ORDER BLUEPRINTS USE THE FORM ON PAGE 15 OR CALL TOLL-FREE 1-877-671-6036
View thousands more home plans online at www.familyhandyman.com/homeplans

Plan #718-077D-0002

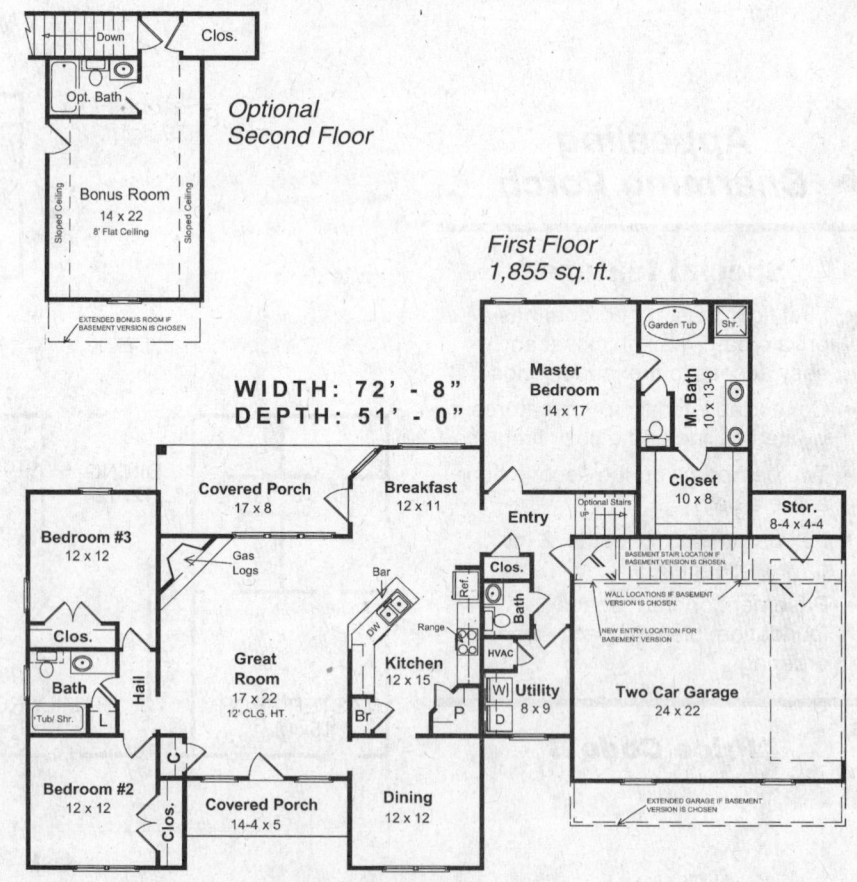

1,855 total square feet of living area

Front And Rear Covered Porches Add Charm

Special features

- The great room boasts a 12' ceiling and corner fireplace
- Bayed breakfast area adjoins the kitchen that features a walk-in pantry
- The relaxing master bedroom includes a private bath with walk-in closet and garden tub
- Optional second floor has an additional 352 square feet of living area
- 3 bedrooms, 2 1/2 baths, 2-car side entry garage
- Basement, crawl space or slab foundation, please specify when ordering

Price Code D

TO ORDER BLUEPRINTS USE THE FORM ON PAGE 15 OR CALL TOLL-FREE 1-877-671-6036
View thousands more home plans online at www.familyhandyman.com/homeplans

Plan #718-038D-0044

1,982 total square feet of living area

Two-Story With Victorian Feel

Special features

- Spacious master bedroom has bath with corner whirlpool tub and sunny skylight above
- Breakfast area overlooks into the great room
- Screened porch with skylight above extends the home outdoors and allows for another entertainment area
- 4 bedrooms, 2 1/2 baths
- Basement foundation

Price Code C

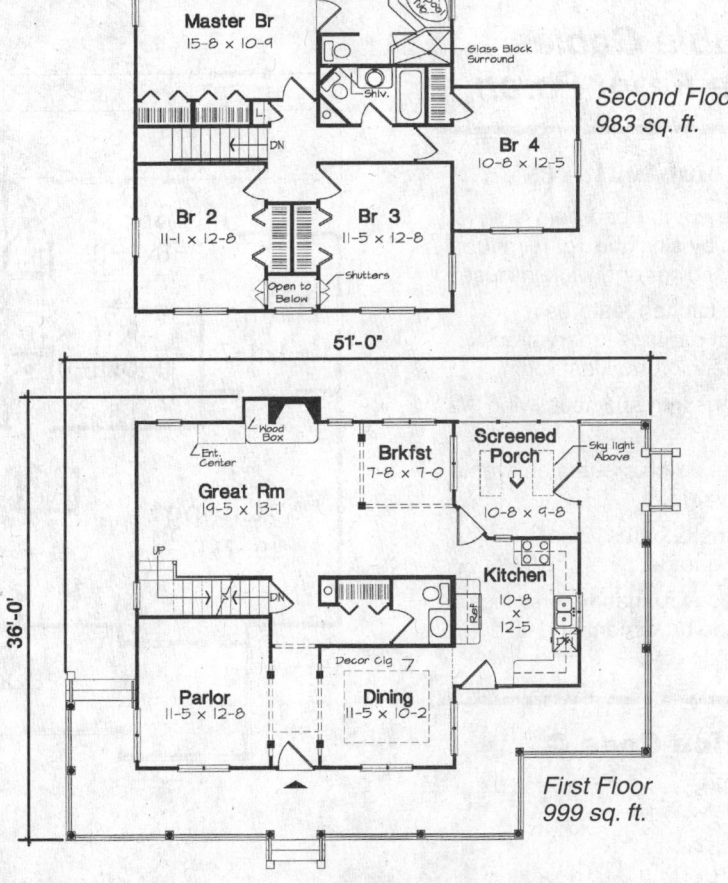

TO ORDER BLUEPRINTS USE THE FORM ON PAGE 15 OR CALL TOLL-FREE 1-877-671-6036
View thousands more home plans online at www.familyhandyman.com/homeplans

The Family Handyman

Plan #718-001D-0080

1,832 total square feet of living area

Double Gables Frame Front Porch

Special features

- Distinctive master bedroom is enhanced by skylights, garden tub, separate shower and walk-in closet
- U-shaped kitchen features a convenient pantry, laundry area and full view to breakfast room
- Foyer opens into spacious living room
- Large front porch creates enjoyable outdoor living
- 3 bedrooms, 2 baths, 2-car detached garage
- Crawl space foundation, drawings also include basement and slab foundations

Price Code C

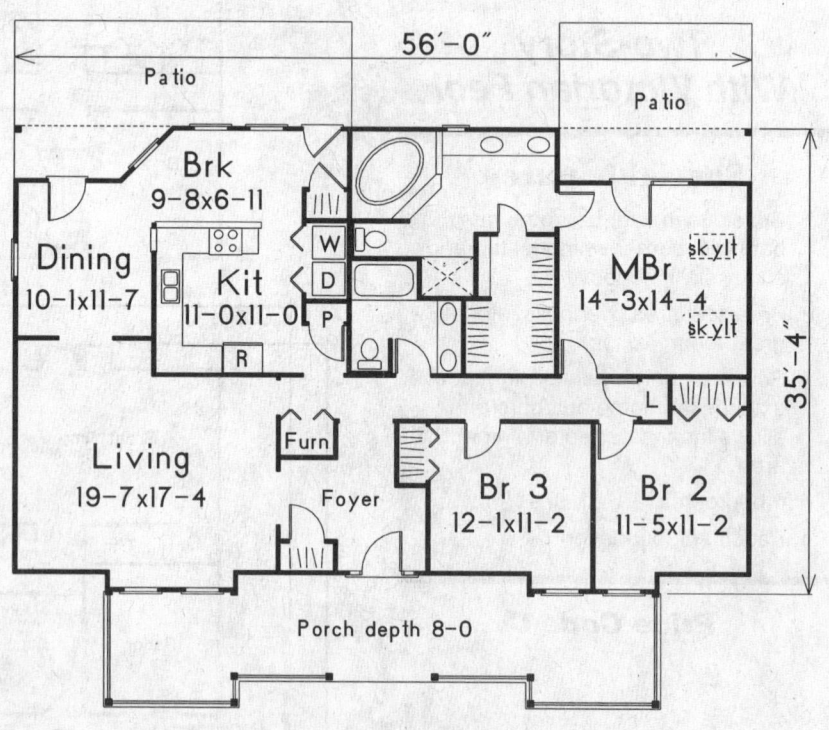

TO ORDER BLUEPRINTS USE THE FORM ON PAGE 15 OR CALL TOLL-FREE 1-877-671-6036
View thousands more home plans online at www.familyhandyman.com/HOMEPLANS

Plan #718-055D-0091

2,499 total square feet of living area

Lovely Master Suite With Sitting Area

Special features

- Convenient snack bar expands the kitchen
- Private study, great room and dining room all have 10' ceilings
- Bedrooms #2 and #3 share a full bath
- Optional second floor has an additional 438 square feet of living area
- 3 bedrooms, 2 baths, 2-car side entry garage
- Slab or crawl space foundation, please specify when ordering

Price Code D

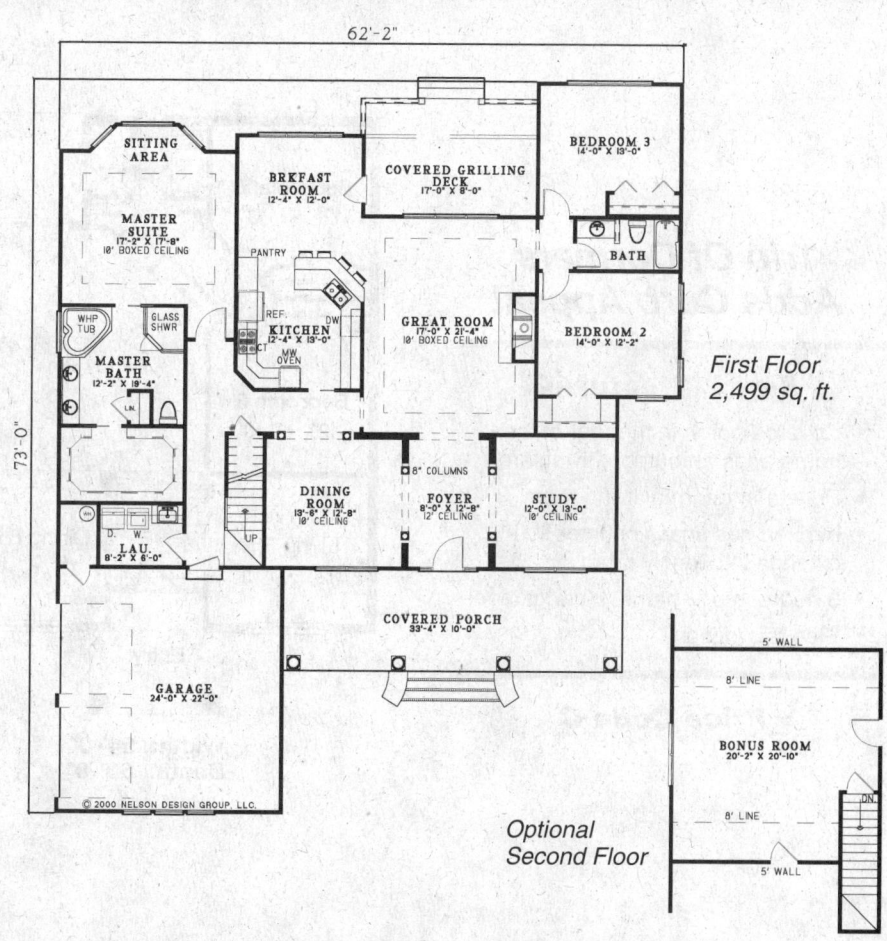

First Floor
2,499 sq. ft.

Optional Second Floor

TO ORDER BLUEPRINTS USE THE FORM ON PAGE 15 OR CALL TOLL-FREE 1-877-671-6036
View thousands more home plans online at www.familyhandyman.com/HOMEPLANS

Plan #718-047D-0025

1,806 total square feet of living area

Trio Of Dormers Adds Curb Appeal

Special features

- Covered porch in the rear of the home adds an outdoor living area
- Private and formal living room
- Kitchen has snack counter that extends into family room
- 3 bedrooms, 2 baths, 2-car garage
- Slab foundation

Price Code C

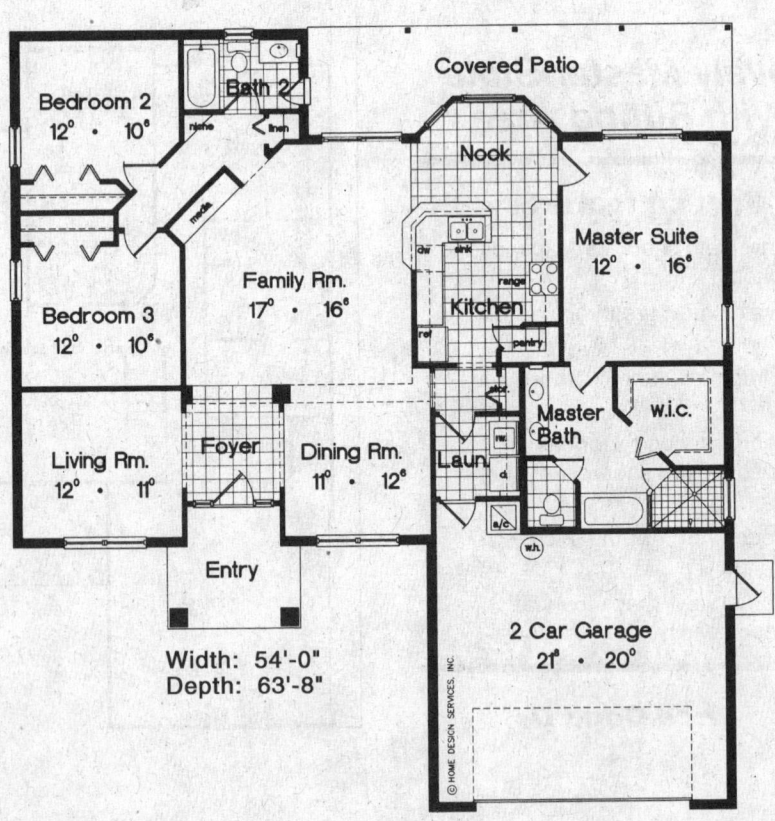

Width: 54'-0"
Depth: 63'-8"

TO ORDER BLUEPRINTS USE THE FORM ON PAGE 15 OR CALL TOLL-FREE 1-877-671-6036
View thousands more home plans online at www.familyhandyman.com/HOMEPLANS

Plan #718-016D-0049

1,793 total square feet of living area

Porch Adds To Farmhouse Style

Special features

- Beautiful foyer leads into the great room that has a fireplace flanked by two sets of beautifully transomed doors both leading to a large covered porch
- Dramatic eat-in kitchen includes an abundance of cabinets and workspace in an exciting angled shape
- Delightful master bedroom has many amenities
- Optional bonus room above the garage has an additional 779 square feet of living area
- 3 bedrooms, 2 baths, 2-car side entry garage
- Basement, crawl space or slab foundation, please specify when ordering

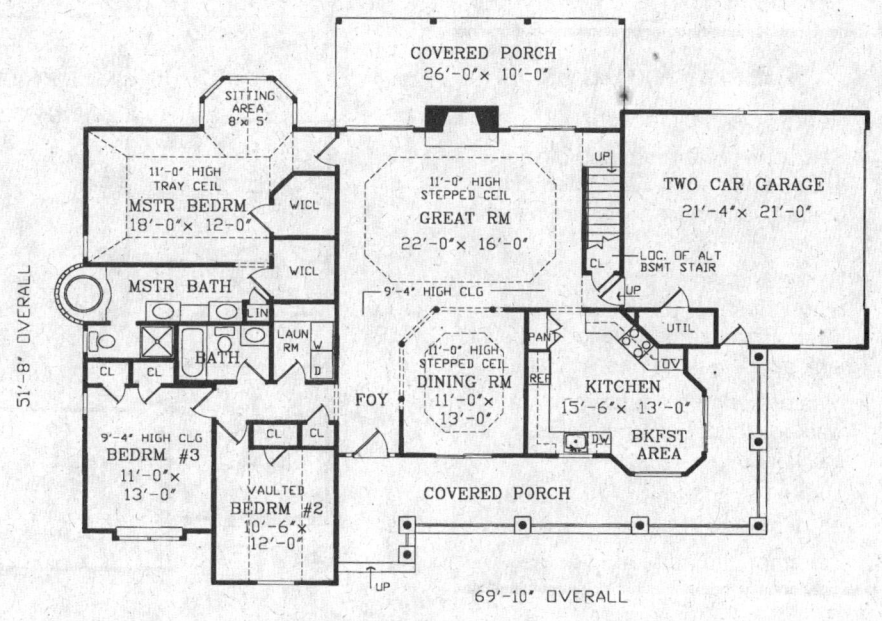

Price Code B

TO ORDER BLUEPRINTS USE THE FORM ON PAGE 15 OR CALL TOLL-FREE 1-877-671-6036
View thousands more home plans online at www.familyhandyman.com/homeplans

Plan #718-007D-0017

1,882 total square feet of living area

Organized Kitchen Is The Center Of Activity

Special features

- Handsome brick facade
- Spacious great room and dining area combination is brightened by unique corner windows and patio access
- Well-designed kitchen incorporates a breakfast bar peninsula, sweeping casement window above sink and a walk-in pantry island
- Master bedroom features a large walk-in closet and private bath with bay window
- 4 bedrooms, 2 baths, 2-car side entry garage
- Basement foundation

Price Code C

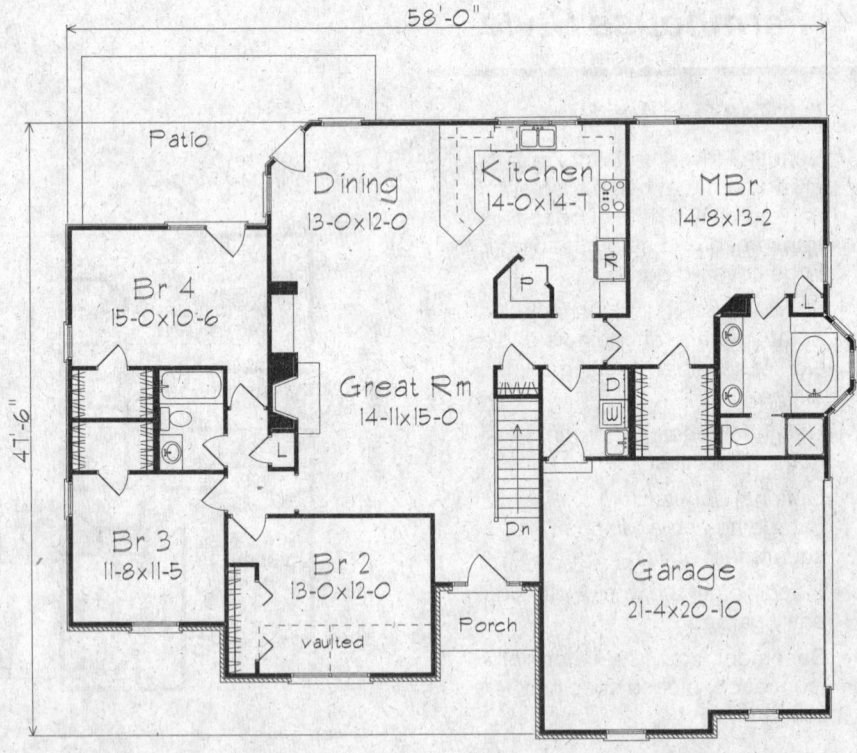

TO ORDER BLUEPRINTS USE THE FORM ON PAGE 15 OR CALL TOLL-FREE 1-877-671-6036
View thousands more home plans online at www.familyhandyman.com/HOMEPLANS

Plan #718-060D-0028

2,287 total square feet of living area

Raised Plantation Styling

Special features

- Two-story foyer has balcony
- Great room includes a fireplace and decorative fixed glass between dining room
- Large kitchen and breakfast room enjoy great view to rear
- Second floor has two bedrooms, balcony and large playroom
- 3 bedrooms, 2 1/2 baths, 2-car side entry garage
- Slab or crawl space foundation, please specify when ordering

Price Code D

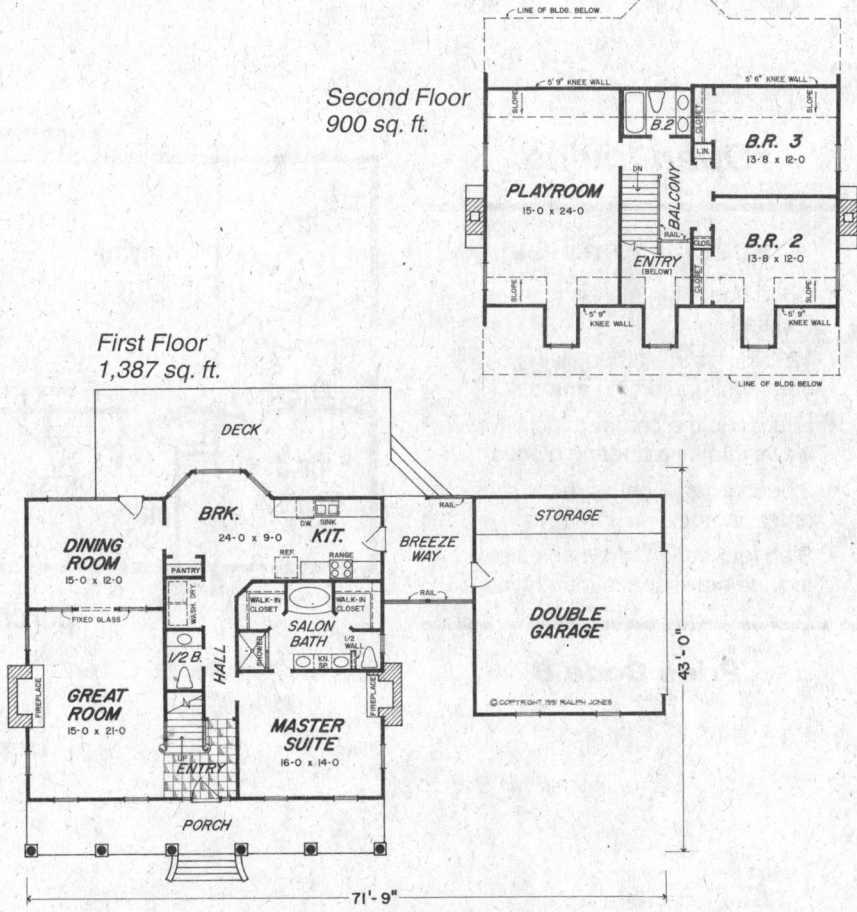

TO ORDER BLUEPRINTS USE THE FORM ON PAGE 15 OR CALL TOLL-FREE 1-877-671-6036

View thousands more home plans online at www.familyhandyman.com/homeplans

The Family Handyman

Plan #718-020D-0005

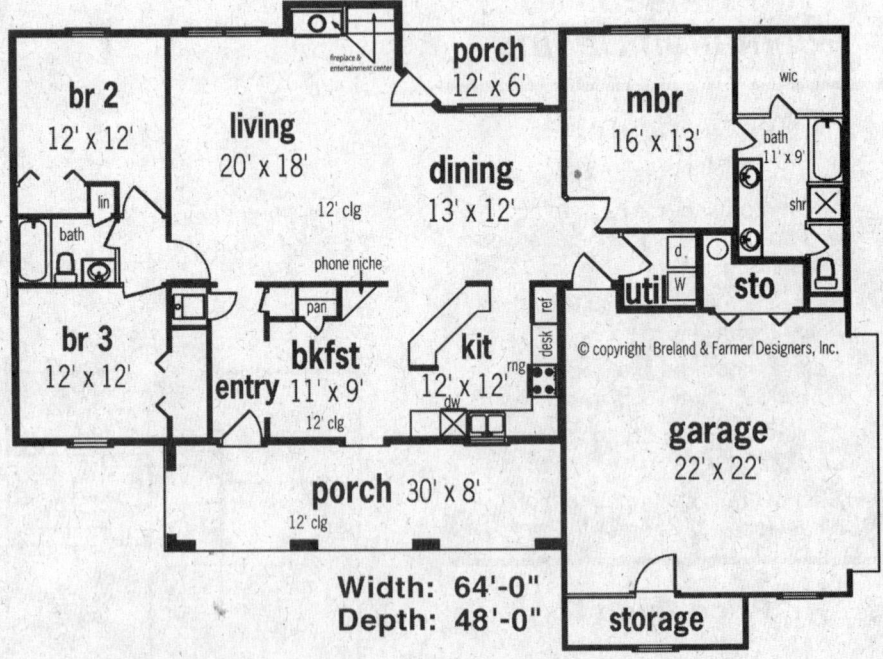

1,770 total square feet of living area

Open Living

Special features

- Open floor plan makes this home feel spacious
- 12' ceilings in kitchen, living, breakfast and dining areas
- Kitchen is the center of activity with views into all gathering places
- 3 bedrooms, 2 baths, 2-car side entry garage
- Slab foundation, drawings also include crawl space foundation

Price Code B

Width: 64'-0"
Depth: 48'-0"

TO ORDER BLUEPRINTS USE THE FORM ON PAGE 15 OR CALL TOLL-FREE 1-877-671-6036
View thousands more home plans online at www.familyhandyman.com/homeplans

Plan #718-035D-0001

1,715 total square feet of living area

Spacious Ranch For A Growing Family

Special features

- Vaulted great room is spacious and bright
- Master suite enjoys a sitting room and private bath
- Kitchen has plenty of counterspace and cabinetry
- 3 bedrooms, 2 baths, 2-car garage
- Walk-out basement, crawl space or slab foundation, please specify when ordering

Price Code B

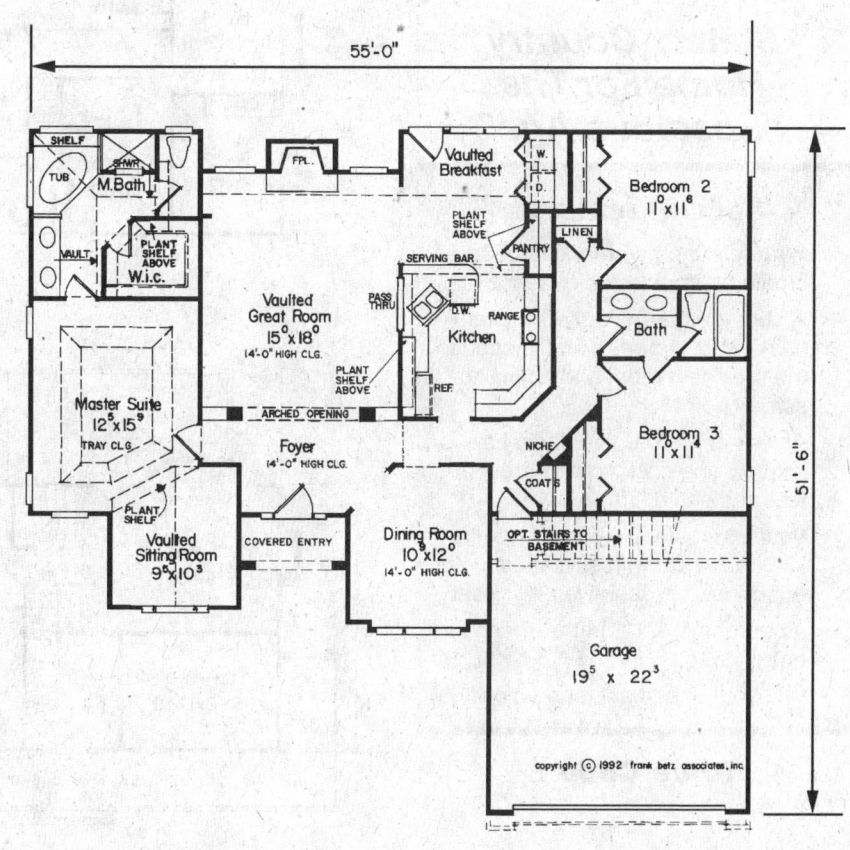

TO ORDER BLUEPRINTS USE THE FORM ON PAGE 15 OR CALL TOLL-FREE 1-877-671-6036
View thousands more home plans online at www.familyhandyman.com/HOMEPLANS

Plan #718-007D-0079

2,727 total square feet of living area

Stately Country Home For The "Spacious Age"

Special features

- Wrap-around porch and large foyer create an impressive entrance
- A state-of-the-art vaulted kitchen has a walk-in pantry and is open to the breakfast room and adjoining screen porch
- A walk-in wet bar, fireplace, bay window and deck access are features of the family room
- Vaulted master bedroom enjoys a luxurious bath with skylight and an enormous 13' deep walk-in closet
- 4 bedrooms, 2 1/2 baths, 2-car side entry garage
- Walk-out basement foundation

Price Code E

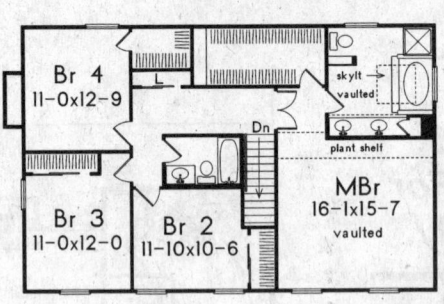

Second Floor 1,204 sq. ft.

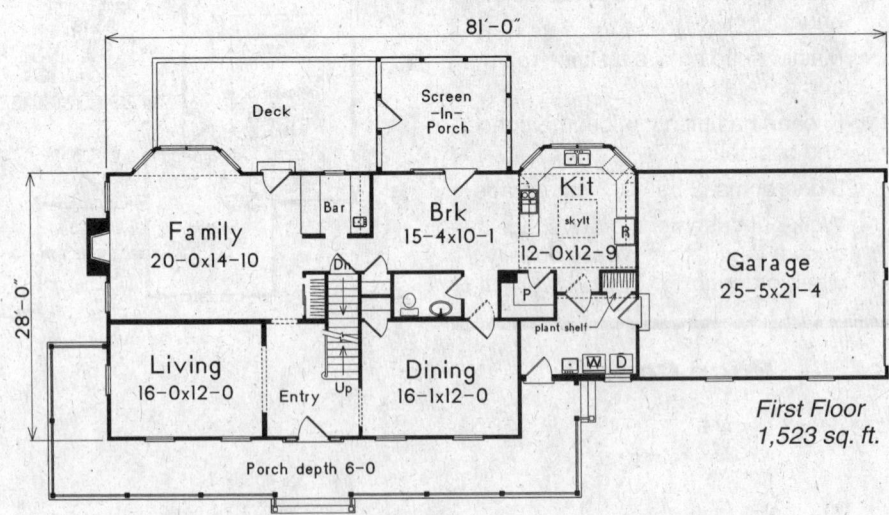

First Floor 1,523 sq. ft.

TO ORDER BLUEPRINTS USE THE FORM ON PAGE 15 OR CALL TOLL-FREE 1-877-671-6036
View thousands more home plans online at www.familyhandyman.com/homeplans

Plan #718-036D-0012

2,470 total square feet of living area

Covered Patio For Outdoor Entertainment

Special features

- 9' ceilings throughout this home
- Family room has cathedral ceiling, fireplace and patio access
- Oversized kitchen features all the amenities
- Gallery opens into living room which includes a fireplace and wet bar
- 3 bedrooms, 2 1/2 baths, 2-car side entry garage
- Crawl space or slab foundation, please specify when ordering

Price Code D

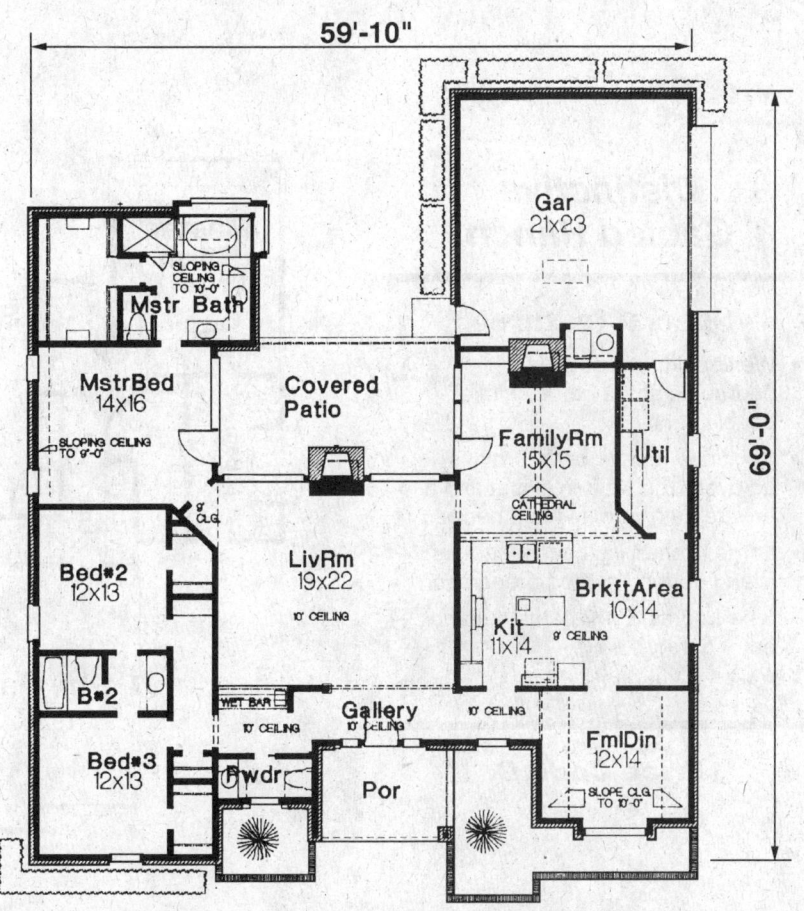

TO ORDER BLUEPRINTS USE THE FORM ON PAGE 15 OR CALL TOLL-FREE 1-877-671-6036
View thousands more home plans online at www.familyhandyman.com/HOMEPLANS

Plan #718-052D-0043

1,854 total square feet of living area

Distinctive Gabled Ranch

Special features

- Well-designed secondary bedrooms share a bath with a double vanity
- Secluded master bedroom has an oversized walk-in closet and a private bath with all the amenities
- Large kitchen includes a center island perfect for food preparation
- 3 bedrooms, 2 1/2 baths, 2-car side entry garage
- Basement foundation

Price Code C

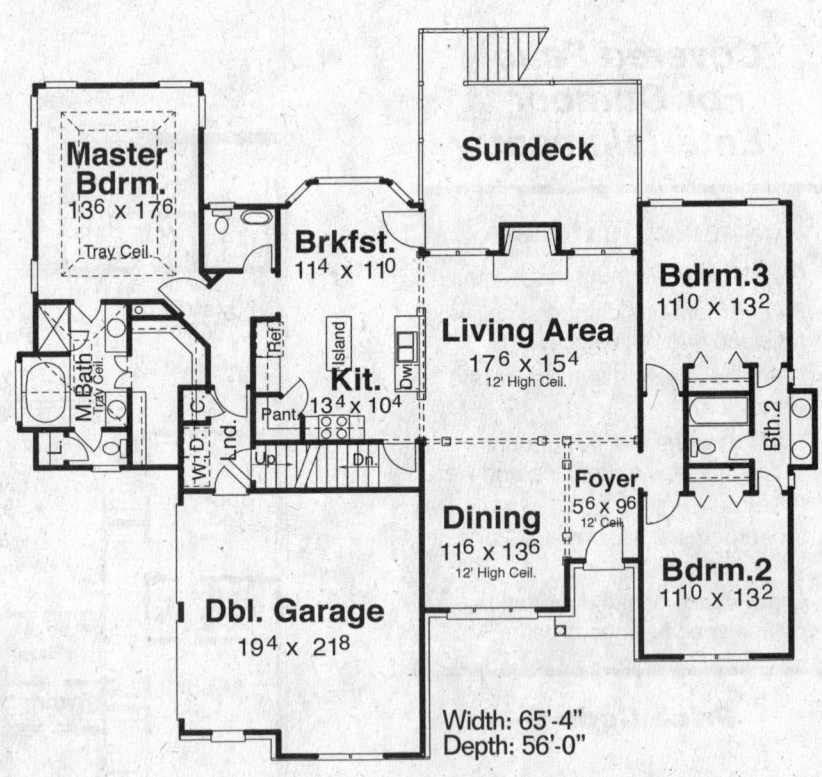

Plan #718-030D-0005

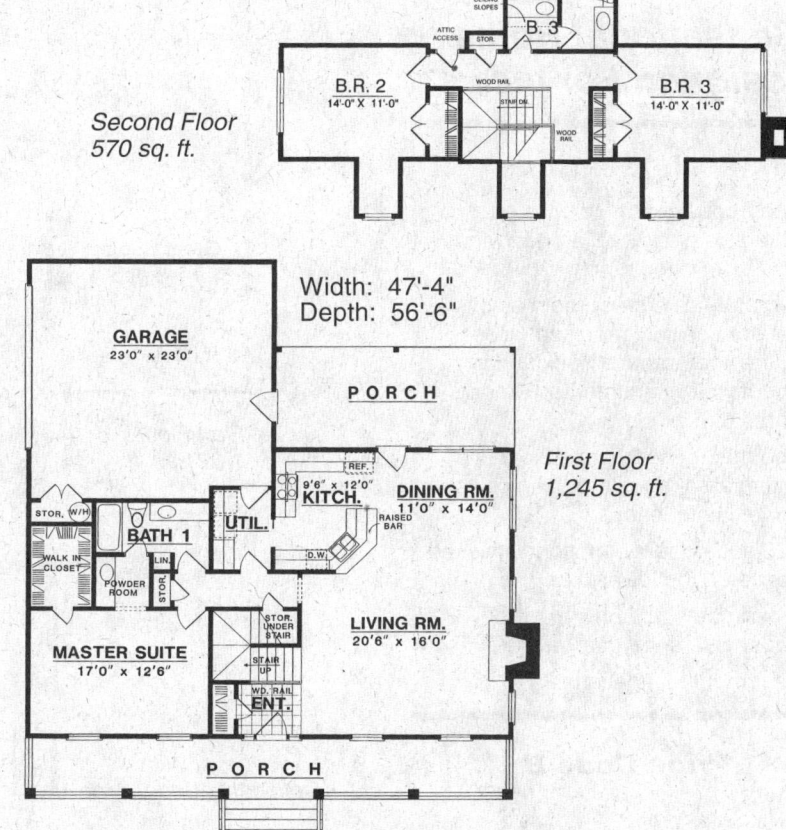

1,815 total square feet of living area

Kitchen Overlooks Living Area

Special features

- Well-designed kitchen opens to the dining room and features a raised breakfast bar
- First floor master suite has a walk-in closet
- Front and back porches unite this home with the outdoors
- 3 bedrooms, 2 baths, 2-car side entry garage
- Basement, crawl space or slab foundation, please specify when ordering

Price Code C

Second Floor 570 sq. ft.

Width: 47'-4"
Depth: 56'-6"

First Floor 1,245 sq. ft.

TO ORDER BLUEPRINTS USE THE FORM ON PAGE 15 OR CALL TOLL-FREE 1-877-671-6036
View thousands more home plans online at www.familyhandyman.com/HOMEPLANS

Plan #718-007D-0119

1,621 total square feet of living area

Sensational Home Designed For Views

Special features

- The front exterior includes an attractive gable-end arched window and extra-deep porch
- A grand-scale great room enjoys a coffered ceiling, fireplace, access to the wrap-around deck and is brightly lit with numerous French doors and windows
- The master bedroom suite has a sitting area, double walk-in closets and a luxury bath
- 223 square feet of optional finished space on the lower level
- 3 bedrooms, 2 baths, 2-car drive under side entry garage
- Basement foundation

Price Code B

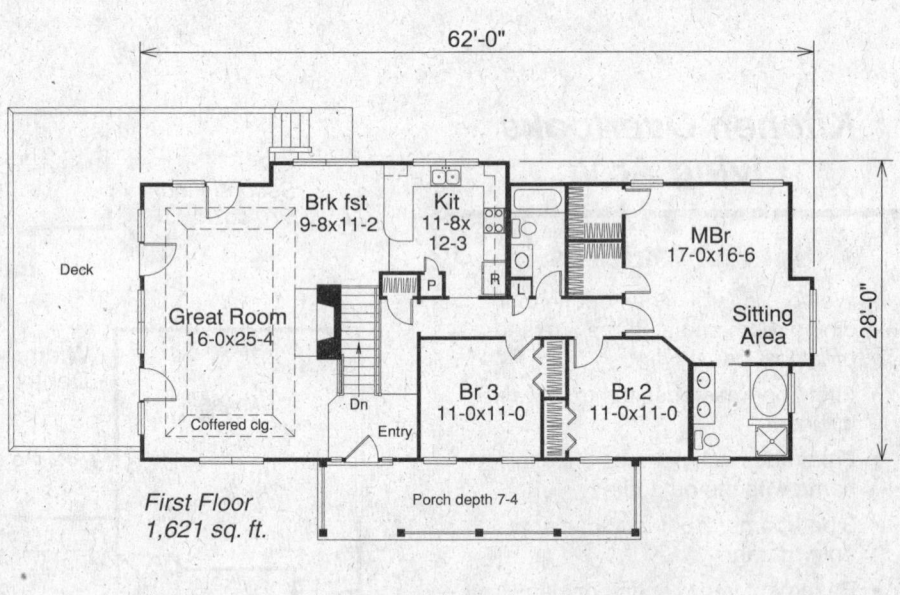

First Floor 1,621 sq. ft.

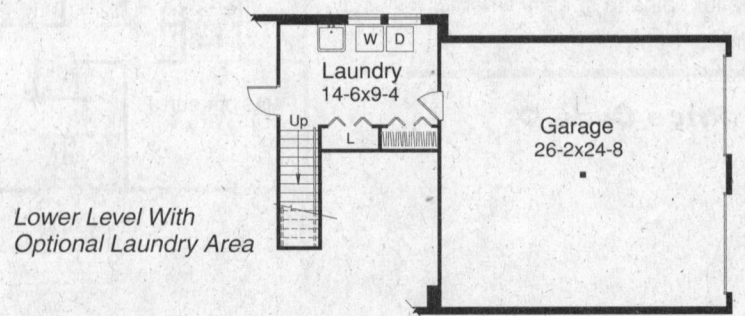

Lower Level With Optional Laundry Area

TO ORDER BLUEPRINTS USE THE FORM ON PAGE 15 OR CALL TOLL-FREE 1-877-671-6036
View thousands more home plans online at www.familyhandyman.com/HOMEPLANS

Plan #718-047D-0032

1,963 total square feet of living area

Charming Covered Porch

Special features

- Spacious breakfast nook is a great gathering place
- Master bedroom has its own wing with a private bath and lots of closet space
- Large laundry room with closet and sink
- 3 bedrooms, 2 baths, 2-car side entry garage
- Slab or crawl space foundation, please specify when ordering

Price Code C

Width: 58'-0"
Depth: 66'-8"

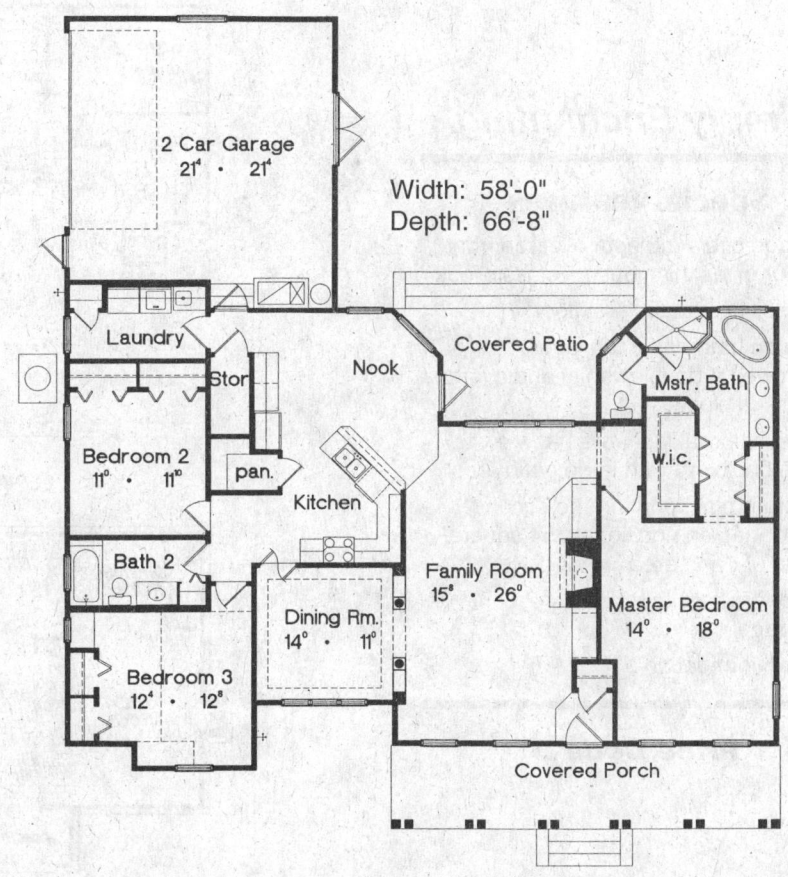

TO ORDER BLUEPRINTS USE THE FORM ON PAGE 15 OR CALL TOLL-FREE 1-877-671-6036
View thousands more home plans online at www.familyhandyman.com/HOMEPLANS

Plan #718-060D-0027

1,628 total square feet of living area

Simply Enchanting

Special features

- Large circle transom over the front door gives this house a classic look
- 9' ceilings on the first floor
- Salon bath has a tub, separate shower, a double vanity and a large walk-in closet
- Well-lit breakfast area has view to the backyard with large patio area
- Future play room on the second floor has an additional 354 square feet of living area
- 3 bedrooms, 2 1/2 baths, 2-car garage
- Slab foundation

Price Code B

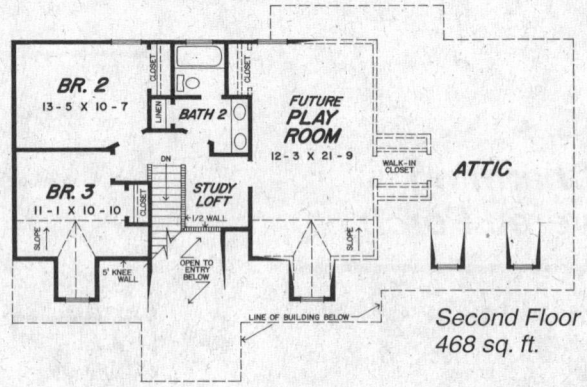

Second Floor
468 sq. ft.

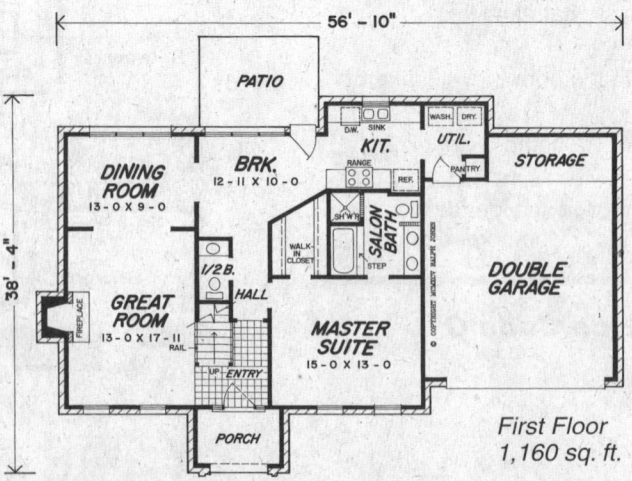

First Floor
1,160 sq. ft.

TO ORDER BLUEPRINTS USE THE FORM ON PAGE 15 OR CALL TOLL-FREE 1-877-671-6036

View thousands more home plans online at www.familyhandyman.com/homeplans

Plan #718-038D-0055

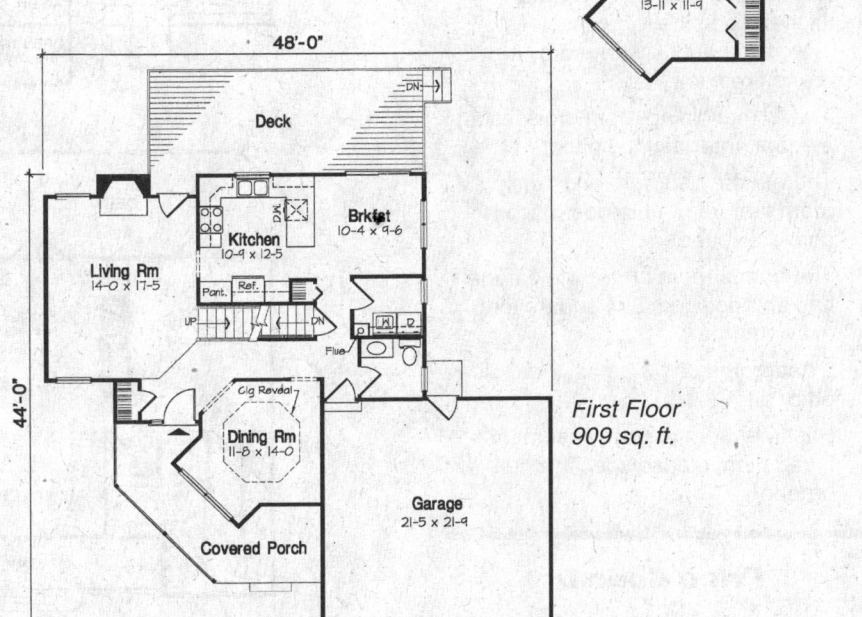

1,763 total square feet of living area

Rear View

Unique, Traditional Style, Farmhouse Flavor

Special features

- Dining room has a large box-bay window and a recessed ceiling
- Kitchen has plenty of workspace, a pantry and a double sink
- Master bedroom features a large bath with walk-in closet
- 3 bedrooms, 2 1/2 baths, 2-car garage
- Basement foundation

Price Code C

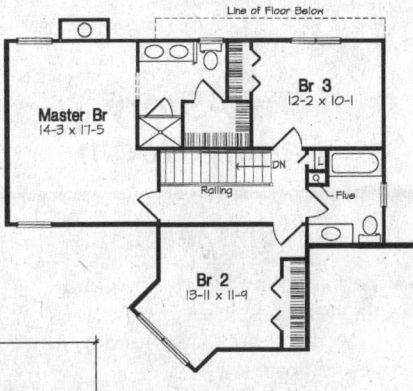

Second Floor 854 sq. ft.

First Floor 909 sq. ft.

TO ORDER BLUEPRINTS USE THE FORM ON PAGE 15 OR CALL TOLL-FREE 1-877-671-6036
View thousands more home plans online at www.familyhandyman.com/homeplans

Plan #718-047D-0079

2,508 total square feet of living area

Two-Story Family Room

Special features

- Family room, bayed nook and kitchen combine for a spacious living area and is warmed by a grand fireplace
- The formal dining room provides an elegant entertaining space
- The master bedroom and family room feature double-door access onto the rear deck
- The bonus room above the garage has an additional 384 square feet of living area
- 3 bedrooms, 2 1/2 baths, 2-car side entry garage
- Basement or walk-out basement foundation, please specify when ordering

Price Code D

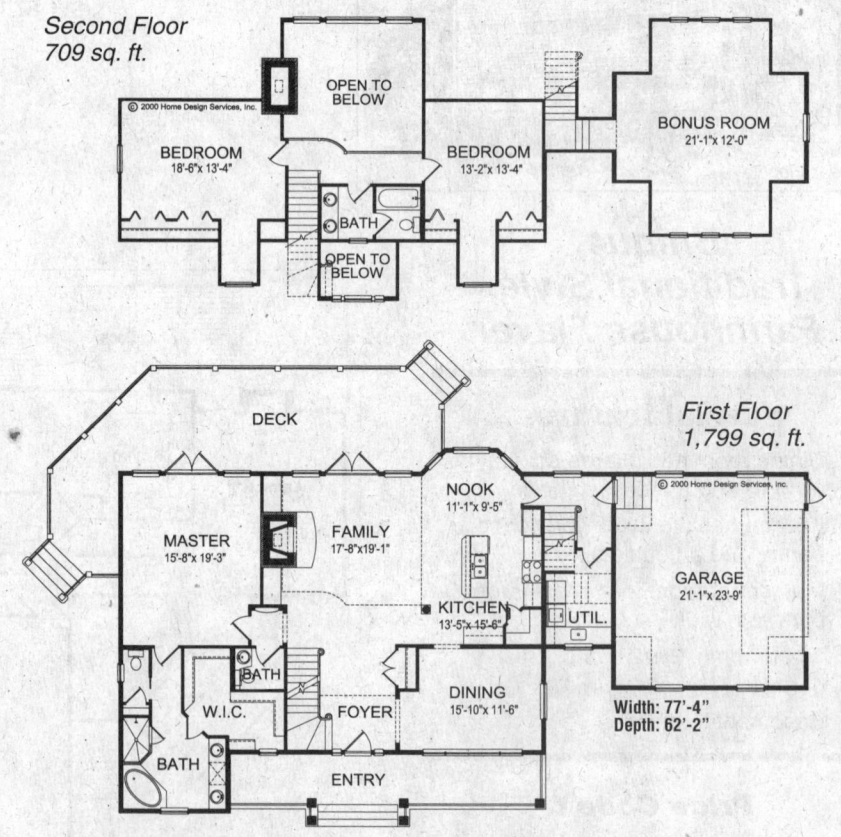

TO ORDER BLUEPRINTS USE THE FORM ON PAGE 15 OR CALL TOLL-FREE 1-877-671-6036
View thousands more home plans online at www.familyhandyman.com/HOMEPLANS

Plan #718-021D-0011

1,800 total square feet of living area

Transom Windows Create Impressive Front Entry

Special features

- Energy efficient home with 2" x 6" exterior walls
- Covered front and rear porches add outdoor living area
- 12' ceilings in the kitchen, breakfast area, dining and living rooms
- Private master bedroom features an expansive bath
- Side entry garage has two storage areas
- Pillared styling with brick and stucco exterior finish
- 3 bedrooms, 2 baths, 2-car side entry garage
- Crawl space foundation, drawings also include slab foundation

Price Code D

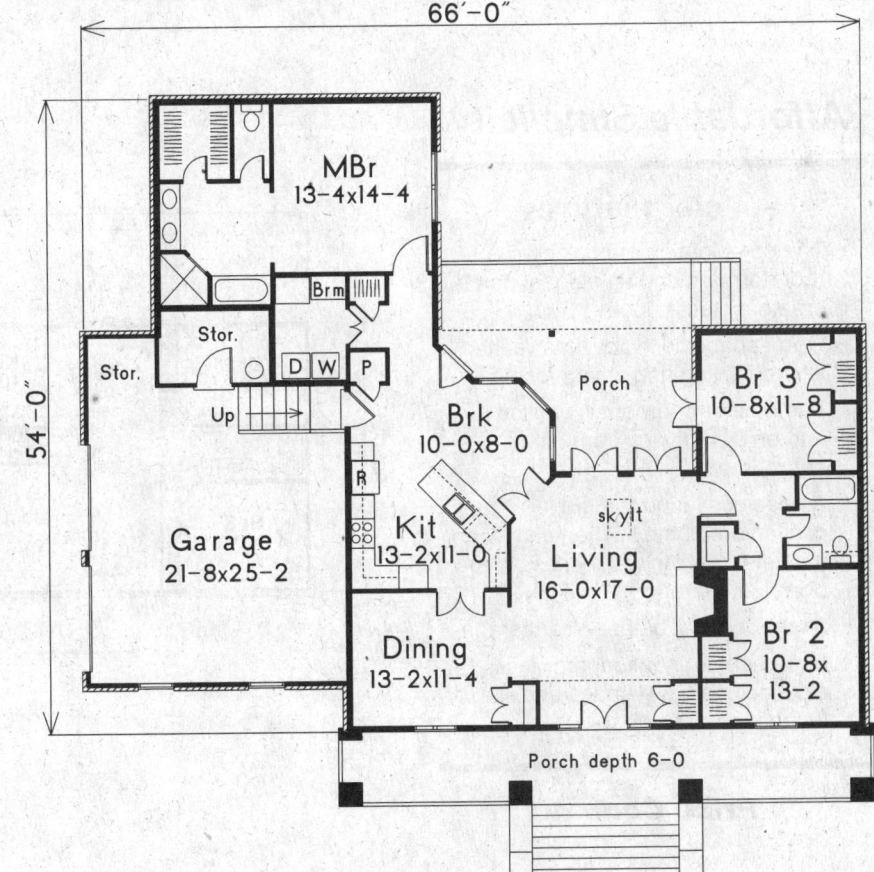

TO ORDER BLUEPRINTS USE THE FORM ON PAGE 15 OR CALL TOLL-FREE 1-877-671-6036
View thousands more home plans online at www.familyhandyman.com/homeplans

Plan #718-007D-0134

1,310 total square feet of living area

Affordable Simplicity

Special features

- The combination of brick quoins, roof dormers and an elegant porch create a classic look
- Open-space floor plan has vaulted kitchen, living and dining rooms
- The master bedroom is vaulted and enjoys privacy from other bedrooms
- A spacious laundry room is convenient to the kitchen and master bedroom with access to an oversized garage
- 3 bedrooms, 2 baths, 2-car garage
- Basement foundation, drawings also include crawl space and slab foundations

Price Code A

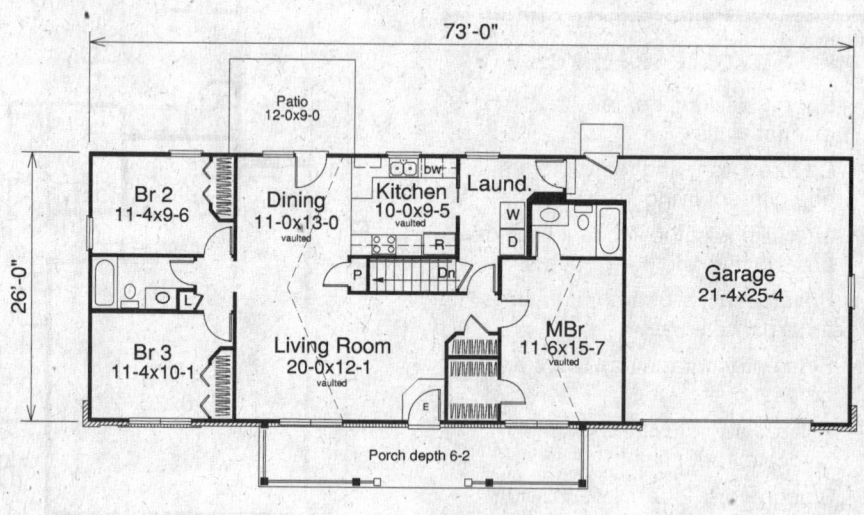

TO ORDER BLUEPRINTS USE THE FORM ON PAGE 15 OR CALL TOLL-FREE 1-877-671-6036
View thousands more home plans online at www.familyhandyman.com/homeplans

Plan #718-053D-0007

1,922 total square feet of living area

Two-Story Foyer Adds To Country Charm

Special features

- Varied front elevation features numerous accents
- Master bedroom suite is well-secluded with double-door entry and private bath
- Formal living and dining rooms located off the entry
- 3 bedrooms, 2 1/2 baths, 2-car garage
- Basement foundation

Price Code C

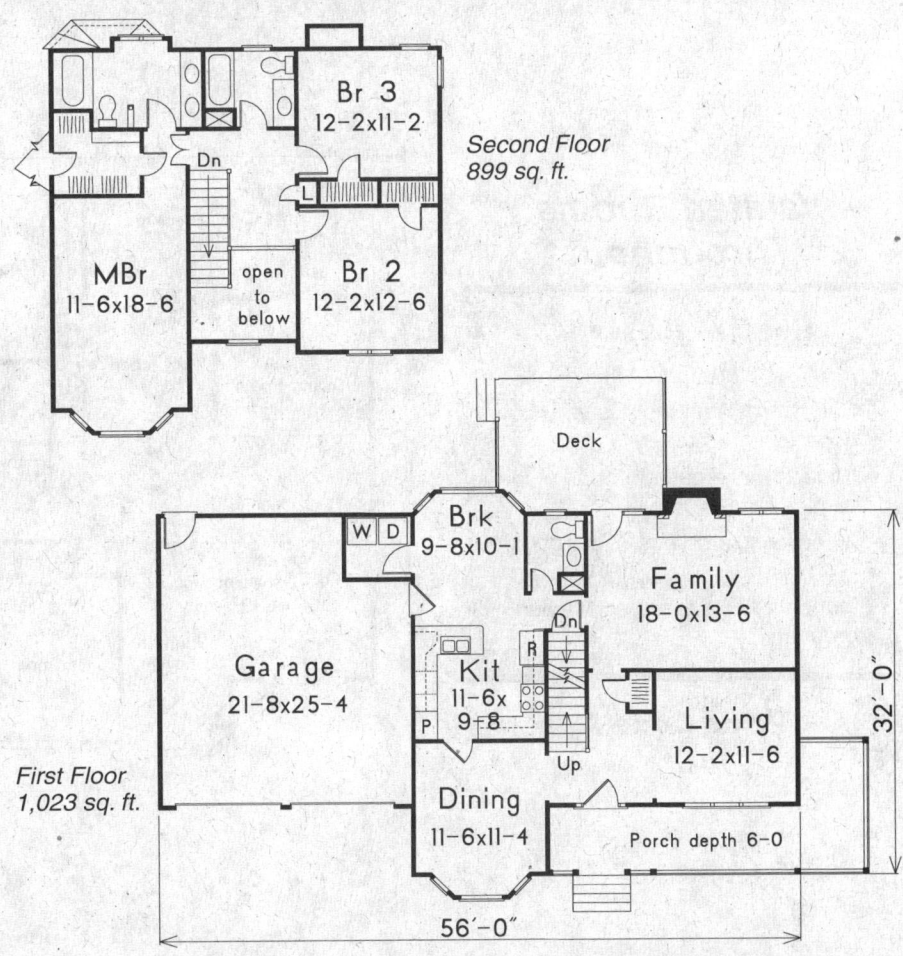

Second Floor 899 sq. ft.

First Floor 1,023 sq. ft.

Plan #718-035D-0017

1,373 total square feet of living area

Vaulted Rooms Throughout

Special features

- 9' ceilings throughout this home
- Sunny breakfast room is very accessible to kitchen
- Kitchen has a pass-through to the vaulted family room
- 3 bedrooms, 2 baths, 2-car garage
- Crawl space or walk-out basement foundation, please specify when ordering

Price Code A

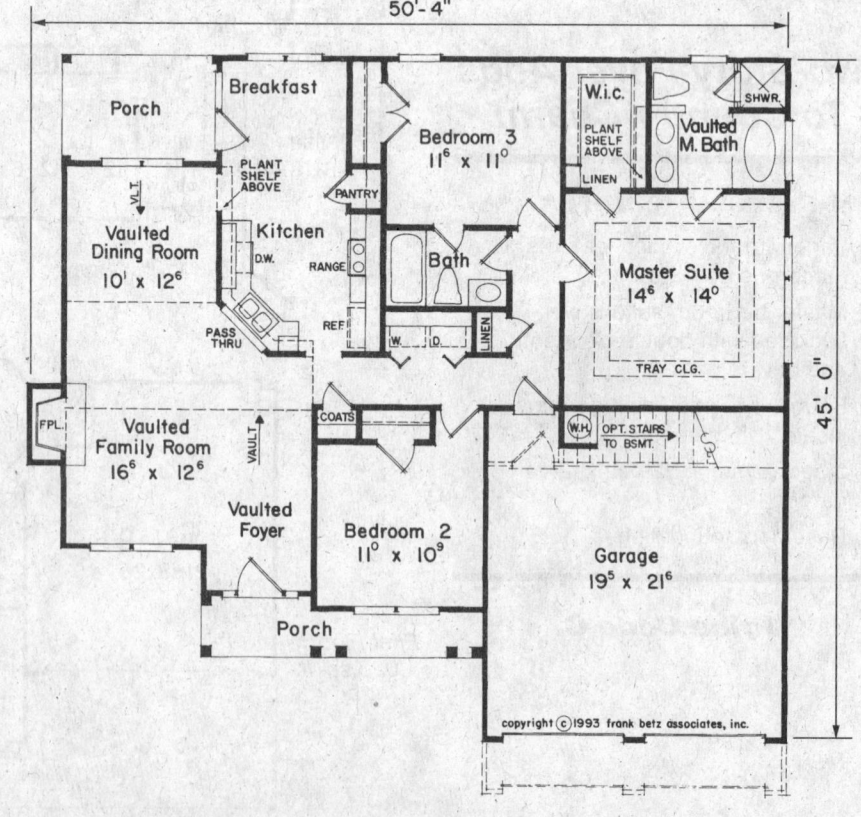

Plan #718-007D-0163

1,580 total square feet of living area

Elegance With Efficiency

Special features

- Home offers great looks with an oversized front porch
- The large great room features a corner fireplace, vaulted ceiling, access to the patio and is open to the bayed dining area and kitchen breakfast bar
- The spacious kitchen enjoys an adjoining multi-purpose room ideal for a study or hobby room
- The master bedroom boasts a vaulted ceiling, two walk-in closets and a plush bath
- 3 bedrooms, 2 baths, 2-car garage
- Crawl space foundation, drawings also include slab and basement foundations

Price Code B

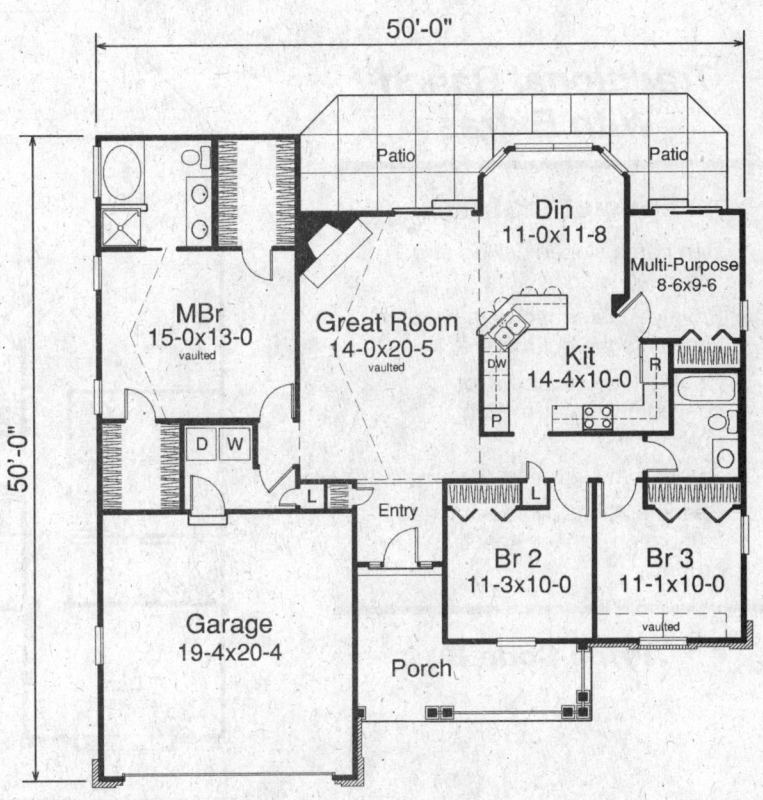

TO ORDER BLUEPRINTS USE THE FORM ON PAGE 15 OR CALL TOLL-FREE 1-877-671-6036
View thousands more home plans online at www.familyhandyman.com/homeplans

Plan #718-038D-0039

1,771 total square feet of living area

Traditional Ranch With Extras

Special features

- Den has a sloped ceiling and charming window seat
- Private master bedroom has access to the outdoors
- Central kitchen allows for convenient access when entertaining
- 2 bedrooms, 2 baths, 2-car garage
- Basement, crawl space or slab foundation, please specify when ordering

Price Code B

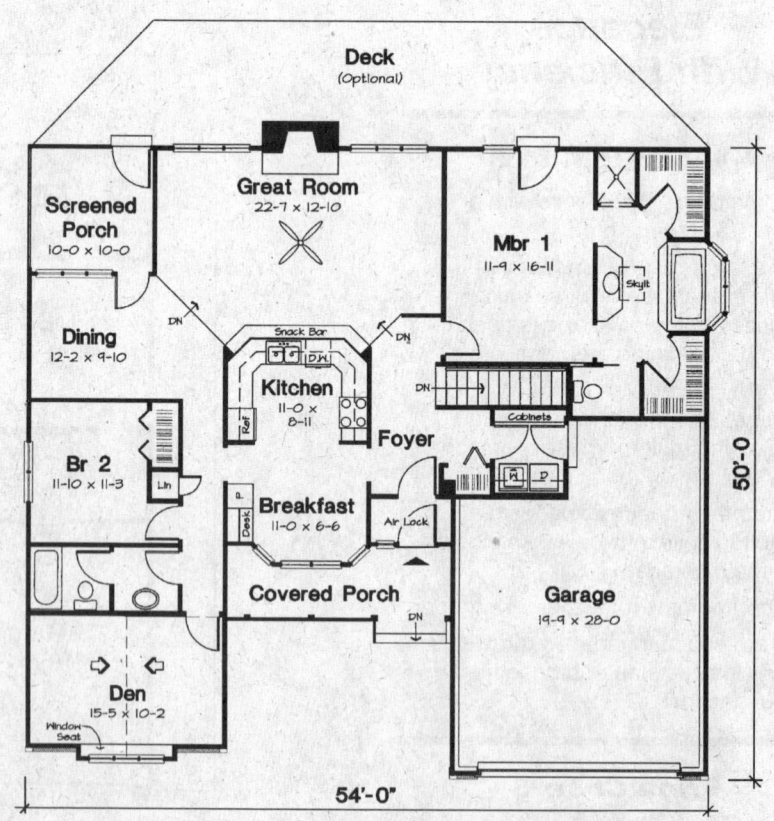

TO ORDER BLUEPRINTS USE THE FORM ON PAGE 15 OR CALL TOLL-FREE 1-877-671-6036
View thousands more home plans online at www.familyhandyman.com/HOMEPLANS

Plan #718-023D-0006

2,357 total square feet of living area

Attractive Entry Created By Full-Length Porch

Special features

- 9' ceilings on the first floor
- Secluded master bedroom includes a private bath with double walk-in closets and vanity
- Balcony overlooks living room with large fireplace
- The future game room on the second floor has an additional 303 square feet of living area
- 4 bedrooms, 3 1/2 baths, 2-car side entry garage
- Slab foundation, drawings also include crawl space foundation

Price Code D

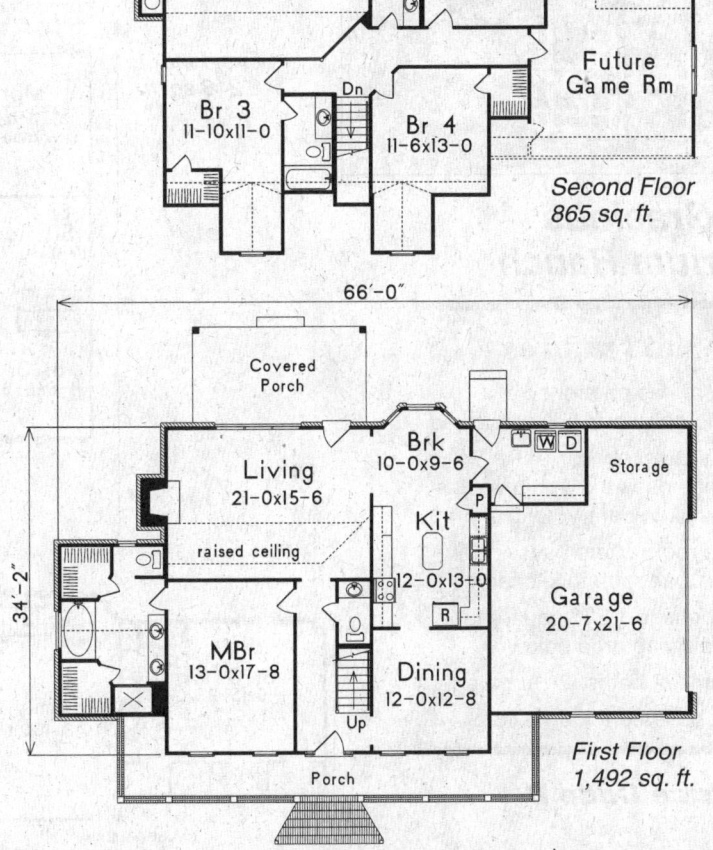

Second Floor 865 sq. ft.

First Floor 1,492 sq. ft.

TO ORDER BLUEPRINTS USE THE FORM ON PAGE 15 OR CALL TOLL-FREE 1-877-671-6036
View thousands more home plans online at www.familyhandyman.com/homeplans

The Family Handyman

Plan #718-007D-0065

2,218 total square feet of living area

Rear View

Gracious Atrium Ranch

Special features

- Great room has an arched colonnade entry and bay windowed atrium
- Kitchen has pass-through breakfast bar and walk-in pantry
- Breakfast room offers bay window and snack bar open to kitchen
- Atrium opens to 1,217 square feet of optional living area below
- 4 bedrooms, 2 baths, 2-car garage
- Walk-out basement foundation

Price Code D

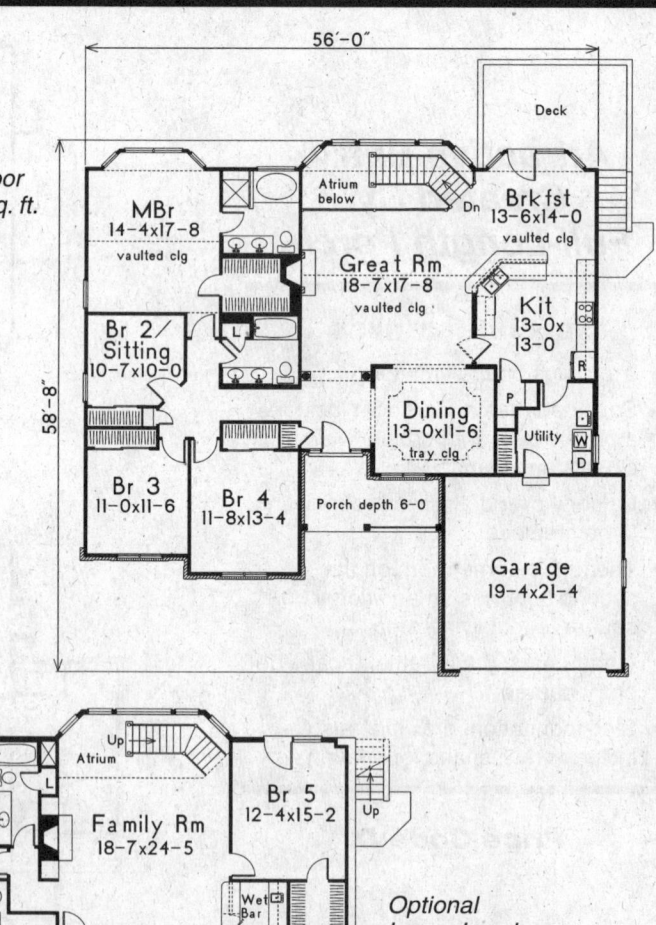

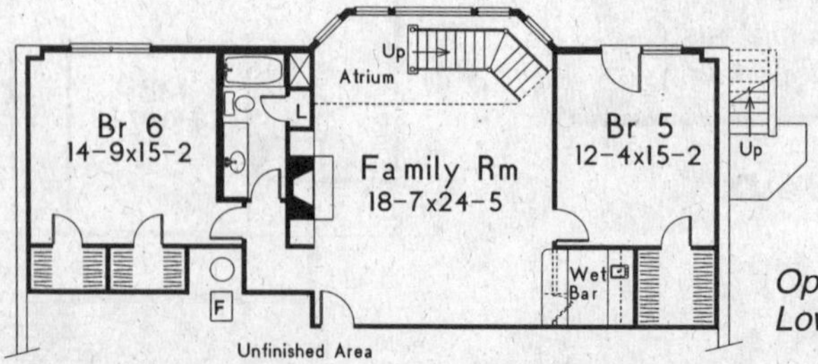

First Floor 2,218 sq. ft.

Optional Lower Level

TO ORDER BLUEPRINTS USE THE FORM ON PAGE 15 OR CALL TOLL-FREE 1-877-671-6036
View thousands more home plans online at www.familyhandyman.com/homeplans

Plan #718-055D-0109

2,217 total square feet of living area

Modest-Sized Home With Much To Offer

Special features

- Great room features a fireplace and is open to the foyer, breakfast and dining rooms
- Laundry room and storage closet are located off the garage
- Secluded master suite includes a bath with a corner whirlpool tub, split vanities, corner shower and a large walk-in closet
- 4 bedrooms, 2 baths, 2-car garage
- Crawl space or slab foundation, please specify when ordering

Price Code C

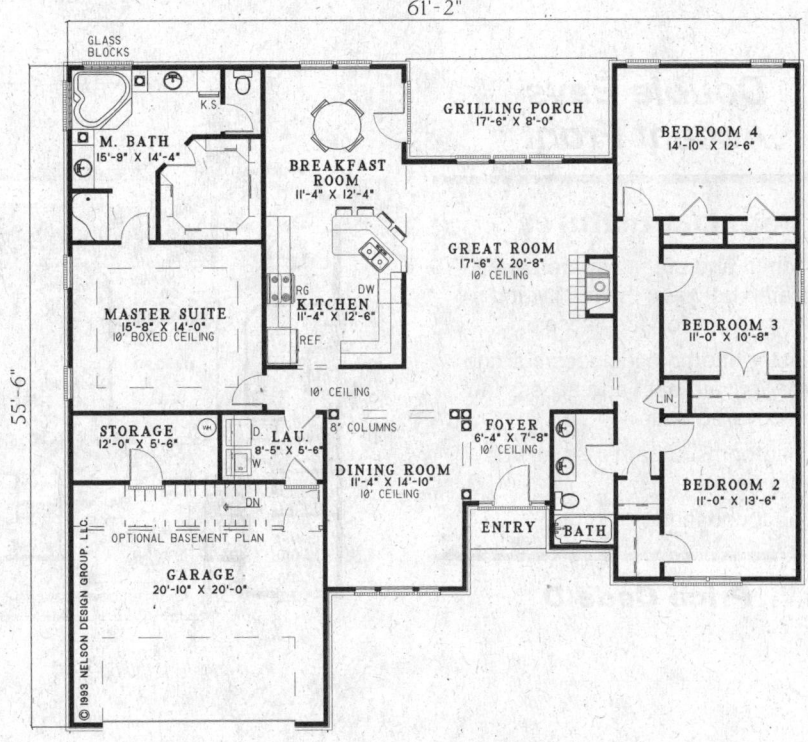

TO ORDER BLUEPRINTS USE THE FORM ON PAGE 15 OR CALL TOLL-FREE 1-877-671-6036
View thousands more home plans online at www.familyhandyman.com/homeplans

Plan #718-036D-0058

2,529 total square feet of living area

Double Bays Accent Front

Special features

- Kitchen and breakfast area are located between the family and living rooms for easy access
- Master bedroom includes a sitting area, private bath and access to the covered patio
- 4 bedrooms, 3 baths, 3-car side entry garage
- Slab foundation

Price Code D

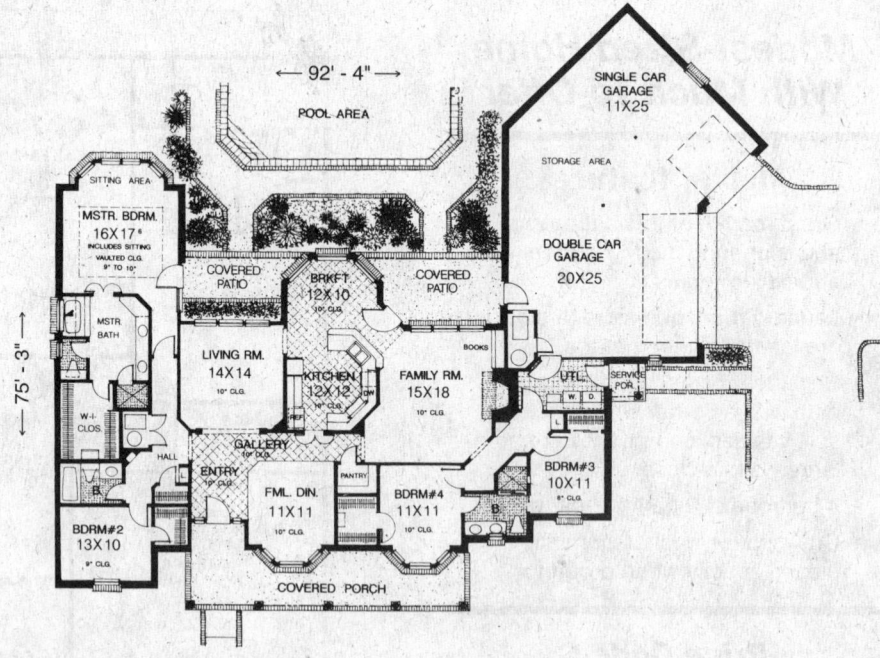

TO ORDER BLUEPRINTS USE THE FORM ON PAGE 15 OR CALL TOLL-FREE 1-877-671-6036
View thousands more home plans online at www.familyhandyman.com/HOMEPLANS

Plan #718-062D-0045

2,516 total square feet of living area

Appealing Victorian Accents

Special features

- Living room has a fireplace, while the formal dining room has a buffet alcove and access to the verandah
- A cozy sitting area and tray ceiling accent the master bedroom
- Spacious bedrooms make this a wonderful family home
- 4 bedrooms, 2 1/2 baths, 2-car side entry garage
- Basement or crawl space foundation, please specify when ordering

Price Code D

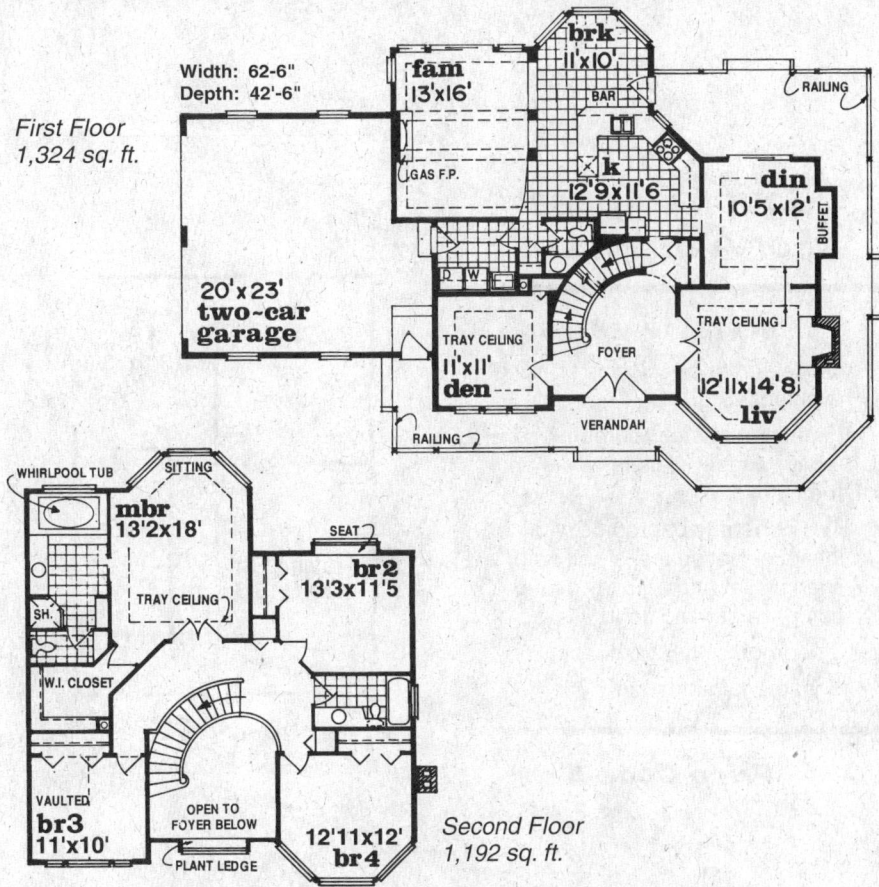

Width: 62'-6"
Depth: 42'-6"

First Floor 1,324 sq. ft.

Second Floor 1,192 sq. ft.

TO ORDER BLUEPRINTS USE THE FORM ON PAGE 15 OR CALL TOLL-FREE 1-877-671-6036
View thousands more home plans online at www.familyhandyman.com/HOMEPLANS

Plan #718-007D-0088

1,299 total square feet of living area

Country Appeal For A Small Lot

Special features

- Large porch for enjoying relaxing evenings
- First floor master bedroom has a bay window, walk-in closet and roomy bath
- Two generous bedrooms with lots of closet space, a hall bath, linen closet and balcony overlook comprise second floor
- 3 bedrooms, 2 1/2 baths
- Basement foundation

Price Code A

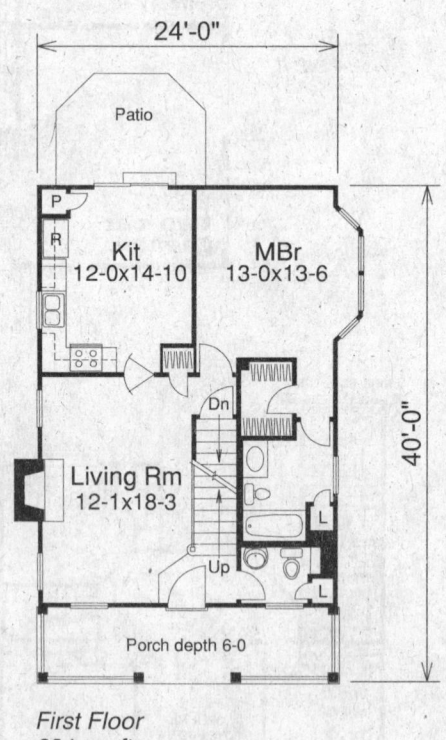

First Floor
834 sq. ft.

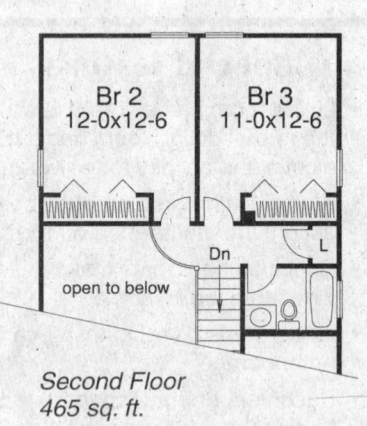

Second Floor
465 sq. ft.

TO ORDER BLUEPRINTS USE THE FORM ON PAGE 15 OR CALL TOLL-FREE 1-877-671-6036
View thousands more home plans online at www.familyhandyman.com/homeplans

Plan #718-047D-0035

2,077 total square feet of living area

Ranch Has A Lot To Offer

Special features

- Lots of storage space throughout
- Enormous covered patio adds a lot of space when entertaining
- Angled walls add appeal throughout this home
- 3 bedrooms, 2 baths, 2-car side entry garage
- Slab foundation

Price Code C

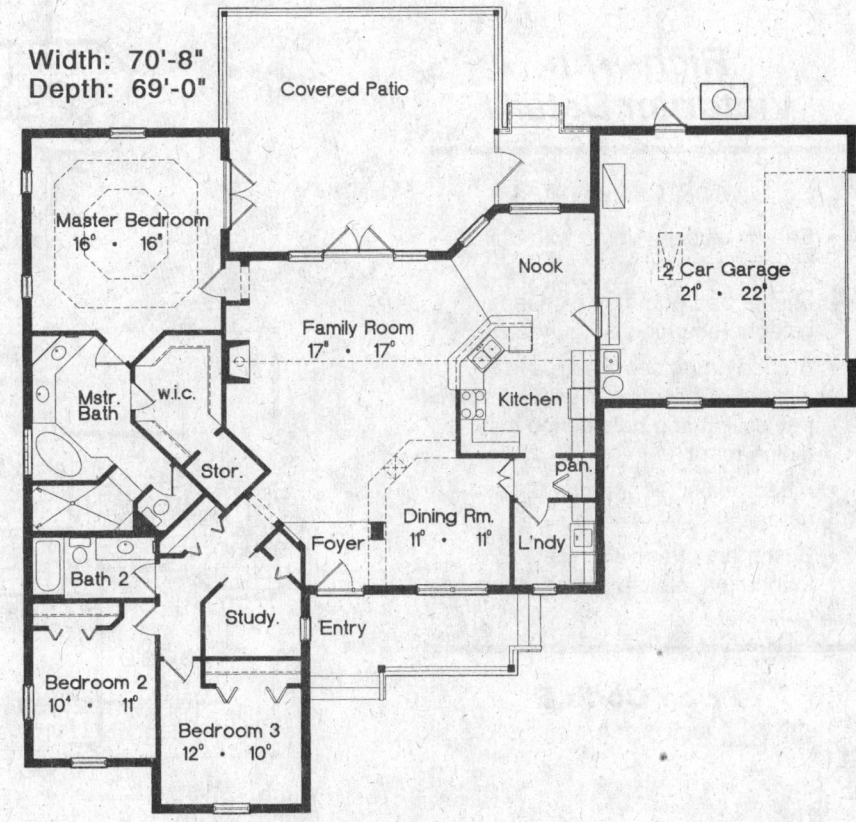

Width: 70'-8"
Depth: 69'-0"

TO ORDER BLUEPRINTS USE THE FORM ON PAGE 15 OR CALL TOLL-FREE 1-877-671-6036
View thousands more home plans online at www.familyhandyman.com/HOMEPLANS

Plan #718-062D-0046

2,632 total square feet of living area

Rich With Victorian Details

Special features

- Energy efficient home with 2" x 6" exterior walls
- Master bedroom has a cheerful octagon-shaped sitting area
- Arched entrances create a distinctive living room with a lovely tray ceiling and help define the dining room
- 4 bedrooms, 2 1/2 baths, 2-car garage
- Basement or crawl space foundation, please specify when ordering

Price Code E

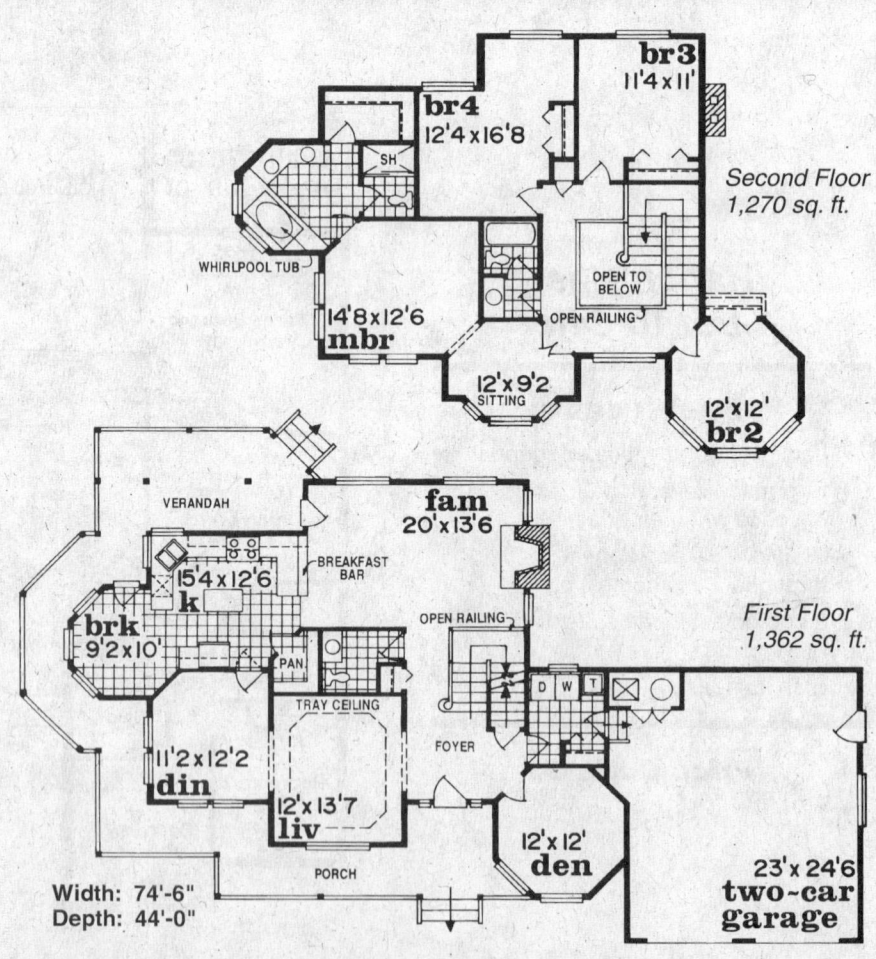

Second Floor 1,270 sq. ft.

First Floor 1,362 sq. ft.

Width: 74'-6"
Depth: 44'-0"

TO ORDER BLUEPRINTS USE THE FORM ON PAGE 15 OR CALL TOLL-FREE 1-877-671-6036
View thousands more home plans online at www.familyhandyman.com/HOMEPLANS

Plan #718-039D-0020

2,010 total square feet of living area

Kitchen With Island Sink

Special features

- Oversized kitchen is a great gathering place with eat-in island bar, dining area nearby and built-in desk
- First floor master bedroom has privacy
- Unique second floor kid's living area for playroom
- Optional bonus room has an additional 313 square feet of living area
- 3 bedrooms, 2 1/2 baths, 2-car side entry garage
- Basement foundation

Price Code C

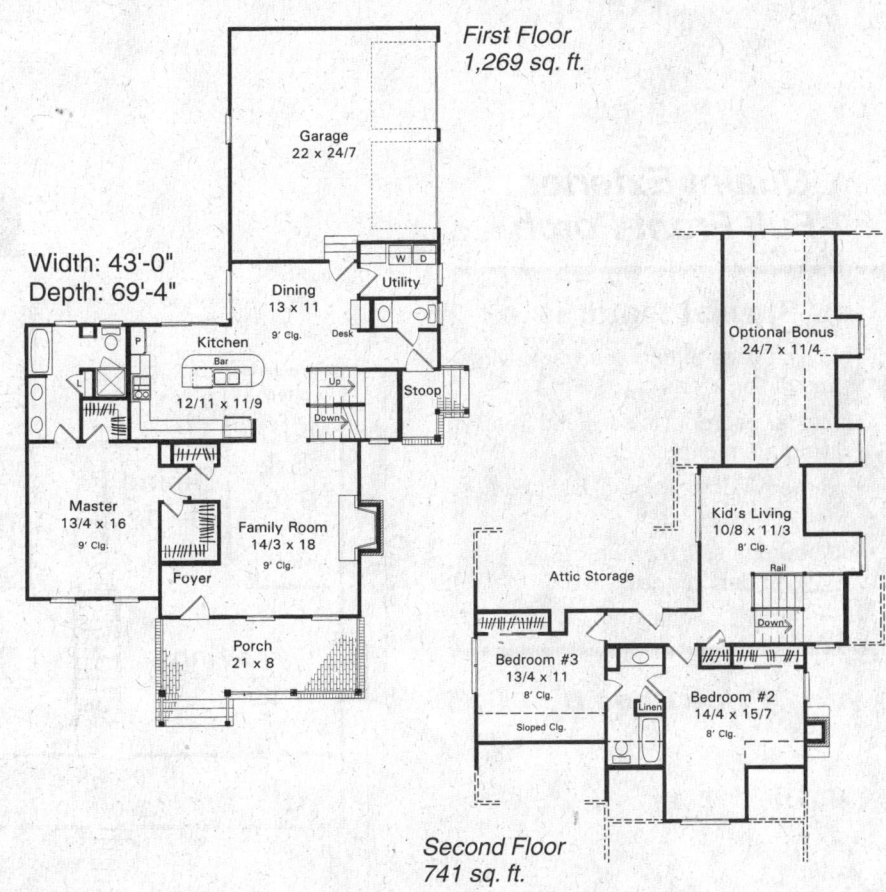

TO ORDER BLUEPRINTS USE THE FORM ON PAGE 15 OR CALL TOLL-FREE 1-877-671-6036
View thousands more home plans online at www.familyhandyman.com/HOMEPLANS

Plan #718-053D-0030

1,657 total square feet of living area

Quaint Exterior, Full Front Porch

Special features

- Stylish pass-through between living and dining areas
- Master bedroom is secluded from living area for privacy
- Large windows in breakfast and dining areas
- 3 bedrooms, 2 1/2 baths, 2-car drive under garage
- Basement foundation

Price Code B

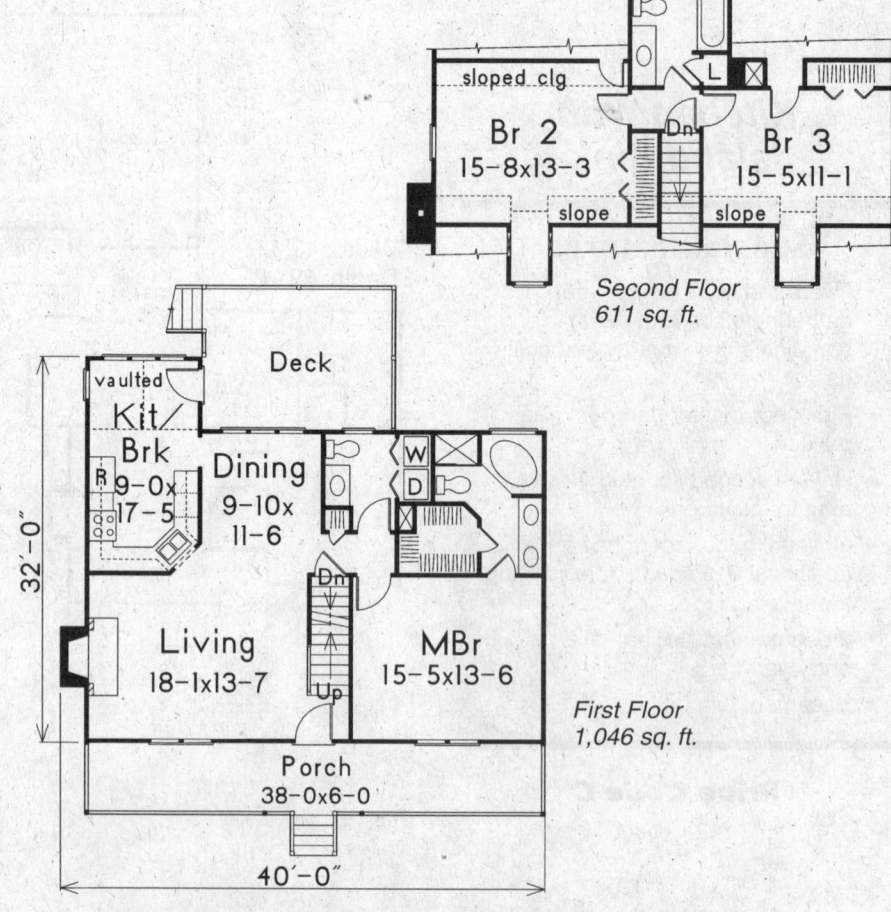

Plan #718-007D-0054

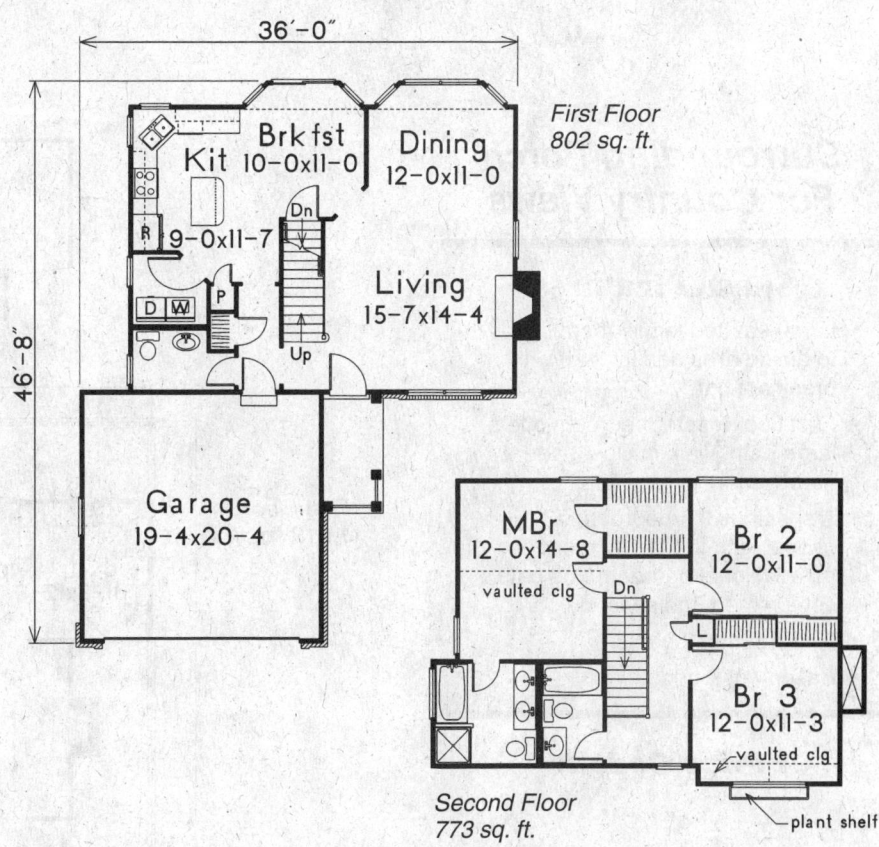

1,575 total square feet of living area

Stylish Living For A Narrow Lot

Special features

- Inviting porch leads to spacious living and dining rooms
- Kitchen with corner windows features an island snack bar, attractive breakfast room bay, convenient laundry area and built-in pantry
- A luxury bath and walk-in closet adorn the master bedroom suite
- 3 bedrooms, 2 1/2 baths, 2-car garage
- Basement foundation, drawings also include crawl space and slab foundations

Price Code B

TO ORDER BLUEPRINTS USE THE FORM ON PAGE 15 OR CALL TOLL-FREE 1-877-671-6036
View thousands more home plans online at www.familyhandyman.com/homeplans

Plan #718-058D-0020

1,428 total square feet of living area

Surrounding Porch For Country Views

Special features

- Large vaulted family room opens to dining area and kitchen with breakfast bar
- First floor master bedroom offers large bath, walk-in closet and nearby laundry facilities
- A spacious loft/bedroom #3 overlooking the family room and an additional bedroom and bath complement the second floor
- 3 bedrooms, 2 baths
- Basement foundation

Price Code A

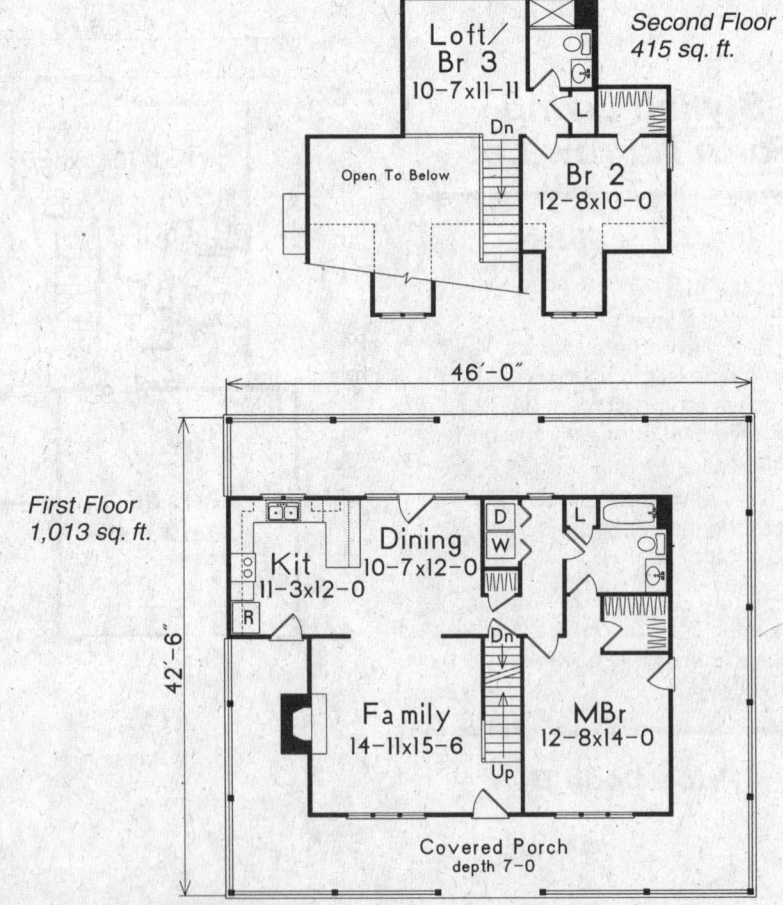

Plan #718-024D-0040

2,503 total square feet of living area

Beautiful Southern Style

Special features

- 10' ceilings throughout the first floor
- A secondary entrance into the kitchen is convenient and casual
- First floor master bedroom has its own bath and walk-in closet
- The living room features a fireplace flanked by doors leading to the rear porch
- 4 bedrooms, 3 1/2 baths, 2-car drive under garage
- Walk-out basement foundation

Price Code D

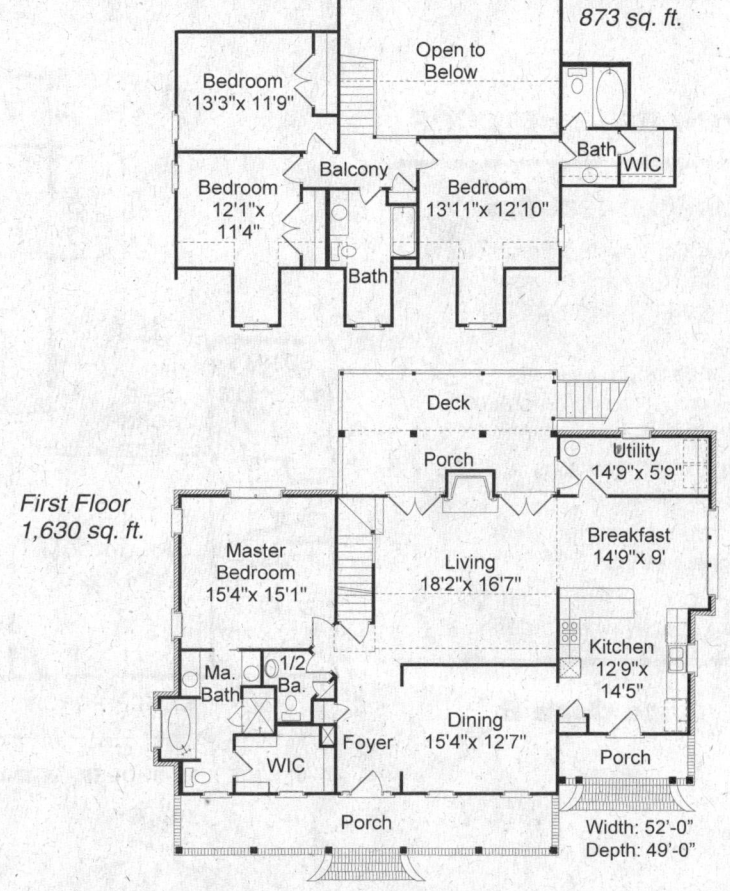

TO ORDER BLUEPRINTS USE THE FORM ON PAGE 15 OR CALL TOLL-FREE 1-877-671-6036
View thousands more home plans online at www.familyhandyman.com/homeplans

Plan #718-028D-0003

1,716 total square feet of living area

Extra-Large Porches

Special features

- Great room boasts a fireplace and access to the kitchen/breakfast area through a large arched opening
- Master bedroom includes a huge walk-in closet and French doors that lead onto an L-shaped porch
- Bedrooms #2 and #3 share a bath and linen closet
- 3 bedrooms, 2 baths, 2-car detached garage
- Crawl space or slab foundation, please specify when ordering

Price Code B

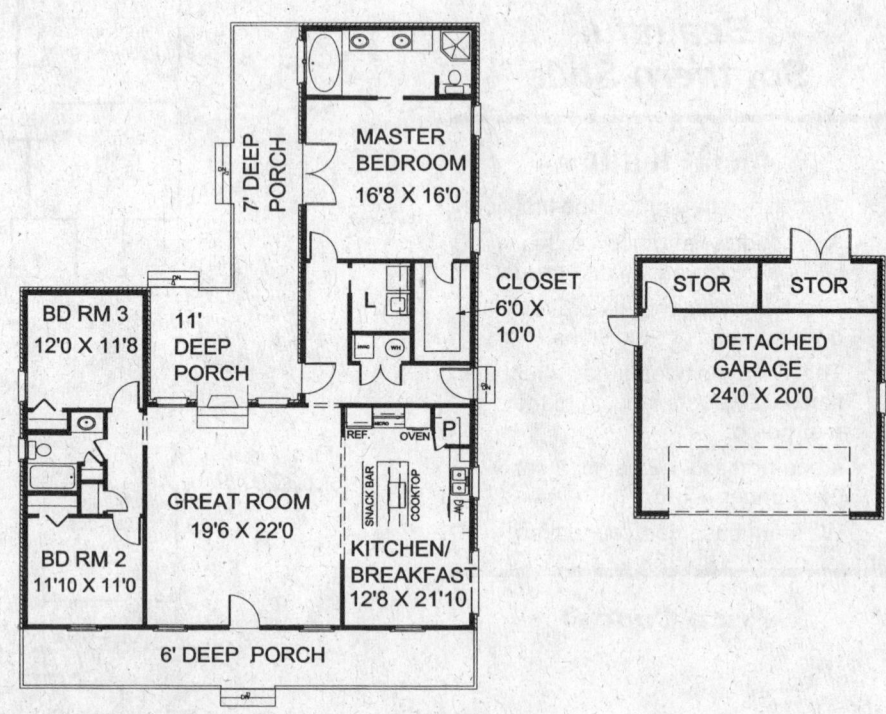

44'-0" WIDE X 65'-0" DEEP - WITHOUT GARAGE

TO ORDER BLUEPRINTS USE THE FORM ON PAGE 15 OR CALL TOLL-FREE 1-877-671-6036

View thousands more home plans online at www.familyhandyman.com/HOMEPLANS

Plan #718-048D-0011

1,550 total square feet of living area

Vaulted Ceilings Add Dimension

Special features
- Alcove in family room can be used as a cozy corner fireplace or as a media center
- Master bedroom features a large walk-in closet, skylight and separate tub and shower
- Convenient laundry closet
- Kitchen with pantry and breakfast bar connects to the family room
- Family room and master bedroom access the covered patio
- 3 bedrooms, 2 baths, 2-car garage
- Slab foundation

Price Code B

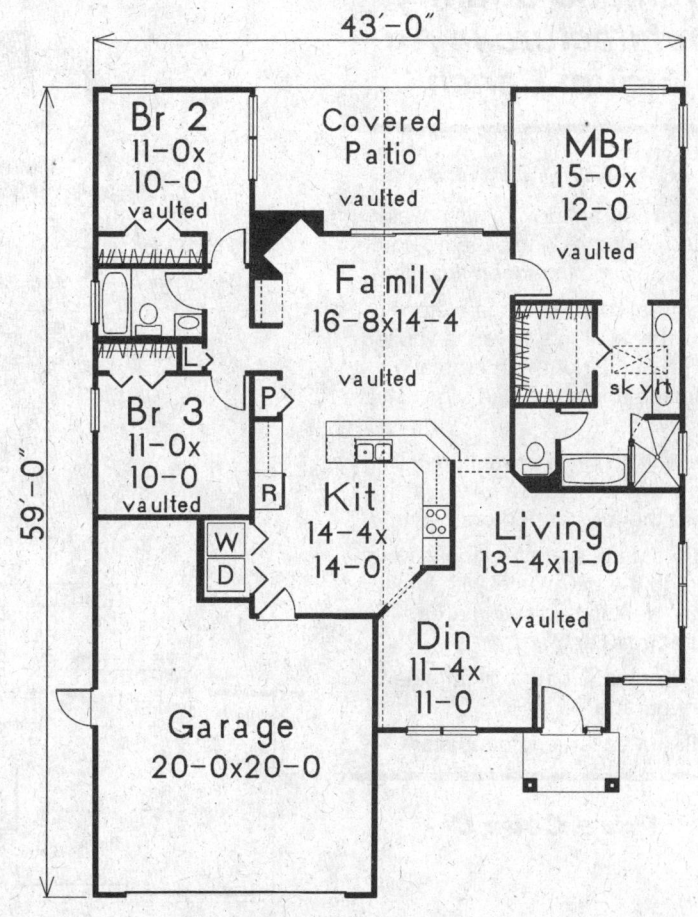

TO ORDER BLUEPRINTS USE THE FORM ON PAGE 15 OR CALL TOLL-FREE 1-877-671-6036
View thousands more home plans online at www.familyhandyman.com/HOMEPLANS

Plan #718-007D-0116

2,100 total square feet of living area

Dramatic Country Architecture In An Atrium Ranch

Special features

- A large courtyard with stone walls, lantern columns and covered porch welcomes you into open spaces
- The great room features a stone fireplace, built-in shelves, a vaulted ceiling and atrium with dramatic staircase and a two and a half story window wall
- Two walk-in closets, vaulted ceiling with plant shelf and a luxury bath adorn the master bedroom suite
- 1,391 square feet of optional living area on the lower level with family room, walk-in bar, sitting area, bedroom #3 and a bath
- 2 bedrooms, 2 baths, 3-car side entry garage
- Walk-out basement foundation

Price Code C

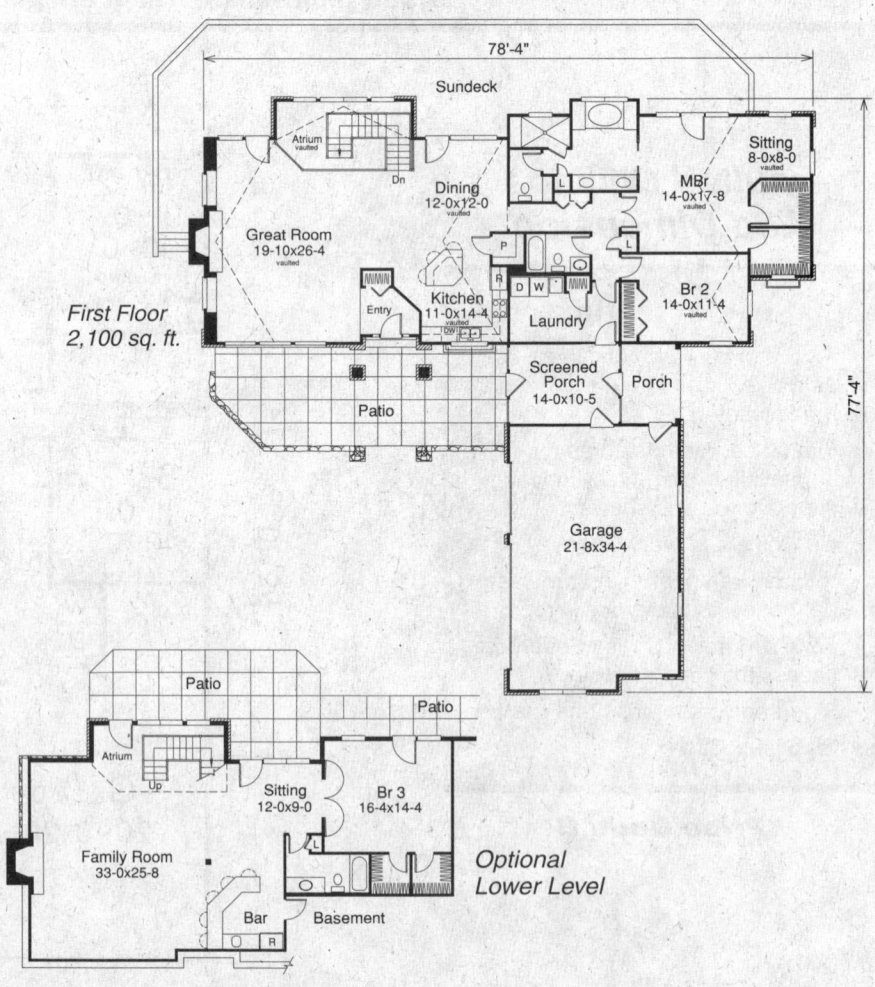

TO ORDER BLUEPRINTS USE THE FORM ON PAGE 15 OR CALL TOLL-FREE 1-877-671-6036
View thousands more home plans online at www.familyhandyman.com/HOMEPLANS

Plan #718-035D-0025

1,614 total square feet of living area

Quaint Two-Story

Special features

- Master suite has all the luxuries including private bath with whirlpool tub and walk-in closet
- Two-story family room has cozy fireplace and plenty of windows adding sunlight
- 9' ceilings throughout home
- 3 bedrooms, 2 1/2 baths, 2-car garage
- Crawl space or walk-out basement foundation, please specify when ordering

Price Code B

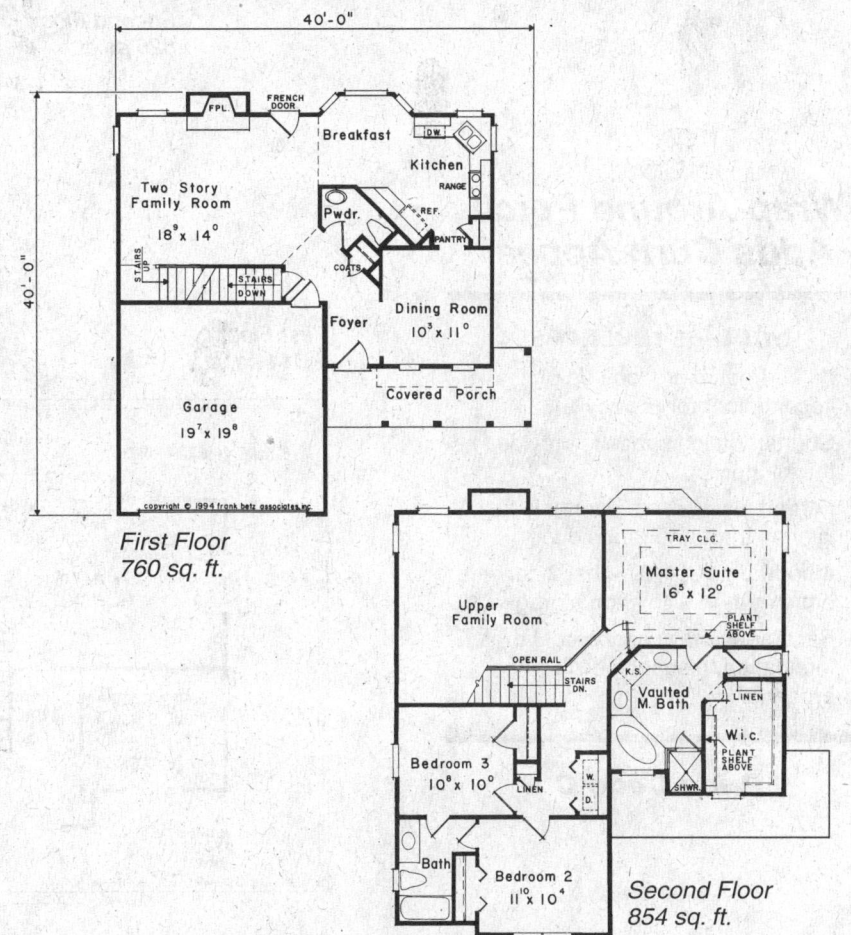

First Floor 760 sq. ft.

Second Floor 854 sq. ft.

TO ORDER BLUEPRINTS USE THE FORM ON PAGE 15 OR CALL TOLL-FREE 1-877-671-6036
View thousands more home plans online at www.familyhandyman.com/HOMEPLANS

Plan #718-067D-0006

1,840 total square feet of living area

Wrap-Around Porch Adds Curb Appeal

Special features
- All bedrooms are located on the second floor for privacy
- Counter dining space is provided in the kitchen
- Formal dining room connects to the kitchen through French doors
- 4 bedrooms, 2 1/2 baths, 2-car side entry garage with shop/storage
- Basement, crawl space or slab foundation, please specify when ordering

Price Code C

Second Floor 826 sq. ft.

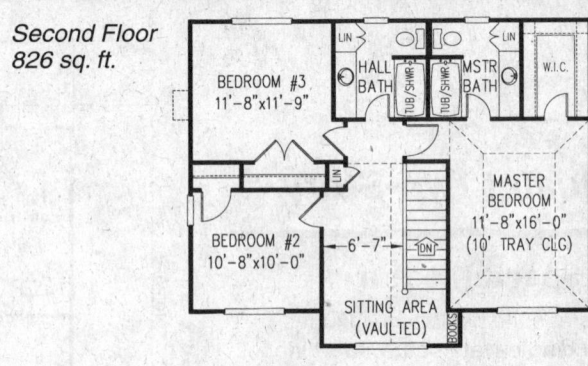

First Floor 1,014 sq. ft.

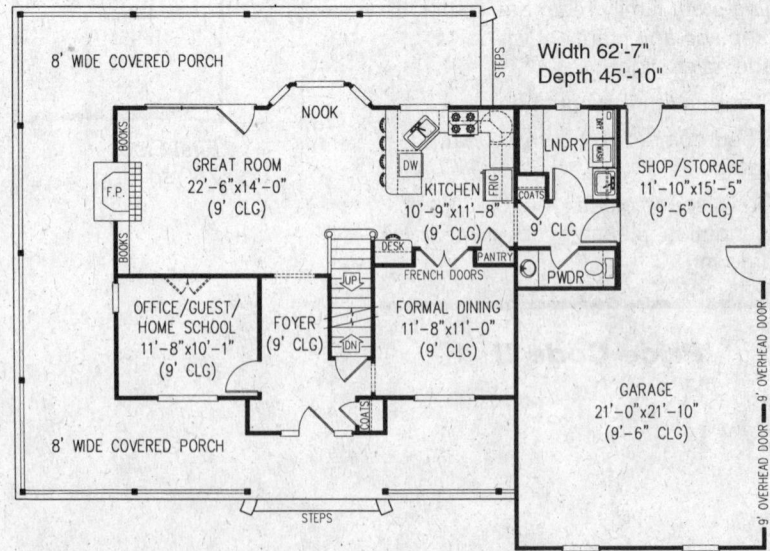

TO ORDER BLUEPRINTS USE THE FORM ON PAGE 15 OR CALL TOLL-FREE 1-877-671-6036
View thousands more home plans online at www.familyhandyman.com/homeplans

Plan #718-037D-0004

2,449 total square feet of living area

Country-Style Home

Special features

- Striking living area features fireplace flanked with windows, cathedral ceiling and balcony
- First floor master bedroom has twin walk-in closets and large linen storage
- Dormers add space for desks or seats
- 3 bedrooms, 2 1/2 baths, 2-car detached garage
- Slab foundation, drawings also include crawl space foundation

Price Code E

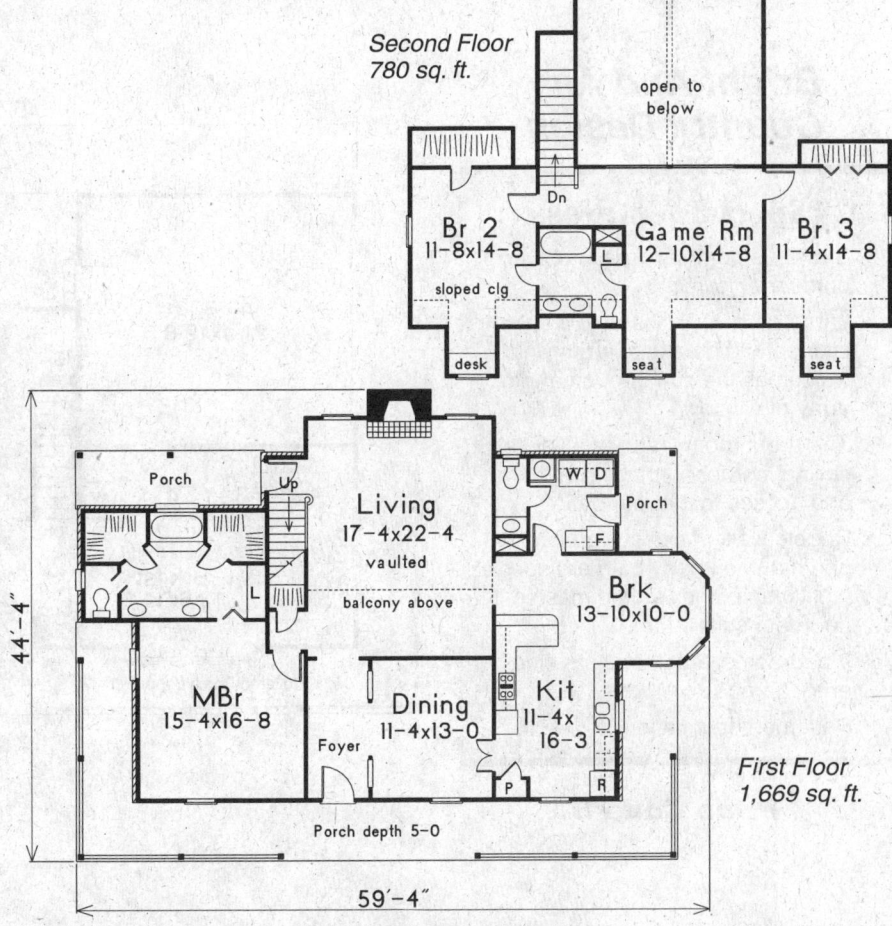

TO ORDER BLUEPRINTS USE THE FORM ON PAGE 15 OR CALL TOLL-FREE 1-877-671-6036
View thousands more home plans online at www.familyhandyman.com/HOMEPLANS

Plan #718-007D-0140

1,591 total square feet of living area

Bright And Airy Country Design

Special features

- Spacious porch and patio provide outdoor enjoyment
- Large entry foyer leads to a cheery kitchen and breakfast room which welcomes the sun through a wide array of windows
- The great room features a vaulted ceiling, corner fireplace, wet bar and access to the rear patio
- Double walk-in closets, private porch and a luxury bath are special highlights of the vaulted master bedroom suite
- 3 bedrooms, 2 baths, 2-car side entry garage
- Basement foundation

Price Code B

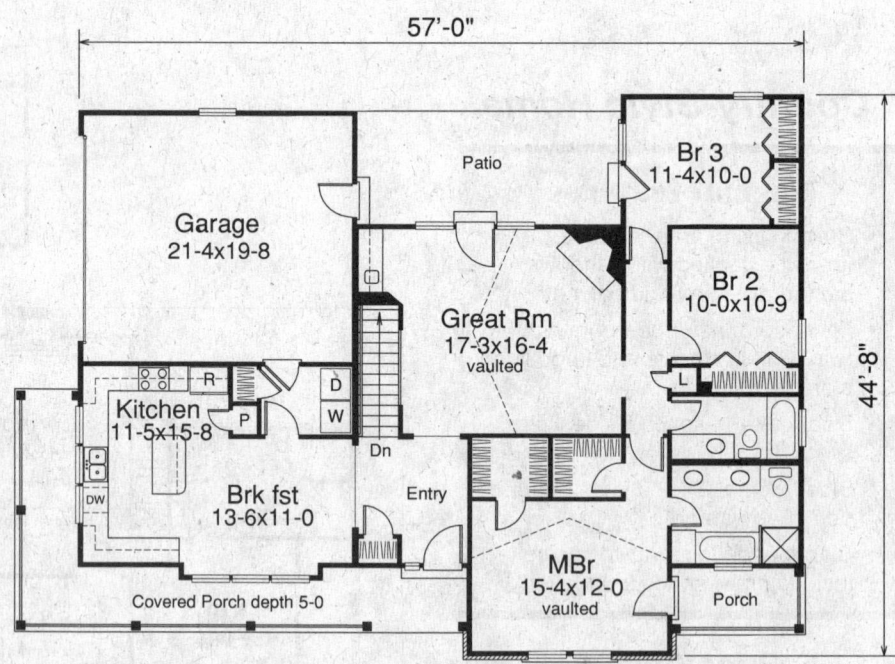

Plan #718-053D-0002

1,668 total square feet of living area

Bay Window Graces Luxury Master Bedroom

Special features

- Large bay windows grace the breakfast area, master bedroom and dining room
- Extensive walk-in closets and storage spaces are throughout the home
- Handy covered entry porch
- Large living room has a fireplace, built-in bookshelves and sloped ceiling
- 3 bedrooms, 2 baths, 2-car drive under garage
- Basement foundation

Price Code C

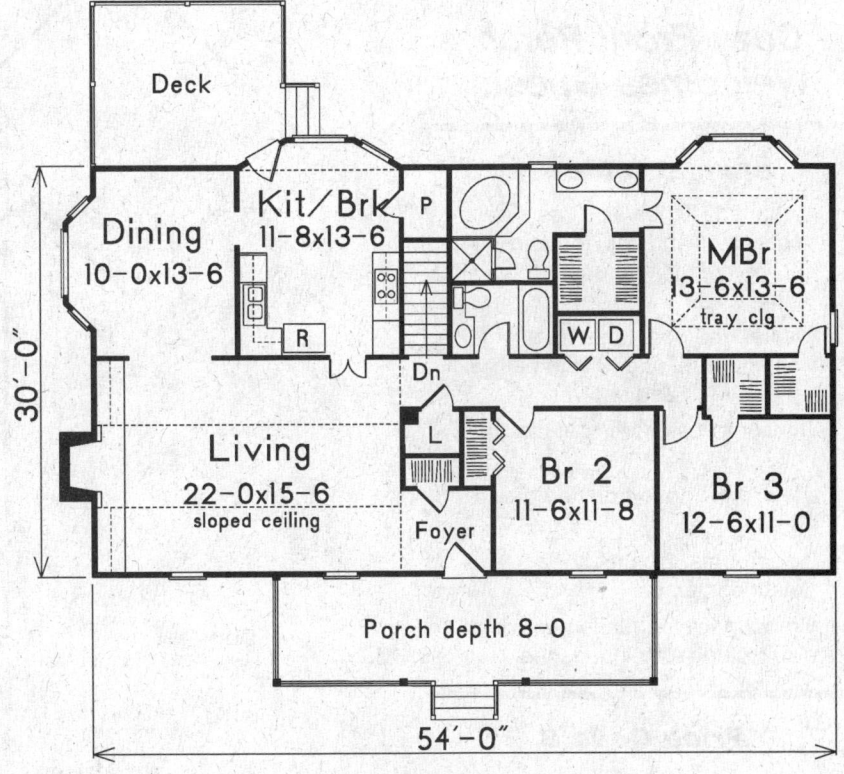

Plan #718-040D-0026

1,393 total square feet of living area

Cozy Front Porch Welcomes Guests

Special features

- L-shaped kitchen features a walk-in pantry, island cooktop and is convenient to the laundry room and dining area
- Master bedroom features a large walk-in closet and private bath with separate tub and shower
- Convenient storage/coat closet in hall
- View to the patio from the dining area
- 3 bedrooms, 2 baths, 2-car detached garage
- Crawl space foundation, drawings also include slab foundation

Price Code B

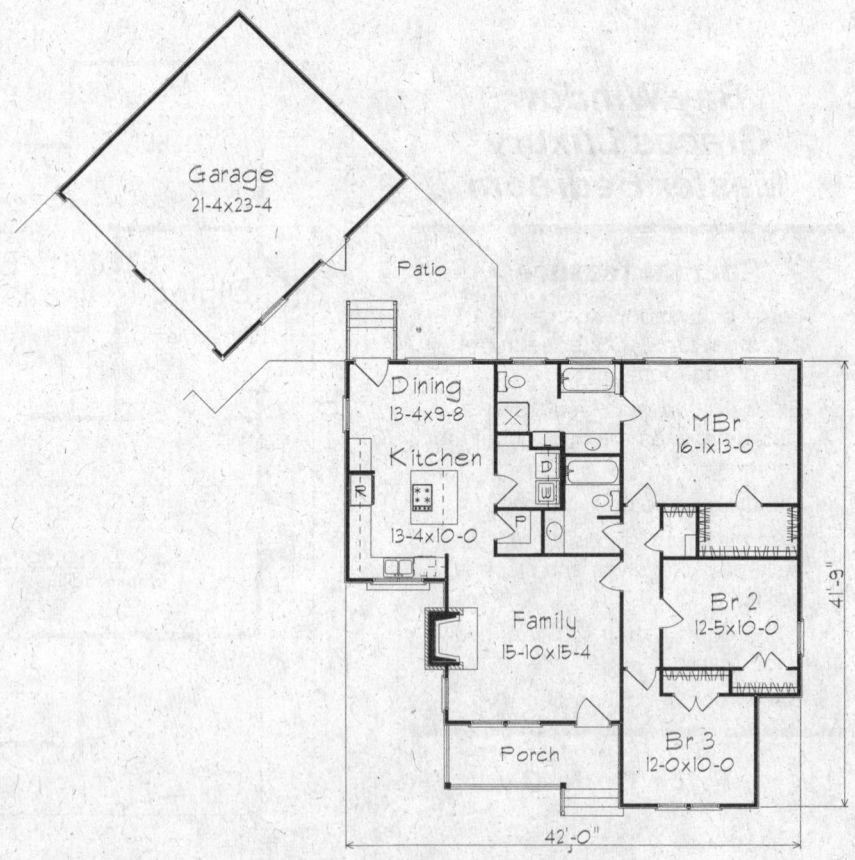

TO ORDER BLUEPRINTS USE THE FORM ON PAGE 15 OR CALL TOLL-FREE 1-877-671-6036
View thousands more home plans online at www.familyhandyman.com/homeplans

Plan #718-065D-0046

2,049 total square feet of living area

Delightful Home For Family Living

Special features

- The large covered porch creates an inviting entrance
- An angled counter defines the kitchen and provides additional seating
- The master bedroom enjoys a large walk-in closet and private bath with double-bowl vanity
- The parlor/library offers an elegant atmosphere
- The second floor bonus room is included in the total square footage
- 3 bedrooms, 2 1/2 baths, 2-car garage
- Basement foundation

Price Code C

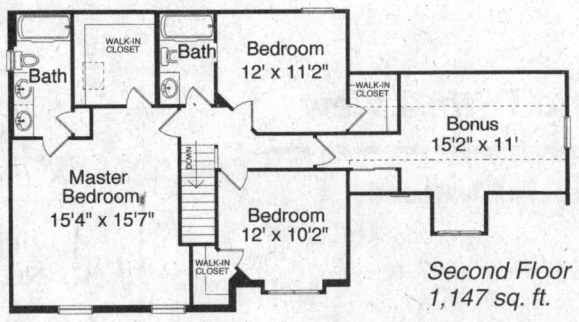

Second Floor 1,147 sq. ft.

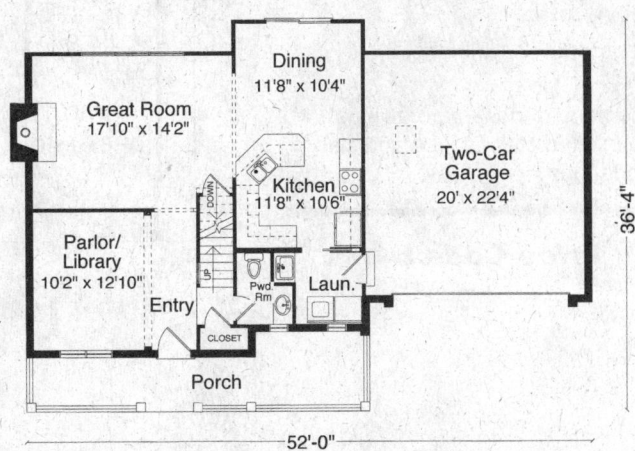

First Floor 902 sq. ft.

TO ORDER BLUEPRINTS USE THE FORM ON PAGE 15 OR CALL TOLL-FREE 1-877-671-6036
View thousands more home plans online at www.familyhandyman.com/homeplans

Plan #718-007D-0038

1,524 total square feet of living area

Dining With A View

Special features

- Delightful balcony overlooks two-story entry illuminated by oval window
- Roomy first floor master bedroom offers quiet privacy
- All bedrooms feature one or more walk-in closets
- 3 bedrooms, 2 1/2 baths, 2-car garage
- Basement foundation, drawings also include crawl space and slab foundations

Price Code B

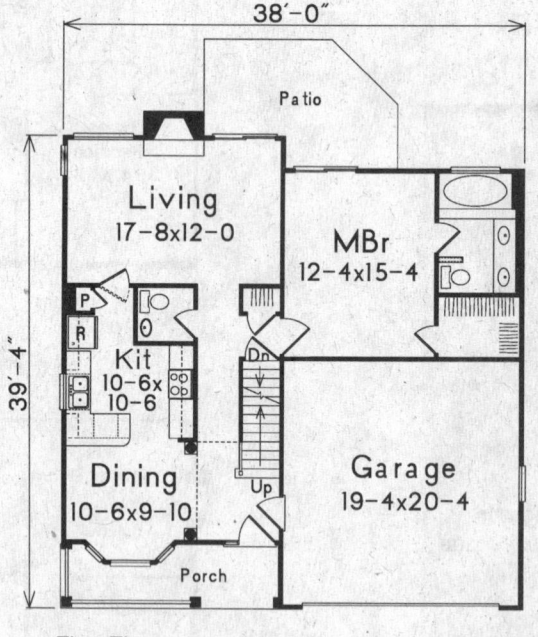

First Floor
951 sq. ft.

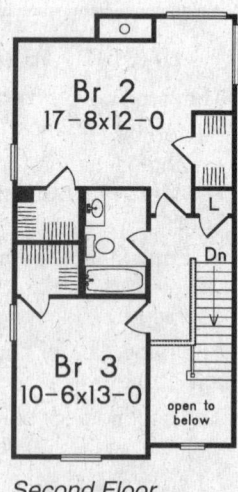

Second Floor
573 sq. ft.

TO ORDER BLUEPRINTS USE THE FORM ON PAGE 15 OR CALL TOLL-FREE 1-877-671-6036
View thousands more home plans online at www.familyhandyman.com/homeplans

Plan #718-043D-0007

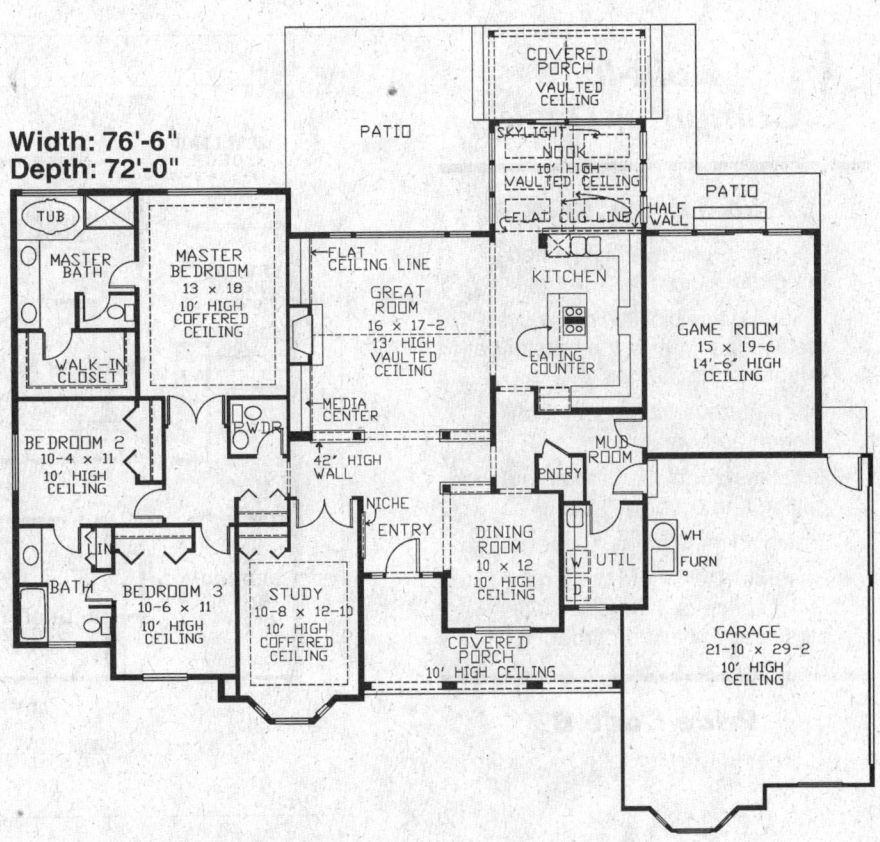

2,788 total square feet of living area

Many Decorative Touches Throughout

Special features

- Breakfast nook is flooded with sunlight from skylights
- Fireplace in great room is framed by media center and shelving
- Large game room is secluded for active children
- 3 bedrooms, 2 1/2 baths, 3-car side entry garage
- Crawl space foundation

Price Code E

TO ORDER BLUEPRINTS USE THE FORM ON PAGE 15 OR CALL TOLL-FREE 1-877-671-6036
View thousands more home plans online at www.familyhandyman.com/homeplans

Plan #718-055D-0017

1,525 total square feet of living area

Built-In Computer Desk

Special features

- Corner fireplace is highlighted in the great room
- Unique glass block window over the whirlpool tub in the master bath brightens the interior
- Open bar overlooks both the kitchen and great room
- Breakfast room leads to an outdoor grilling and covered porch
- 3 bedrooms, 2 baths, 2-car garage
- Basement, walk-out basement, crawl space or slab foundation, please specify when ordering

Price Code B

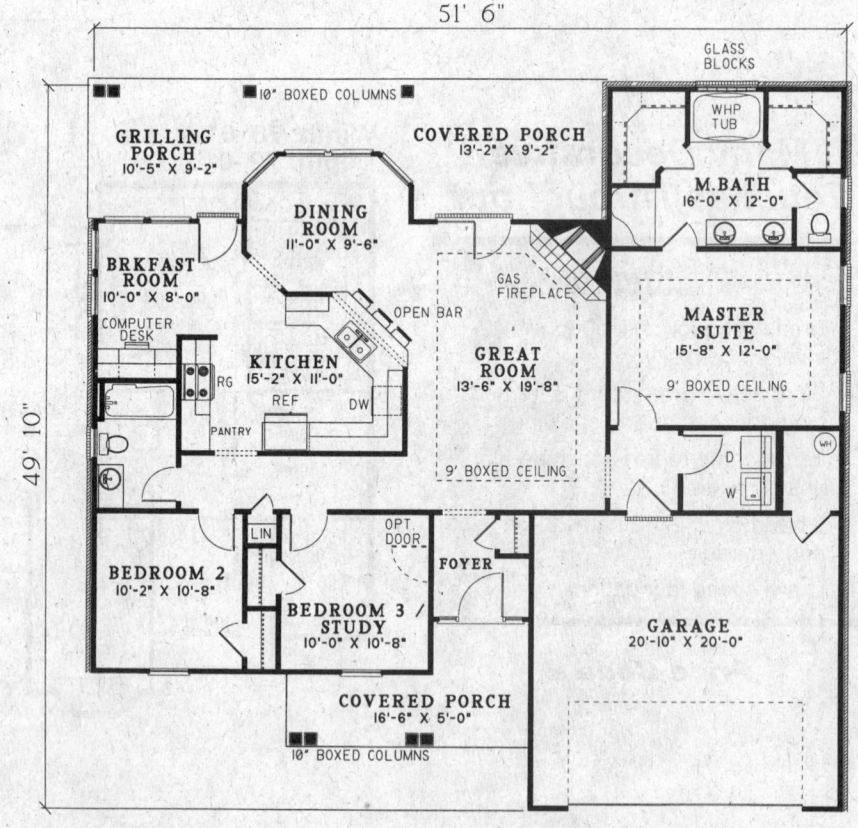

TO ORDER BLUEPRINTS USE THE FORM ON PAGE 15 OR CALL TOLL-FREE 1-877-671-6036
View thousands more home plans online at www.familyhandyman.com/homeplans

Plan #718-013D-0033

2,340 total square feet of living area

Farmhouse Style Is Inviting

Special features

- Large family room has a vaulted ceiling, bookcases and an entertainment center which surrounds a brick fireplace
- Highly functional kitchen is easily accessible from many parts of this home
- The second floor consists of two secondary bedrooms each having direct access to the bath
- The loft can serve as a recreation area or fifth bedroom
- 3 bedrooms, 2 1/2 baths, 2-car side entry garage
- Walk-out basement foundation

Price Code D

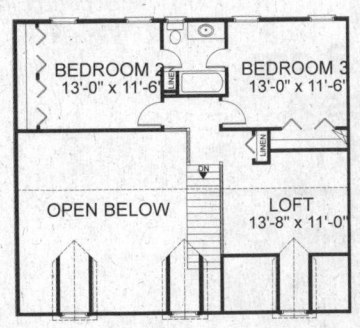

Second Floor 651 sq. ft.

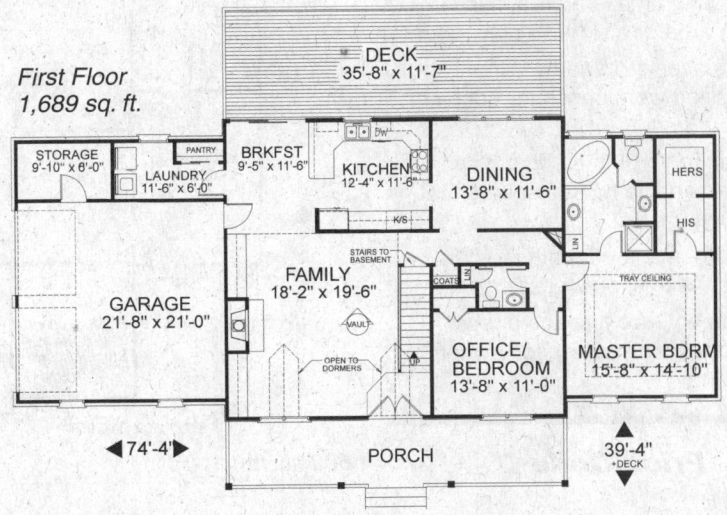

First Floor 1,689 sq. ft.

TO ORDER BLUEPRINTS USE THE FORM ON PAGE 15 OR CALL TOLL-FREE 1-877-671-6036
View thousands more home plans online at www.familyhandyman.com/homeplans

Plan #718-067D-0014

2,599 total square feet of living area

Vaulted Two-Story Foyer Makes A Grand Entry

Special features

- Office/home school room could easily be converted to a fifth bedroom
- Recreation room on the second floor would make a great casual living area or children's play room
- Large shop/storage has an oversized work bench for hobbies or projects
- Bonus room on the second floor has an additional 385 square feet of living area
- 4 bedrooms, 2 1/2 baths, 2-car garage with shop/storage
- Basement, crawl space or slab foundation, please specify when ordering

Price Code D

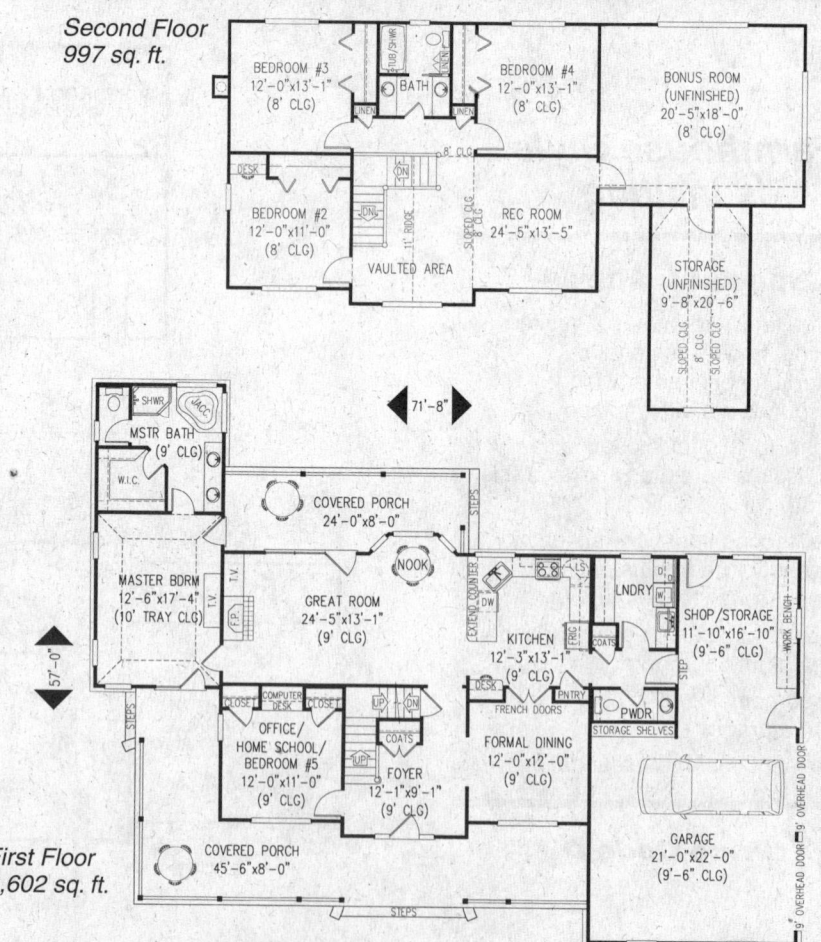

TO ORDER BLUEPRINTS USE THE FORM ON PAGE 15 OR CALL TOLL-FREE 1-877-671-6036
View thousands more home plans online at www.familyhandyman.com/homeplans

The Family Handyman

Plan #718-007D-0072

2,900 total square feet of living area

Two-Story Atrium For Great Views

Special features

- Elegant entry foyer leads to the second floor balcony overlook of the vaulted two-story atrium
- Spacious kitchen features an island breakfast bar, walk-in pantry, bayed breakfast room and adjoining screened porch
- Two large second floor bedrooms and stair balconies overlook a sun-drenched two-story vaulted atrium
- 4 bedrooms, 3 1/2 baths, 2-car side entry garage
- Basement foundation

Price Code E

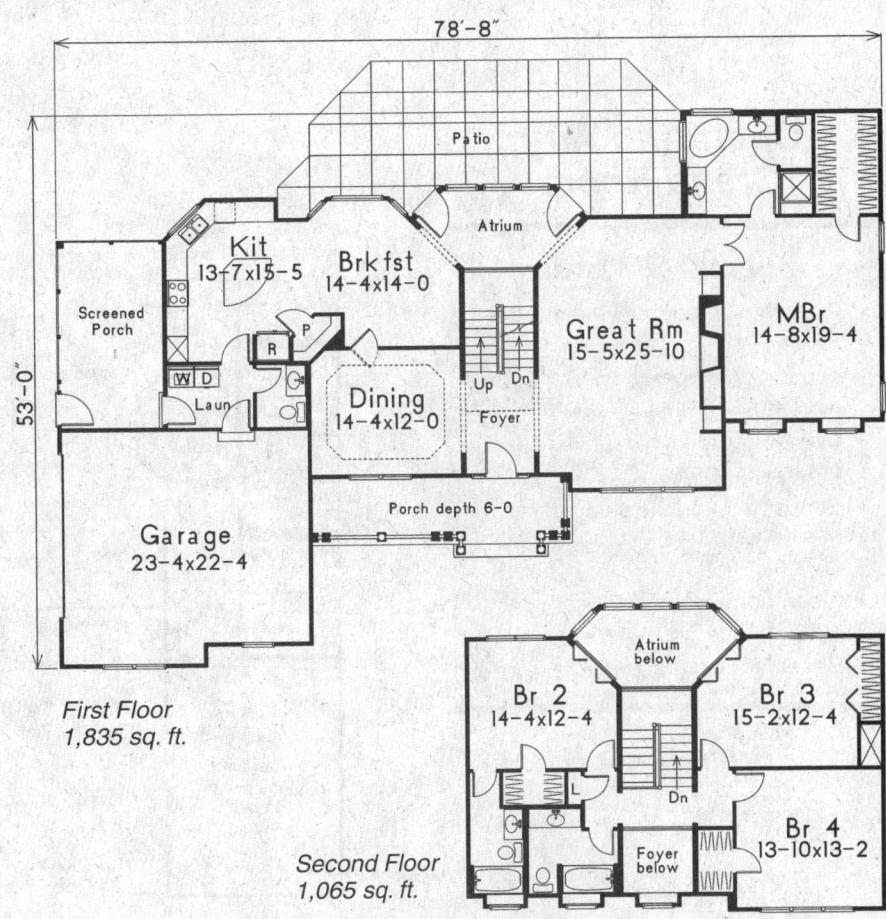

First Floor 1,835 sq. ft.

Second Floor 1,065 sq. ft.

TO ORDER BLUEPRINTS USE THE FORM ON PAGE 15 OR CALL TOLL-FREE 1-877-671-6036
View thousands more home plans online at www.familyhandyman.com/homeplans

Plan #718-056D-0005

2,111 total square feet of living area

Open And Airy Grand Room

Special features

- 9' ceilings throughout the first floor
- Formal dining room has columns separating it from other areas while allowing it to maintain an open feel
- Master bedroom has privacy from other bedrooms
- Bonus room on the second floor has an additional 345 square feet of living area
- 3 bedrooms, 2 baths, 2-car side entry garage
- Basement foundation

Price Code H

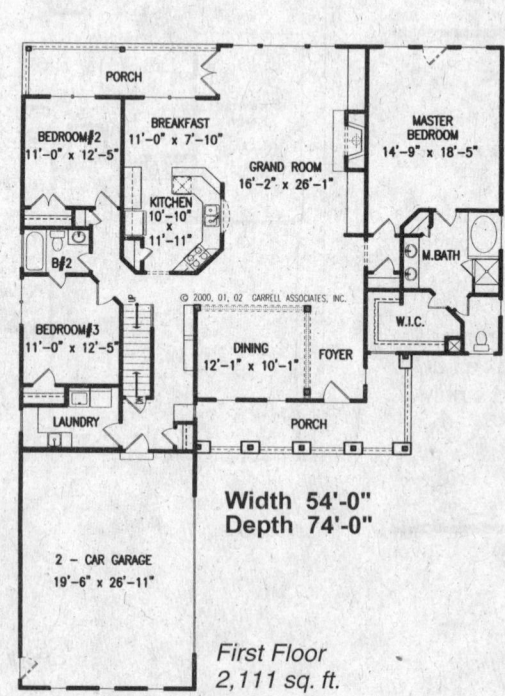

First Floor
2,111 sq. ft.

Width 54'-0"
Depth 74'-0"

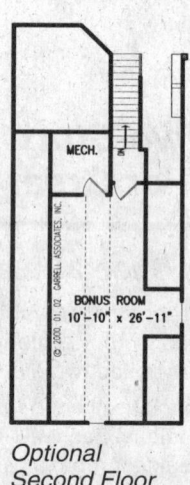

Optional Second Floor

TO ORDER BLUEPRINTS USE THE FORM ON PAGE 15 OR CALL TOLL-FREE 1-877-671-6036
View thousands more home plans online at www.familyhandyman.com/homeplans

The Family Handyman

Plan #718-037D-0009

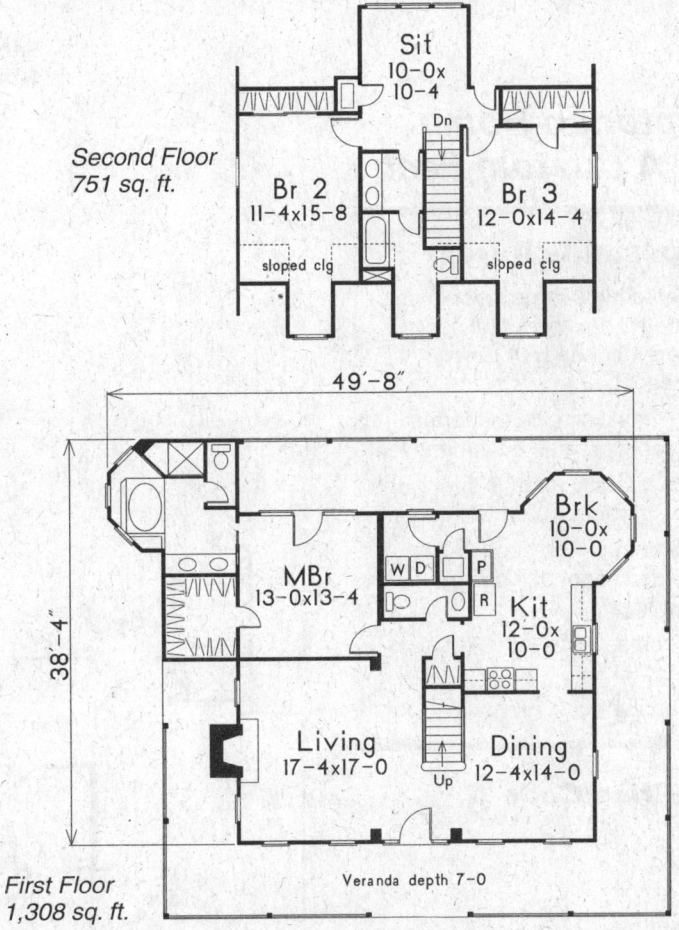

2,059 total square feet of living area

Country Charm Wrapped In A Veranda

Special features

- Octagon-shaped breakfast room offers plenty of windows and creates a view to the veranda
- First floor master bedroom has a large walk-in closet and deluxe bath
- 9' ceilings throughout the home
- Secondary bedrooms and bath feature dormers and are adjacent to the cozy sitting area
- 3 bedrooms, 2 1/2 baths, 2-car detached garage
- Slab foundation, drawings also include basement and crawl space foundations

Price Code C

Second Floor 751 sq. ft.

Sit 10-0 x 10-4
Br 2 11-4 x 15-8
Br 3 12-0 x 14-4
sloped clg

49'-8"
38'-4"
Brk 10-0 x 10-0
MBr 13-0 x 13-4
Kit 12-0 x 10-0
Living 17-4 x 17-0
Dining 12-4 x 14-0
Veranda depth 7-0

First Floor 1,308 sq. ft.

TO ORDER BLUEPRINTS USE THE FORM ON PAGE 15 OR CALL TOLL-FREE 1-877-671-6036
View thousands more home plans online at www.familyhandyman.com/homeplans

Plan #718-071D-0006

3,746 total square feet of living area

Victorian Home Has A Custom Feel

Special features

- Upon entering a large foyer guests are greeted by a beautiful central two-story rotunda with circular staircase
- An oval tray ceiling in the formal dining room creates a Victorian feel
- Two-story family room is sunny and bright with windows on two floors
- Bonus room on the second floor has an additional 314 square feet of living area
- 4 bedrooms, 3 1/2 baths, 3-car garage
- Crawl space foundation

Price Code G

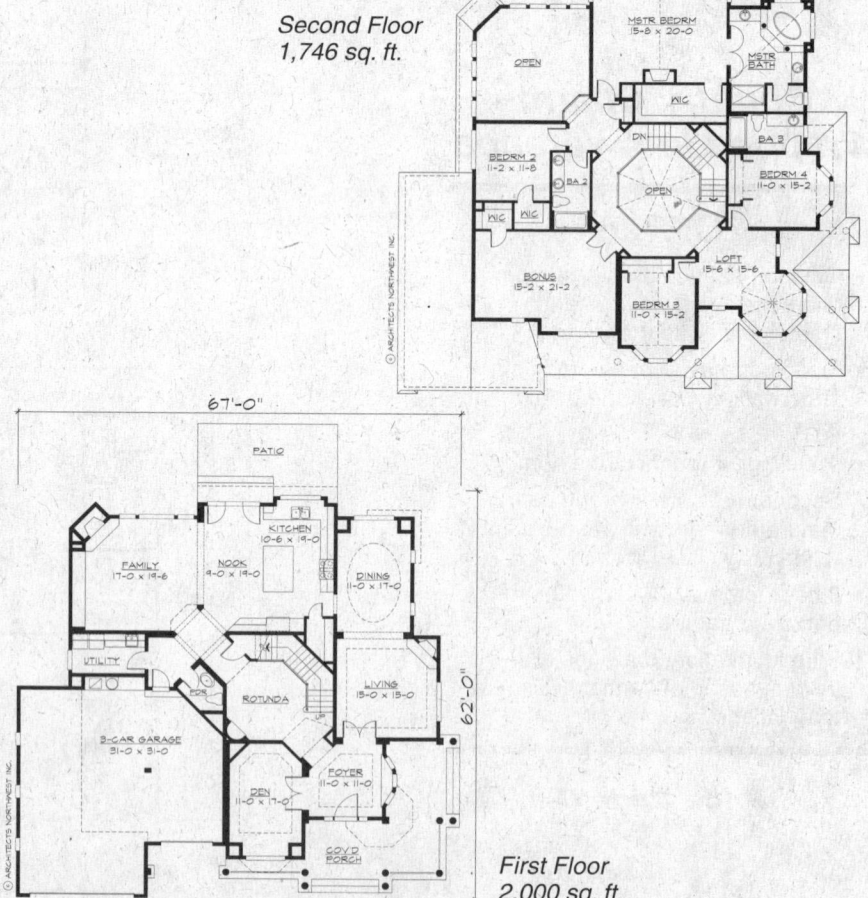

Second Floor 1,746 sq. ft.

First Floor 2,000 sq. ft.

TO ORDER BLUEPRINTS USE THE FORM ON PAGE 15 OR CALL TOLL-FREE 1-877-671-6036
View thousands more home plans online at www.familyhandyman.com/homeplans

Plan #718-007D-0123

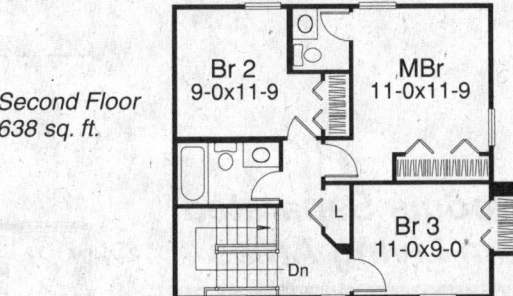

1,308 total square feet of living area

Affordable Two-Story Has It All

Special features

- Multi-gabled facade and elongated porch create a pleasing country appeal
- Large dining room with bay window and view to rear patio opens to a full-functional kitchen with snack bar
- An attractive U-shaped stair with hall overlook leads to the second floor
- 3 bedrooms, 1 full bath, 2 half baths, 2-car garage
- Basement foundation

Price Code A

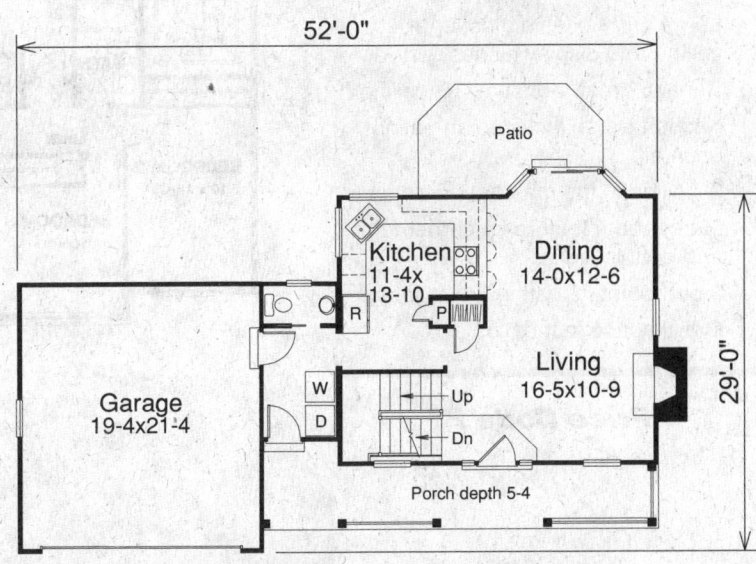

Second Floor 638 sq. ft.

First Floor 670 sq. ft.

TO ORDER BLUEPRINTS USE THE FORM ON PAGE 15 OR CALL TOLL-FREE 1-877-671-6036
View thousands more home plans online at www.familyhandyman.com/homeplans

Plan #718-043D-0005

1,734 total square feet of living area

Bedrooms Separated From Living Areas

Special features

- Large entry boasts a coffered ceiling and display niches
- Sunken great room has 10' ceiling
- Kitchen island includes an eating counter
- 9' ceiling in the master bedroom
- Master bath features a corner tub and double sinks
- 3 bedrooms, 2 baths, 2-car garage
- Crawl space foundation

Price Code B

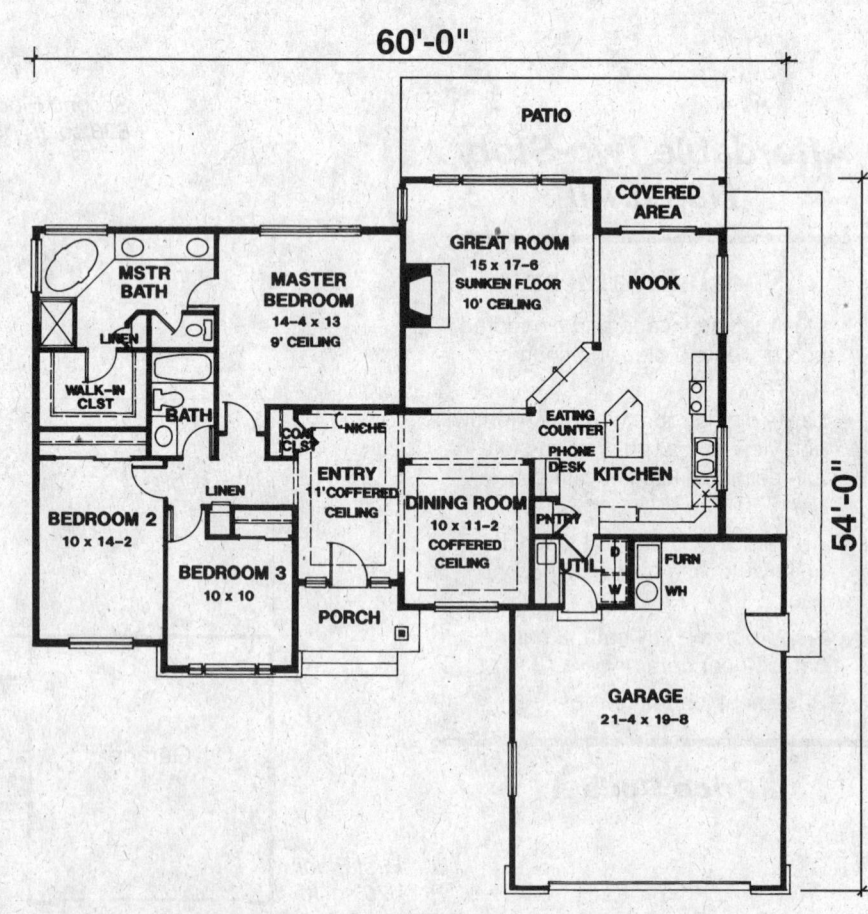

TO ORDER BLUEPRINTS USE THE FORM ON PAGE 15 OR CALL TOLL-FREE 1-877-671-6036
View thousands more home plans online at www.familyhandyman.com/homeplans

Plan #718-051D-0020

2,491 total square feet of living area

Bayed Sunroom Brightens Farmhouse

Special features

- Entry is flanked by formal living and dining rooms
- Hallway between dining room and kitchen includes a butler's pantry to ease serving a party
- The kitchen, breakfast nook and family room combine for an expansive gathering space
- All bedrooms are located on the second floor for privacy
- 4 bedrooms, 2 1/2 baths, 2-car side entry garage
- Basement foundation

Price Code D

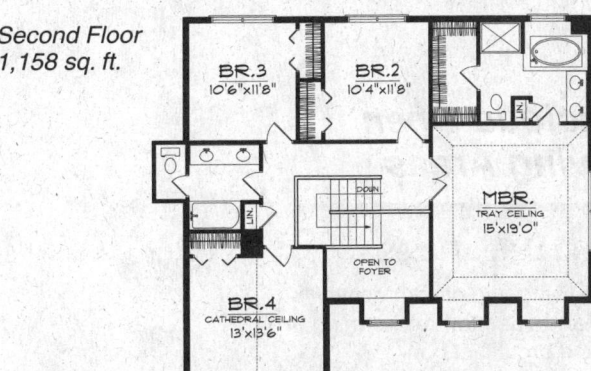

Second Floor 1,158 sq. ft.

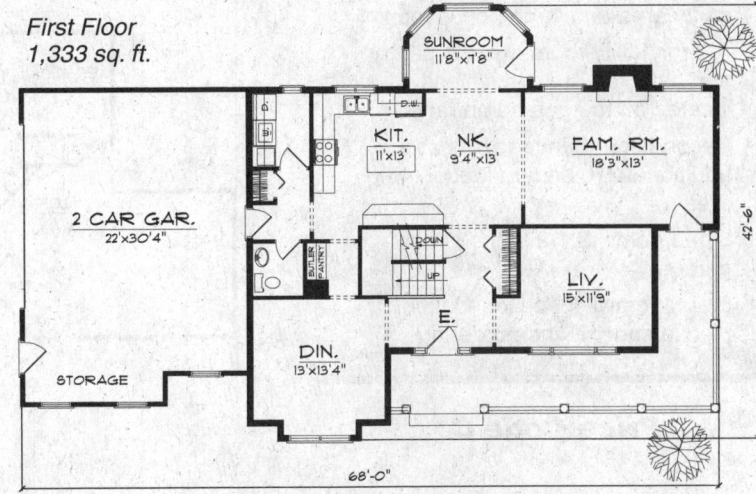

First Floor 1,333 sq. ft.

TO ORDER BLUEPRINTS USE THE FORM ON PAGE 15 OR CALL TOLL-FREE 1-877-671-6036
View thousands more home plans online at www.familyhandyman.com/homeplans

Plan #718-030D-0011

2,089 total square feet of living area

Spacious Open Living Areas

Special features

- The large living and dining rooms combine and open to the charming kitchen and breakfast nook
- The second floor is designed with children in mind with a unique study area and large bonus room
- A large utility room, walk-in pantry and half bath are conveniently located off the garage entrance
- Second floor bonus room has an additional 270 square feet of living area
- 3 bedrooms, 2 1/2 baths, 2-car garage
- Slab or crawl space foundation, please specify when ordering

Price Code C

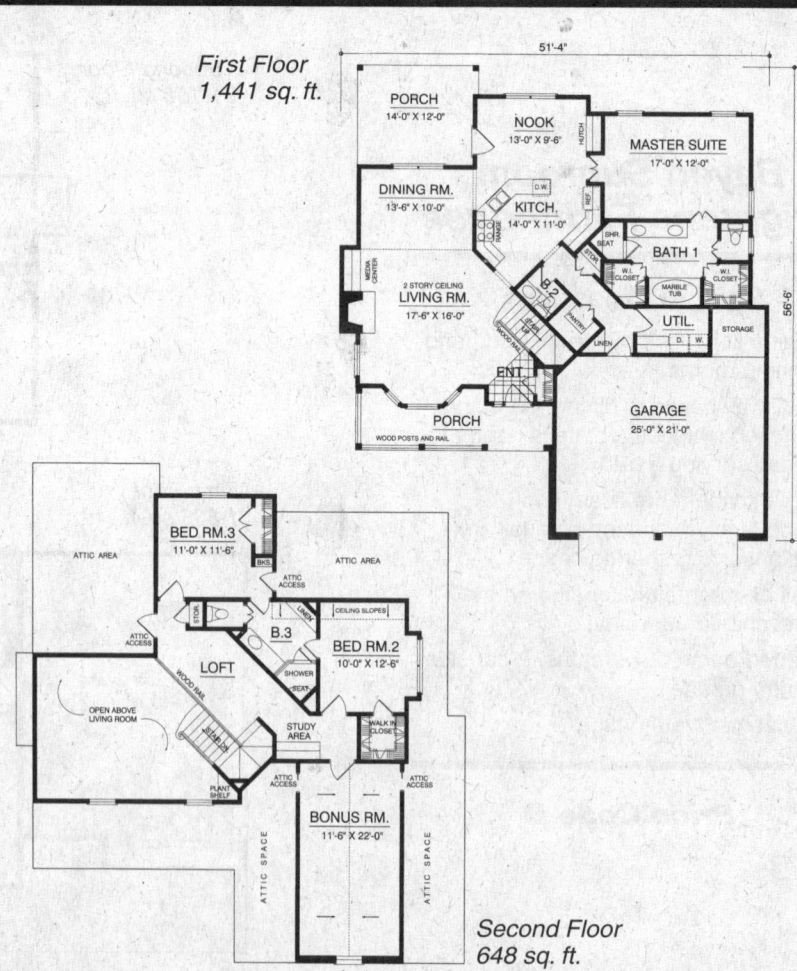

First Floor 1,441 sq. ft.

Second Floor 648 sq. ft.

TO ORDER BLUEPRINTS USE THE FORM ON PAGE 15 OR CALL TOLL-FREE 1-877-671-6036
View thousands more home plans online at www.familyhandyman.com/homeplans

The Family Handyman

Plan #718-011D-0045

2,850 total square feet of living area

A True Victorian Treasure

Special features

- An enormous wrap-around porch surrounds the home on one side creating a lot of outdoor living area
- A double-door entry leads to the master bedroom which features a private bath with a spa tub
- Extra space in the garage allows for storage or work area
- Bonus room is included in the second floor square footage
- 3 bedrooms, 3 baths, 2-car side entry garage
- Crawl space foundation

Price Code F

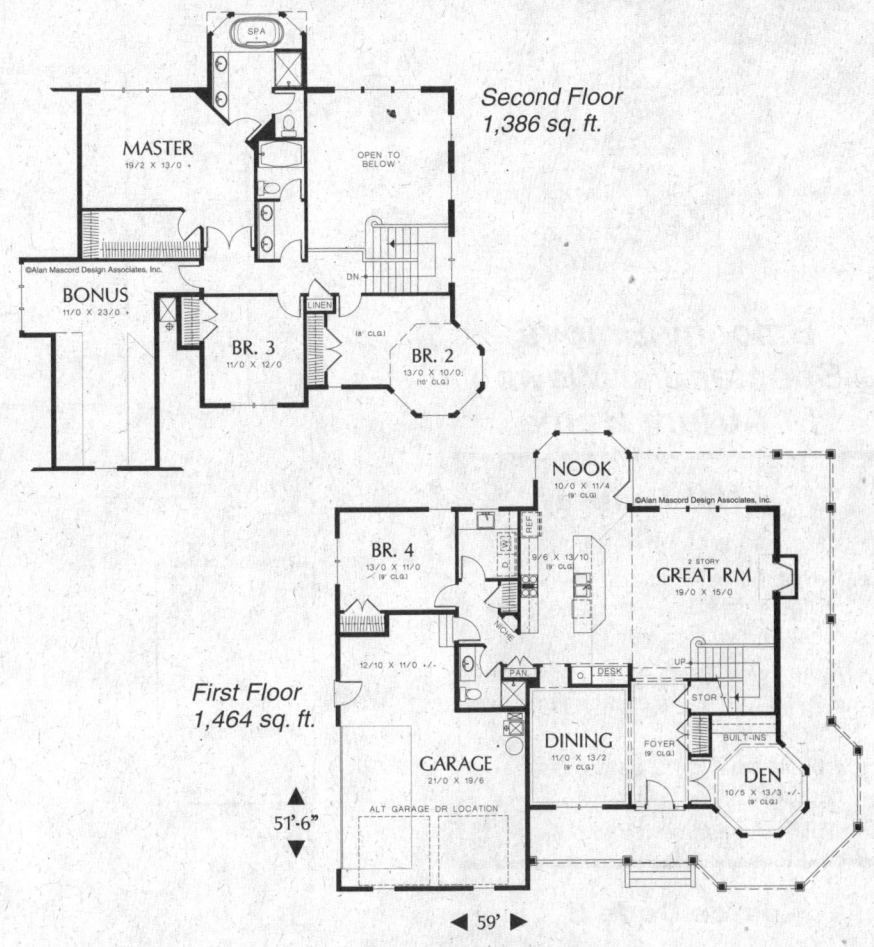

Second Floor 1,386 sq. ft.

First Floor 1,464 sq. ft.

Plan #718-007D-0003

2,806 total square feet of living area

Rear View

Balcony Enjoys Spectacular Views In Atrium Home

Special features

- Harmonious charm throughout
- Sweeping balcony and vaulted ceiling soar above spacious great room and walk-in bar
- Atrium with lower level family room is a unique touch, creating an open and airy feeling
- 4 bedrooms, 2 1/2 baths, 2-car garage
- Walk-out basement foundation

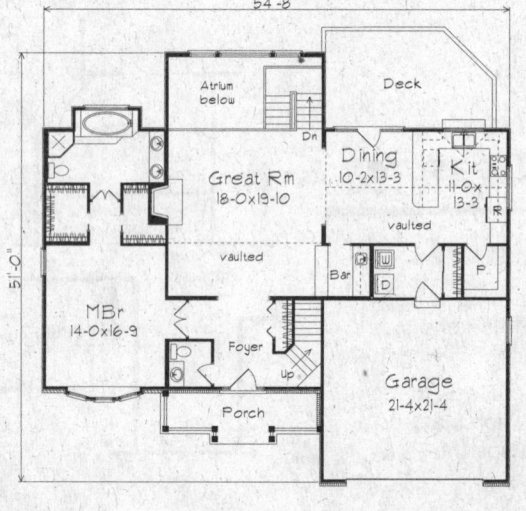

First Floor
1,473 sq. ft.

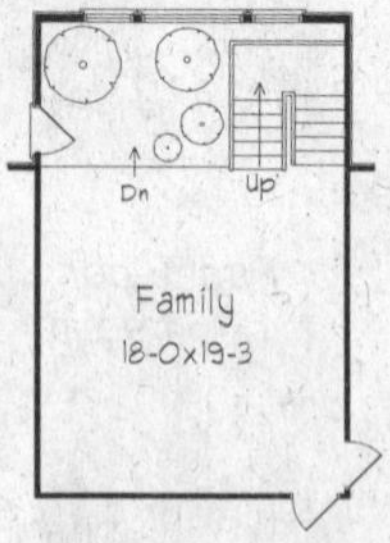

Lower Level
548 sq. ft.

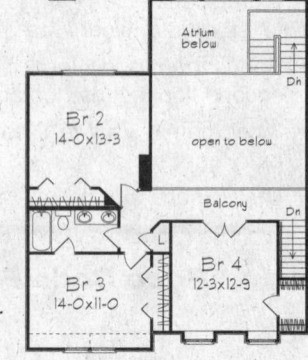

Second Floor
785 sq. ft.

Price Code E

TO ORDER BLUEPRINTS USE THE FORM ON PAGE 15 OR CALL TOLL-FREE 1-877-671-6036
View thousands more home plans online at www.familyhandyman.com/HOMEPLANS

Plan #718-058D-0048

3,556 total square feet of living area

Wrap-Around Porch And Turret Accent Design

Special features

- Jack and Jill bath is located between two of the bedrooms on the second floor
- Second floor features three bedrooms and overlooks the great room
- Formal entrance and additional family entrance from covered porch to laundry/mud room
- First floor master bedroom features a coffered ceiling, double walk-in closets, luxury bath and direct access to the study
- 4 bedrooms, 3 1/2 baths, 3-car side entry garage
- Basement foundation

Price Code F

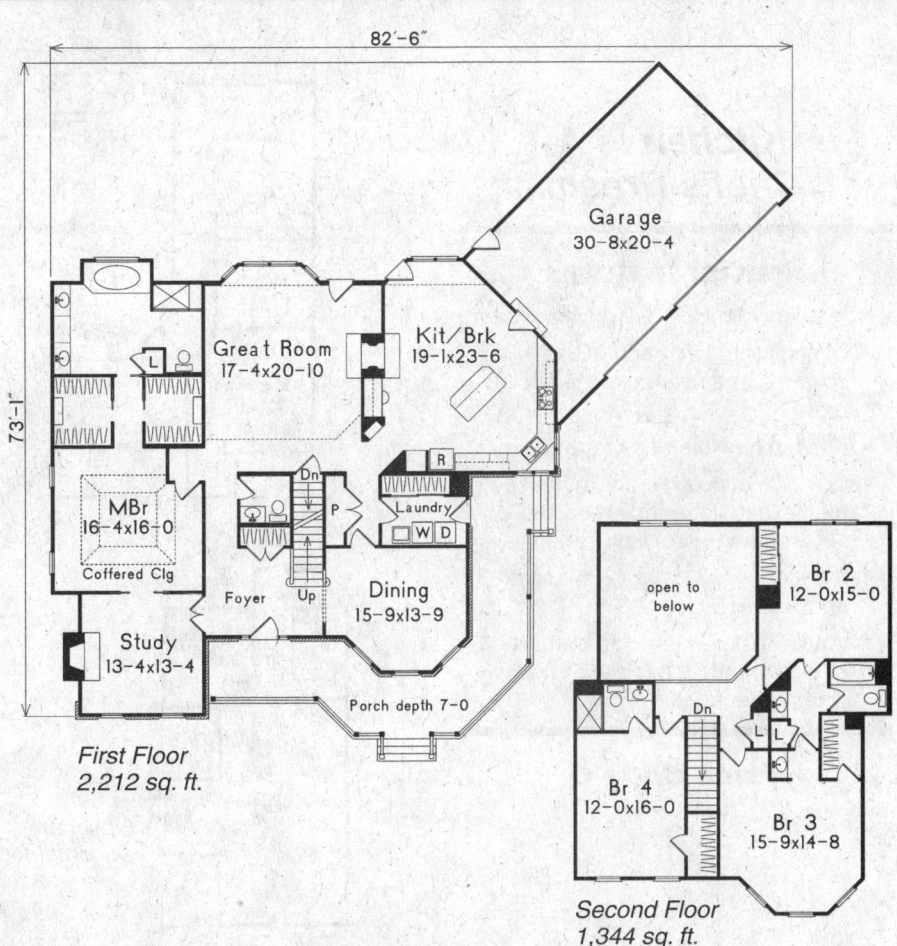

First Floor 2,212 sq. ft.

Second Floor 1,344 sq. ft.

TO ORDER BLUEPRINTS USE THE FORM ON PAGE 15 OR CALL TOLL-FREE 1-877-671-6036
View thousands more home plans online at www.familyhandyman.com/HOMEPLANS

Plan #718-035D-0036

2,193 total square feet of living area

Kitchen Is A Chef's Dream

Special features

- Master suite includes a sitting room
- Dining room has decorative columns and overlooks the family room
- Kitchen has lots of storage
- Optional bonus room with bath on the second floor has an additional 400 square feet of living area
- 3 bedrooms, 3 baths, 2-car side entry garage
- Walk-out basement, crawl space or slab foundation, please specify when ordering

Price Code C

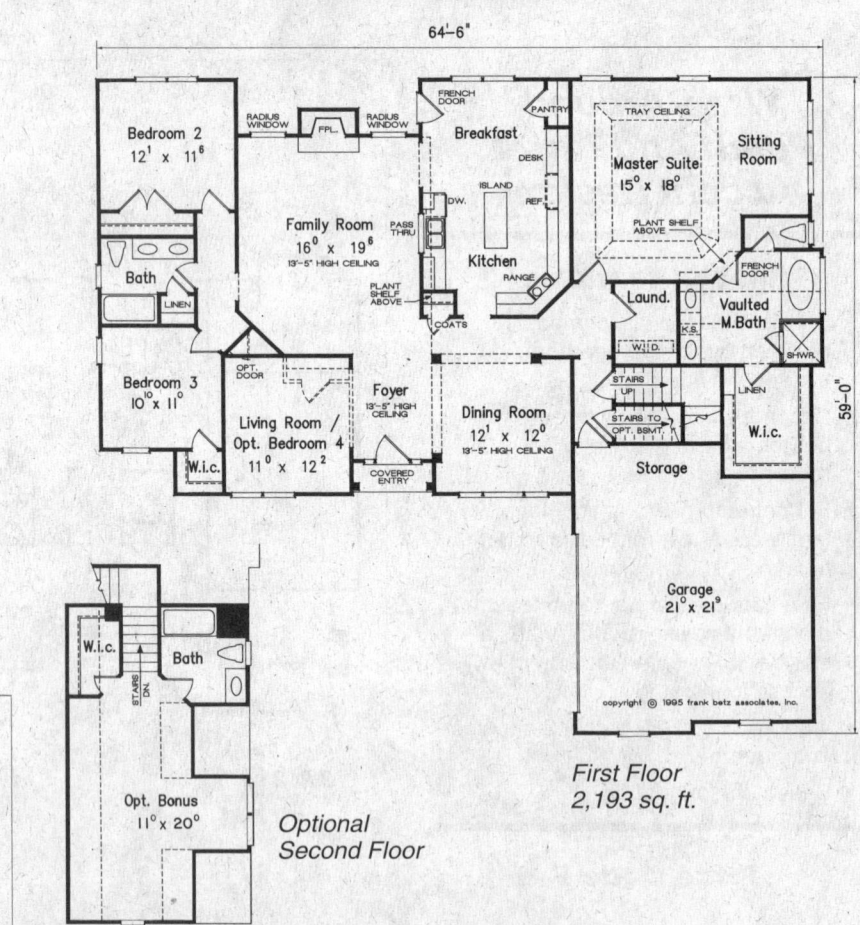

Optional Second Floor

First Floor
2,193 sq. ft.

TO ORDER BLUEPRINTS USE THE FORM ON PAGE 15 OR CALL TOLL-FREE 1-877-671-6036
View thousands more home plans online at www.familyhandyman.com/HOMEPLANS

Plan #718-003D-0005

1,708 total square feet of living area

Private Breakfast Room Provides Casual Dining

Special features

- Massive family room is enhanced with several windows, a fireplace and access to the porch
- Deluxe master bath is accented by a step-up corner tub flanked by double vanities
- Closets throughout maintain organized living
- Bedrooms are isolated from living areas
- 3 bedrooms, 2 baths, 2-car garage
- Basement foundation, drawings also include crawl space foundation

Price Code B

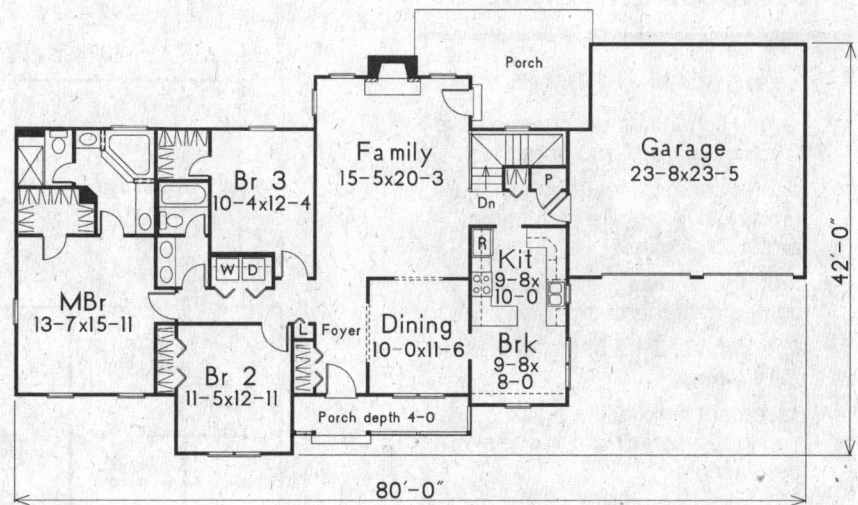

TO ORDER BLUEPRINTS USE THE FORM ON PAGE 15 OR CALL TOLL-FREE 1-877-671-6036
View thousands more home plans online at www.familyhandyman.com/homeplans

Plan #718-001D-0059

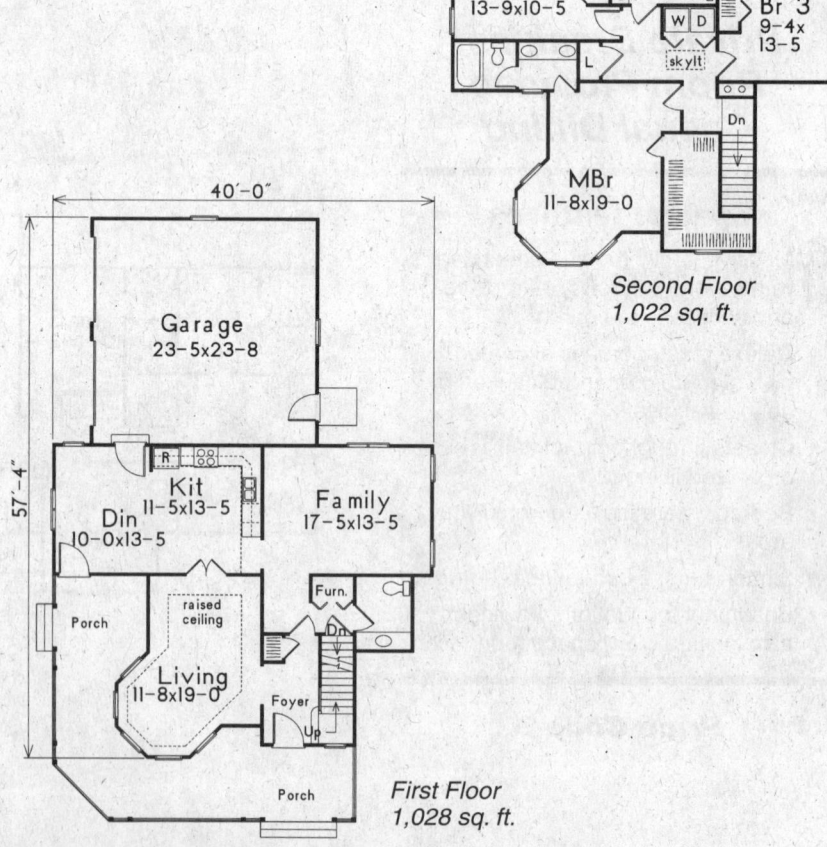

2,050 total square feet of living area

Dramatic Layout Created By Victorian Turret

Special features

- Large kitchen and dining area have access to garage and porch
- Master bedroom features a unique turret design, private bath and large walk-in closet
- Laundry facilities are conveniently located near the bedrooms
- 3 bedrooms, 2 1/2 baths, 2-car side entry garage
- Basement foundation, drawings also include crawl space and slab foundations

Price Code C

TO ORDER BLUEPRINTS USE THE FORM ON PAGE 15 OR CALL TOLL-FREE 1-877-671-6036
View thousands more home plans online at www.familyhandyman.com/HOMEPLANS

Plan #718-001D-0003

2,286 total square feet of living area

Impressive Victorian Blends Charm And Efficiency

Special features

- Fine architectural detail makes this home a showplace with its large windows, intricate brickwork and fine woodwork and trim
- Stunning two-story entry with attractive wood railing and balustrades in foyer
- Convenient wrap-around kitchen enjoys a window view, planning center and pantry
- Oversized master bedroom includes a walk-in closet and master bath
- 4 bedrooms, 2 1/2 baths, 2-car garage
- Basement foundation, drawings also include crawl space and slab foundations

Price Code E

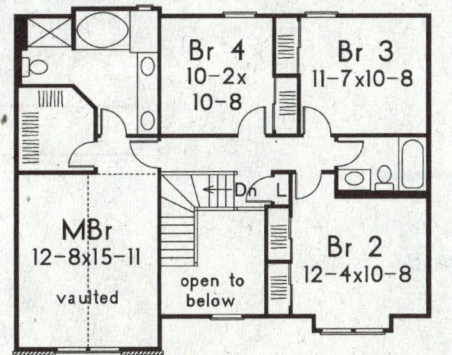

Second Floor 1,003 sq. ft.

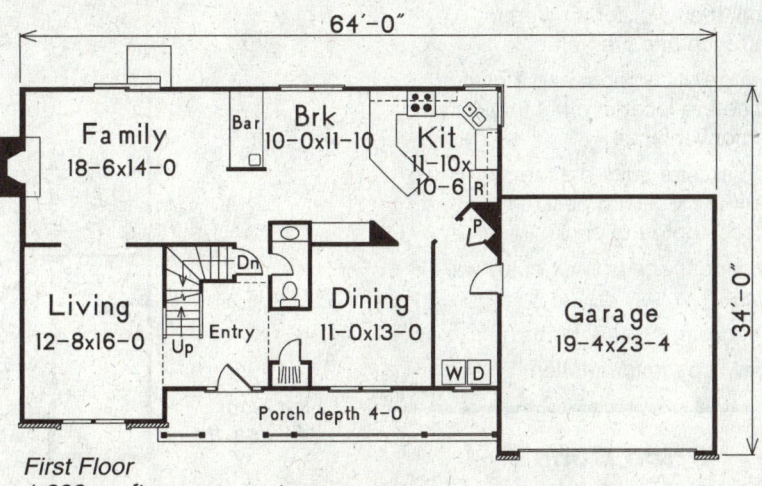

First Floor 1,283 sq. ft.

TO ORDER BLUEPRINTS USE THE FORM ON PAGE 15 OR CALL TOLL-FREE 1-877-671-6036
View thousands more home plans online at www.familyhandyman.com/HOMEPLANS

Plan #718-047D-0086

3,570 total square feet of living area

Covered Porch Decorates This Mountain Home

Special features

- The vaulted living room with grand fireplace features double-door access onto the rear deck
- A formal study and dining room flank the foyer for an elegant entrance into the home
- A large utility room and a private office are located off of the kitchen for convenience
- The master suite pampers with two walk-in closets, a deluxe bath and access onto the deck
- Secondary bedrooms enjoy walk-in closets
- 4 bedrooms, 3 1/2 baths
- Crawl space foundation

Price Code F

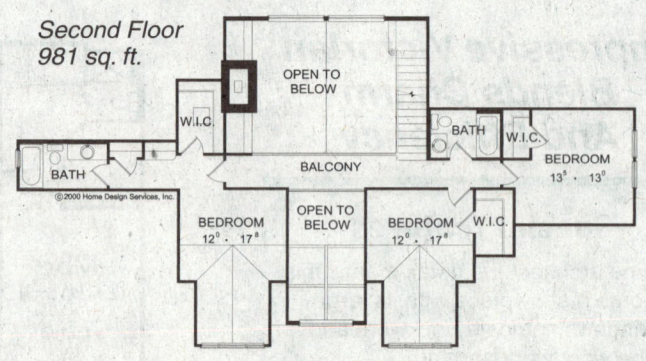

Second Floor 981 sq. ft.

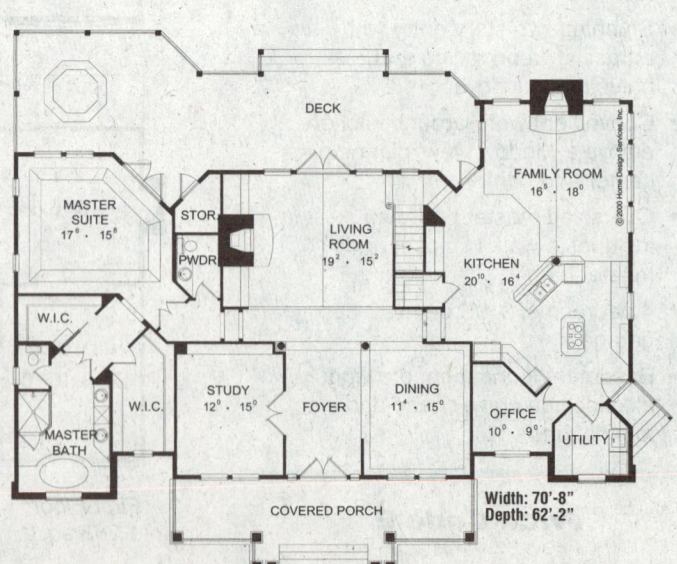

First Floor 2,589 sq. ft.

Width: 70'-8"
Depth: 62'-2"

TO ORDER BLUEPRINTS USE THE FORM ON PAGE 15 OR CALL TOLL-FREE 1-877-671-6036
View thousands more home plans online at www.familyhandyman.com/HOMEPLANS

Plan #718-024D-0017

2,697 total square feet of living area

Traditional Brick Ranch

Special features

- Secluded study with full bath nearby is an ideal guest room or office
- Master bedroom has access to outdoor patio
- 351 square feet of additional unfinished living space available in the attic
- 3 bedrooms, 3 baths, 2-car side entry garage
- Slab foundation

Price Code E

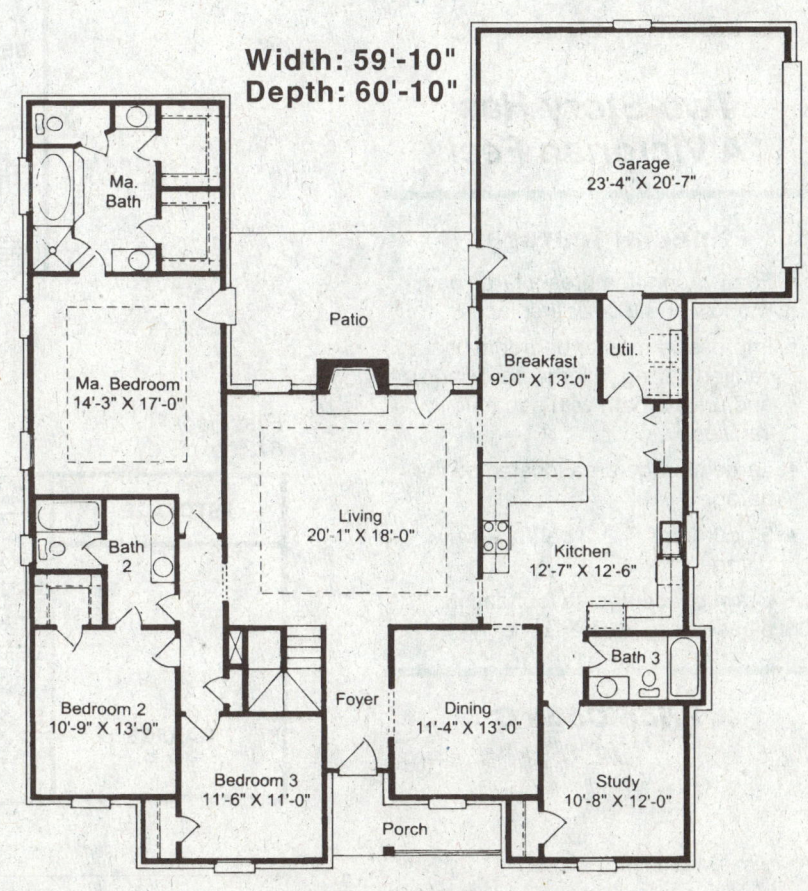

Width: 59'-10"
Depth: 60'-10"

TO ORDER BLUEPRINTS USE THE FORM ON PAGE 15 OR CALL TOLL-FREE 1-877-671-6036
View thousands more home plans online at www.familyhandyman.com/homeplans

Plan #718-013D-0009

1,598 total square feet of living area

Two-Story Has A Victorian Feel

Special features

- Family room features a large bay window and a cozy fireplace
- Impressive master bedroom has a vaulted ceiling, a large bay window and private bath with separate vanities
- Large storage area located off the garage
- 3 bedrooms, 2 1/2 baths, 2-car garage
- Crawl space or slab foundation, please specify when ordering

Price Code C

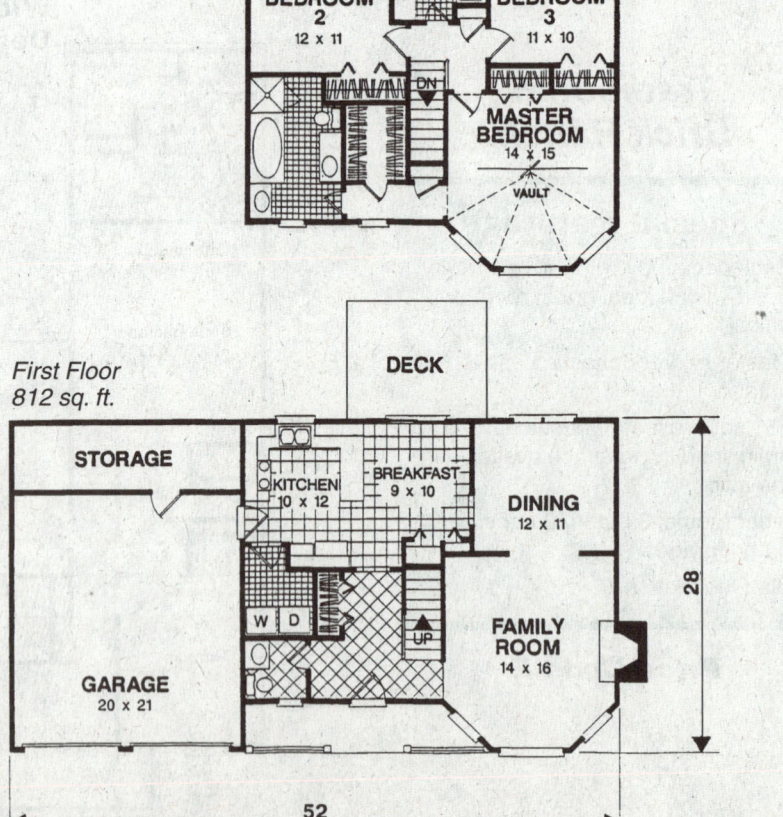

TO ORDER BLUEPRINTS USE THE FORM ON PAGE 15 OR CALL TOLL-FREE 1-877-671-6036
View thousands more home plans online at www.familyhandyman.com/HOMEPLANS

Plan #718-001D-0028

2,461 total square feet of living area

Great Traffic Flow On Both Floors

Special features

- Unique corner tub, double vanities and walk-in closet enhance the large master bedroom
- Fireplace provides focus in the spacious family room
- Centrally located half bath for guests
- 4 bedrooms, 2 1/2 baths, 2-car garage
- Basement foundation, drawings also include slab and crawl space foundations

Price Code D

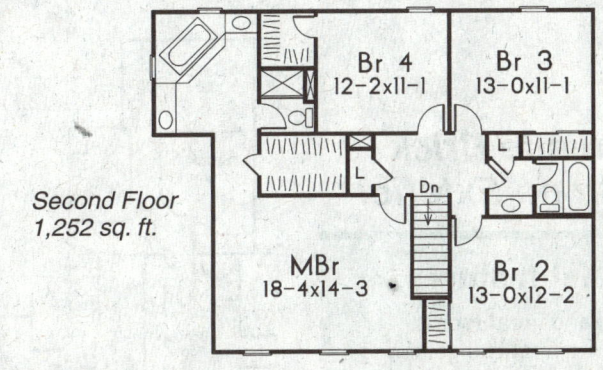

Second Floor 1,252 sq. ft.

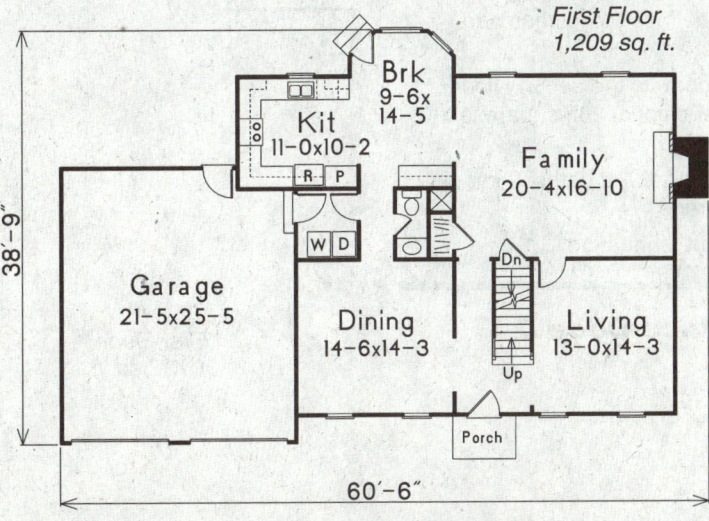

First Floor 1,209 sq. ft.

Plan #718-065D-0037

2,241 total square feet of living area

Exquisite Brick And Stone Exterior

Special features

- The dining and great rooms combine for a beautiful gathering place
- An island with extended counter seating defines the kitchen and breakfast area
- Bonus room on the second floor has an additional 283 square feet of living area
- 4 bedrooms, 2 1/2 baths, 2-car side entry garage
- Basement foundation

Price Code D

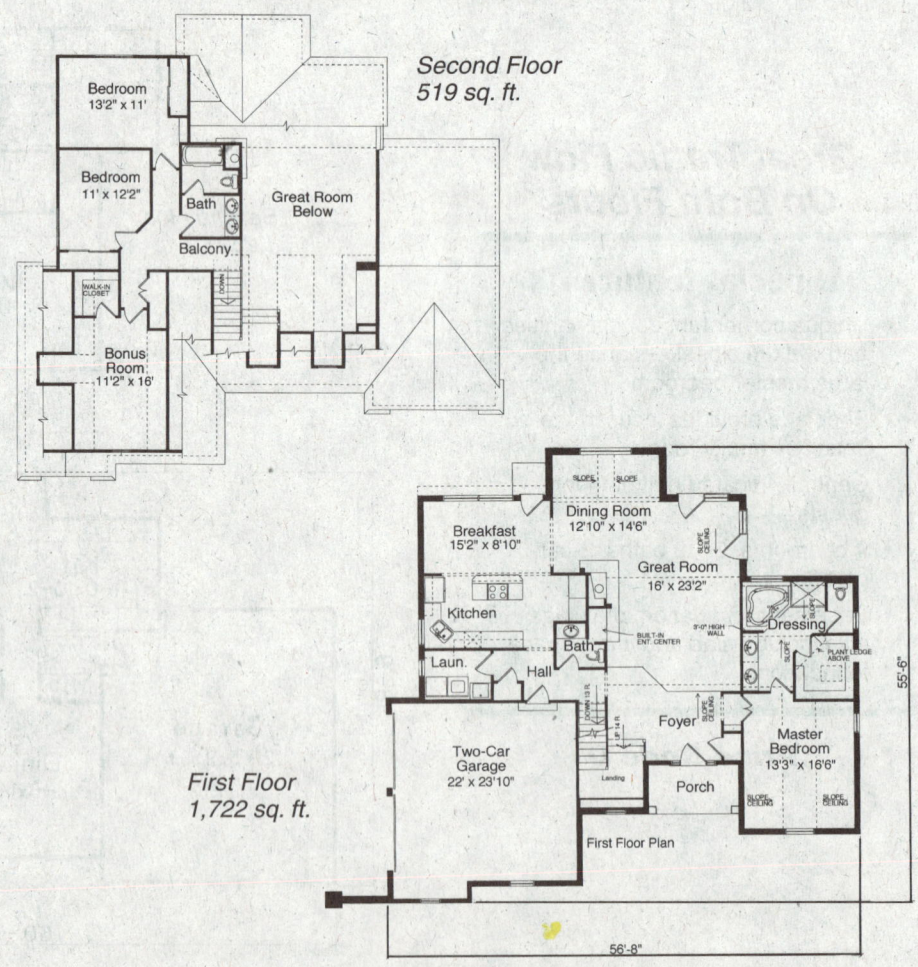

Plan #718-028D-0043

2,052 total square feet of living area

Classic Southern Style

Special features

- The master bedroom, great room and bedroom #3 access the rear porch which is ideal for relaxing
- The unique kitchen features a large cooktop island with snack bar, walk-in pantry and wall oven with built-in microwave
- The master bedroom boasts a walk-in closet and deluxe bath with whirlpool tub and double-bowl vanity
- 3 bedrooms, 2 baths, 2-car detached garage
- Slab or crawl space foundation, please specify when ordering

Price Code C

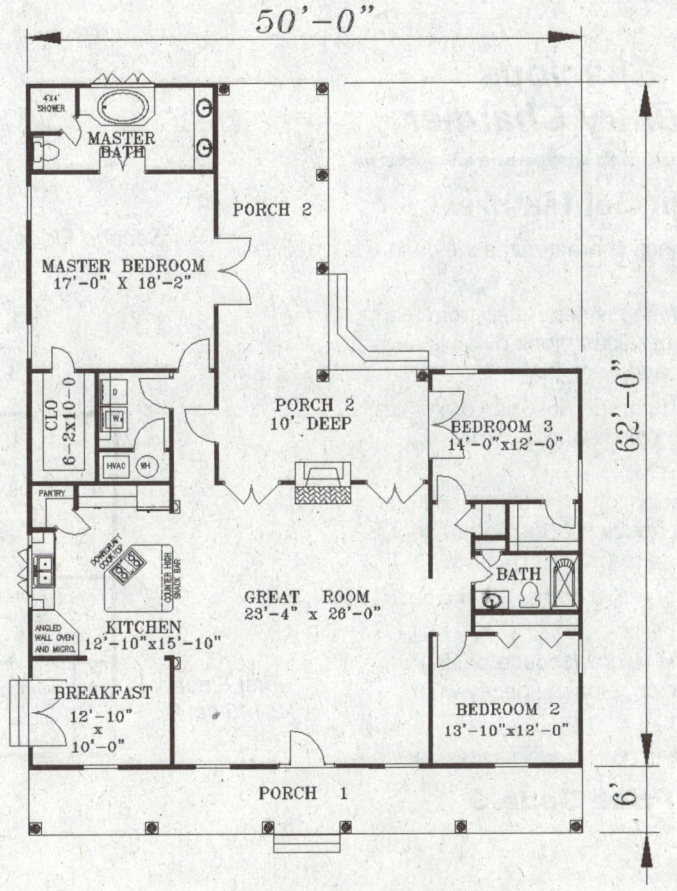

Plan #718-016D-0058

2,874 total square feet of living area

Spacious Country Charmer

Special features

- Openness characterizes the casual areas
- The kitchen is separated from the bayed breakfast nook by an island workspace
- Stunning great room has dramatic vaulted ceiling and a corner fireplace
- Unfinished loft on the second floor has an additional 300 square feet of living area
- 4 bedrooms, 3 baths, 3-car side entry garage
- Basement, crawl space or slab foundation, please specify when ordering

Price Code G

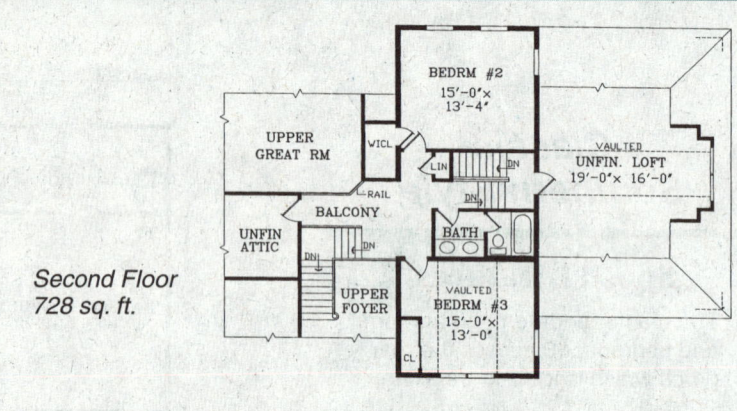

Second Floor 728 sq. ft.

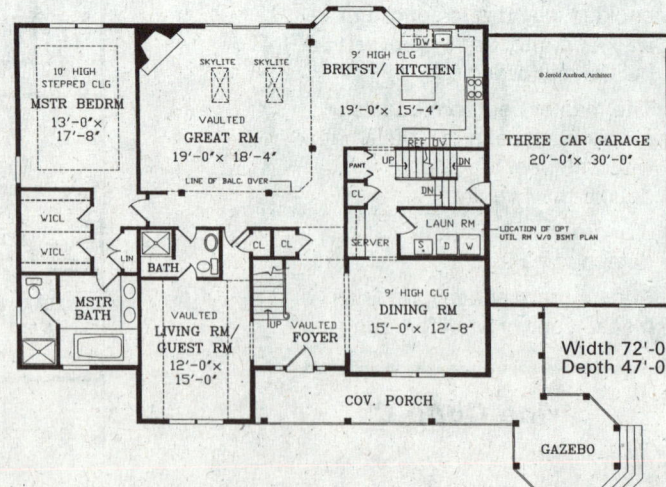

First Floor 2,146 sq. ft.

Width 72'-0"
Depth 47'-0"

TO ORDER BLUEPRINTS USE THE FORM ON PAGE 15 OR CALL TOLL-FREE 1-877-671-6036
View thousands more home plans online at www.familyhandyman.com/homeplans

Plan #718-040D-0016

3,013 total square feet of living area

Comfortable Living At Its Finest

Special features

- Oversized rooms throughout
- Kitchen features an island sink, large pantry and opens into the breakfast room with a sunroom feel
- Large family room with fireplace accesses the rear deck and front porch
- Master bedroom includes a large walk-in closet and private deluxe bath
- 4 bedrooms, 3 1/2 baths, 2-car side entry garage
- Basement foundation

Price Code E

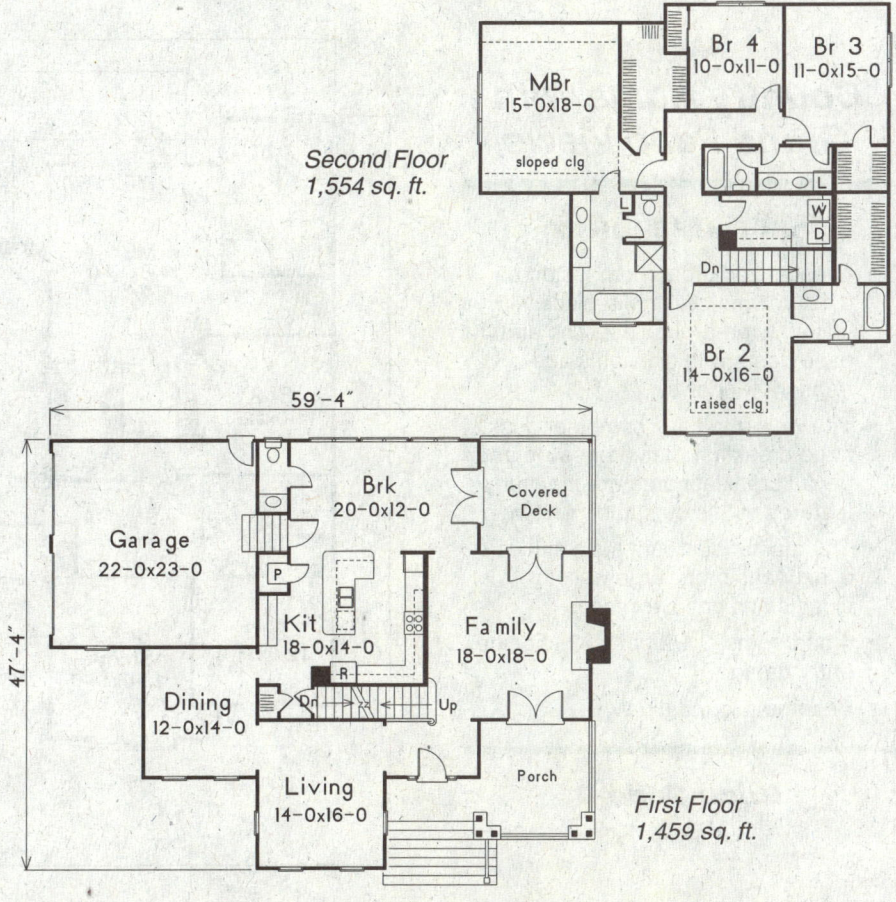

Second Floor 1,554 sq. ft.

First Floor 1,459 sq. ft.

TO ORDER BLUEPRINTS USE THE FORM ON PAGE 15 OR CALL TOLL-FREE 1-877-671-6036
View thousands more home plans online at www.familyhandyman.com/homeplans

The Family Handyman

Plan #718-007D-0113

2,547 total square feet of living area

Country Home With Grand Patio Views

Special features

- Grand-sized great room features a 12' volume ceiling, fireplace with built-in wrap-around shelving and patio doors with sidelights and transom windows
- The walk-in pantry, computer desk, large breakfast island for seven and bayed breakfast area are the many features of this outstanding kitchen
- The master bedroom suite enjoys a luxurious bath, large walk-in closets and patio access
- 4 bedrooms, 2 1/2 baths, 3-car side entry garage
- Basement foundation

Price Code D

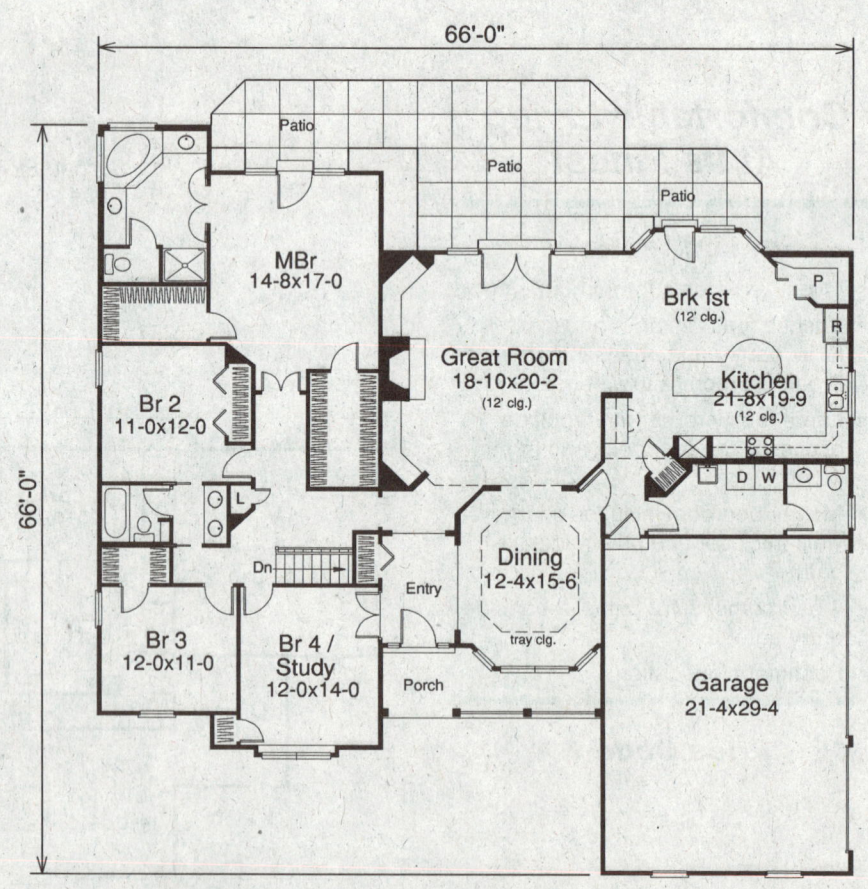

298 — TO ORDER BLUEPRINTS USE THE FORM ON PAGE 15 OR CALL TOLL-FREE 1-877-671-6036
View thousands more home plans online at www.familyhandyman.com/homeplans

Plan #718-027D-0006

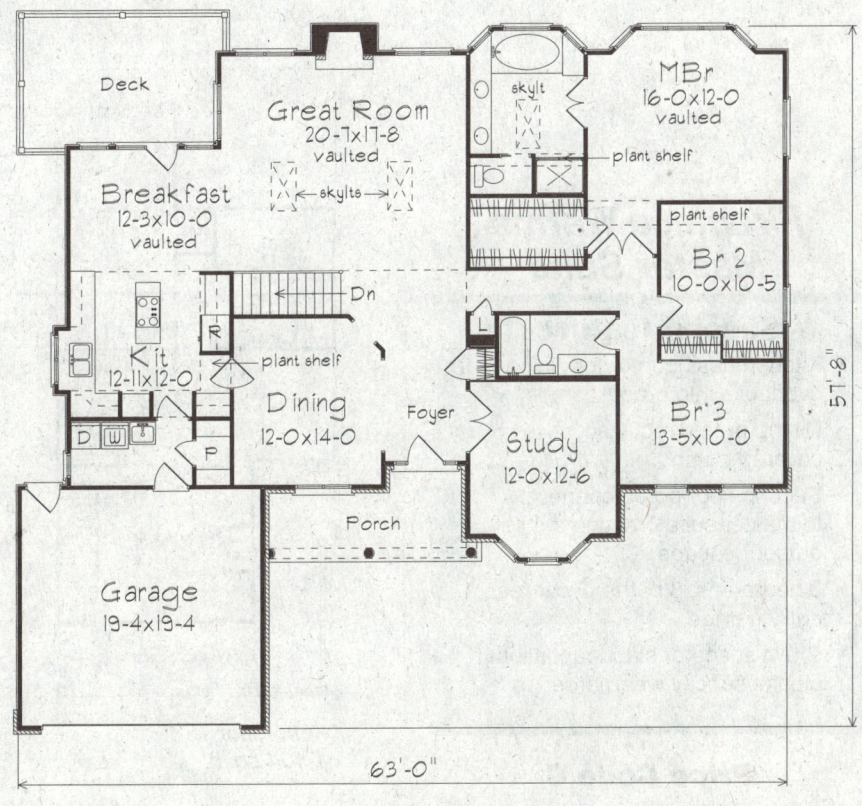

2,076 total square feet of living area

Great Room Forms Core Of This Home

Special features

- Vaulted great room has a fireplace flanked by windows and skylights that welcome the sun
- Kitchen leads to the vaulted breakfast room and rear deck
- Study located off the foyer provides a great location for a home office
- Large bay windows grace the master bedroom and bath
- 3 bedrooms, 2 baths, 2-car garage
- Basement foundation

Price Code C

TO ORDER BLUEPRINTS USE THE FORM ON PAGE 15 OR CALL TOLL-FREE 1-877-671-6036
View thousands more home plans online at www.familyhandyman.com/homeplans

Plan #718-055D-0099

1,897 total square feet of living area

Fireplace Warms Master Suite

Special features

- Kitchen has counter for dining that overlooks into great room
- Dining area directly accesses covered porch
- Second floor porch connects to master suite creating a quiet outdoor escape
- 3 bedrooms, 3 baths, 2-car rear entry garage
- Crawl space or slab foundation, please specify when ordering

Price Code C

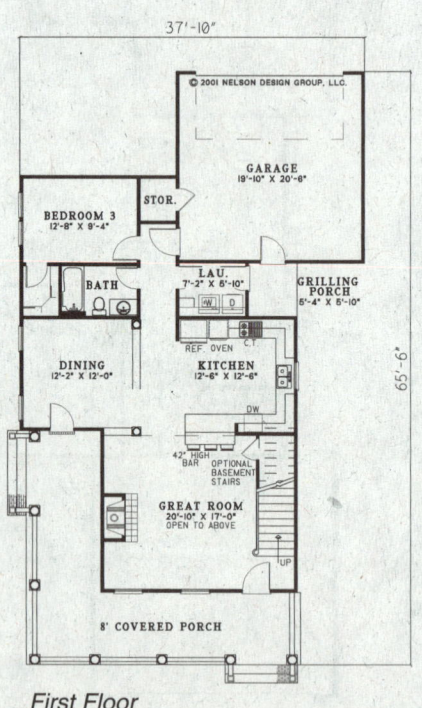

First Floor
1,104 sq. ft.

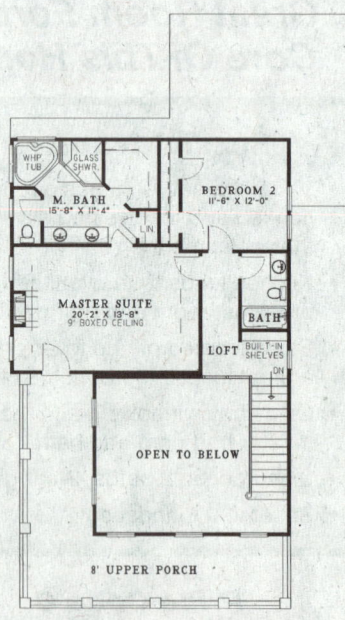

Second Floor
793 sq. ft.

TO ORDER BLUEPRINTS USE THE FORM ON PAGE 15 OR CALL TOLL-FREE 1-877-671-6036
View thousands more home plans online at www.familyhandyman.com/homeplans

Plan #718-030D-0010

1,919 total square feet of living area

Charming Dormers Enhance Facade

Special features

- The spacious kitchen and bayed dining area features a raised bar island with sink, window seat and large pantry
- The relaxing master suite boasts double-door access to a private porch and a lavish bath including two walk-in closets and a whirlpool tub
- Both secondary bedrooms include a walk-in closet and charming dormer
- Second floor bonus room has an additional 306 square feet of living area
- 3 bedrooms, 2 1/2 baths, 2-car side entry garage
- Slab or crawl space foundation, please specify when ordering

Price Code C

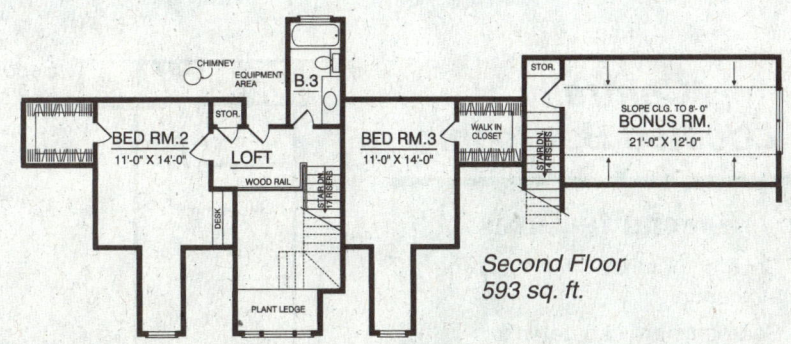

Second Floor 593 sq. ft.

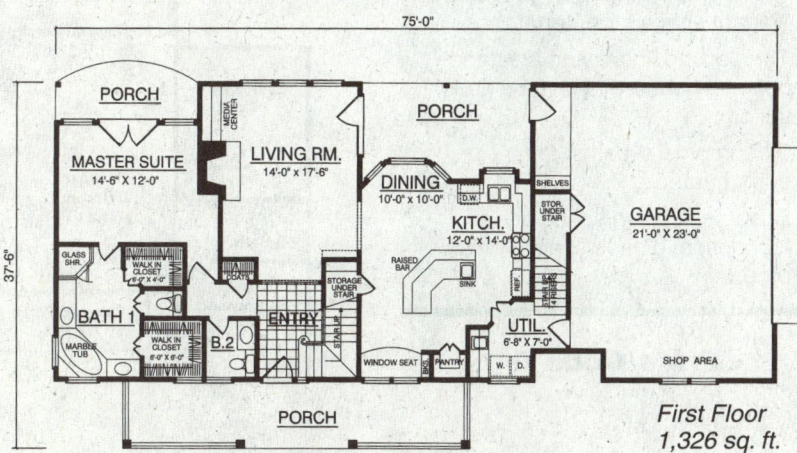

First Floor 1,326 sq. ft.

TO ORDER BLUEPRINTS USE THE FORM ON PAGE 15 OR CALL TOLL-FREE 1-877-671-6036
View thousands more home plans online at www.familyhandyman.com/HOMEPLANS

The Family Handyman

Plan #718-077D-0004

2,024 total square feet of living area

Centrally Located Bedroom

Special features

- Covered porches offer a relaxing atmosphere
- Bedrooms are separated for privacy
- The formal dining room provides an elegant space for entertaining
- The second floor living area and optional bath are ideal for a guest suite
- 3 bedrooms, 2 baths, 2-car side entry garage
- Basement, crawl space or slab foundation, please specify when ordering

Price Code D

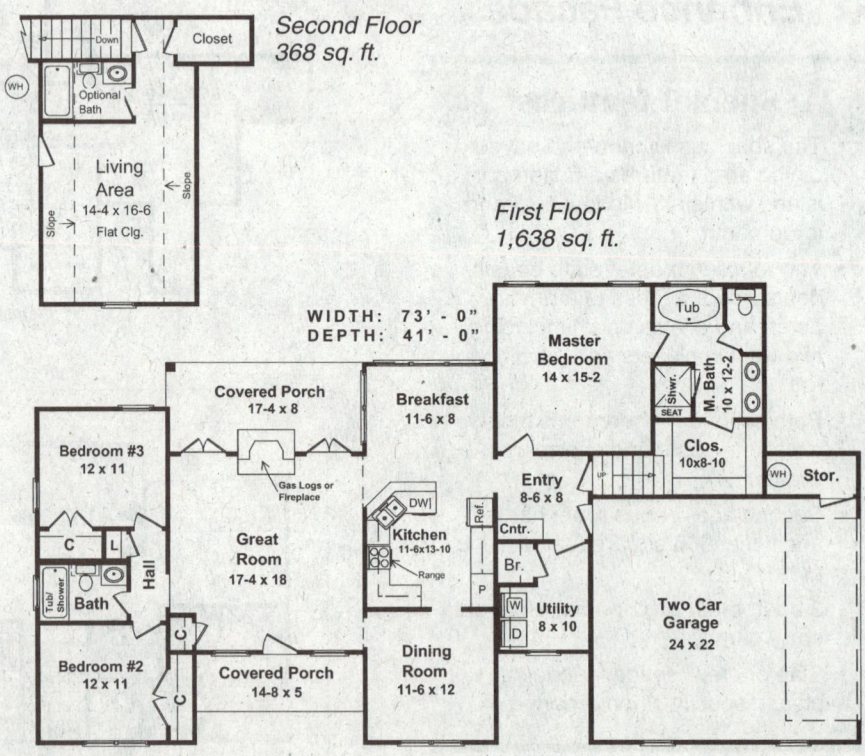

The Family Handyman

Plan #718-007D-0075

1,684 total square feet of living area

Rear View

A Special Home For Views

Special features

- Delightful wrap-around porch is anchored by a full masonry fireplace
- The vaulted great room includes a large bay window, fireplace, dining balcony and atrium window wall
- Double walk-in closets, large luxury bath and sliding doors to exterior balcony are a few fantastic features of the master bedroom
- Atrium opens to 611 square feet of optional living area
- 3 bedrooms, 2 baths, 2-car drive under garage
- Walk-out basement foundation

Price Code B

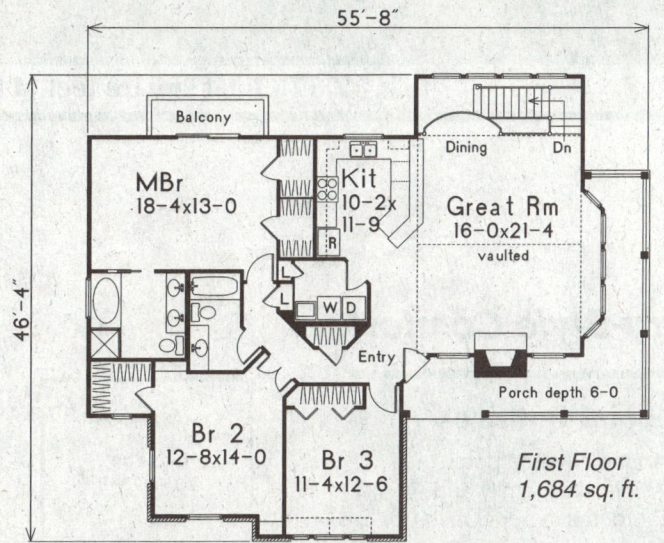

First Floor 1,684 sq. ft.

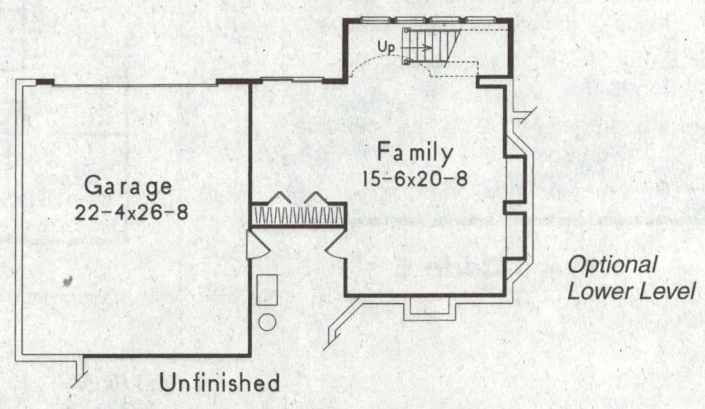

Optional Lower Level

TO ORDER BLUEPRINTS USE THE FORM ON PAGE 15 OR CALL TOLL-FREE 1-877-671-6036
View thousands more home plans online at www.familyhandyman.com/HOMEPLANS

Plan #718-053D-0021

2,826 total square feet of living area

Country-Style Comfort

Special features

- Wrap-around covered porch is accessible from family and breakfast rooms in addition to front entrance
- Bonus room, which is included in the square footage, has a separate entrance and is suitable for an office or private accommodations
- Large, full-windowed breakfast room
- 4 bedrooms, 2 1/2 baths, 2-car side entry garage
- Basement foundation

Price Code E

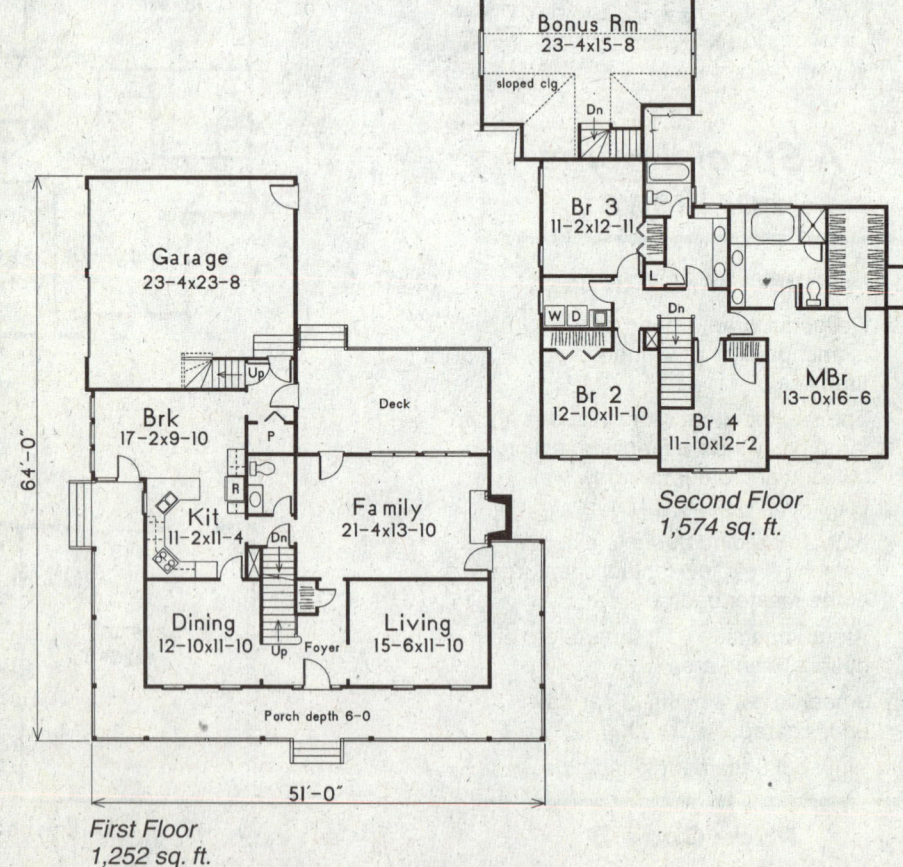

First Floor
1,252 sq. ft.

Second Floor
1,574 sq. ft.

TO ORDER BLUEPRINTS USE THE FORM ON PAGE 15 OR CALL TOLL-FREE 1-877-671-6036
View thousands more home plans online at www.familyhandyman.com/homeplans

Plan #718-020D-0010

2,194 total square feet of living area

Two-Story Living Room

Special features

- Energy efficient home with 2" x 6" exterior walls
- Utility room has a laundry drop conveniently located next to the kitchen
- Both second floor bedrooms have large closets and their own bath
- Bonus room on the second floor has an additional 352 square feet of living space
- 3 bedrooms, 3 1/2 baths, 2-car side entry garage
- Crawl space foundation, drawings also include slab and basement foundations

Price Code C

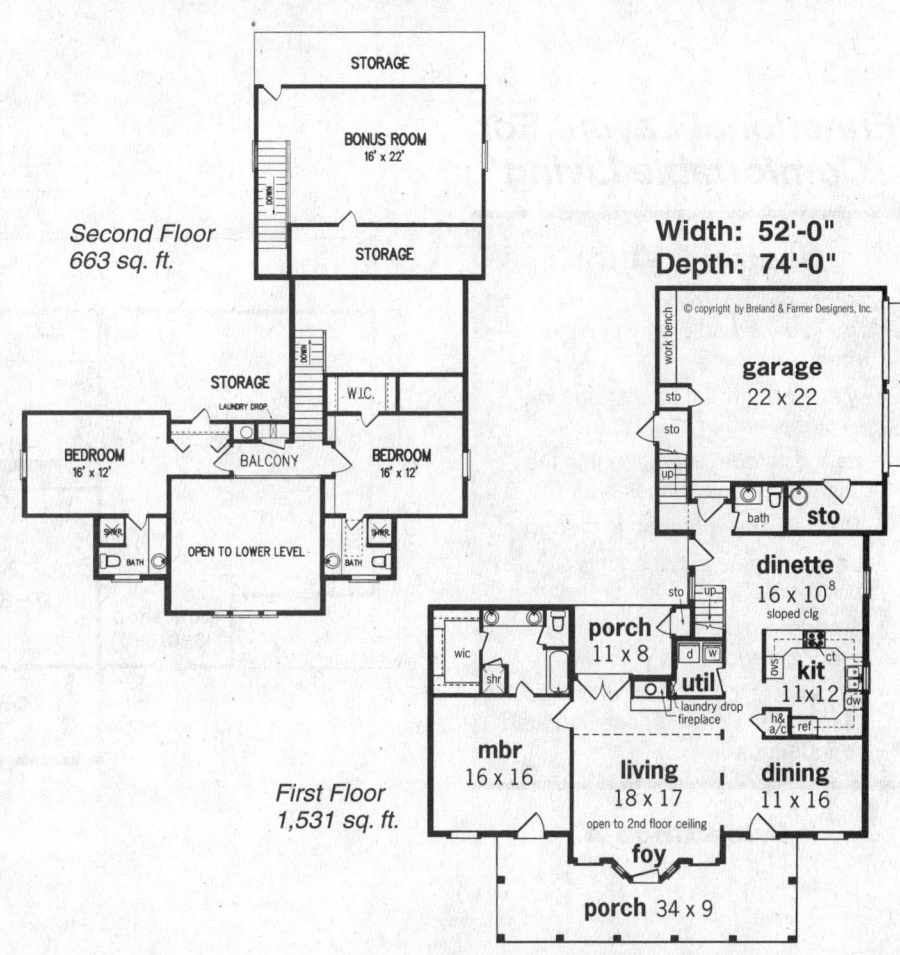

Width: 52'-0"
Depth: 74'-0"

Second Floor 663 sq. ft.

First Floor 1,531 sq. ft.

TO ORDER BLUEPRINTS USE THE FORM ON PAGE 15 OR CALL TOLL-FREE 1-877-671-6036
View thousands more home plans online at www.familyhandyman.com/HOMEPLANS

Plan #718-001D-0024

1,360 total square feet of living area

Functional Layout For Comfortable Living

Special features

- Kitchen/dining room features island workspace and plenty of dining area
- Master bedroom has a large walk-in closet and private bath
- Laundry room is adjacent to the kitchen for easy access
- Convenient workshop in garage
- Large closets in secondary bedrooms
- 3 bedrooms, 2 baths, 2-car side entry garage
- Basement foundation, drawings also include crawl space and slab foundations

Price Code A

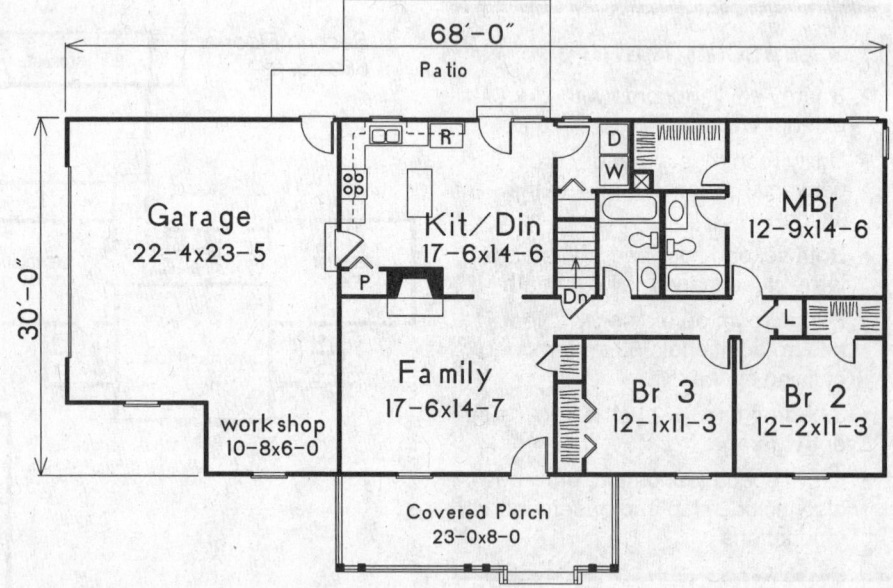

TO ORDER BLUEPRINTS USE THE FORM ON PAGE 15 OR CALL TOLL-FREE 1-877-671-6036
View thousands more home plans online at www.familyhandyman.com/homeplans

Plan #718-060D-0032

2,969 total square feet of living area

Classic Columned Colonial

Special features

- Formal entry with open stairwell to second floor and balcony overlook with upper porch access
- 9' ceilings on first floor
- Large great room has fireplace, access to patio/deck and view to rear
- Kitchen with center island, walk-in pantry and bayed breakfast room
- 3 bedrooms, 2 1/2 baths, 2-car side entry garage
- Slab or crawl space foundation, please specify when ordering

Price Code E

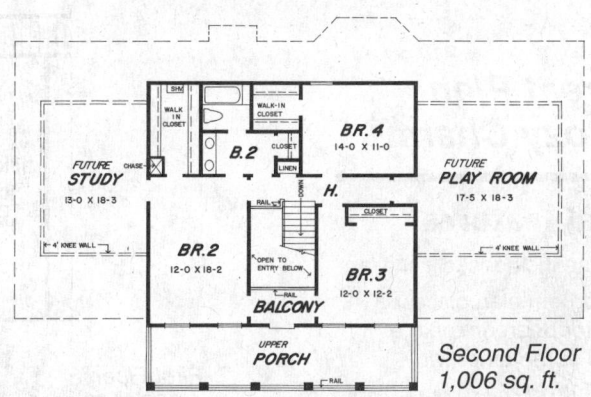

Second Floor 1,006 sq. ft.

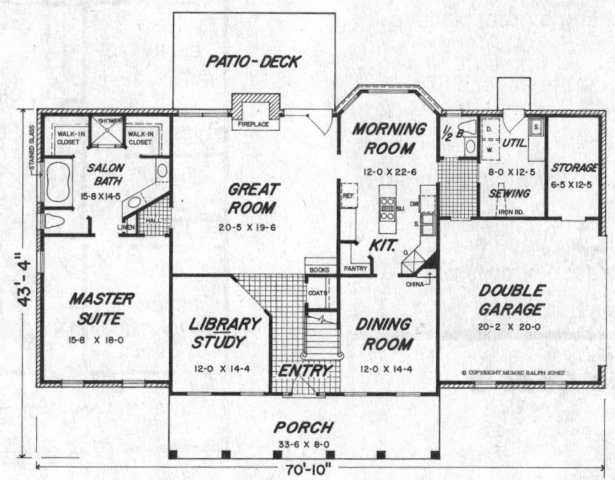

First Floor 1,963 sq. ft.

TO ORDER BLUEPRINTS USE THE FORM ON PAGE 15 OR CALL TOLL-FREE 1-877-671-6036
View thousands more home plans online at www.familyhandyman.com/HOMEPLANS

Plan #718-016D-0021

1,892 total square feet of living area

A Great Plan With Cozy Charm

Special features

- Victorian home includes folk charm
- This split bedroom plan places a lovely master bedroom on the opposite end of the other two bedrooms for privacy
- Central living and dining areas combine creating a great place for entertaining
- Bonus room on the second floor has an additional 285 square feet of living area
- 3 bedrooms, 2 1/2 baths, 2-car side entry garage
- Basement, crawl space or slab foundation, please specify when ordering

Price Code D

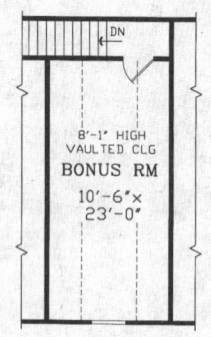

Optional Second Floor

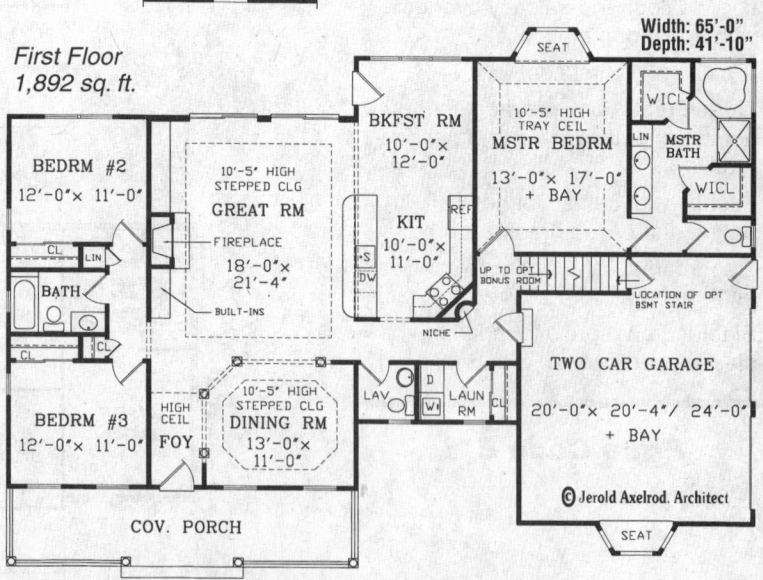

First Floor 1,892 sq. ft.

308   **TO ORDER BLUEPRINTS USE THE FORM ON PAGE 15 OR CALL TOLL-FREE 1-877-671-6036**
View thousands more home plans online at www.familyhandyman.com/HOMEPLANS

Plan #718-024D-0011

1,819 total square feet of living area

Double Dormers Add Curb Appeal

Special features

- Unique bath layout on the second floor allows for both bedrooms to have their own private sink area while connecting to main bath
- Window wall in dining area floods area with sunlight
- Walk-in closets in every bedroom
- 3 bedrooms, 2 1/2 baths
- Crawl space or slab foundation, please specify when ordering

Price Code C

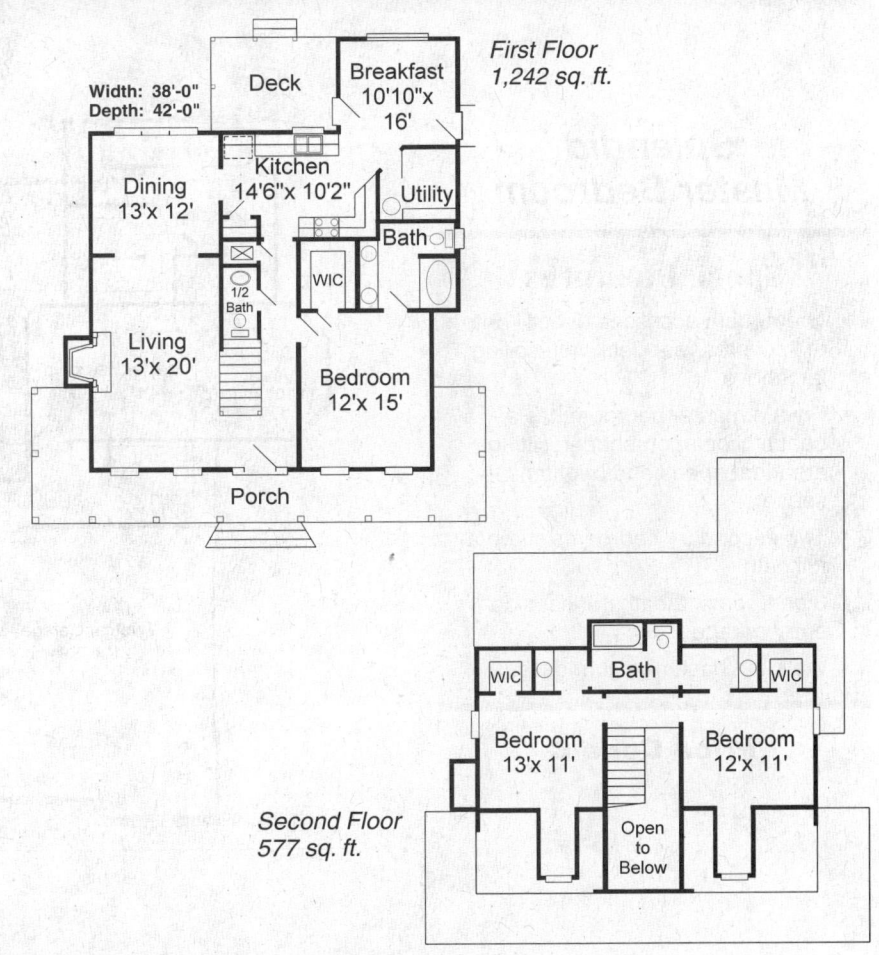

TO ORDER BLUEPRINTS USE THE FORM ON PAGE 15 OR CALL TOLL-FREE 1-877-671-6036
View thousands more home plans online at www.familyhandyman.com/homeplans

The Family Handyman

Plan #718-065D-0013

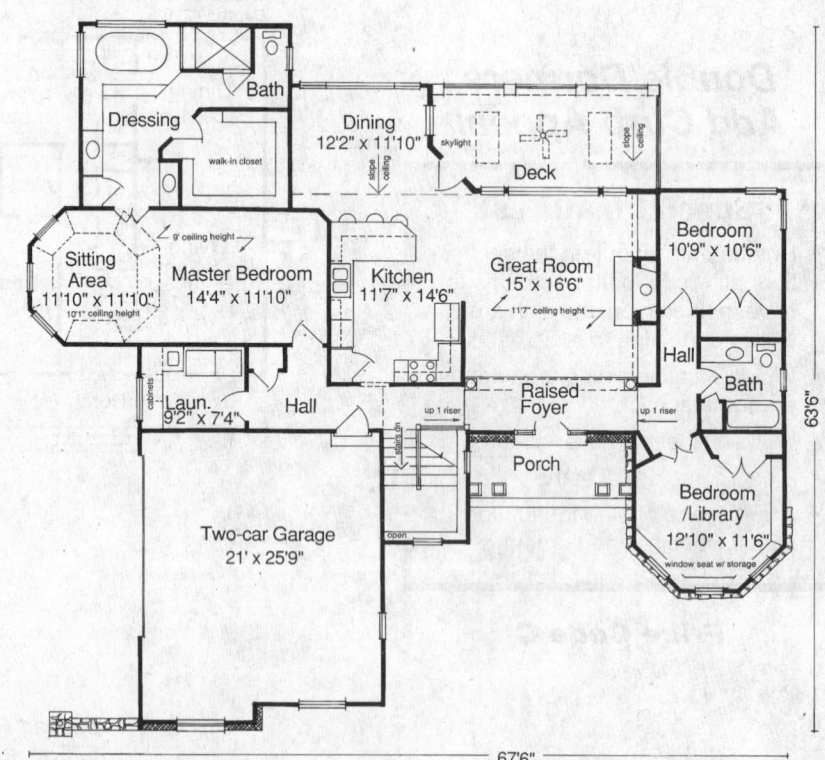

2,041 total square feet of living area

Splendid Master Bedroom

Special features

- Great room accesses directly onto the covered rear deck with ceiling fan above
- Private master bedroom has a beautiful octagon-shaped sitting area that opens and brightens the space
- Two secondary bedrooms share a full bath
- 3 bedrooms, 2 baths, 2-car side entry garage
- Walk-out basement foundation

Price Code C

TO ORDER BLUEPRINTS USE THE FORM ON PAGE 15 OR CALL TOLL-FREE 1-877-671-6036
View thousands more home plans online at www.familyhandyman.com/HOMEPLANS

Plan #718-053D-0060

2,636 total square feet of living area

Country Comfort

Special features

- Master bedroom has a generous walk-in closet, luxurious bath and a vaulted sitting area
- Spacious kitchen has an island cooktop and vaulted breakfast nook
- Bonus room above garage has an additional 389 square feet of living area
- 4 bedrooms, 3 1/2 baths, 2-car side entry garage, 1-car drive under garage
- Basement foundation

Price Code E

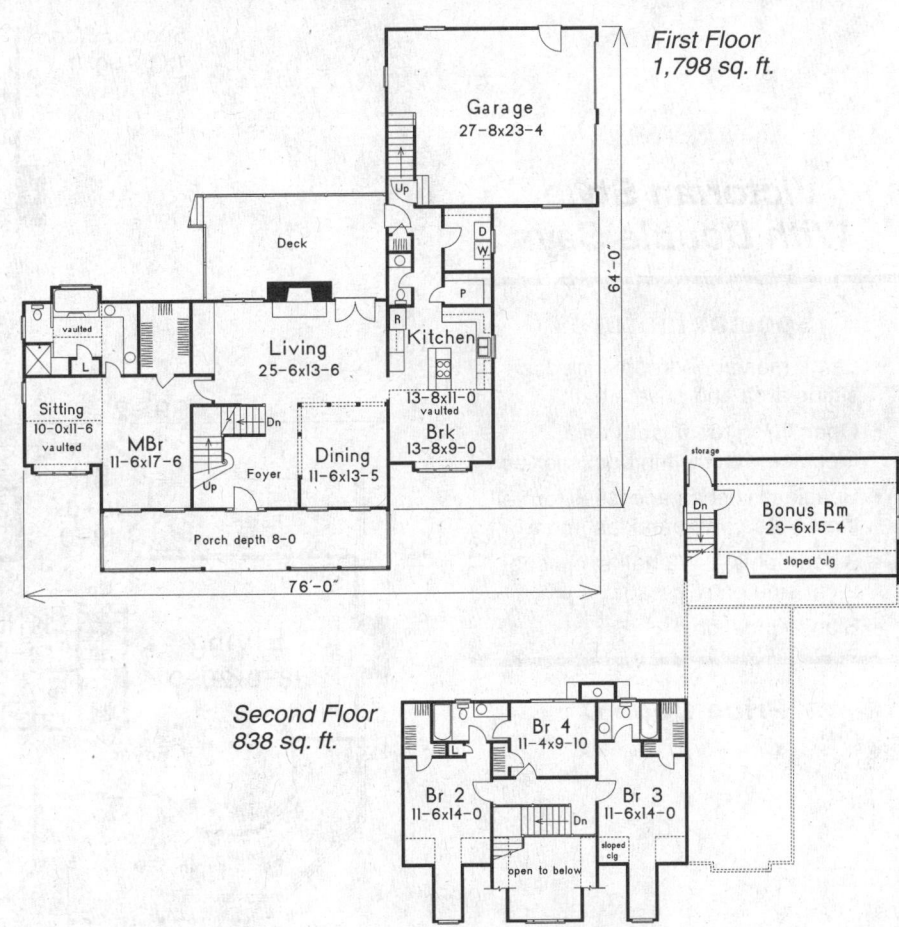

TO ORDER BLUEPRINTS USE THE FORM ON PAGE 15 OR CALL TOLL-FREE 1-877-671-6036
View thousands more home plans online at www.familyhandyman.com/HOMEPLANS

Plan #718-037D-0016

2,066 total square feet of living area

Victorian Style With Double Bays

Special features

- Large master bedroom includes sitting area and private bath
- Open living room features a fireplace with built-in bookshelves
- Spacious kitchen accesses formal dining area and breakfast room
- 3 bedrooms, 2 1/2 baths, optional 2-car side entry garage
- Slab foundation

Price Code C

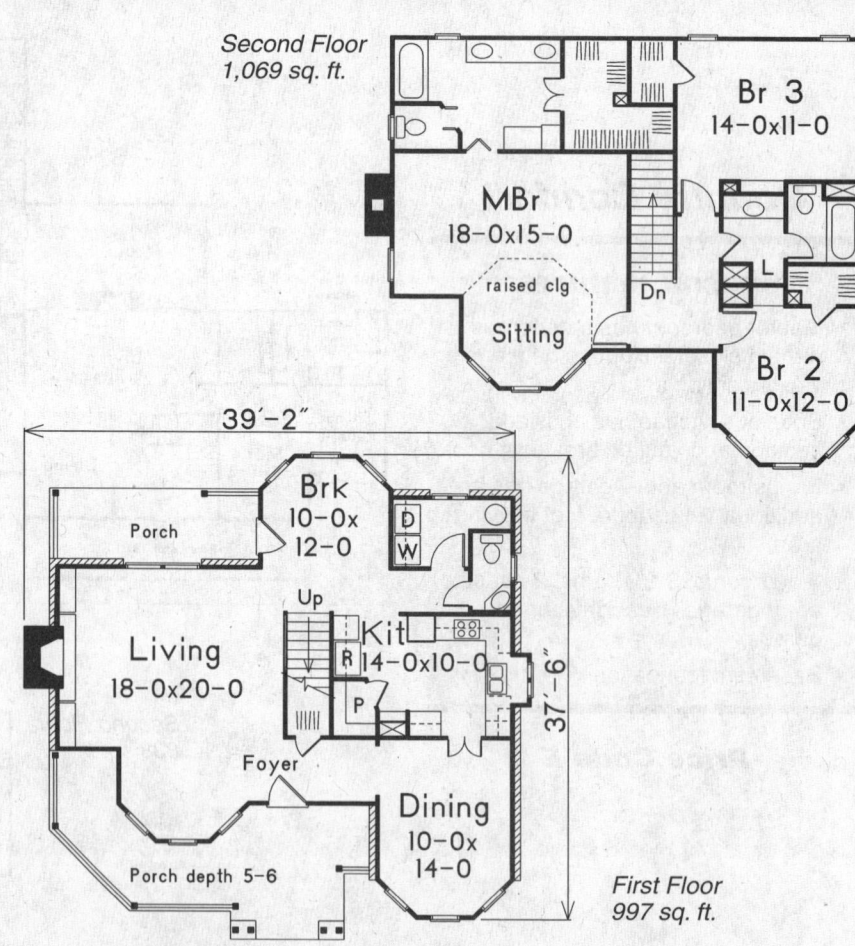

TO ORDER BLUEPRINTS USE THE FORM ON PAGE 15 OR CALL TOLL-FREE 1-877-671-6036

View thousands more home plans online at www.familyhandyman.com/homeplans

Plan #718-013D-0028

2,239 total square feet of living area

Casual Farmhouse Appeal

Special features

- Two sets of French doors in the family room lead to a covered porch ideal for relaxing
- The master bedroom has a spacious bath with an oversized tub placed in a sunny bay window
- Both second floor bedrooms have storage closets for terrific organizing
- 3 bedrooms, 2 1/2 baths, 2-car detached garage
- Basement or crawl space foundation, please specify when ordering

Price Code D

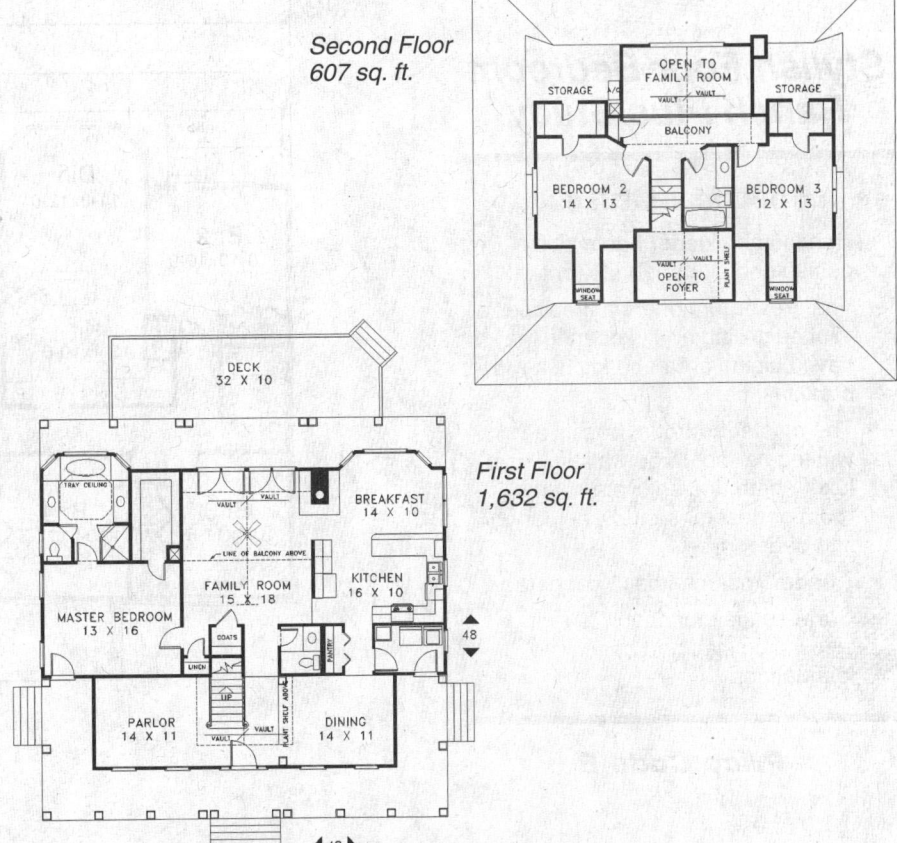

Second Floor 607 sq. ft.

First Floor 1,632 sq. ft.

TO ORDER BLUEPRINTS USE THE FORM ON PAGE 15 OR CALL TOLL-FREE 1-877-671-6036
View thousands more home plans online at www.familyhandyman.com/HOMEPLANS

The Family Handyman

Plan #718-007D-0164

1,741 total square feet of living area

Stylish Four Bedroom Ranch Plus Study

Special features

- Handsome exterior has multiple gables and elegant brickwork
- The great room offers a fireplace, vaulted ceiling and is open to the bayed dining area and kitchen with breakfast bar
- The master bedroom boasts a vaulted ceiling, large walk-in closet, luxury bath and enjoys a nearby room perfect for a study, nursery or fifth bedroom
- 4 bedrooms, 2 baths, 2-car garage
- Crawl space foundation, drawings also inclue slab and basement foundations

Price Code B

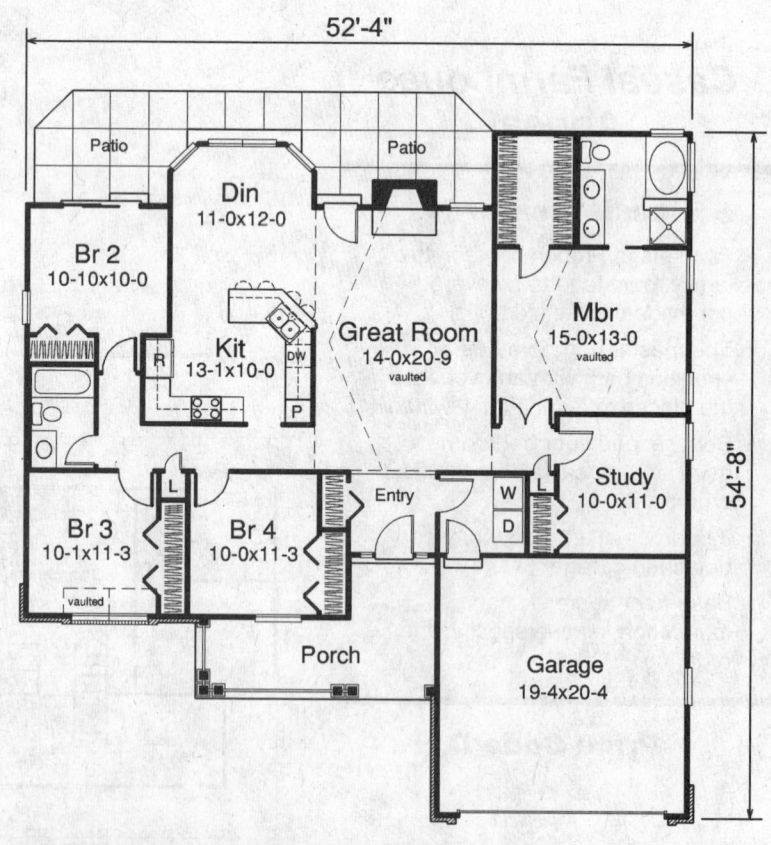

TO ORDER BLUEPRINTS USE THE FORM ON PAGE 15 OR CALL TOLL-FREE 1-877-671-6036

View thousands more home plans online at www.familyhandyman.com/homeplans

Plan #718-035D-0051

1,491 total square feet of living area

Southern Styling With Covered Porch

Special features

- Two-story family room has a vaulted ceiling
- Well-organized kitchen has serving bar which overlooks the family and dining rooms
- First floor master suite has a tray ceiling, walk-in closet and private bath
- 3 bedrooms, 2 1/2 baths, 2-car drive under garage
- Walk-out basement foundation

Price Code A

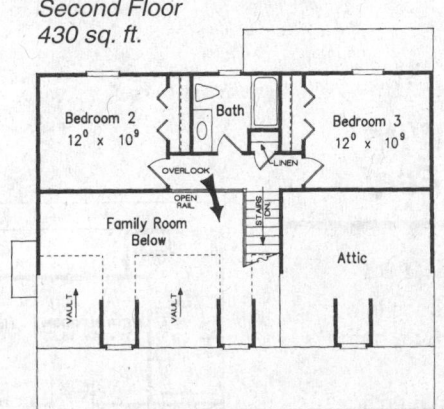

Second Floor
430 sq. ft.

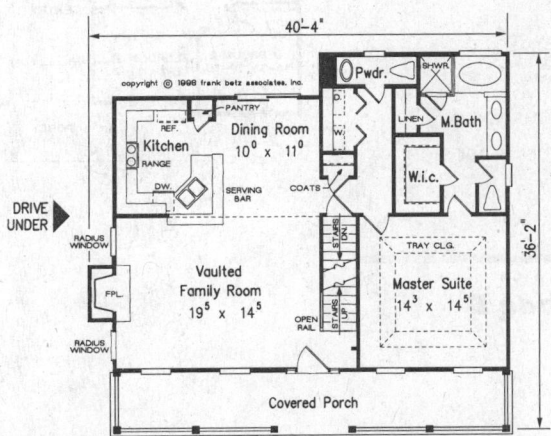

First Floor
1,061 sq. ft.

TO ORDER BLUEPRINTS USE THE FORM ON PAGE 15 OR CALL TOLL-FREE 1-877-671-6036
View thousands more home plans online at www.familyhandyman.com/homeplans

Plan #718-043D-0006

2,355 total square feet of living area

A Ranch With A Rustic Feel

Special features

- A double-door entry leads into a private den perfect for a home office
- Vaulted ceilings and a fireplace make the family room a terrific gathering spot
- Cheerful nook off kitchen makes an ideal breakfast area
- 9' ceilings throughout home
- 3 bedrooms, 3 baths, 3-car side entry garage
- Crawl space foundation

Price Code D

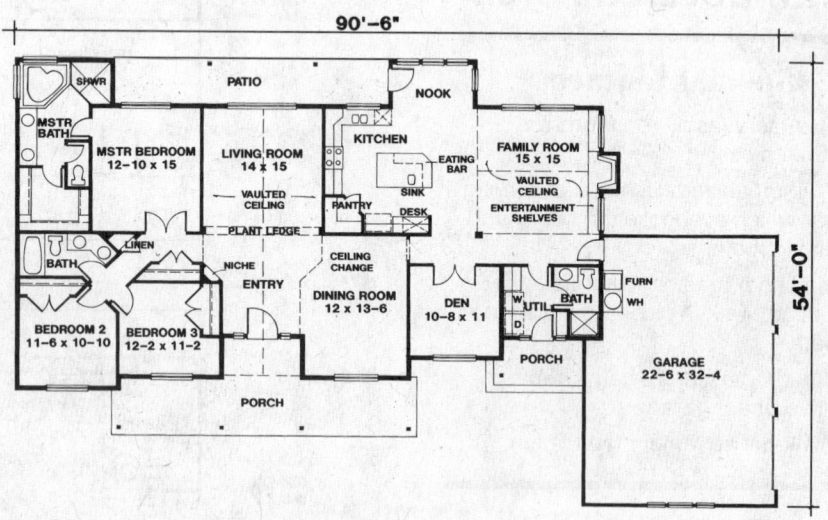

Plan #718-065D-0038

1,663 total square feet of living area

Spacious Ranch Home

Special features

- The open great room, dining area and kitchen combine to form the main living area
- An 11' ceiling tops the great room and foyer for added openness
- The rear covered porch provides a cozy and relaxing atmosphere
- The master bedroom enjoys a sloped ceiling and a private entrance to the covered porch
- 3 bedrooms, 2 baths, 2-car side entry garage
- Basement foundation

Price Code B

Width: 60'-8"
Depth: 48'-3"

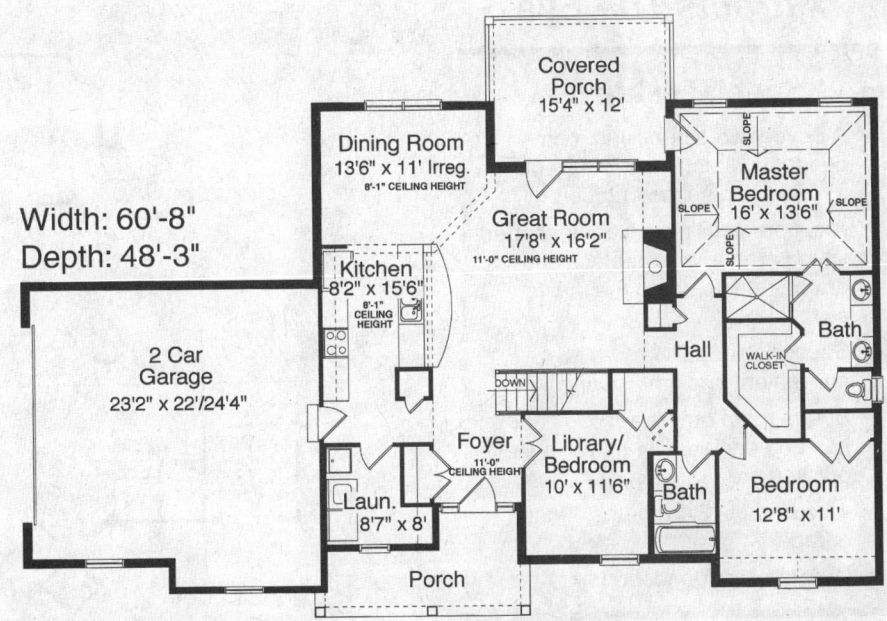

TO ORDER BLUEPRINTS USE THE FORM ON PAGE 15 OR CALL TOLL-FREE 1-877-671-6036
View thousands more home plans online at www.familyhandyman.com/homeplans

Plan #718-071D-0005

3,688 total square feet of living area

Charming Gazebo Attracts The Eye

Special features

- A bayed two-story living room connects directly to the gazebo for added living space outdoors
- A coffered ceiling, octagon-shaped sitting area and a fireplace add drama and luxury to the master suite
- Second floor utility room is convenient and time saving
- Bonus room on the second floor has an additional 342 square feet of living area
- 4 bedrooms, 3 1/2 baths, 3-car garage
- Crawl space foundation

Price Code G

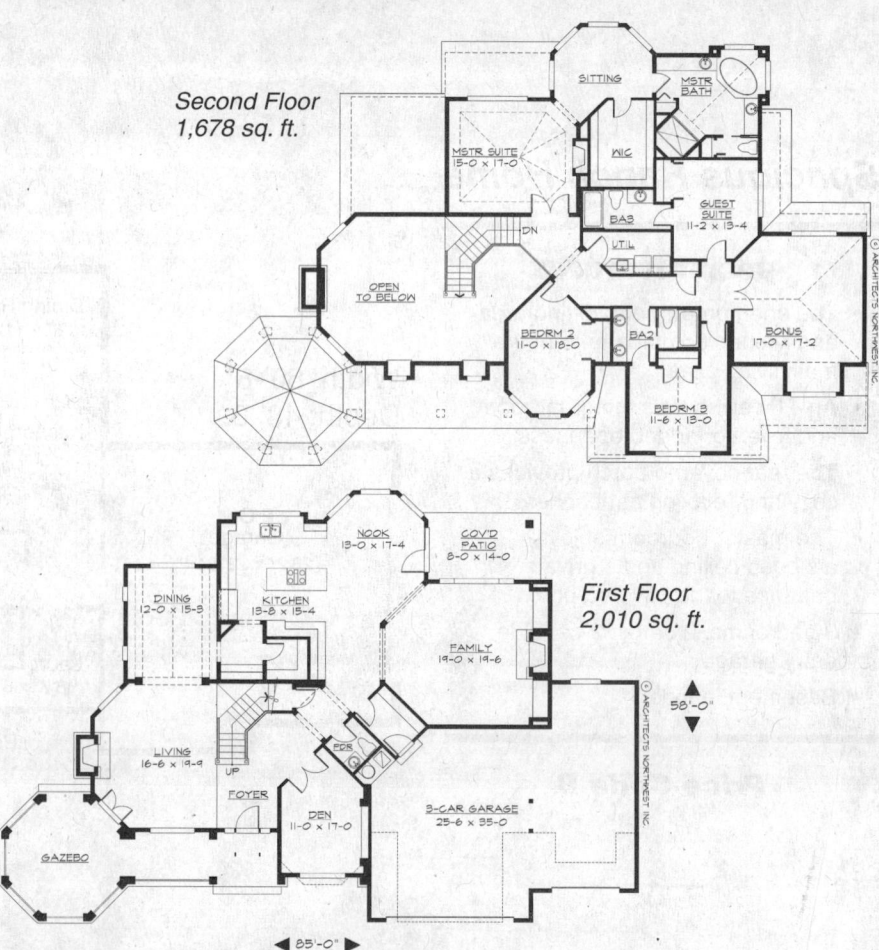

Second Floor 1,678 sq. ft.

First Floor 2,010 sq. ft.

TO ORDER BLUEPRINTS USE THE FORM ON PAGE 15 OR CALL TOLL-FREE 1-877-671-6036
View thousands more home plans online at www.familyhandyman.com/homeplans

The Family Handyman

Plan #718-052D-0044

1,856 total square feet of living area

Popular First Floor Master Bedroom

Special features

- Large secondary bedrooms include plenty of extra storage and share a full bath
- Dining area has direct access to a sundeck and flows into the living area
- The breakfast nook is a cheerful place to spend the morning with plenty of sunshine through many windows
- 3 bedrooms, 2 1/2 baths, 2-car drive under garage
- Basement foundation

Price Code C

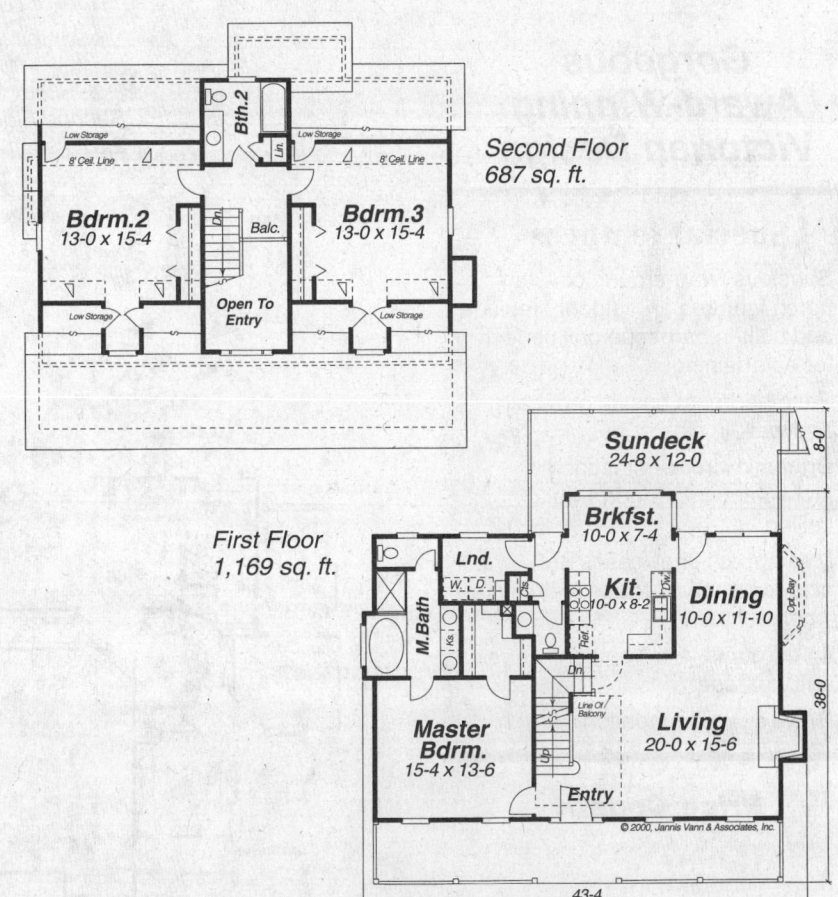

Second Floor 687 sq. ft.

First Floor 1,169 sq. ft.

TO ORDER BLUEPRINTS USE THE FORM ON PAGE 15 OR CALL TOLL-FREE 1-877-671-6036
View thousands more home plans online at www.familyhandyman.com/HOMEPLANS

The Family Handyman

Plan #718-071D-0010

5,250 total square feet of living area

Gorgeous Award-Winning Victorian Design

Special features

- Spacious wrap-around covered porch features an outdoor fireplace and built-in barbecue grill perfect for entertaining
- Each bedroom has its own bath and walk-in closet
- Dramatic circular staircase is highlighted in rotunda with 27' ceiling
- Master bath showcases an octagon-shaped space featuring a whirlpool tub
- 4 bedrooms, 4 1/2 baths, 4-car side entry garage
- Crawl space foundation

Price Code H

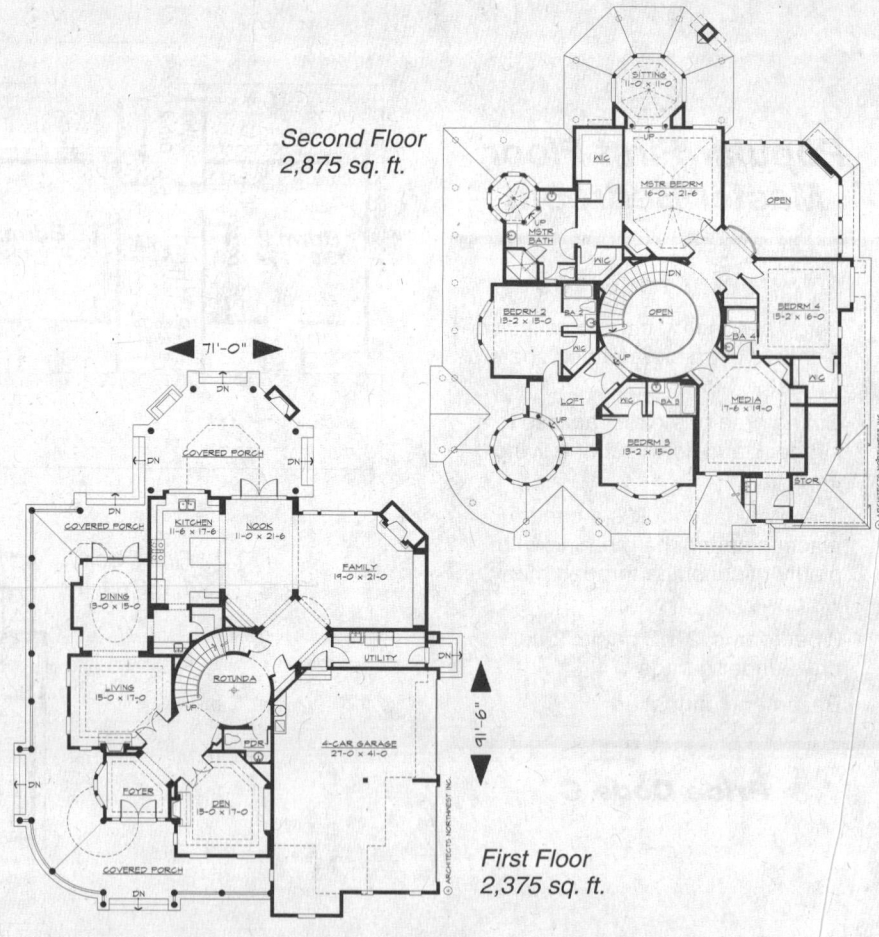

Second Floor 2,875 sq. ft.

First Floor 2,375 sq. ft.

TO ORDER BLUEPRINTS USE THE FORM ON PAGE 15 OR CALL TOLL-FREE 1-877-671-6036
View thousands more home plans online at www.familyhandyman.com/homeplans

Made in United States
Troutdale, OR
01/11/2026

45497429R00029

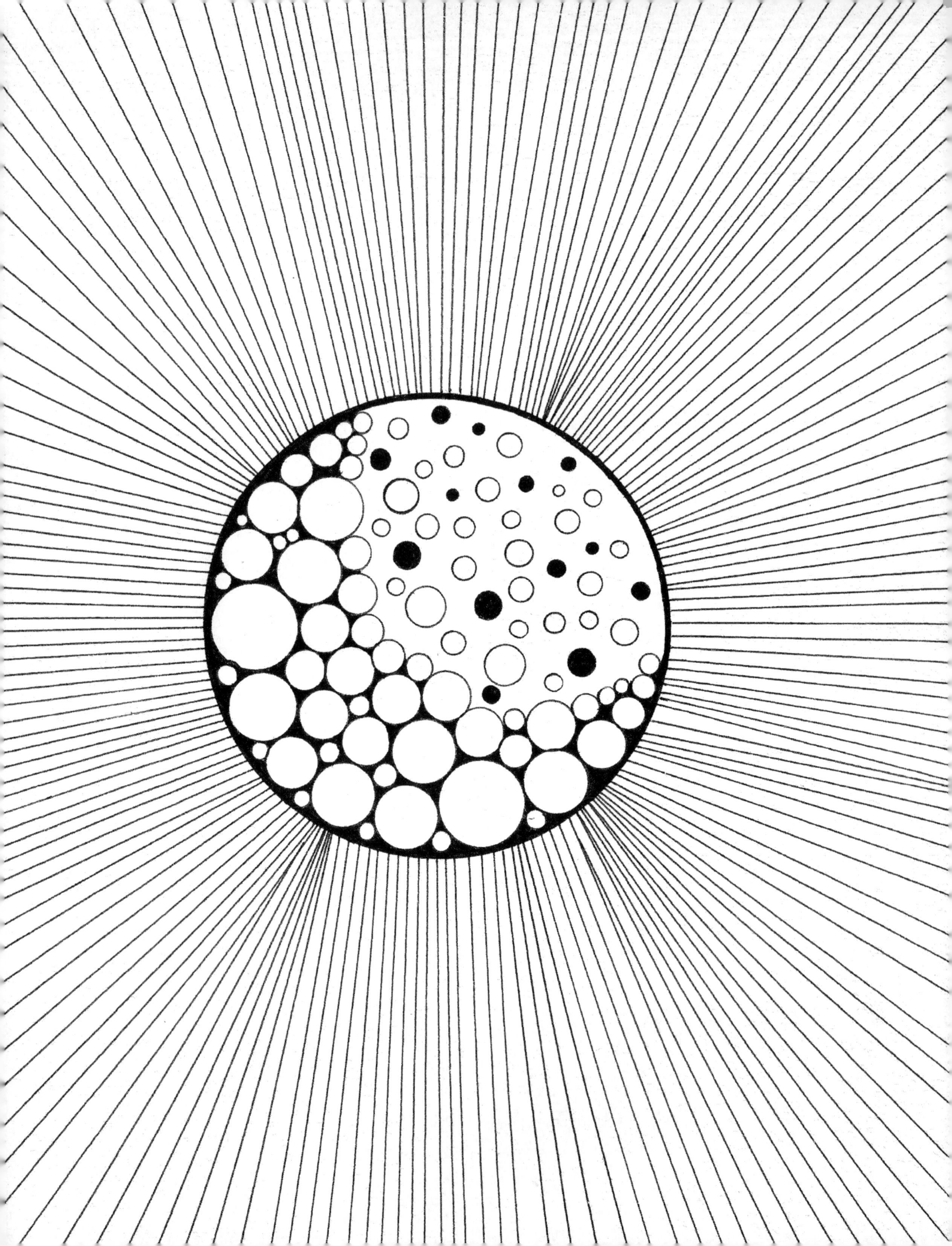